Mathematics I
Volume 2

Randall I. Charles
Basia Hall
Dan Kennedy
Laurie E. Bass
Allan E. Bellman
Sadie Chavis Bragg
William G. Handlin
Art Johnson
Stuart J. Murphy
Grant Wiggins

Owner: James Balinski

PEARSON

Boston, Massachusetts · Chandler, Arizona · Glenview, Illinois · Upper Saddle River, New Jersey

Acknowledgments appear on page Z60, which constitutes an extension of this copyright page.

PEARSON

ISBN-13:   978-0-13-323462-6
ISBN-10:   0-13-323462-2

5 6 7 8 9 10 V031 17 16 15 14

From the *Authors*

Welcome

Math is a powerful tool with far-reaching applications throughout your life. We have designed a unique and engaging program that will enable you to tap into the power of mathematics and mathematical reasoning. This award-winning program has been developed to align fully to the Common Core State Standards.

Developing mathematical understanding and problem-solving abilities is an ongoing process—a journey both inside and outside the classroom. This course is designed to help make sense of the mathematics you encounter in and out of class each day and to help you develop mathematical proficiency.

You will learn important mathematical principles. You will also learn how the principles are connected to one another and to what you already know. You will learn to solve problems and learn the reasoning that lies behind your solutions. You will also develop the key mathematical practices of the Common Core State Standards.

Each chapter begins with the "big ideas" of the chapter and some essential questions that you will learn to answer. Through this question-and-answer process you will develop your ability to analyze problems independently and solve them in different applications.

Your skills and confidence will increase through practice and review. Work through the problems so you understand the concepts and methods presented and the thinking behind them. Then do the exercises. Ask yourself how new concepts relate to old ones. Make the connections!

Everyone needs help sometimes. You will find that this program has built-in opportunities, both in this text and online, to get help whenever you need it.

The problem-solving and reasoning habits and problem-solving skills you develop in this program will serve you in all your studies and in your daily life. They will prepare you for future success not only as a student, but also as a member of a changing technological society.

Best wishes,

Series *Authors*

Randall I. Charles, Ph.D., is Professor Emeritus in the Department of Mathematics at San Jose State University, San Jose, California. He began his career as a high school mathematics teacher, and he was a mathematics supervisor for five years. Dr. Charles has been a member of several NCTM committees including the writing team for the Curriculum Focal Points. He is the former Vice President of the National Council of Supervisors of Mathematics. Much of his writing and research has been in the area of problem solving. He has authored more than 90 mathematics textbooks for kindergarten through college.

Dan Kennedy, Ph.D., is a classroom teacher and the Lupton Distinguished Professor of Mathematics at the Baylor School in Chattanooga, Tennessee. A frequent speaker at professional meetings on the subject of mathematics education reform, Dr. Kennedy has conducted more than 50 workshops and institutes for high school teachers. He is coauthor of textbooks in calculus and precalculus, and from 1990 to 1994 he chaired the College Board's AP Calculus Development Committee. He is a 1992 Tandy Technology Scholar and a 1995 Presidential Award winner.

Basia Hall currently serves as Manager of Instructional Programs for the Houston Independent School District. With 33 years of teaching experience, Ms. Hall has served as a department chair, instructional supervisor, school improvement facilitator, and professional development trainer. She has developed curricula for Algebra 1, Geometry, and Algebra 2 and co-developed the Texas state mathematics standards. A 1992 Presidential Awardee, Ms. Hall is past president of the Texas Association of Supervisors of Mathematics and is a state representative for the National Council of Supervisors of Mathematics (NCSM).

Consulting *Authors*

Stuart J. Murphy is a visual learning author and consultant. He is a champion of helping students develop visual learning skills so they become more successful students. He is the author of MathStart, a series of children's books that presents mathematical concepts in the context of stories, and *I See I Learn,* a Pre-Kindergarten and Kindergarten learning initiative that focuses on social and emotional skills. A graduate of the Rhode Island School of Design, he has worked extensively in educational publishing and has been on the authorship teams of a number of elementary and high school mathematics programs. He is a frequent presenter at meetings of the National Council of Teachers of Mathematics, the International Reading Association, and other professional organizations.

Grant Wiggins, Ed.D., is the President of Authentic Education in Hopewell, New Jersey. He earned his B.A. from St. John's College in Annapolis and his Ed.D. from Harvard University Dr. Wiggins consults with schools, districts, and state education departments on a variety of reform matters; organizes conferences and workshops; and develops print materials and web resources on curricular change. He is perhaps best known for being the coauthor, with Jay McTighe, of *Understanding by Design* and *The Understanding by Design Handbook*[1], the award-winning and highly successful materials on curriculum published by ASCD. His work has been supported by the Pew Charitable Trusts, the Geraldine R. Dodge Foundation, and the National Science Foundation.

[1] ASCD, publisher of the "Understanding by Design Handbook" co-authored by Grant Wiggins and registered owner of the trademark "Understanding by Design", has not authorized or sponsored this work and is in no way affiliated with Pearson or its products.

Program *Authors*

Algebra Topics

Allan E. Bellman, Ph.D., is an Associate Professor of Mathematics Education at the University of Mississippi. He previously taught at the University of California, Davis for 12 years and in public school in Montgomery County, Maryland for 31. He has been an instructor for both the Woodrow Wilson National Fellowship Foundation and the Texas Instruments' T^3 program. Dr. Bellman has expertise in the use of technology in education and assessment-driven instruction and speaks frequently on these topics. He is a recipient of the Tandy Award for Teaching Excellence and has twice been listed in Who's Who Among America's Teachers.

Sadie Chavis Bragg, Ed.D., is Senior Vice President of Academic Affairs and professor of mathematics at the Borough of Manhattan Community College of the City University of New York. She is a past president of the American Mathematical Association of Two-Year Colleges (AMATYC). In recognition for her service to the field of mathematics locally, statewide, nationally, and internationally, she was awarded AMATYC's most prestigious award, The Mathematics Excellence Award for 2010. Dr. Bragg has coauthored more than 60 mathematics textbooks for kindergarten through college.

William G. Handlin, Sr., is a classroom teacher and Department Chair of Mathematics and former Department Chair of Technology Applications at Spring Woods High School in Houston, Texas. Awarded Life Membership in the Texas Congress of Parents and Teachers for his contributions to the well-being of children, Mr. Handlin is also a frequent workshop and seminar leader in professional meetings.

Geometry Topics

Laurie E. Bass is a classroom teacher at the 9–12 division of the Ethical Culture Fieldston School in Riverdale, New York. A classroom teacher for more than 30 years, Ms. Bass has a wide base of teaching experiences, ranging from Grade 6 through Advanced Placement Calculus. She was the recipient of a 2000 Honorable Mention for the Radio Shack National Teacher Awards. She has been a contributing writer for a number of publications, including software-based activities for the Algebra 1 classroom. Among her areas of special interest are cooperative learning for high school students and geometry exploration on the computer. Ms. Bass is a frequent presenter at local, regional, and national conferences.

Art Johnson, Ed.D., is a professor of mathematics education at Boston University. He is a mathematics educator with 32 years of public school teaching experience, a frequent speaker and workshop leader, and the recipient of a number of awards: the Tandy Prize for Teaching Excellence, the Presidential Award for Excellence in Mathematics Teaching, and New Hampshire Teacher of the Year. He was also profiled by the Disney Corporation in the American Teacher of the Year Program. Dr. Johnson has contributed 18 articles to NCTM journals and has authored over 50 books on various aspects of mathematics.

Using **Your Book** with *Success*

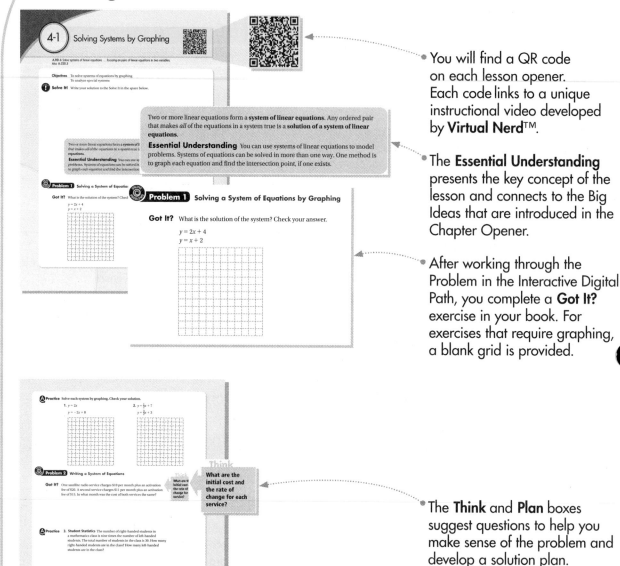

You will find a QR code on each lesson opener. Each code links to a unique instructional video developed by **Virtual Nerd**™.

The **Essential Understanding** presents the key concept of the lesson and connects to the Big Ideas that are introduced in the Chapter Opener.

After working through the Problem in the Interactive Digital Path, you complete a **Got It?** exercise in your book. For exercises that require graphing, a blank grid is provided.

The **Think** and **Plan** boxes suggest questions to help you make sense of the problem and develop a solution plan.

Each **Got It?** exercise is followed by additional exercises that focus on the same math concept and skill. You complete these exercises in your book.

Two or more linear equations form a **system of linear equations**. Any ordered pair that makes *all* of the equations in a system true is a **solution of a system of linear equations**.

Essential Understanding You can use systems of linear equations to model problems. Systems of equations can be solved in more than one way. One method is to graph each equation and find the intersection point, if one exists.

Problem 1 Solving a System of Equations by Graphing

Got It? What is the solution of the system? Check your answer.

$y = 2x + 4$
$y = x + 2$

Think
What are the initial cost and the rate of change for each service?

Practice 3. **Student Statistics** The number of right-handed students in a mathematics class is nine times the number of left-handed students. The total number of students in the class is 30. How many right-handed students are in the class? How many left-handed students are in the class?

4. **Plants** A plant nursery is growing a tree that is 3 ft tall and grows at an average rate of 1 ft per year. Another tree at the nursery is 4 ft tall and grows at an average rate of 0.5 ft per year. After how many years will the trees be the same height?

You can use the instructional summaries in the **Take Note** boxes to review concepts when completing homework or studying for an assessment.

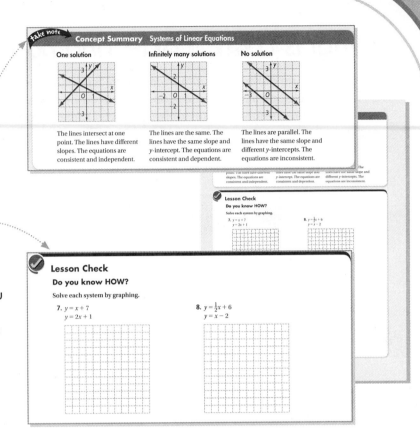

At the end of each lesson is a **Lesson Check** that you complete in your book. The Do you know HOW? section focuses on skills and the Do you UNDERSTAND? section targets your understanding of the math concepts related to the skills.

Lesson Check

Do you know HOW?

Solve each system by graphing.

7. $y = x + 7$
   $y = 2x + 1$

8. $y = \frac{1}{2}x + 6$
   $y = x - 2$

Each lesson ends with **More Practice and Problem Solving** Exercises. You will complete these exercises in your homework notebook or on a separate sheet of paper.

The exercises with the **Common Core logo** help you become more proficient with the Standards for Mathematical Practice. Those with the **STEM** logo provide practice with science, technology, or engineering topics.

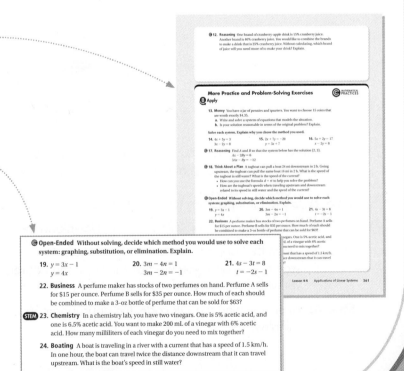

Open-Ended Without solving, decide which method you would use to solve each system: graphing, substitution, or elimination. Explain.

19. $y = 3x - 1$
    $y = 4x$

20. $3m - 4n = 1$
    $3m - 2n = -1$

21. $4s - 3t = 8$
    $t = -2s - 1$

22. **Business** A perfume maker has stocks of two perfumes on hand. Perfume A sells for $15 per ounce. Perfume B sells for $35 per ounce. How much of each should be combined to make a 3-oz bottle of perfume that can be sold for $63?

STEM 23. **Chemistry** In a chemistry lab, you have two vinegars. One is 5% acetic acid, and one is 6.5% acetic acid. You want to make 200 mL of a vinegar with 6% acetic acid. How many milliliters of each vinegar do you need to mix together?

24. **Boating** A boat is traveling in a river with a current that has a speed of 1.5 km/h. In one hour, the boat can travel twice the distance downstream that it can travel upstream. What is the boat's speed in still water?

What is a **QR code** and how do I use it?

A unique feature of Pearson's *Integrated High School Mathematics* is the QR code on every lesson opener. QR codes can be scanned by any electronic device with a camera, such as a smart phone, tablet, and even some laptop computers. The QR codes on the lesson openers link to Virtual Nerd™ tutorial videos that directly relate to the content in the lesson. To learn more about Virtual Nerd tutorial videos and its exclusive dynamic whiteboard, go to virtualnerd.com.

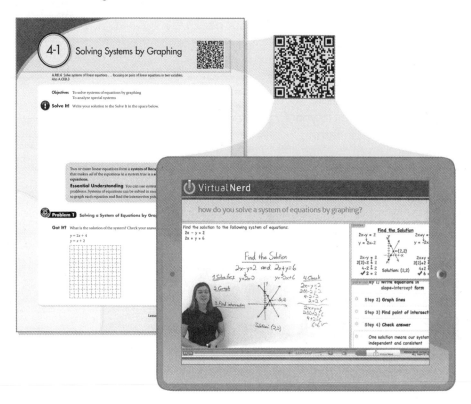

You must have a QR code reader on your mobile device or computer. You can download a QR reader app at the app store for your mobile device.

Step 1: Go to the app store for your camera-enabled smart phone or tablet.

Step 2: Search for "QR" or "QR readers". Download the QR reader app.

Step 3: Open that app and follow the instructions to scan. Whenever you want to scan a QR code, you will need to open the QR reader app first, otherwise you will just end up taking a picture of a QR code.

Step 4: After scanning the QR code, the appropriate Virtual Nerd tutorial video will play.

What **Resources** can I use when studying?

Pearson's *Integrated High School Mathematics* offers a range of resources that you can use out of class.

Student Worktext Your book is more than a textbook. Not only does it have important summaries of key math concepts and skills, it will also have your worked-out solutions to the *Got It?* and *Practice* exercises and your own notes for each lesson or problem. Use your book to:

- Refer back to your worked-out solutions and notes.
- Review the key concepts of each lesson by rereading the *Essential Understanding* and *Take Note* boxes.
- Access video tutorials of the concepts addressed in the lesson by scanning the QR codes.

Pearson SuccessNet You have full access to all of the resources on Pearson SuccessNet, including the **Interactive Digital Path** where you will find all of the *Solve Its!* and Problems presented in class. Revisit the animated, stepped-out problems presented in-class to clarify and solidify your math knowledge. Additional resources available to you include:

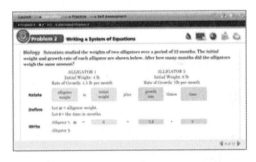

- Interactive Student Worktext
- Homework Video Tutors in English and Spanish
- Online Glossary with audio in English and Spanish
- MathXL for School Interactive Math Practice
- Math Tools and Online Manipulatives
- Multilingual Handbook
- Assessments with immediate feedback

Mobile eText You may wish to access your student book on the go, either online or offline via download. Pearson's *Integrated High School Mathematics* also offers you a complete mobile etext of the Student Worktext.

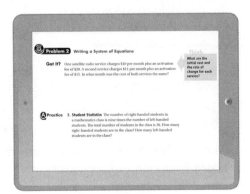

- Use the notes, highlight, and bookmark features to personalize your eText.
- Watch animated problem videos with step-by-step instruction for every lesson.

Pearson SuccessNet

Pearson SuccessNet is the gateway to all of the digital components of the program. You can use the online content to review the day's lesson, complete lessons independently, get help with your homework assignments, and prepare for and/or take an assessment. You will be given a username and password to log into www.pearsonsuccessnet.com.

The Homepage

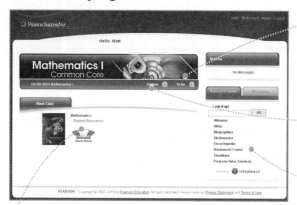

The **To Do** tab contains a list of assignments that you need to complete. You can also access your gradebook and review past assignments.

The **Explore** tab provides you access to the Table of Contents and all of the digital content for the program.

You can also access the following student resources: Practice Worksheets, Homework Video Tutors, and a Multilingual Handbook

Your eText includes links to animated lesson videos, highlighting and note taking tools, and a visual glossary with audio.

Table of Contents

To access the Table of Contents, click on *Explore* from your Homepage.

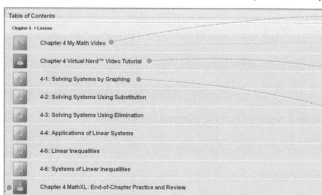

Student-developed videos bring real-life context to mathematics.

Step-by-step video tutorials offer additional support for every lesson.

Digital lessons include access to animated problems, math tools, homework exercises, and self-assessments.

MathXL for School exercises provide additional practice. Examples and tutorials support every problem, and instant feedback is provided as you complete each exercise.

Interactive Digital Path

To access the **Interactive Digital Path**, click on the appropriate lesson from the Table of Contents.

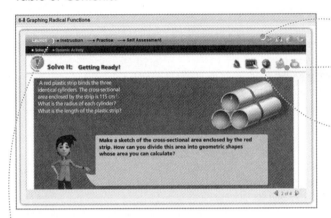

Math Tools help you explore and visualize concepts.

You'll find opportunities to review formulas, properties, and other key concepts.

Interactive Glossary is available in English and Spanish with audio.

Every lesson includes the following:

Launch: Interactive lesson opener connects the math to real-world applications.

Instruction: All lesson problems are stepped out with detailed instruction. You can complete the subsequent *Got It?* exercises in your Student Worktext.

Practice: Exercises from your Student Worktext are available for view.

Self-Assessment: You can take the self-check lesson quiz, and then check your answers on the second screen.

MathXL for School

To access *MathXL for School*, click on the Chapter Review and Practice link from the Table of Contents.

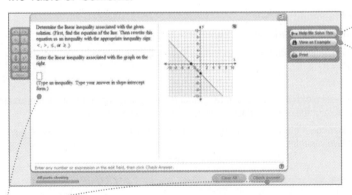

Select **Help Me Solve This** for an interactive step-by-step tutorial.

Select **View an Example** to see a similar worked out problem.

Input your answer and select **Check Answer** to get immediate feedback. After completing the exercise, a new exercise automatically regenerates, so you have unlimited practice opportunities.

Common Core *State Standards*

Mathematics I

Hi, I'm Max. Here is a list of the Common Core State Standards that Integrated Mathematics I addressess.

Number and Quantity

Quantities

Reason quantitatively and use units to solve problems

N.Q.1   Use units as a way to understand problems and to guide the solution of multi-step problems; choose and interpret units consistently in formulas; choose and interpret the scale and the origin in graphs and data displays.

N.Q.2   Define appropriate quantities for the purpose of descriptive modeling.

N.Q.3   Choose a level of accuracy appropriate to limitations on measurement when reporting quantities.

Algebra

Seeing Structure in Expressions

Interpret the structure of expressions

A.SSE.1.a Interpret expressions that represent a quantity in terms of its context. ★ Interpret parts of an expression, such as terms, factors, and coefficients.

A.SSE.1.b Interpret expressions that represent a quantity in terms of its context. ★ Interpret complicated expressions by viewing one or more of their parts as a single entity.

Write expressions in equivalent forms to solve problems

A.SSE.3.c Choose and produce an equivalent form of an expression to reveal and explain properties of the quantity represented by the expression. ★ Use the properties of exponents to transform expressions for exponential functions.

Creating Equations ★

Create equations that describe numbers or relationships

A.CED.1   Create equations and inequalities in one variable and use them to solve problems. Include equations arising from linear and exponential functions.

A.CED.2   Create equations in two or more variables to represent relationships between quantities; graph equations on coordinate axes with labels and scales.

A.CED.3   Represent constraints by equations or inequalities, and by systems of equations and/or inequalities, and interpret solutions as viable or nonviable options in a modeling context.

A.CED.4   Rearrange formulas to highlight a quantity of interest, using the same reasoning as in solving equations.

Reasoning with Equations and Inequalities

Solve equations and inequalities in one variable

A.REI.3   Solve linear equations and inequalities in one variable, including equations with coefficients represented by letters.

Solve systems of equations

A.REI.5   Prove that, given a system of two equations in two variables, replacing one equation by the sum of that equation and a multiple of the other produces a system with the same solutions.

A.REI.6   Solve systems of linear equations exactly and approximately (e.g., with graphs), focusing on pairs of linear equations in two variables.

★ Indicates a modeling standard

Represent and solve equations and inequalities graphically

A.REI.10 Understand that the graph of an equation in two variables is the set of all its solutions plotted in the coordinate plane, often forming a curve (which could be a line).

A.REI.11 Explain why the x-coordinates of the points where the graphs of the equations $y = f(x)$ and $y = g(x)$ intersect are the solutions of the equation $f(x) = g(x)$; find the solutions approximately, e.g., using technology to graph the functions, make tables of values, or find successive approximations. Include cases where $f(x)$ and/or $g(x)$ are linear and exponential functions. ★

A.REI.12 Graph the solutions to a linear inequality in two variables as a half-plane (excluding the boundary in the case of a strict inequality), and graph the solution set to a system of linear inequalities in two variables as the intersection of the corresponding half-planes.

Functions

Interpreting Functions

Understand the concept of a function and use function notation

F.IF.1 Understand that a function from one set (called the domain) to another set (called the range) assigns to each element of the domain exactly one element of the range. If f is a function and x is an element of its domain, then $f(x)$ denotes the output of f corresponding to the input x. The graph of f is the graph of the equation $y = f(x)$.

F.IF.2 Use function notation, evaluate functions for inputs in their domains, and interpret statements that use function notation in terms of a context.

F.IF.3 Recognize that sequences are functions, sometimes defined recursively, whose domain is a subset of the integers.

Interpret functions that arise in applications in terms of the context

F.IF.4 For a function that models a relationship between two quantities, interpret key features of graphs and tables in terms of the quantities, and sketch graphs showing key features given a verbal description of the relationship. *Key features include: intercepts; intervals where the function is increasing, decreasing, positive, or negative; relative maximums and minimums; symmetries; end behavior; and periodicity.* ★

F.IF.5 Relate the domain of a function to its graph and, where applicable, to the quantitative relationship it describes. ★

F.IF.6 Calculate and interpret the average rate of change of a function (presented symbolically or as a table) over a specified interval. Estimate the rate of change from a graph. ★

Analyze functions using different representations

F.IF.7.a Graph functions expressed symbolically and show key features of the graph, by hand in simple cases and using technology for more complicated cases. ★ Graph linear functions and show intercepts, maxima, and minima.

F.IF.9 Compare properties of two functions each represented in a different way (algebraically, graphically, numerically in tables, or by verbal descriptions).

Building Functions

Build a function that models a relationship between two quantities

F.BF.1.a Write a function that describes a relationship between two quantities. ★ Determine an explicit expression, a recursive process, or steps for calculation from a context.

F.BF.2 Write arithmetic and geometric sequences both recursively and with an explicit formula, use them to model situations, and translate between the two forms. ★

Linear, Quadratic, and Exponential Models

Construct and compare linear and exponential models and solve problems.

F.LE.1.a Distinguish between situations that can be modeled with linear functions and with exponential functions. Prove that linear functions grow by equal differences over equal intervals, and that exponential functions grow by equal factors over equal intervals.

F.LE.1.b Distinguish between situations that can be modeled with linear functions and with exponential functions. Recognize situations in which one quantity changes at a constant rate per unit interval relative to another.

F.LE.1.c Distinguish between situations that can be modeled with linear functions and with exponential functions. Recognize situations in which a quantity grows or decays by a constant percent rate per unit interval relative to another.

F.LE.2 Construct linear and exponential functions, including arithmetic and geometric sequences, given a graph, a description of a relationship, or two input-output pairs (include reading these from a table).

F.LE.3 Observe using graphs and tables that a quantity increasing exponentially eventually exceeds a quantity increasing linearly.

Interpret expressions for functions in terms of the situation they model

F.LE.5 Interpret the parameters in a linear or exponential function in terms of a context.

Look at the domains in bold and the cluster to get a good idea of the topics you'll study this year.

Geometry

Congruence

Experiment with Transformations in the Plane

G.CO.1 Know precise definitions of angle, circle, perpendicular line, parallel line, and line segment, based on the undefined notions of point, line, distance along a line, and distance around a circular arc.

G.CO.2 Represent transformations in the plane using, e.g., transparencies and geometry software; describe transformations as functions that take points in the plane as inputs and give other points as outputs. Compare transformations that preserve distance and angle to those that do not (e.g., translation versus horizontal stretch).

G.CO.3 Given a rectangle, parallelogram, trapezoid, or regular polygon, describe the rotations and reflections that carry it onto itself.

G.CO.4 Develop definitions of rotations, reflections, and translations in terms of angles, circles, perpendicular lines, parallel lines, and line segments.

G.CO.5 Given a geometric figure and a rotation, reflection, or translation, draw the transformed figure using, e.g., graph paper, tracing paper, or geometry software. Specify a sequence of transformations that will carry a given figure onto another.

Understand congruence in terms of rigid motions

G.CO.6 Use geometric descriptions of rigid motions to transform figures and to predict the effect of a given rigid motion on a given figure; given two figures, use the definition of congruence in terms of rigid motions to decide if they are congruent.

G.CO.7 Use the definition of congruence in terms of rigid motions to show that two triangles are congruent if and only if corresponding pairs of sides and corresponding pairs of angles are congruent.

G.CO.8 Explain how the criteria for triangle congruence (ASA, SAS, and SSS) follow from the definition of congruence in terms of rigid motions.

Prove geometric theorems

G.CO.9 Prove theorems about lines and angles. *Theorems include: vertical angles are congruent; when a transversal crosses parallel lines, alternate interior angles are congruent and corresponding angles are congruent; points on a perpendicular bisector of a line segment are exactly those equidistant from the segment's endpoints*

G.CO.10 Prove theorems about triangles. *Theorems include: measures of interior angles of a triangle sum to 180°; base angles of isosceles triangles are congruent; the segment joining midpoints of two sides of a triangle is parallel to the third side and half the length; the medians of a triangle meet at a point.*

G.CO.11 Prove theorems about parallelograms. *Theorems include: opposite sides are congruent, opposite angles are congruent, the diagonals of a parallelogram bisect each other and conversely, rectangles are parallelograms with congruent diagonals.*

Statistics and Probability★

Interpreting Categorical and Quantitative Data

Summarize, represent, and interpret data on a single count or measurement variable

S.ID.1   Represent data with plots on the real number line (dot plots, histograms, and box plots).

S.ID.2   Use statistics appropriate to the shape of the data distribution to compare center (median, mean) and spread (interquartile range, standard deviation) of two or more different data sets.

S.ID.3   Interpret differences in shape, center, and spread in the context of the data sets, accounting for possible effects of extreme data points (outliers).

Summarize, represent, and interpret data on two categorical and quantitative variables

S.ID.5   Summarize categorical data for two categories in two-way frequency tables. Interpret relative frequencies in the context of the data (including joint, marginal, and conditional relative frequencies). Recognize possible associations and trends in the data.

S.ID.6.a   Represent data on two quantitative variables on a scatter plot, and describe how the variables are related. Fit a function to the data; use functions fitted to data to solve problems in the context of the data. Use given functions or choose a function suggested by the context. Emphasize linear and exponential models.

S.ID.6.c   Represent data on two quantitative variables on a scatter plot, and describe how the variables are related. Fit a linear function for a scatter plot that suggests a linear association.

Interpret linear models

S.ID.7   Interpret the slope (rate of change) and the intercept (constant term) of a linear model in the context of the data.

S.ID.8   Compute (using technology) and interpret the correlation coefficient of a linear fit.

S.ID.9   Distinguish between correlation and causation.

BIGideas

These Big Ideas are the organizing ideas for the study of important areas of mathematics: algebra, geometry, and statistics.

Stay connected! These Big Ideas will help you understand how the math you study in high school fits together.

Algebra

Properties

- In the transition from arithmetic to algebra, attention shifts from arithmetic operations (addition, subtraction, multiplication, and division) to the use of the *properties* of these operations.
- All of the facts of arithmetic and algebra follow from certain properties.

Variable

- Quantities are used to form expressions, equations, and inequalities.
- An expression refers to a quantity but does not make a statement about it. An equation (or an inequality) is a statement about the quantities it mentions.
- Using variables in place of numbers in equations (or inequalities) allows the statement of relationships among numbers that are unknown or unspecified.

Equivalence

- A single quantity may be represented by many different expressions.
- The facts about a quantity may be expressed by many different equations (or inequalities).

Solving Equations & Inequalities

- Solving an equation is the process of rewriting the equation to make what it says about its variable(s) as simple as possible.
- Properties of numbers and equality can be used to transform an equation (or inequality) into equivalent, simpler equations (or inequalities) in order to find solutions.
- Useful information about equations and inequalities (including solutions) can be found by analyzing graphs or tables.
- The numbers and types of solutions vary predictably, based on the type of equation.

Proportionality

- Two quantities are *proportional* if they have the same ratio in each instance where they are measured together.
- Two quantities are *inversely proportional* if they have the same product in each instance where they are measured together.

Function

- A function is a relationship between variables in which each value of the input variable is associated with a unique value of the output variable.
- Functions can be represented in a variety of ways, such as graphs, tables, equations, or words. Each representation is particularly useful in certain situations.
- Some important families of functions are developed through transformations of the simplest form of the function.
- New functions can be made from other functions by applying arithmetic operations or by applying one function to the output of another.

Modeling

- Many real-world mathematical problems can be represented algebraically. These representations can lead to algebraic solutions.
- A function that models a real-world situation can be used to make estimates or predictions about future occurrences.

Statistics and Probability

Data Collection and Analysis
- Sampling techniques are used to gather data from real-world situations. If the data are representative of the larger population, inferences can be made about that population.
- Biased sampling techniques yield data unlikely to be representative of the larger population.
- Sets of numerical data are described using measures of central tendency and dispersion.

Data Representation
- The most appropriate data representations depend on the type of data—quantitative or qualitative, and univariate or bivariate.
- Line plots, box plots, and histograms are different ways to show distribution of data over a possible range of values.

Probability
- Probability expresses the likelihood that a particular event will occur.
- Data can be used to calculate an experimental probability, and mathematical properties can be used to determine a theoretical probability.
- Either experimental or theoretical probability can be used to make predictions or decisions about future events.
- Various counting methods can be used to develop theoretical probabilities.

Geometry

Visualization
- Visualization can help you see the relationships between two figures and help you connect properties of real objects with two-dimensional drawings of these objects.

Transformations
- Transformations are mathematical functions that model relationships with figures.
- Transformations may be described geometrically or by coordinates.
- Symmetries of figures may be defined and classified by transformations.

Measurement
- Some attributes of geometric figures, such as length, area, volume, and angle measure, are measurable. Units are used to describe these attributes.

Reasoning & Proof
- Definitions establish meanings and remove possible misunderstanding.
- Other truths are more complex and difficult to see. It is often possible to verify complex truths by reasoning from simpler ones using deductive reasoning.

Similarity
- Two geometric figures are similar when corresponding lengths are proportional and corresponding angles are congruent.
- Areas of similar figures are proportional to the squares of their corresponding lengths.
- Volumes of similar figures are proportional to the cubes of their corresponding lengths.

Coordinate Geometry
- A coordinate system on a line is a number line on which points are labeled, corresponding to the real numbers.
- A coordinate system in a plane is formed by two perpendicular number lines, called the x- and y-axes, and the quadrants they form. The coordinate plane can be used to graph many functions.
- It is possible to verify some complex truths using deductive reasoning in combination with the distance, midpoint, and slope formulas.

8

Transformations

Geometry

Congruence
Experiment with transformations in the plane.

Chapter 8

Connecting Algebra and Geometry

Number and Quantity

Quantities
Reason quantitatively and use units to solve problems.

Geometry

Expressing Geometric Properties with Equations
Use coordinates to prove simple geometric theorems algebraically.

Chapter 9

10

Reasoning and Proof

Geometry

Congruence
Prove geometric theorems
Make geometric constructions

Chapter 10

Proving Theorems About Lines and Angles

Geometry

Congruence
  Prove geometric theorems
  Make geometric constructions

Chapter 11

Congruent Triangles

Geometry

Congruence
Make geometric constructions

Similarity, Right Triangles, and Trigonometry
Prove theorems involving similarity

Chapter 12

13

Proving Theorems About Triangles

Geometry

Congruence
Prove geometric theorems

Circles
Understand and apply theorems about circles

Chapter 13

Proving Theorems About Quadrilaterals

Geometry

Congruence
Prove geometric theorems

Similarity, Right Triangles, and Trigonometry
Prove theorems involving similarity

Chapter 14

Get Ready!

Identifying Polygons

Identify each polygon.

1. a polygon with 5 sides

2. a polygon with 10 congruent angles and 10 congruent sides

3. a parallelogram with 4 congruent sides

4. a parallelogram with 4 right angles

5. a quadrilateral with exactly 2 parallel sides

Translating Graphs

Describe how each function is a translation of the parent function $y = |x|$.

6. $g(x) = |x| + 4$

7. $h(x) = |x + 1| - 2$

8. $j(x) = |x - 5| + 1$

Writing a Function Rule

Write a function rule for each situation.

9. the area A of a rectangle when you know the length ℓ is 7 ft more than the width w

10. the cost C to buy p pounds of pasta at $1.29 per lb

11. the perimeter P of a rectangular garden whose width w is 3 ft less than its length ℓ

 Looking Ahead Vocabulary

12. Think about your *reflection* in a mirror. If you raise your right hand, which hand appears to be raised in your *reflection*? If you are standing 2 ft from the mirror, how far away from you does your *reflection* appear to be?

13. The minute hand of a clock *rotates* as the minutes go by. What point of the minute hand stays fixed as the hand *rotates*?

Transformations

Big Ideas

1 Transformations
Essential Question How can you change a figure's position without changing its size and shape?

2 Coordinate Geometry
Essential Question How can you represent a transformation in the coordinate plane?

ⓒ Domain

- Congruence

Chapter Preview

 Vocabulary

English/Spanish Vocabulary Audio Online:

English	Spanish
image, *p. 495*	imagen
isometry, *p. 532*	isometría
preimage, *p. 495*	preimagen
reflection, *p. 508*	reflexión
rigid motion, *p. 495*	movimiento rígido
rotation, *p. 515*	rotación
translation, *p. 498*	traslación

In this activity, you will use tracing paper to perform translations, rotations, and reflections.

Activity

Step 1 Copy $\triangle ABC$ and the x- and y-axis on graph paper. Trace the copy of $\triangle ABC$ on tracing paper.

Step 2 Translate $\triangle ABC$ up 4 units and to the right 2 units by sliding the tracing paper. Draw the new triangle on the graph paper and label it $\triangle A'B'C'$ so that the original vertices A, B, and C correspond to the vertices A', B', and C' of the new triangle. What are the coordinates of the vertices of $\triangle A'B'C'$? What is the same about the triangles? What is different?

Step 3 Align your tracing of $\triangle ABC$ with the original and then trace the positive x-axis and the origin.

Step 4 Rotate $\triangle ABC$ 90° counterclockwise about the origin by keeping the origin in place and aligning the traced axis with the positive y-axis. You can use the point of your pencil to hold the origin in place as you rotate the triangle. Draw the image of $\triangle ABC$ after the rotation on the graph paper and label it $\triangle A''B''C''$. Compare the coordinates of the vertices of $\triangle ABC$ with the coordinates of the vertices of $\triangle A''B''C''$. Describe the pattern.

Step 5 Flip your tracing of $\triangle ABC$ over and align the origin and the traced positive x-axis to reflect $\triangle ABC$ across the x-axis. Draw and label the reflected triangle $\triangle A'''B'''C'''$ on the graph paper. What do you notice about the orientations of the triangles?

In Exercises 1 and 2 on the next page, you will find the images of other triangles after translating, rotating, and reflecting.

Exercises

Use tracing paper. Find the images of each triangle for a translation 3 units left and 5 units down, a 90° rotation counterclockwise about the origin, and a reflection across the *x*-axis.

1.

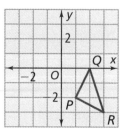

 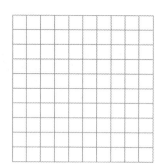 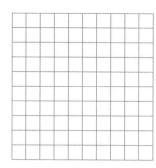

translation   rotation   reflection

2.

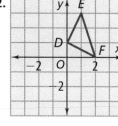

translation   rotation   reflection

8-1 Translations

G.CO.5 Given a geometric figure and a . . . translation, draw the transformed figure . . . Specify a sequence of transformations that will carry a given figure onto another. Also **G.CO.2, G.CO.4**

Objectives To identify rigid motions
To find translation images of figures

Solve It! Write your solution to the Solve It in the space below.

In the Solve It, you described changes in positions of letters. In this lesson, you will learn some of the mathematical language used to describe changes in positions of geometric figures.

Essential Understanding You can change the position of a geometric figure so that the angle measures and the distance between any two points of a figure stay the same.

A **transformation** of a geometric figure is a function, or *mapping*, that results in a change in the position, shape, or size of the figure. When you play dominoes, you often move the dominoes by flipping them, sliding them, or turning them. Each move is a type of transformation. The diagrams below illustrate some basic transformations that you will study.

The domino flips.

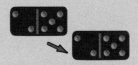
The domino slides.

The domino turns.

In a transformation, the original figure is the **preimage**. The resulting figure is the **image**. Some transformations, like those shown by the dominoes, preserve distance and angle measures. To preserve distance means that the distance between any two points of the image is the same as the distance between the corresponding points of the preimage. To preserve angles means that the angles of the image have the same angle measure as the corresponding angles of the preimage. A transformation that preserves distance and angle measures is called a **rigid motion**.

Problem 1 Identifying a Rigid Motion

Got It? Does the transformation appear to be a rigid motion? Explain.

a.

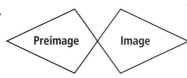

b.

Practice Tell whether the transformation appears to be a rigid motion. Explain.

1.

Image

Preimage

2.

Preimage   Image

A transformation maps every point of a figure onto its image and may be described with arrow notation (→). Prime notation (ʹ) is sometimes used to identify image points. In the diagram below, K' is the image of K.

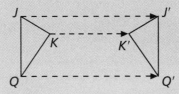

$\triangle JKQ \rightarrow \triangle J'K'Q'$
$\triangle JKQ$ maps onto $\triangle J'K'Q'$.

Notice that you list corresponding points of the preimage and image in the same order.

Problem 2 Naming Images and Corresponding Parts

Got It? In the diagram, $\triangle NID \rightarrow \triangle SUP$.

 a. What are the images of $\angle I$ and point D?

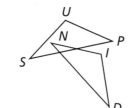

Plan

How do you identify corresponding points?

 b. What are the pairs of corresponding sides?

Ⓐ Practice In each diagram, the red figure is an image of the blue figure.

 (a) Choose an angle or point from the preimage and name its image.

 (b) List all pairs of corresponding sides.

 3.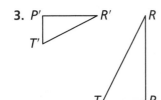

 4.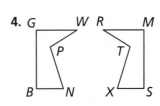

Key Concept Translation

A **translation** is a transformation that maps all points of a figure the same distance in the same direction.

You write the translation that maps $\triangle ABC$ onto $\triangle A'B'C'$ as $T(\triangle ABC) = \triangle A'B'C'$. A translation is a rigid motion with the following properties.

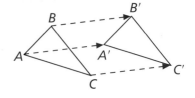

If $T(\triangle ABC) = \triangle A'B'C'$, then
- $AA' = BB' = CC'$
- $AB = A'B', BC = B'C', AC = A'C'$
- $m\angle A = m\angle A', m\angle B = m\angle B', m\angle C = m\angle C'$

The diagram at the right shows a translation in the coordinate plane. Each point of $ABCD$ is translated 4 units right and 2 units down. So each (x, y) pair in $ABCD$ is mapped to $(x + 4, y - 2)$. You can use the function notation $T_{<4, -2>}(ABCD) = A'B'C'D'$ to describe this translation, where 4 represents the translation of each point of the figure 4 units right and -2 represents the translation 2 units down.

> B moves 4 units right and 2 units down.

Problem 3   Finding the Image of a Translation

Got It?   **a.** What are the vertices of $T_{<1, -4>}(\triangle ABC)$? Copy $\triangle ABC$ and graph its image.

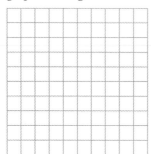

Think

What does the rule tell you about the direction each point moves?

b. Reasoning Draw $\overline{AA'}$, $\overline{BB'}$, and $\overline{CC'}$. What relationships exist among these three segments? How do you know?

Copy each graph. Graph the image of each figure under the given translation.

5. $T_{<5,-1>}(x, y)$

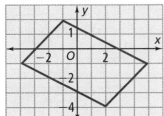

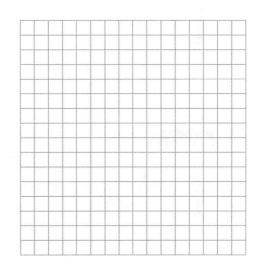

6. $T_{<-2, 5>}(x, y)$

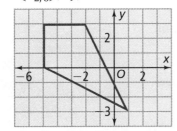

Problem 4 Writing a Rule to Describe a Translation

Got It? The translation image of $\triangle LMN$ is $\triangle L'M'N'$ with L' $(1,-2)$, M' $(3,-4)$, and N' $(6,-2)$. What is a rule that describes the translation?

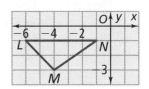

The red figure is a translation image of the blue figure. Write a rule to describe each translation.

7.

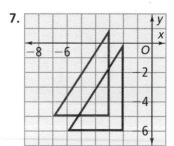

8.

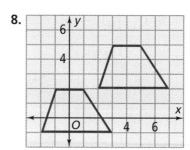

A **composition of transformations** is a combination of two or more transformations. In a composition, you perform each transformation on the image of the preceding transformation.

In the diagram at the right, the field hockey ball can move from Player 3 to Player 5 by a direct pass. This translation is represented by the blue arrow. The ball can also be passed from Player 3 to Player 9, and then from Player 9 to Player 5. The two red arrows represent this composition of translations.

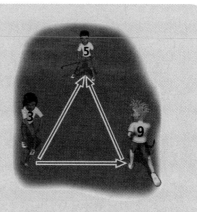

In general, the composition of any two translations is another translation.

Problem 5 Composing Translations

Got It? In Problem 5, the bishop next moves 3 squares left and 3 squares down. Where is the bishop in relation to its original position?

9. **Travel** You are visiting San Francisco. From your hotel near Union Square, you walk 4 blocks east and 4 blocks north to the Wells Fargo History Museum. Then you walk 5 blocks west and 3 blocks north to the Cable Car Barn Museum. Where is the Cable Car Barn Museum in relation to your hotel?

10. **Travel** Your friend and her parents are visiting colleges. They leave their home in Enid, Oklahoma, and drive to Tulsa, which is 107 mi east and 18 mi south of Enid. From Tulsa, they go to Norman, 83 mi west and 63 mi south of Tulsa. Where is Norman in relation to Enid?

Lesson Check

Do you know HOW?

11. If $\triangle JPT \rightarrow \triangle J'P'T'$, what are the images of P and $\overline{TJ}$?

12. Graph $T_{<-3, -4>}(NILE)$.

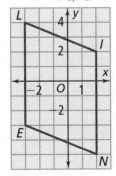

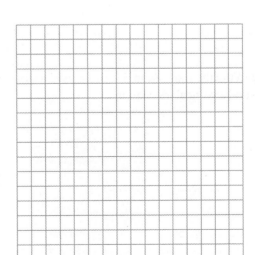

13. Point $H(x, y)$ moves 12 units left and 4 units up. What is a rule that describes this translation?

Do you UNDERSTAND?

14. Vocabulary What is true about a transformation that is not a rigid motion? Include a sketch of an example.

15. Error Analysis Your friend says the transformation $\triangle ABC \rightarrow \triangle PQR$ is a translation. Explain and correct her error.

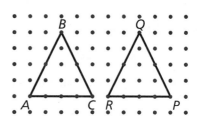

16. Reasoning Write the translation $T_{<1, -3>}(x, y)$ as a composition of a horizontal translation and a vertical translation.

More Practice and Problem-Solving Exercises

B Apply

17. In the diagram at the right, the red figure is a translation image of the blue figure. Write a rule that describes the translation.

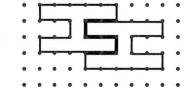

© 18. Think About a Plan $\triangle MUG$ has coordinates $M(2, -4)$, $U(6, 6)$, and $G(7, 2)$. A translation maps point M to $M'(-3, 6)$. What are the coordinates of U' and G' for this translation?

- How can you use a graph to help you visualize the problem?
- How can you find a rule that describes the translation?

Geometry in 3 Dimensions Follow the sample below. Use each figure, graph paper, and the given translation to draw a three-dimensional figure.

SAMPLE Use the rectangle and the translation $T_{<3, 1>}(x, y)$ to draw a box.

Step 1 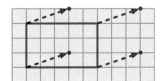   **Step 2**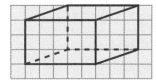

19. $T_{<2, -1>}(x, y)$ **20.** $T_{<-2, 2>}(x, y)$ **21.** $T_{<-3, -5>}(x, y)$

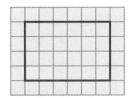   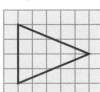   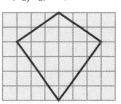

© 22. Open-Ended You are a graphic designer for a company that manufactures wrapping paper. Make a design for wrapping paper that involves translations.

© 23. Reasoning If $T_{<5, 7>}(\triangle MNO) = \triangle M'N'O'$, what translation rule maps $\triangle M'N'O'$ onto $\triangle MNO$?

24. Landscaping The diagram at the right shows the site plan for a backyard storage shed. Local law, however, requires the shed to sit at least 15 ft from property lines. Describe how to move the shed to comply with the law.

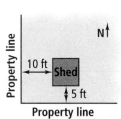

STEM 25. Computer Animation You write a computer animation program to help young children learn the alphabet. The program draws a letter, erases the letter, and makes it reappear in a new location two times. The program uses the following composition of translations to move the letter.

$$T_{<5, 7>}(x, y) \text{ followed by } T_{<-9, -2>}(x, y)$$

Suppose the program makes the letter W by connecting the points $(1, 2)$, $(2, 0)$, $(3, 2)$, $(4, 0)$, and $(5, 2)$. What points does the program connect to make the last W?

26. Use the graph at the right. Write three different translation rules for which the image of $\triangle JKL$ has a vertex at the origin.

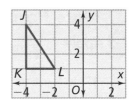

Find a translation that has the same effect as each composition of translations.

27. $T_{<2,\,5>}(x, y)$ followed by $T_{<-4,\,9>}(x, y)$

28. $T_{<12,\,0.5>}(x, y)$ followed by $T_{<1,\,-3>}(x, y)$

© Challenge

29. Coordinate Geometry $\triangle ABC$ has vertices $A(-2, 5)$, $B(-4, -1)$, and $C(2, -3)$. If $T_{<4,\,2>}(\triangle ABC) = \triangle A'B'C'$, show that the images of the midpoints of the sides of $\triangle ABC$ are the midpoints of the sides of $\triangle A'B'C'$.

© **30. Writing** Explain how to use translations to draw a parallelogram.

Paper Folding and Reflections

In Activity 1, you will see how a figure and its *reflection* image are related. In Activity 2, you will use these relationships to construct a reflection image.

Activity 1

Step 1 Use a piece of tracing paper and a straightedge. Using less than half the page, draw a large, scalene triangle. Label its vertices *A*, *B*, and *C*.

Step 2 Fold the paper so that your triangle is covered. Trace △*ABC* using a straightedge.

Step 3 Unfold the paper. Label the traced points corresponding to *A*, *B*, and *C* as *A′* , *B′* , and *C′*, respectively. △*A′B′C′* is a reflection image of △*ABC*. The fold is the reflection line.

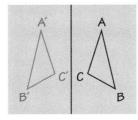

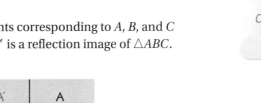

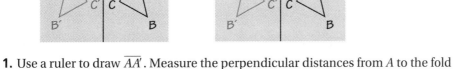

1. Use a ruler to draw $\overline{AA'}$. Measure the perpendicular distances from *A* to the fold and from *A′* to the fold. What do you notice?

2. Measure the angles formed by the fold and $\overline{AA'}$. What are the angle measures?

3. Repeat Exercises 1 and 2 for B and B' and for C and C'. Then, make a conjecture: How is the reflection line related to the segment joining a point and its image?

Activity 2

Step 1 On regular paper, draw a simple shape or design made of segments. Use less than half the page. Draw a reflection line near your figure.

Step 2 Draw a line perpendicular to the reflection line through one point of your drawing.

4. Explain how you can use a ruler and the perpendicular you drew to find the reflection image of the point you chose.

5. Connect the reflection images for several points of your shape and complete the image. Check the accuracy of the reflection image by folding the paper along the reflection line and holding it up to a light source.

G.CO.5 Given a geometric figure and a rotation . . . draw the transformed figure . . . Specify a sequence of transformations that will carry a given figure onto another. Also **G.CO.2, G.CO.4**

Objective To find reflection images of figures

 Solve It! Write your solution to the Solve It in the space below.

In the Solve It, you reflected shapes across lines. Notice that when you reflect a figure, the shapes have *opposite orientations*. Two figures have opposite orientations if the corresponding vertices of the preimage and image read in opposite directions.

The vertices of △*BUG* read clockwise.

The vertices of △*B′U′G′* read counterclockwise.

Essential Understanding When you reflect a figure across a line, each point of the figure maps to another point the same distance from the line but on the other side. The orientation of the figure reverses.

In order to precisely define reflections, you need to use the *perpendicular bisector* of a segment, which is the line perpendicular to the segment at its midpoint. A point (or line) is *equidistant* from a set of other points when it is the same distance from each of those other points.

Key Concept   Reflection Across a Line

A **reflection** across a line *m*, called the **line of reflection**, is a transformation with the following properties:

- If a point *A* is on line *m*, then the image of *A* is itself (that is, $A' = A$).
- If a point *B* is not on line *m*, then *m* is the perpendicular bisector of $\overline{BB'}$.

You write the reflection across *m* that takes *P* to *P'* as $R_m(P) = P'$.

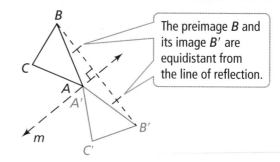

The preimage *B* and its image *B'* are equidistant from the line of reflection.

You can use the equation of a line of reflection in the function notation. For example, $R_{y=x}$ describes the reflection across the line $y = x$.

Problem 1   **Reflecting a Point Across a Line**

Got It? Point *P* has coordinates (3, 4). If $R_{x=1}(P) = P'$, what are the coordinates of *P'*?

Think

How does a graph help you visualize the problem?

 Practice Find the coordinates of each image.

1. $R_{x=-3}(U)$

2. $R_{x\text{-axis}}(V)$

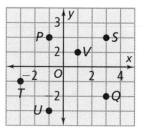

You can also use the notation R_m to describe reflections of figures. The diagram on the next page shows $R_m(\triangle ABC)$, and function notation is used to describe some of the properties of reflections.

Property   Properties of Reflections

- Reflections preserve distance.
  If $R_m(A) = A'$, and $R_m(B) = B'$, then $AB = A'B'$.
- Reflections preserve angle measure.
  If $R_m(\angle ABC) = \angle A'B'C'$, then $m\angle ABC = m\angle A'B'C'$.
- Reflections map each point of the preimage to one and only one corresponding point of its image.
  $R_m(A) = A'$ if and only if $R_m(A') = A$.

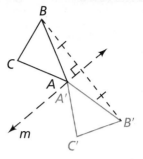

Observe that the above properties mean that reflections are rigid motions, which you learned about in Lesson 8-1.

Problem 2   Graphing a Reflection Image

Got It?   Graph $\triangle ABC$ from Problem 2. Graph and label $R_{x\text{-axis}}(\triangle ABC)$.

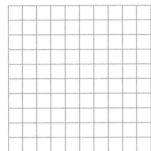

Practice   Coordinate Geometry Given points $J(1, 4)$, $A(3, 5)$, and $G(2, 1)$, graph $\triangle JAG$ and its reflection image as indicated.

3. $R_{y=5}$

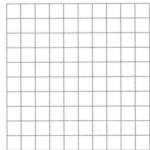

4. $R_{x=2}$

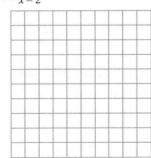

Got It?   Use the figure in Problem 3. How can you use a reflection rule to describe Triangle 1? Explain.

 Practice   **5.** Each figure in the diagram at the right is a reflection of another figure across one of the reflection lines.

    a. Write a reflection rule to describe Figure 3. Justify your answer.

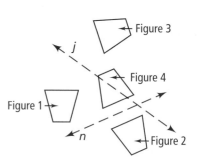

    b. Write a reflection rule to describe Figure 2. Justify your answer.

    c. Write a reflection rule to describe Figure 4. Justify your answer.

You can use the properties of reflections to prove statements about figures.

 Problem 4 **Using Properties of Reflections**

Got It? Can you use properties of reflections to prove that △*GHJ* is equilateral? Explain.

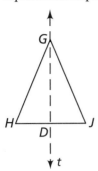

Think

What do you need to prove to show that △***GHJ*** is equilateral?

Practice **6.** In the diagram below, *LMNP* is a rectangle with *LM* = 2*MN*.

    a. Sketch $R_{\overline{LM}}(LMNP)$.

    b. What figure results from the reflection? Use properties of reflections to justify your solution.

Lesson Check

Do you know HOW?

Use the graph of △*FGH*.

7. What are the coordinates of $R_{y\text{-axis}}(H)$?

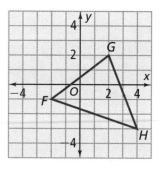

8. What are the coordinates of $R_{x=3}(G)$?

9. Graph and label $R_{y=4}(\triangle FGH)$.

Do you UNDERSTAND?

MATHEMATICAL
PRACTICES

10. Vocabulary What is the relationship between a line of reflection and a segment joining corresponding points of the preimage and image?

11. Error Analysis A classmate sketched $R_s(A) = A'$ as shown in the diagram.

   a. Explain your classmate's error.

   b. Copy point *A* and line *s* and show the correct location of *A'*.

12. What are the coordinates of a point $P(x, y)$ reflected across the y-axis? Across the x-axis? Use reflection notation to write your answer.

More Practice and Problem-Solving Exercises

B **Apply**

Copy each figure and line ℓ. Draw each figure's reflection image across line ℓ.

13.

14.

15. Think About a Plan The coordinates of the vertices of $\triangle FGH$ are
$F(2, -1)$, $G(-2, -2)$, and $H(-4, 3)$. Graph $\triangle FGH$ and $R_{y=x-3}(\triangle FGH)$.
- What is the relationship between the line $y = x - 3$ and $\overline{FF'}$, $\overline{GG'}$ and $\overline{HH'}$?
- How can you use slope to find the image of each vertex?

16. In the diagram $R(ABCDE) = A'B'C'D'E'$.
   a. What are the midpoints of $\overline{AA'}$ and $\overline{DD'}$?
   b. What is the equation of the line of reflection?
   c. Write a rule that describes this reflection.

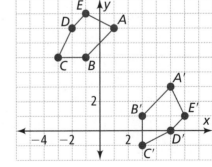

Copy each pair of figures. Then draw the line of reflection you can use to map one figure onto the other.

17.

18.

19. History The work of artist and scientist Leonardo da Vinci (1452–1519) has an unusual characteristic. His handwriting is a mirror image of normal handwriting.

    a. Write the mirror image of the sentence, "Leonardo da Vinci was left-handed." Use a mirror to check how well you did.

    b. Explain why the fact about da Vinci in part (a) might have made mirror writing seem natural to him.

Ⓒ **20. Open-Ended** Give three examples from everyday life of objects or situations that show or use reflections.

Find the image of $O(0, 0)$ after two reflections, first across line ℓ_1 and then across line ℓ_2.

21. $\ell_1 : y = 3, \ell_2 : x\text{-axis}$ **22.** $\ell_1 : x = -2, \ell_2 : y\text{-axis}$ **23.** $\ell_1 : x\text{-axis}, \ell_2 : y\text{-axis}$

Ⓒ **24. Reasoning** When you reflect a figure across a line, does every point on the preimage move the same distance? Explain.

25. Use the diagram at the right. Find the coordinates of each image point.

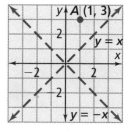

    a. $R_{y = x}(A) = A'$

    b. $R_{y = -x}(A') = A''$

    c. $R_{y = x}(A'') = A'''$

    d. $R_{y = -x}(A''') = A''''$

    e. How are A and A'''' related?

Ⓒ **Challenge**

Ⓒ **Reasoning** Can you form the given type of quadrilateral by drawing a triangle and then reflecting one or more times? Explain.

26. parallelogram   **27.** isosceles trapezoid   **28.** kite

29. rhombus   **30.** rectangle   **31.** square

8-3 Rotations

G.CO.4 Develop definitions of rotations . . . in terms of angles, circles, perpendicular lines, . . . and line segments. Also **G.CO.2, G.CO.5**

Objective To draw and identify rotation images of figures

 Solve It! Write your solution to the Solve It in the space below.

In the Solve It, you thought about how the coordinates of a point change as it turns, or *rotates*, about the origin on a coordinate grid. In this lesson, you will learn how to recognize and draw rotations of geometric figures.

Essential Understanding Rotations preserve distance, angle measures, and orientation of figures.

take note

Key Concept Rotation About a Point

A **rotation** of $x°$ about a point Q, called the **center of rotation**, is a transformation with these two properties:

- The image of Q is itself (that is, $Q' = Q$).
- For any other point V, $QV' = QV$ and $m\angle VQV' = x$.

The preimage V and its image V' are equidistant from the center of rotation.

The number of degrees a figure rotates is the **angle of rotation**.

A rotation about a point is a rigid motion. You write the $x°$ rotation of $\triangle UVW$ about point Q as $r_{(x°, Q)}(\triangle UVW) = \triangle U'V'W'$.

Unless stated otherwise, rotations in this book are counterclockwise.

Got It? Copy △*LOB* from Problem 1. What is the image of △*LOB* for a 50° rotation about *B*?

Practice Draw the image of each figure for the given rotation about *P*. Use prime notation to label the vertices of the image.

1. 60°

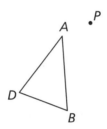

2. 90°

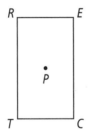

When a figure is rotated 90°, 180°, 270°, or 360° about the origin O in a coordinate plane, you can use the following rules.

Key Concept   Rotation in the Coordinate Plane

$r_{(90°, O)}(x, y) = (-y, x)$

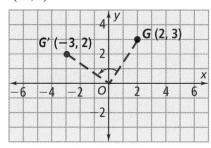

$r_{(180°, O)}(x, y) = (-x, -y)$

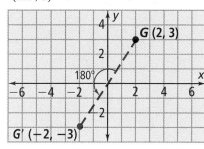

$r_{(270°, O)}(x, y) = (y, -x)$

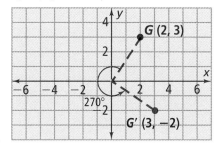

$r_{(360°, O)}(x, y) = (x, y)$

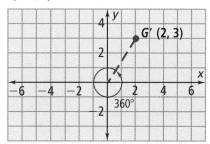

Problem 2   Drawing Rotations in a Coordinate Plane

Got It?   Graph $r_{(270°, O)}(FGHI)$.

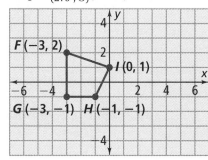

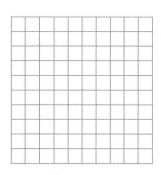

Plan

How do you know where to draw the vertices on the coordinate plane?

Practice For Exercises 3 and 4, use the graph at the right.

3. Graph $r_{(90°, O)}(FGHJ)$.

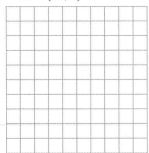

4. Graph $r_{(270°, O)}(FGHJ)$.

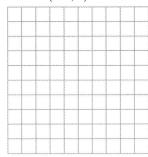

You can use the properties of rotations to solve problems.

Problem 3 **Using Properties of Rotations**

Got It? Use the figure in Problem 3. Can you use the properties of rotations to prove that *WXYZ* is a rhombus? Explain.

Plan

What would you need to show that *WXYZ* is a rhombus?

Practice For Exercises 5 and 6, use the diagram at the right. *TQNV* is a rectangle. *M* is the midpoint of the diagonals.

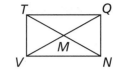

5. Use the properties of rotations to show that the measures of both pairs of opposite sides are equal in length.

 6. Reasoning Can you use the properties of rotations to show that the measures of the lengths of the diagonals are equal?

Lesson Check

Do you know HOW?

7. Draw $r_{(70°, P)}(\triangle ABC)$.

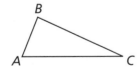

In the figure at the right, point *A* is equidistant from the vertices of square *SQRE*.

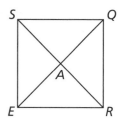

8. What is $r_{(90°, A)}(E)$?

9. What is the image of $\overline{RQ}$ for a 180° rotation about *A*?

10. Use the properties of rotations to describe how you know that the lengths of the diagonals of the square are equal.

Do you UNDERSTAND?

© 11. Vocabulary $\triangle A'B'C'$ is a rotation image of $\triangle ABC$ about point *O*. Describe how to find the angle of rotation.

© 12. Error Analysis A classmate drew a 115° rotation of $\triangle PQR$ about point *P*, as shown at the right. Explain and correct your classmate's error.

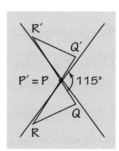

13. Compare and Contrast Compare rotating a figure about a point to reflecting the figure across a line. How are the transformations alike? How are they different?

 14. Reasoning Point $P(x, y)$ is rotated about the origin by $135°$ and then by $45°$. What are the coordinates of the image of point P? Explain.

More Practice and Problem-Solving Exercises

MATHEMATICAL PRACTICES

B Apply

15. In the diagram at the right, $\overline{M'N'}$ is the rotation image of $\overline{MN}$ about point E. Name all pairs of angles and all pairs of segments that have equal measures in the diagram.

16. **Language Arts** Symbols are used in dictionaries to help users pronounce words correctly. The ə symbol is called a *schwa*. It is used in dictionaries to represent neutral vowel sounds such as *a* in *ago*, *i* in *sanity*, and *u* in *focus*. What transformation maps a ə to a lowercase e?

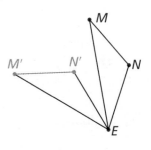

Find the angle of rotation about C that maps the blue figure to the red figure.

17.

18.

19.
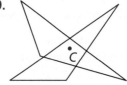

20. Think About a Plan The Millenium Wheel, also known as the London Eye, contains 32 observation cars. Determine the angle of rotation that will bring Car 3 to the position of Car 18.
- How do you find the angle of rotation that a car travels when it moves one position counterclockwise?
- How many positions does Car 3 move?

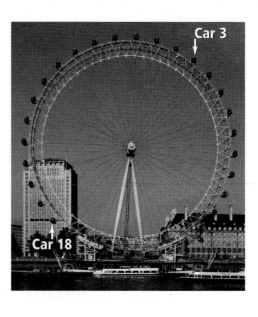

Car 3

Car 18

21. Reasoning For center of rotation P, does an $x°$ rotation followed by a $y°$ rotation give the same image as a $y°$ rotation followed by an $x°$ rotation? Explain.

22. Writing Describe how a series of rotations can have the same effect as a 360° rotation about a point X.

23. Coordinate Geometry Graph $A(5, 2)$. Graph B, the image of A for a 90° rotation about the origin O. Graph C, the image of A for a 180° rotation about O. Graph D, the image of A for a 270° rotation about O. What type of quadrilateral is $ABCD$? Explain.

Point O is equidistant from the vertices of the regular nonagon shown at the right.

24. Find the angle of rotation that maps F to H.

25. Open-Ended Describe a rotation that maps H to C.

26. Error Analysis Your friend says that $\overline{AB}$ is the image of $\overline{ED}$ for a 120° rotation about O. What is wrong with your friend's statement?

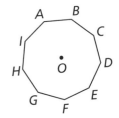

In the figure at the right, the large triangle, the quadrilateral, and the hexagon are regular. Find the image of each point or segment for the given rotation or composition of rotations. (Hint: Adjacent red segments form 30° angles.)

27. $r_{(120°, O)}(B)$

28. $r_{(270°, O)}(L)$

29. $r_{(300°, O)}(\overline{IB})$

30. $r_{(60°, O)}(E)$

31. $r_{(180°, O)}(\overline{JK})$

32. $r_{(240°, O)}(G)$

33. $r_{(120°, H)}(F)$

34. $r_{(270°, L)}(M)$

35. $r_{(180°, O)}(I)$

36. $r_{(270°, O)}(M)$

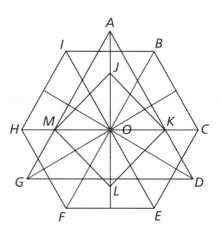

Challenge

37. Coordinate Geometry Draw $\triangle LMN$ with vertices $L(2, -1)$, $M(6, -2)$, and $N(4, 2)$. Find the coordinates of the vertices after a 90° rotation about the origin and about each of the points L, M, and N.

38. Reasoning If you are given a figure and a rotation image of the figure, how can you find the center and angle of rotation?

Symmetry

G.CO.3 Given a . . . polygon, describe the rotations and reflections that carry it onto itself.

You can use what you know about reflections and rotations to identify types of **symmetry**. A figure has symmetry if there is a rigid motion that maps the figure onto itself.

A figure has **line symmetry**, or **reflectional symmetry**, if there is a reflection for which the figure is its own image. The line of reflection is called the **line of symmetry**.

A figure has a **rotational symmetry**, if its image, after a rotation of less than 360°, is exactly the same as the original figure. A figure has **point symmetry** if a 180° rotation about a center of rotation maps the figure onto itself.

Activity 1

1. Refer to the rhombus at the right.

   a. How many lines of reflection, or lines of symmetry, does the rhombus have?

   b. Draw all of the lines of symmetry.

2. Do all parallelograms have reflectional symmetry? Explain your reasoning.

3. The isosceles trapezoid at the right has only 1 pair of parallel sides. How many lines of symmetry does the trapezoid have?

4. Do all isosceles trapezoids have reflectional symmetry? Do all trapezoids have reflectional symmetry? Explain.

Activity 2

5. Refer to the regular hexagon at the right.

    a. How many lines of symmetry does a regular hexagon have?

    b. Draw all of the lines of symmetry.

6. What are the center and angle(s) of the rotations that map the regular hexagon onto itself?

7. Do all regular polygons have rotational symmetry? Explain your reasoning.

8. Do all regular polygons have point symmetry? Explain.

Activity 3

Copy and cut out the shapes below. Shade $\frac{1}{2}$ of each square to represent the darker sections. Arrange the shapes to make a design that has both reflectional symmetry and rotational symmetry.

9. Draw the design you made.

10. How many lines of symmetry does your design have? Sketch each line of symmetry.

11. Why is the shading of the tiles important to the symmetry?

12. Does your design have more than one of angle of rotation that maps it onto itself? If so, what are they?

13. Can you change the center of rotation and still map the figure onto itself? Explain.

Exercises

Tell what type(s) of symmetry each figure has. Sketch the figure and the line(s) of symmetry, and give the angle(s) of rotation when appropriate.

14.

15.

16.

ⓔ **17. Vocabulary** If a figure has point symmetry, must it also have rotational symmetry? Explain.

© **18. Writing** A quadrilateral with vertices $(1, 5)$ and $(-2, -3)$ has point symmetry about the origin.

    a. How can you use point symmetry to find the other vertices?

    b. Show that the quadrilateral is a parallelogram.

© **19. Error Analysis** Your friend thinks that the regular pentagon in the diagram has 10 lines of symmetry. Explain and correct your friend's error.

Exploring Multiple Transformations

G.CO.2 Represent transformations in the plane using, e.g., . . . geometry software . . . Also **G.CO.5**

MATHEMATICAL
PRACTICES

You can use geometry software to explore compositions of transformations.

Activity 1

Step 1 Draw $\triangle ABC$. Construct two parallel lines that do not intersect the triangle, and label them m and s.

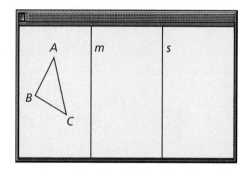

Step 2 Reflect $\triangle ABC$ across line m. Label the vertices of the reflected triangle as shown.

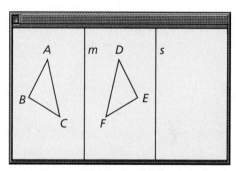

Step 3 Reflect $\triangle DEF$ across line s. Label the vertices of the reflected triangle as shown.

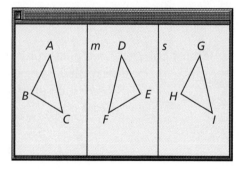

Step 4 Drag elements of the construction to different parts of the display window, including $\triangle ABC$ and lines m and s. Observe how the three triangles move relative to each other.

Activity 2

Step 1   Draw △*LMN* and two intersecting lines that do not intersect the triangle. Label the lines *j* and *k*.

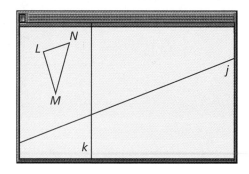

Step 2   Reflect △*LMN* across line *k*. Label the vertices of the reflected triangle as shown.

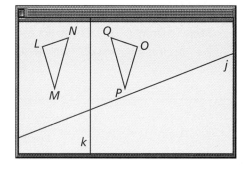

Step 3   Reflect △*OPQ* across line *j*. Label the vertices of the reflected triangle as shown.

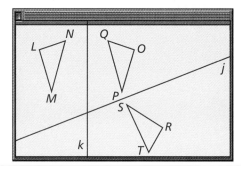

Step 4   Drag elements of the construction to different parts of the display window, including △*LMN* and lines *k* and *j*. Observe how the three triangles move relative to each other.

Exercises

© **1. Make a Conjecture** In Activity 1, what is a single transformation that will map $\triangle ABC$ onto $\triangle GHI$? Make a conjecture about the result of a composition of reflections of a preimage across two parallel lines.

2. In Activity 2, suppose that the intersecting lines were perpendicular. What rotation could you use to get the same result as reflecting the preimage across two perpendicular lines?

© **3. Reasoning** Use geometry software to measure the side lengths and angle measures of all of the triangles in Activity 1 and in Activity 2. What can you conclude about the relationships between corresponding sides and angles of the preimage and image after a composition of transformations?

8-4 Compositions of Isometries

G.CO.5 Given a geometric figure and a rotation, reflection, or translation, draw the transformed figure . . .
Specify a sequence of transformations that will carry a given figure onto another. Also **G.CO.2**

Objectives To find compositions of isometries, including glide reflections
To classify isometries

 Solve It! Write your solution to the Solve It in the space below.

In the Solve It, you looked for a way to use two reflections to produce the same image as a given horizontal translation. In this lesson, you will learn that any rigid motion can be expressed as a composition of reflections.

The term *isometry* means "same distance." An **isometry** is a transformation that preserves distance, or length. So, translations, reflections, and rotations are isometries.

Essential Understanding You can express all isometries as compositions of reflections.

Expressing isometries as compositions of reflections depends on the following fact.

take note

Key Concept Composition of Isometries

The composition of two or more isometries is an isometry.

There are only four kinds of isometries.

Translation	Rotation	Reflection	Glide Reflection
R ⤏ R	↶⤏R	R|Я	R ⤏ R / Я

You will learn about *glide reflections* later in the lesson.

In Lesson 8-1, you learned that a composition of transformations is a combination of two or more transformations, one performed after the other.

Key Concept Reflections Across Parallel Lines

A composition of reflections across two parallel lines is a translation.

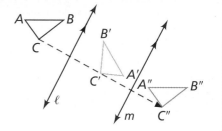

You can write this composition as
$(R_m \circ R_\ell)(\triangle ABC) = \triangle A''B''C''$
or $R_m(R_\ell(\triangle ABC)) = \triangle A''B''C''$.

$\overline{AA''}$, $\overline{BB''}$, and $\overline{CC''}$ are all perpendicular to lines ℓ and m.

ONLINE PROBLEMS

Problem 1 Composing Reflections Across Parallel Lines

Got It?   **a.** Draw parallel lines ℓ and m as in Problem 1. Draw J between ℓ and m. What is the image of $(R_m \circ R_\ell)(J)$? What is the distance of the resulting translation?

Think

Which line do you reflect over first?

ⓒ b. Reasoning Use the results of part (a) and Problem 1. Make a conjecture about the distance of any translation that is the result of a composition of reflections across two parallel lines.

Practice Find the image of each letter after the transformation $R_m \circ R_\ell$.
Describe the resulting translation.

1.

F

$\longleftrightarrow \quad \ell$

$\longleftrightarrow \quad m$

2.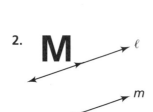

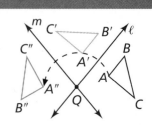

---

take note

Key Concept   Reflections Across Intersecting Lines

A composition of reflections across two intersecting lines is a rotation.

You can write this composition as $(R_m \circ R_\ell)(\triangle ABC) = \triangle A''B''C''$ or
$R_m(R_\ell(\triangle ABC)) = \triangle A''B''C''$.

The figure is rotated about the point where the two lines intersect, in
this case, point Q.

Problem 2 **Composing Reflections Across Intersecting Lines**

Got It?   **a.** Use the diagram below. What is $(R_b \circ R_a)(J)$? What are the center and the angle of rotation for the resulting rotation?

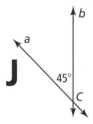

b. Reasoning Use the results of part (a) and Problem 2. Make a conjecture about the center of rotation and the angle of rotation for any rotation that is the result of any composition of reflections across two intersecting lines.

Ⓐ Practice Find the image of each letter after the transformation $R_m \circ R_\ell$. What are the center and angle of rotation for the resulting rotation?

3.

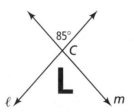

4.

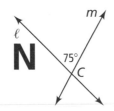

Any composition of isometries can be represented by a
reflection, translation, rotation, or glide reflection. A **glide
reflection** is the composition of a translation (a glide) and a
reflection across a line parallel to the direction of translation.
You can map a left paw print onto a right paw print with a
glide reflection.

ONLINE PROBLEMS **Problem 3**   **Finding a Glide Reflection Image**

Got It?   Graph △*TEX* from Problem 3. What is the image of △*TEX* for the
glide reflection $(R_{y=-2} \circ T_{<1, 0>})(\triangle TEX)$?

Think
What is the
direction of the
translation?

A Practice   Graph △*PNB* and its image after the given transformation.

5. $(R_{y=0} \circ T_{<2, 2>})(\triangle PNB)$

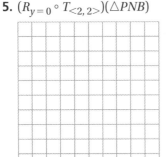

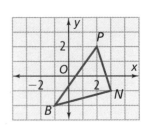

6. $(R_{y=x} \circ T_{<-1,\,1>})(\triangle PNB)$

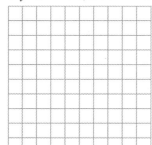

Lesson Check

Do you know HOW?

Sketch the image of Z reflected across line *a*, then across line *b*.

7.

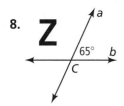

8.

Z /a
65° b
C

9. $\triangle PQR$ has vertices $P(0, 5)$, $Q(5, 3)$, and $R(3, 1)$. What are the vertices of the image of $\triangle PQR$ for the glide reflection $(R_{y=-2} \circ T_{<3,\,-1>})(\triangle PQR)$?

Do you UNDERSTAND?

© 10. Vocabulary In a glide reflection, what is the relationship between the direction of the translation and the line of reflection?

© 11. Error Analysis You reflect $\triangle DEF$ first across line m and then across line n. Your friend says you can get the same result by reflecting $\triangle DEF$ first across line n and then across line m. Explain your friend's error.

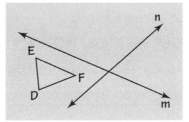

More Practice and Problem-Solving Exercises

Ⓑ Apply

Use the given points and lines. Graph $\overline{AB}$ and its image $\overline{A''B''}$ after a reflection first across ℓ_1 and then across ℓ_2. Is the resulting transformation a translation or a rotation? For a translation, describe the direction and distance. For a rotation, tell the center of rotation and the angle of rotation.

12. $A(1, 5)$ and $B(2, 1)$; $\ell_1 : x = 3$; $\ell_2 : x = 7$

13. $A(2, 4)$ and $B(3, 1)$; $\ell_1 : x$-axis; $\ell_2 : y$-axis

14. $A(-4, -3)$ and $B(-4, 0)$; $\ell_1 : y = x$; $\ell_2 : y = -x$

15. $A(2, -5)$ and $B(-1, -3)$; $\ell_1 : y = 0$; $\ell_2 : y = 2$

16. $A(6, -4)$ and $B(5, 0)$; $\ell_1 : x = 6$; $\ell_2 : x = 4$

17. $A(-1, 0)$ and $B(0, -2)$; $\ell_1 : y = -1$; $\ell_2 : y = 1$

© 18. Think About a Plan Let A' be the point $(1, 5)$. If $(R_{y=1} \circ T_{<3, 0>})(A) = A'$, then what are the coordinates of A?
- How can you *work backwards* to find the coordinates of A?
- Should A be to the left or to the right of A'?
- Should A be above or below A'?

Describe the isometry that maps the blue figure onto the red figure.

19.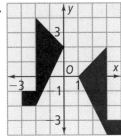

20.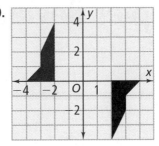

21. Which transformation maps the blue triangle onto the red triangle?

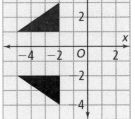

Ⓐ $R_{x=2} \circ T_{<0,-3>}$

Ⓑ $r_{(180°,\,O)}$

Ⓒ $R_{y=-\frac{1}{2}}$

Ⓓ $r_{(180°,\,O)} \circ R_{x\text{-axis}}$

Ⓒ **22. Writing** Reflections and glide reflections are *odd isometries*, while translations and rotations are *even isometries*. Use what you have learned in this lesson to explain why these categories make sense.

Ⓒ **23. Open-Ended** Draw $\triangle ABC$. Describe a reflection, a translation, a rotation, and a glide reflection. Then draw the image of $\triangle ABC$ for each transformation.

Ⓒ **24. Reasoning** The definition states that a glide reflection is the composition of a translation and a reflection. Explain why these can occur in either order.

Identify each mapping as a translation, reflection, rotation, or glide reflection. Write the rule for each translation, reflection, rotation, or glide reflection. For glide reflections, write the rule as a composition of a translation and a reflection.

25. $\triangle ABC \rightarrow \triangle EDC$

26. $\triangle EDC \rightarrow \triangle PQM$

27. $\triangle MNJ \rightarrow \triangle EDC$

28. $\triangle HIF \rightarrow \triangle HGF$

29. $\triangle PQM \rightarrow \triangle JLM$

30. $\triangle MNP \rightarrow \triangle EDC$

31. $\triangle JLM \rightarrow \triangle MNJ$

32. $\triangle PQM \rightarrow \triangle KJN$

33. $\triangle KJN \rightarrow \triangle ABC$

34. $\triangle HGF \rightarrow \triangle KJN$

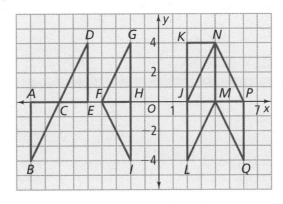

Ⓒ **Challenge**

35. Describe a glide reflection that maps the blue R to the red.

Ⓒ **36. Reasoning** Does an $x°$ rotation about a point P followed by a reflection across a line ℓ give the same image as a reflection across ℓ followed by an $x°$ rotation about P? Explain.

R

MathXL® for School
Go to pearsonsuccessnet.com

8-1 Translations

Quick Review

A **transformation** of a geometric figure is a change in its position, shape, or size.

A **translation** is a rigid motion that maps all points of a figure the same distance in the same direction.

In a **composition of transformations**, each transformation is performed on the image of the preceding transformation.

Example

What are the coordinates of $T_{<-2, 3>}(5, -9)$?

Add -2 to the x-coordinate, and 3 to the y-coordinate.

$(5, -9) \rightarrow (5 - 2, -9 + 3)$, or $(3, -6)$.

Exercises

1. a. A transformation maps $ZOWE$ onto $LFMA$. Does the transformation appear to be a rigid motion? Explain.

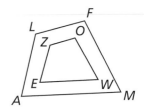

  b. What is the image of $\overline{ZE}$? What is the preimage of M?

2. $\triangle RST$ has vertices $R(0, -4)$, $S(-2, -1)$, and $T(-6, 1)$. Graph $T_{<-4, 7>}(\triangle RST)$.

3. Write a rule to describe a translation 5 units left and 10 units up.

4. Find a single translation that has the same effect as the following composition of translations.

$T_{<-4, 7>}$ followed by $T_{<3, 0>}$

8-2 Reflections

Quick Review

The diagram shows a **reflection** across line r. A reflection is a rigid motion that preserves distance and angle measure. The image and preimage of a reflection have opposite orientations.

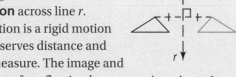

Example

Use points $P(1, 0)$, $Q(3, -2)$, and $R(4, 0)$. What is $R_{y\text{-axis}}(\triangle PQR)$?

Graph $\triangle PQR$. Find P', Q', and R' such that the y-axis is the perpendicular bisector of $\overline{PP'}$, $\overline{QQ'}$, and $\overline{RR'}$. Draw $\triangle P'Q'R'$.

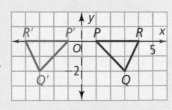

Exercises

Given points $A(6, 4)$, $B(-2, 1)$, and $C(5, 0)$, graph $\triangle ABC$ and each reflection image.

5. $R_{x\text{-axis}}(\triangle ABC)$ **6.** $R_{x = 4}(\triangle ABC)$

7. $R_{y = x}(\triangle ABC)$

8. Copy the diagram. Then draw $R_{y\text{-axis}}(BGHT)$. Label the vertices of the image by using prime notation.

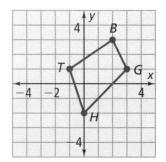

8-3 Rotations

Quick Review

The diagram shows a **rotation** of $x°$ about point R. A rotation is a rigid motion in which a figure and its image have the same orientation.

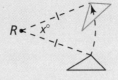

Example

GHIJ has vertices $G(0, -3)$, $H(4, 1)$, $I(-1, 2)$, and $J(-5, -2)$. **What are the vertices of** $r_{(90°, O)}(GHIJ)$**?**

Use the rule $r_{(90°, O)}(x, y) = (-y, x)$.

$$r_{(90°, O)}(G) = (3, 0)$$

$$r_{(90°, O)}(H) = (-1, 4)$$

$$r_{(90°, O)}(I) = (-2, -1)$$

$$r_{(90°, O)}(J) = (2, -5)$$

Exercises

9. Copy the diagram below. Then draw $r_{(90°, P)}(\triangle ZXY)$. Label the vertices of the image by using prime notation.

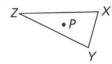

10. What are the coordinates of $r_{(180°, O)}(-4, 1)$?

11. *WXYZ* is a quadrilateral with vertices $W(3, -1)$, $X(5, 2)$, $Y(0, 8)$, and $Z(2, -1)$. Graph *WXYZ* and $r_{(270°, O)}(WXYZ)$.

8-4 Compositions of Isometries

Quick Review

An **isometry** is a transformation that preserves distance. All of the rigid motions, translations, reflections, and rotations, are isometries. A composition of isometries is also an isometry. All rigid motions can be expressed as a composition of reflections.

The diagram shows a **glide reflection** of N. A glide reflection is an isometry in which a figure and its image have opposite orientations.

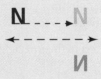

Example

Describe the result of reflecting P first across line ℓ and then across line m.

A composition of two reflections across intersecting lines is a rotation. The angle of rotation is twice the measure of the acute angle formed by the intersecting lines. P is rotated $100°$ about C.

Exercises

12. Sketch and describe the result of reflecting E first across line ℓ and then across line m.

Each figure is an isometry image of the figure at the right. Tell whether their orientations are the same or opposite. Then classify the isometry.

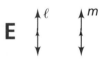

13.

14.

15.

16. $\triangle TAM$ has vertices $T(0, 5)$, $A(4, 1)$, and $M(3, 6)$. Find $R_{y = -2} \circ T_{<-4, 0>}(\triangle TAM)$.

Pull It All Together

Programming a Video Game

 ASSESSMENT

Alicia is a programmer for a company that makes video games. She is working on an interactive jigsaw puzzle. She needs to use transformations to write a program that will move the puzzle piece, shown by $\triangle ABC$, into the target area, $\triangle A'B'C'$.

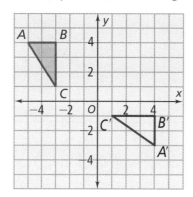

Alicia wants to write the program for two different cases, which correspond to two different levels of the game.

- Case 1: Reflections across any line are allowed.
- Case 2: Reflections across only the axes are allowed.

Alicia must convince her boss that the transformations she uses in each case move the puzzle piece to the target area in the minimum number of moves.

Task Description

Determine a composition of transformations that moves the puzzle piece to the target area for Case 1 and for Case 2. In each case, explain how you know that you have moved the piece in the minimum number of moves.

- What can you conclude by looking at the orientation of the puzzle piece and the orientation of the target area?
- How can you show that there is no single transformation that maps $\triangle ABC$ to $\triangle A'B'C'$?

Get Ready!

Squaring Numbers

Simplify.

1. 6^2

2. 5^2

3. 12^2

Simplifying Expressions

Simplify each expression. Use 3.14 for π.

4. $3 \cdot 2.5 + 3 \cdot 1.5$

5. $\pi(2)^2$

6. $\sqrt{8^2 + 15^2}$

Evaluating Expressions

Evaluate the following expressions for $a = -3$ and $b = 7$.

7. $\frac{a + b}{2}$

8. $\frac{b - 8}{4 + a}$

9. $\sqrt{(2 - a)^2 + (-5 - b)^2}$

Finding Absolute Value

Simplify each absolute value expression.

10. $|-4|$

11. $|1 - 10|$

12. $|-6 - (-5)|$

Solving Equations

Algebra Solve each equation.

13. $8 = 3x - 7$

14. $4x - 5 = 7 - 2x$

15. $-1 - 3x = 5 - 3(2x + 4)$

 Looking Ahead Vocabulary

16. A building or a monument can have a *base* and a *height*. What are the *base* and the *height* of a parallelogram?

17. The *altitude* of an airplane is the height of the airplane above ground. What do you think an *altitude* of a parallelogram is?

CHAPTER 9

Connecting Algebra and Geometry

Big Ideas

1 Measurement
Essential Question How do you find the area and perimeter of a polygon?

2 Coordinate Geometry
Essential Question How can you use coordinate geometry to prove general relationships?

© Domains

- Expressing Geometric Properties with Equations
- Quantities

Chapter Preview

9-1 Perimeter and Area in the Coordinate Plane

9-2 Areas of Parallelograms and Triangles

9-3 Areas of Trapezoids, Rhombuses, and Kites

9-4 Polygons in the Coordinate Plane

Interactive Digital Path

Log in to **pearsonsuccessnet.com** and click on Interactive Digital Path to access the Solve Its and animated Problems.

Vocabulary

English/Spanish Vocabulary Audio Online:

English	Spanish
area, *p. 545*	segmentos congruentes
base of a parallelogram, *p. 559*	base de paralelogramo
base of a triangle, *p. 561*	base de un triangulo
height of a parallelogram, *p. 559*	alture de un paralelogramo
height of a trapezoid, *p. 568*	altura de un trapecio
height of a triangle, *p. 561*	altura de un triangulo
perimeter, *p. 545*	perímetro

9-1 Perimeter and Area in the Coordinate Plane

G.GPE.7 Use coordinates to compute perimeters of polygons and areas of triangles and rectangles . . . Also **N.Q.1**

Objectives To find the perimeter or circumference of basic shapes
To find the area of basic shapes

 Solve It! Write your solution to the Solve It in the space below.

In the Solve It, you considered various ideas of what it means to take up space on a flat surface.

Essential Understanding Perimeter and area are two different ways of measuring geometric figures.

The **perimeter** P of a polygon is the sum of the lengths of its sides. The **area** A of a polygon is the number of square units it encloses. For figures such as squares, rectangles, triangles, and circles, you can use formulas for perimeter (or *circumference C* for circles) and area.

---

take note

Key Concept Perimeter, Circumference, and Area

Square

side length s

$P = 4s$

$A = s^2$

Triangle

side lengths a, b, and c, base b, and height h

$P = a + b + c$

$A = \frac{1}{2}bh$

Rectangle

base b and height h

$P = 2b + 2h$, or $2(b + h)$

$A = bh$

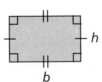

Circle

radius r and diameter d

$C = \pi d$, or $C = 2\pi r$

$A = \pi r^2$

The units of measurement for perimeter and circumference include inches, feet, yards, miles, centimeters, and meters. When measuring area, use square units such as square inches (in.^{2}), square feet (ft^2), square yards (yd^2), square miles (mi^2), square centimeters (cm^2), and square meters (m^2).

 **Problem 1** **Finding the Perimeter and Area of a Rectangle in the Coordinate Plane**

Got It? Rectangle *HIJK* has vertices *H*(−5, −3), *I*(−5, 2), *J*(2, 2), and *K*(2, −3). What is the perimeter of rectangle *HIJK*? What is the area of rectangle *HIJK*?

Ⓐ Practice Find the perimeter and area of each rectangle.

1. rectangle *ABCD* with vertices *A*(2, 4), *B*(2, 9), *C*(5, 9), and *D*(5, 4)

2. rectangle *EFGH* with vertices *E*(−3, 1), *F*(−3, 6), *G*(2, 6), and *H*(2, 1)

You can name a circle with the symbol $\odot$. For example, the circle with center A is written $\odot A$.

The formulas for a circle involve the special number pi (π). Pi is the ratio of any circle's circumference to its diameter. Since π is an irrational number,

$$\pi = 3.1415926\ldots,$$

you cannot write it as a terminating decimal. For an approximate answer, you can use 3.14 or $\frac{22}{7}$ for π. You can also use the π key on your calculator to get a rounded decimal for π. For an exact answer, leave the result in terms of π.

 **Problem 2** **Finding Circumference**

Plan

> **How do you decide which formula to use?**

Got it?   **a.** What is the circumference of a circle with radius 24 m in terms of π?

b. What is the circumference of a circle with diameter 24 m to the nearest tenth?

Ⓐ Practice Find the circumference of $\odot C$ in terms of π.

3.

5 ft

C

4.

$\frac{1}{4}$ m

C

Problem 3 Finding Perimeter and Area of a Triangle in the Coordinate Plane

Got It? Triangle ABC has vertices $A(-6, 4)$, $B(6, 4)$, and $C(-6, -1)$. What is the perimeter of $\triangle ABC$? What is the area of $\triangle ABC$?

Practice Find the perimeter and area of each triangle.

5. triangle JKL with vertices $J(1, -1)$, $K(1, 5)$, and $L(9, -1)$

6. triangle *MNP* with vertices *M*(−5, −3), *N*(5, 2), and *P*(5, −3)

Problem 4 **Finding the Perimeter of a Pentagon in the Coordinate Plane**

Think

Do you need to calculate the length of each side?

Got It? Pentagon *JKLMN* has vertices *J*(−2, 5), *K*(1, 1), *L*(1, −4), *M*(−5, −4), and *N*(−5, 1). What is the perimeter of *JKLMN*?

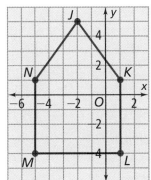

Practice In Exercises 7 and 8, find the perimeter of each pentagon.

7. pentagon *MNPQR* with vertices *M*(1, 6), *N*(5, 10), *P*(9, 6), *Q*(9, 1), and *R*(1, 1)

8. pentagon *RSTUV* with vertices *R*(−6, 2), *S*(−3, 6), *T*(5, 6), *U*(5, −2), and *V*(−3, −2)

 **Problem 5** **Finding Area of a Circle**

Got It?   The diameter of a circle is 14 ft.

   a. What is the area of the circle in terms of π?

   b. What is the area of the circle using an approximation of π?

   c. Reasoning Which approximation of π did you use in part (b)? Why?

(A) **Practice** Find the area of each circle in terms of π.

9.

20 m

10.

$\frac{3}{4}$ in.

The following postulate is useful in finding areas of figures with irregular shapes.

take note ➤

Postulate 10 Area Addition Postulate

The area of a region is the sum of the areas of its nonoverlapping parts.

ONLINE PROBLEMS

Problem 6 **Finding Area of an Irregular Shape**

Got It? **a. Reasoning** What is another way to separate the figure in Problem 6?

b. What is the area of the figure at the right?

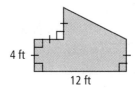

4 ft

12 ft

11.

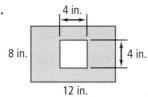

4 in.

8 in.   4 in.

12 in.

12. 4 ft

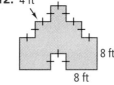

8 ft

8 ft

 ## Lesson Check

Do you know HOW?

13. What is the perimeter and area of a rectangle with base 3 in. and height 7 in.?

14. What is the circumference and area of each circle to the nearest tenth?

    a. $r = 9$ in.   **b.** $d = 7.3$ m

15. What is the perimeter and area of the figure at the right?

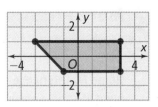

Do you UNDERSTAND?

 MATHEMATICAL PRACTICES

© **16. Writing** Describe a real-world situation in which you would need to find a perimeter. Then describe a situation in which you would need to find an area.

© **17. Compare and Contrast** Your friend can't remember whether $2\pi r$ computes the circumference or the area of a circle. How would you help your friend? Explain.

© **18. Error Analysis** A classmate finds the area of a circle with radius 30 in. to be 900 in.². What error did your classmate make?

More Practice and Problem-Solving Exercises

B Apply

Home Maintenance To determine how much of each item to buy, tell whether you need to know area or perimeter. Explain your choice.

19. wallpaper for a bedroom

20. crown molding for a ceiling

21. fencing for a backyard

22. paint for a basement floor

© 23. Think About a Plan A light-year unit describes the distance that one photon of light travels in one year. The Milky Way galaxy has a diameter of about 100,000 light-years. The distance to Earth from the center of the Milky Way galaxy is about 30,000 light-years. How many more light-years does a star on the outermost edge of the Milky Way travel in one full revolution around the galaxy compared to Earth?
- What do you know about the shape of each orbital path?
- Are you looking for circumference or area?
- How do you compare the paths using algebraic expressions?

24. a. What is the area of a square with sides 12 in. long? 1 ft long?
   b. How many square inches are in a square foot?

© 25. a. Count squares to find the area of the entire figure at the right.
   b. Use a formula to find the area of each square outlined in red.
   c. Writing How does the sum of your results in part (b) compare to your result in part (a)? Which postulate does this support?

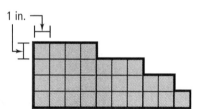

1 in.

26. The area of an 11-cm-wide rectangle is 176 cm². What is its length?

27. Garden A scale drawing on a coordinate plane shows a rectangular garden. One unit represents one yard. The vertices of the garden are located at $(-12, -6)$, $(-12, -1)$, $(-2, -1)$, and $(-2, -6)$. What are the perimeter and area of the garden?

28. Tiling A scale drawing on a coordinate plane shows the plans for a rectangular kitchen. One unit represents one foot. The vertices of the kitchen are at $(-6, 7)$, $(2, 7)$, $(2, -5)$, and $(-6, -5)$. You want to tile the kitchen floor. Each tile is 2 feet by 2 feet. How many tiles will you need for the kitchen floor?

29. A square and a rectangle have equal areas. The rectangle is 64 cm by 81 cm. What is the perimeter of the square?

30. A rectangle has perimeter 40 cm and base 12 cm. What is its area?

Find the area of each shaded figure.

31. compact disc

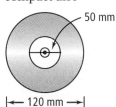

50 mm

|← 120 mm →|

32. drafting triangle

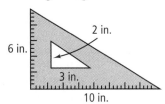

2 in.

6 in.

3 in.

10 in.

33. picture frame

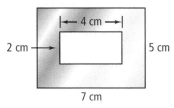

|← 4 cm →|

2 cm →

5 cm

7 cm

Ⓒ **34. Open-Ended** Draw a right triangle on a coordinate plane that has an area of 27 square units.

35. Baseball Sarah drew the outline of a pentagonal home plate on a coordinate plane where each unit represents one centimeter. The vertices of home plate are $(-22.5, 0)$, $(-22.5, 22)$, $(0, 44.5)$, $(22.5, 22)$, and $(22.5, 0)$. What is the perimeter of the home plate? Round to the nearest tenth.

Ⓒ **36. a. Reasoning** Can you use the formula for the perimeter of a rectangle to find the perimeter of any square? Explain.
    b. Can you use the formula for the perimeter of a square to find the perimeter of any rectangle? Explain.
    c. Use the formula for the perimeter of a square to write a formula for the area of a square in terms of its perimeter.

Ⓒ **37. Estimation** On an art trip to England, a student sketches the floor plan of the main body of Salisbury Cathedral. The shape of the floor plan is called the building's "footprint." The student estimates the dimensions of the cathedral on her sketch at the right. Use the student's lengths to estimate the area of Salisbury Cathedral's footprint.

38. Coordinate Geometry The endpoints of a diameter of a circle are $A(2, 1)$ and $B(5, 5)$. Find the area of the circle in terms of π.

39. Algebra A rectangle has a base of x units. The area is $(4x^2 - 2x)$ square units. What is the height of the rectangle in terms of x?

   Ⓐ $(4 - x)$ units   Ⓒ $(x - 2)$ units

   Ⓑ $(4x^3 - 2x^2)$ units   Ⓓ $(4x - 2)$ units

Coordinate Geometry Graph each rectangle in the coordinate plane. Find its perimeter and area.

40. $A(-3, 2)$, $B(-2, 2)$, $C(-2, -2)$, $D(-3, -2)$

41. $A(-2, -6)$, $B(-2, -3)$, $C(3, -3)$, $D(3, -6)$

42. You are drawing a right triangle on a coordinate plane. Two of the vertices are $(3, 0)$ and $(3, -4)$. Name a third point that you can plot so that the perimeter of the right triangle is 12 units.

43. You are drawing a pentagon on a coordinate plane. Four of the vertices are $(-1, 5)$, $(3, 5)$, $(3, -3)$, and $(-1, -3)$. Name a fifth point that can you can plot so that the perimeter of the pentagon is 26 units.

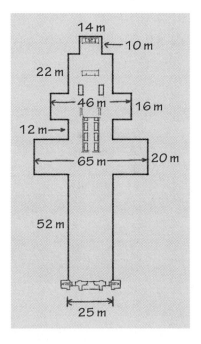

14 m

←10 m

22 m

←46 m→ 16 m

12 m→

←65 m→ 20 m

52 m

25 m

44. The surface area of a three-dimensional figure is the sum of the areas of all of its surfaces. You can find the surface area by finding the area of a net for the figure.

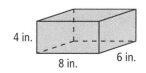

4 in.

8 in.   6 in.

a. Draw a net for the solid shown. Label the dimensions.

b. What is the area of the net? What is the surface area of the solid?

45. Coordinate Geometry On graph paper, draw polygon *ABCDEFG* with vertices $A(1, 1)$, $B(10, 1)$, $C(10, 8)$, $D(7, 5)$, $E(4, 5)$, $F(4, 8)$, and $G(1, 8)$. Find the perimeter and the area of the polygon.

46. Pet Care You want to adopt a puppy from your local animal shelter. First, you plan to build an outdoor playpen along the side of your house, as shown on the right. You want to lay down special dog grass for the pen's floor. If dog grass costs $1.70 per square foot, how much will you spend?

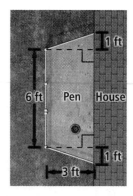

1 ft

6 ft   Pen   House

1 ft

3 ft

47. A rectangular garden has an 8-ft walkway around it. How many more feet is the outer perimeter of the walkway than the perimeter of the garden?

C Challenge

Algebra Find the area of each figure.

48. a rectangle with side lengths $\frac{2a}{5b}$ units and $\frac{3b}{8}$ units

49. a square with perimeter $10n$ units

50. a triangle with base $(5x - 2y)$ units and height $(4x + 3y)$ units

Partitioning a Segment

G.GPE.6 Find the point on a directed line segment . . . that partitions the segment in a given ratio.

You have used the Midpoint Formula to find an endpoint of a segment. You can also use proportional reasoning to find points on a segment other than the endpoints.

Example

The endpoints of $\overline{LM}$ are $L(-4, 1)$ and $M(5, -5)$. Point N lies on $\overline{LM}$ and is $\frac{2}{3}$ of the way from L to M. What are the coordinates of point N?

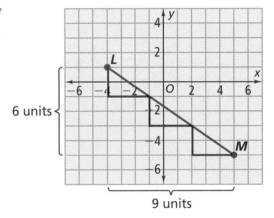

6 units

9 units

Step 1 Plot $\overline{LM}$ on a coordinate plane.

Step 2 Notice that the segment drops 6 units vertically and runs 9 units horizontally as you go from L to M.

Divide the horizontal and vertical distances by 3 to break $\overline{LM}$ into thirds.

vertical distance: $\frac{6}{3} = 2$

horizontal distance: $\frac{9}{3} = 3$

Step 3 Beginning at point L, drop 2 units down and move 3 units to the right to arrive at $(-1, -1)$. Repeat this process twice more to find the points $(2, -3)$ and $M(5, -5)$.

The points $(-1, -1)$ and $(2, -3)$ divide $\overline{LM}$ into thirds. The point $(2, -3)$ lies on $\overline{LM}$ and is $\frac{2}{3}$ of the way from L to M. The coordinates of point N are $(2, -3)$.

Exercises

1. The endpoints of $\overline{RS}$ are $R(-5, -2)$ and $S(3, 2)$. Point T lies on $\overline{RS}$ and is $\frac{1}{4}$ of the way from R to S. What are the coordinates of point T?

2. The endpoints of $\overline{CD}$ are $C(-6, -2)$ and $D(6, 4)$. Point E lies on $\overline{CD}$ and is $\frac{1}{3}$ of the way from C to D. What are the coordinates of point E?

3. Clarence is making a scale model of his neighborhood using a coordinate grid. He plots his school at point $S(4, 5)$ and the park at point $P(16, 11)$ along Elm Street as shown.

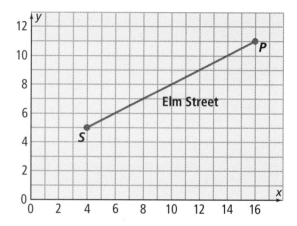

a. The bank is located on Elm Street and is $\frac{1}{6}$ of the way from the school to the park. What are the coordinates of the bank?

b. The grocery store is located on Elm Street and is $\frac{2}{3}$ of the way from the school to the park. What are the coordinates of the grocery store?

Areas of Parallelograms and Triangles

G.GPE.7 Use coordinates to compute perimeters of polygons and areas of triangles and rectangles . . . Also **G.MG.1**

Objective To find the area of parallelograms and triangles

 Solve It! Write your solution to the Solve It in the space below.

Essential Understanding You can find the area of a parallelogram or a triangle when you know the length of its base and its height.

A parallelogram with the same base and height as a rectangle has the same area as the rectangle.

take note

Key Concept   Area of a Rectangle

The area of a rectangle is the product of its base and height.

$A = bh$

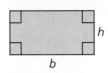

Key Concept   Area of a Parallelogram

The area of a parallelogram is the product of a base and the corresponding height.

$A = bh$

A **base of a parallelogram** can be any one of its sides. The corresponding **altitude** is a segment perpendicular to the line containing that base, drawn from the side opposite the base. The **height** is the length of an altitude.

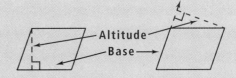

 **Problem 1** Finding the Area of a Parallelogram

Got It? What is the area of a parallelogram with base length 12 m and height 9 m?

Practice Find the area of each parallelogram.

1.
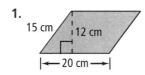
15 cm   12 cm
|← 20 cm →|

2.
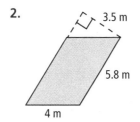
3.5 m
5.8 m
4 m

 Problem 2 Finding a Missing Dimension

Got It? A parallelogram has sides of length 15 cm and 18 cm. The height corresponding to a 15-cm base is 9 cm. What is the height corresponding to an 18-cm base?

Think
How can a diagram help you visualize the problem?

(A) Practice Find the value of *h* for each parallelogram.

3.

4.

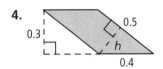

You can rotate a triangle about the midpoint of a side to form a parallelogram.

 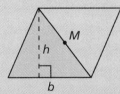

The area of the triangle is half the area of the parallelogram.

take note

Key Concept   Area of a Triangle

The area of a triangle is half the product of a base and the corresponding height.

$A = \frac{1}{2}bh$

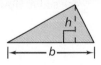

A **base of a triangle** can be any of its sides. The corresponding **height** is the length of the altitude to the line containing that base.

Think

In what units should your final answer be written?

Got It? What is the area of the triangle?

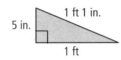

1 ft 1 in.

5 in.

1 ft

 Practice Find the area of each triangle.

5.

5.7 m 5 m

4 m

4 m 3 m

6.

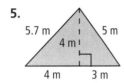

3 ft

2 ft 2 ft

 Problem 4 Finding the Area of an Irregular Figure

Got It? **Reasoning** Suppose the base lengths of the square and triangle in Problem 4 are doubled to 12 in., but the height of each polygon remains the same. How is the area of the figure affected?

7. Urban Design A bakery has a 50 ft-by-31 ft parking lot. The four parking spaces are parallelograms with the same dimensions, the driving region is a rectangle, and the two areas for flowers are triangles with the same dimensions.

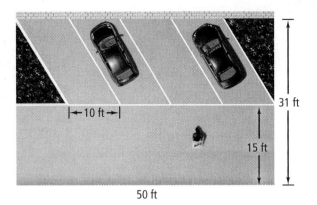

a. Find the area of the paved surface by adding the areas of the driving region and the four parking spaces.

b. Describe another method for finding the area of the paved surface.

c. Use your method from part (b) to find the area. Then compare answers from parts (a) and (b) to check your work.

Lesson Check

Do you know HOW?

Find the area of each parallelogram.

8.

10 m
20 m

9.

8 ft
8 ft

Find the area of each triangle.

10.
12 cm
16 cm

11.

8 in.
9 in.

Do you UNDERSTAND?

MATHEMATICAL
PRACTICES

12. Vocabulary Does an altitude of a triangle have to lie inside the triangle? Explain.

13. Writing How can you show that a parallelogram and a rectangle with the same bases and heights have equal areas?

14. $\square ABCD$ is divided into two triangles along diagonal $\overline{AC}$. If you know the area of the parallelogram, how do you find the area of $\triangle ABC$?

More Practice and Problem-Solving Exercises

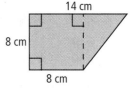

B Apply

15. The area of a parallelogram is 24 in.² and the height is 6 in. Find the length of the corresponding base.

16. What is the area of the figure shown at the right?

  Ⓐ 64 cm²   Ⓒ 96 cm²

  Ⓑ 88 cm²   Ⓓ 112 cm²

17. A right isosceles triangle has area 98 cm². Find the length of each leg.

18. Algebra The area of a triangle is 108 in.². A base and corresponding height are in the ratio 3 : 2. Find the length of the base and the corresponding height.

19. Think About a Plan Ki used geometry software to create the figure shown at the right. She constructed $\overleftrightarrow{AB}$ and a point C not on $\overleftrightarrow{AB}$. Then she constructed line k parallel to $\overleftrightarrow{AB}$ through point C. Next, Ki constructed point D on line k as well as $\overline{AD}$ and $\overline{BD}$. She dragged point D along line k to manipulate $\triangle ABD$. How does the area of $\triangle ABD$ change? Explain.

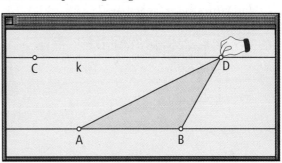

- Which dimensions of the triangle change when Ki drags point D?
- Do the lengths of $\overline{AD}$ and $\overline{BD}$ matter when calculating area?

20. Open-Ended Using graph paper, draw an acute triangle, an obtuse triangle, and a right triangle, each with area 12 units².

Find the area of each figure.

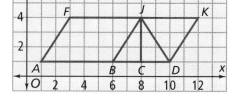

21. $\square ABJF$

22. $\triangle BDJ$

23. $\triangle DKJ$

24. $\square BDKJ$

25. $\square ADKF$

26. $\triangle BCJ$

27. trapezoid $ADJF$

 28. Reasoning Suppose the height of a triangle is tripled. How does this affect the area of the triangle? Explain.

For Exercises 29–32, (a) graph the lines and (b) find the area of the triangle enclosed by the lines.

29. $y = x$, $x = 0$, $y = 7$

30. $y = x + 2$, $y = 2$, $x = 6$

31. $y = -\frac{1}{2}x + 3$, $y = 0$, $x = -2$

32. $y = \frac{3}{4}x - 2$, $y = -2$, $x = 4$

 33. Probability Your friend drew these three figures on a grid. A fly lands at random at a point on the grid.

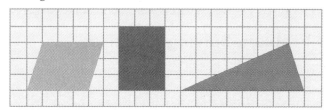

a. **Writing** Is the fly more likely to land on one of the figures or on the blank grid? Explain.

b. Suppose you know the fly lands on one of the figures. Is the fly more likely to land on one figure than on another? Explain.

Coordinate Geometry Find the area of a polygon with the given vertices.

34. $A(3, 9)$, $B(8, 9)$, $C(2, -3)$, $D(-3, -3)$

35. $E(1, 1)$, $F(4, 5)$, $G(11, 5)$, $H(8, 1)$

36. $D(0, 0)$, $E(2, 4)$, $F(6, 4)$, $G(6, 0)$

37. $K(-7, -2)$, $L(-7, 6)$, $M(1, 6)$, $N(7, -2)$

Find the area of each figure.

38.

39.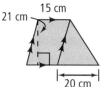

40.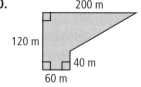

History The Greek mathematician Heron is most famous for this formula
for the area of a triangle in terms of the lengths of its sides *a*, *b*, and *c*.

$$A = \sqrt{s(s-a)(s-b)(s-c)}, \text{ where } s = \frac{1}{2}(a+b+c)$$

**Use Heron's Formula and a calculator to find the area of each triangle.
Round your answer to the nearest whole number.**

41. $a = 8$ in., $b = 9$ in., $c = 10$ in.

42. $a = 15$ m, $b = 17$ m, $c = 21$ m

43. **a.** Use Heron's Formula to find the area of this triangle.
    b. Verify your answer to part (a) by using the formula $A = \frac{1}{2}bh$.

15 in.   9 in.
    12 in.

9-3 | Areas of Trapezoids, Rhombuses, and Kites

G.MG.1 Use geometric shapes, their measures, and their properties to describe objects . . . Also Extends **G.GPE.7**

Objective To find the area of a trapezoid, rhombus, or kite

Solve It! Write your solution to the Solve It in the space below.

Essential Understanding You can find the area of a trapezoid when you know its height and the lengths of its bases.

The **height of a trapezoid** is the perpendicular distance between the bases.

take note

> ### Key Concept   Area of a Trapezoid
>
> The area of a trapezoid is half the product of the height and the sum of the bases.
>
> $$A = \frac{1}{2}h(b_1 + b_2)$$
>
>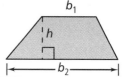

 **Problem 1** **Area of a Trapezoid**

Got It? What is the area of a trapezoid with height 7 cm and bases 12 cm and 15 cm?

Think

What information do you need to find the area of a trapezoid?

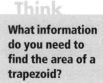

A Practice Find the area of each trapezoid.

1.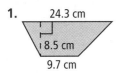
24.3 cm
8.5 cm
9.7 cm

2.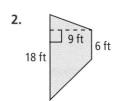
9 ft
6 ft
18 ft

Essential Understanding You can find the area of a rhombus or a kite when you know the lengths of its diagonals.

Key Concept Area of a Rhombus or a Kite

The area of a rhombus or a kite is half the product of the lengths of its diagonals.

$A = \frac{1}{2}d_1d_2$

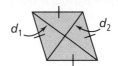
Rhombus

Kite

Problem 2 Finding the Area of a Kite

Got It? What is the area of a kite with diagonals that are 12 in. and 9 in. long?

Ⓐ Practice Find the area of each kite.

3.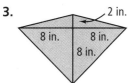

4.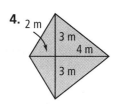

Problem 3 **Finding the Area of a Rhombus**

Got It? A rhombus has sides 10 cm long. If the length of the longer diagonal is 16 cm, what is the area of the rhombus?

Think

How can drawing a diagram help you visualize the problem?

Ⓐ Practice Find the area of each rhombus.

5.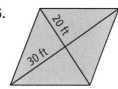

6.

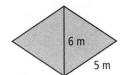

Lesson Check

Do you know HOW?

Find the area of each figure.

7.

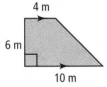

4 m
6 m
10 m

8.

15 in.
18 in.
27 in.

9.

3 ft
5 ft

10.

12 in.
12 in.

11.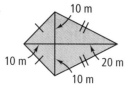

12.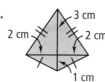

Do you UNDERSTAND?

© **13. Vocabulary** Can a trapezoid and a parallelogram with the same base and height have the same area? Explain.

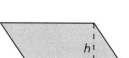

© **14. Reasoning** Do you need to know all the side lengths to find the area of a trapezoid?

© **15. Reasoning** Can you find the area of a rhombus if you only know the lengths of its sides? Explain.

© 16. Reasoning Do you need to know the lengths of the sides to find the area of a kite? Explain.

More Practice and Problem-Solving Exercises

MATHEMATICAL PRACTICES

Ⓑ Apply

© 17. Think About a Plan A trapezoid has two right angles, 12-m and 18-m bases, and an 8-m height. Sketch the trapezoid and find its perimeter and area.
- Are the right angles consecutive or opposite angles?
- How does knowing the height help you find the perimeter?

18. Metallurgy The end of a gold bar has the shape of a trapezoid with the measurements shown. Find the area of the end.

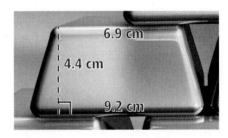

© 19. Open-Ended Draw a kite. Find the lengths of its diagonals. Find its area.

Find the area of each trapezoid to the nearest tenth.

20.

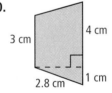

21.

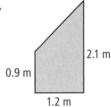

Coordinate Geometry Find the area of quadrilateral *QRST*.

22.

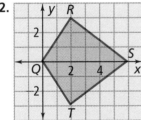

23.

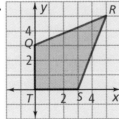

24.

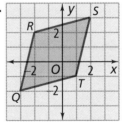

25. a. Coordinate Geometry Graph the lines $x = 0$, $x = 6$, $y = 0$, and $y = x + 4$.
   b. What type of quadrilateral do the lines form?
   c. Find the area of the quadrilateral.

26. Visualization The kite has diagonals d_1 and d_2 congruent to the sides of the rectangle. Explain why the area of the kite is $\frac{1}{2}d_1d_2$.

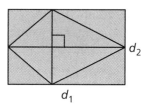

Ⓒ **27.** Draw a trapezoid. Label its bases b_1 and b_2 and its height h. Then draw a diagonal of the trapezoid.
    a. Write equations for the area of each of the two triangles formed.
    b. Writing Explain how you can justify the trapezoid area formula using the areas of the two triangles.

Ⓒ Challenge

28. Algebra One base of a trapezoid is twice the other. The height is the average of the two bases. The area is 324 cm². Find the height and the bases. (*Hint:* Let the smaller base be x.)

29. Sports Ty wants to paint one side of the skateboarding ramp he built. The ramp is 4 m wide. Its surface is modeled by the equation $y = 0.25x^2$. Use the trapezoids and triangles shown to estimate the area to be painted.

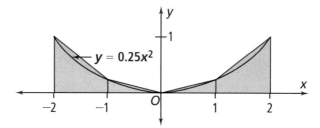

Proving Slope Criteria for Parallel and Perpendicular Lines

G.GPE.5 Prove the slope criteria for parallel and perpendicular lines and use them to solve geometric problems . . .

You can determine whether two nonvertical lines on a coordinate plane are parallel by examining their slopes.

Activity 1

Let two nonvertical parallel lines in the coordinate plane be given in slope-intercept form by the equations $y = m_1x + b_1$ and $y = m_2x + b_2$.

1. How are b_1 and b_2 related? Can $b_2 - b_1$ be equal to 0? Explain.

2. How many solutions does the equation $m_1x + b_1 = m_2x + b_2$ have? Explain.

3. Show that the equation in Exercise 2 is equivalent to $(m_1 - m_2)x = b_2 - b_1$.

4. When are there no solutions to the equation in Exercise 3? Explain.

5. Explain how your answer to Exercise 4 shows that if nonvertical lines are parallel, then their slopes are equal.

6. Show that if two distinct lines have the same slope, then they are parallel by showing that the equation $mx + b_1 = mx + b_2$ has no solutions when $b_1 \neq b_2$.

You can also determine whether two nonvertical lines on a coordinate plane are perpendicular by examining their slopes.

Activity 2

Let two perpendicular lines, neither of which is vertical, be given in slope-intercept form by the equations $y = m_1x + b_1$ and $y = m_2x + b_2$. Let the point of intersection be point A. Draw a horizontal segment $\overline{AP}$ with length 1. Draw a vertical line through point P that intersects the two perpendicular lines at points B and C. This is shown in the figure at the right.

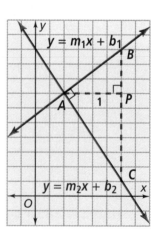

7. Use the slopes of the perpendicular lines to find the lengths of $\overline{BP}$ and $\overline{CP}$.

8. Use your results from Exercise 7 to find the lengths of $\overline{AB}$ and $\overline{AC}$.

9. Let the coordinates of A be (p, q). Show that the y-coordinates of B and C are $q + m_1$ and $q + m_2$, respectively.

10. Use your results from Exercise 9 to find the length of $\overline{BC}$.

11. Use the Pythagorean theorem to show that $m_1 m_2 = -1$.

Exercises

Determine whether the lines are *parallel, perpendicular,* or *neither.*

12. $y = 3x + 1$
$y = -\frac{1}{3}x - 1$

13. $y = \frac{1}{2}x + \frac{3}{2}$
$y = \frac{1}{2}x - \frac{2}{3}$

14. $y = \frac{2}{3}x - 4$
$y = \frac{3}{2}x - 4$

15. $y - 2 = 2(x + 1)$
$4x - 2y = -8$

ⓒ **16. Reasoning** Can you use slope criteria for determining whether lines are parallel or perpendicular if one of the lines is vertical? Explain.

Polygons in the Coordinate Plane

G.GPE.4 . . . Prove simple geometric theorems algebraically.

Objective   To classify polygons in the coordinate plane

Solve It!   Write your solution to the Solve It in the space below.

In the Solve It, you formed a polygon on a grid. In this lesson, you will classify polygons in the coordinate plane.

Essential Understanding   You can classify figures in the coordinate plane using the formulas for slope, distance, and midpoint.

The chart below reviews these formulas and tells when to use them.

take note

Key Concept   Formulas and the Coordinate Plane

Formula	When to Use It
Distance Formula $d = \sqrt{(x_2 - x_1)^2 + (y_2 - y_1)^2}$	To determine whether • sides are congruent • diagonals are congruent
Midpoint Formula $M = \left(\dfrac{x_1 + x_2}{2}, \dfrac{y_1 + y_2}{2}\right)$	To determine • the coordinates of the midpoint of a side • whether diagonals bisect each other
Slope Formula $m = \dfrac{y_2 - y_1}{x_2 - x_1}$	To determine whether • opposite sides are parallel • diagonals are perpendicular • sides are perpendicular

Problem 1 **Classifying a Triangle**

Got It? $\triangle DEF$ has vertices $D(0, 0)$, $E(1, 4)$, and $F(5, 2)$. Show that $\triangle DEF$ is scalene.

Think

What formula should you use?

Ⓐ Practice Determine whether $\triangle ABC$ is *scalene, isosceles,* or *equilateral.* Explain.

1.

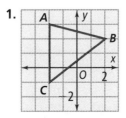

2.

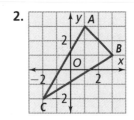

Problem 2 Classifying a Quadrilateral

Got It? Parallelogram *MNPQ* has vertices *M*(0, 1), *N*(−1, 4), *P*(2, 5), and *Q*(3, 2). Show that □*MNPQ* is a rectangle.

Think

How can you use slope to get information about the sides of a figure?

Ⓐ Practice Show that the parallelogram with the given vertices is a rhombus.

3. *L*(1, 2), *M*(3, 3), *N*(5, 2), *P*(3, 1)

4. *S*(1, 3), *P*(4, 4), *A*(3, 1), *T*(0, 0)

Problem 3 Classifying a Quadrilateral

Got It? An isosceles trapezoid has vertices *A*(0, 0), *B*(2, 4), *C*(6, 4), and *D*(8, 0). Show that the quadrilateral formed by connecting the midpoints of the sides of *ABCD* is a rhombus.

A Practice What is the most precise classification of the quadrilateral formed by connecting the consecutive midpoints of each figure below?

5. rectangle *EFGH*

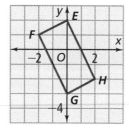

6. isosceles trapezoid *JKLM*

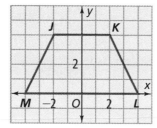

Lesson Check

Do you know HOW?

7. △*TRI* has vertices *T*(−3, 4), *R*(3, 4), and *I*(0, 0). Is △*TRI* *scalene, isosceles,* or *equilateral*?

8. Is *QRST* at the right a rectangle? Explain.

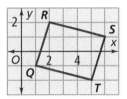

Do you UNDERSTAND?

9. Writing In the figure at the right, the blue points bisect the sides of the triangle. Describe how you would determine whether the lengths of the blue segments are equal.

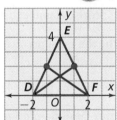

10. Error Analysis A student says that the quadrilateral with vertices *D*(1, 2), *E*(2, 0), *F*(5, 4), and *G*(6, 2) is a square because it has four right angles. What is the student's error?

More Practice and Problem-Solving Exercises

B Apply

Graph and label each triangle with the given vertices. Determine whether each triangle is *scalene, isosceles,* or *equilateral*. Then tell whether each triangle is a right triangle.

11. $T(1, 1), R(3, 8), I(6, 4)$ **12.** $J(-5, 0), K(5, 8), L(4, -1)$

13. $A(3, 2), B(-10, 4), C(-5, -8)$ **14.** $H(1, -2), B(-1, 4), F(5, 6)$

Graph and label each quadrilateral with the given vertices. Then determine the most precise name for each quadrilateral.

15. $P(-5, 0), Q(-3, 2), R(3, 2), S(5, 0)$ **16.** $S(0, 0), T(4, 0), U(3, 2), V(-1, 2)$

17. $F(0, 0), G(5, 5), H(8, 4), I(7, 1)$ **18.** $M(-14, 4), N(1, 6), P(3, -9), Q(-12, -11)$

19. $A(3, 5), B(7, 6), C(6, 2), D(2, 1)$ **20.** $N(-6, 4), P(-3, 1), Q(0, 2), R(-3, 5)$

21. $J(2, 1), K(5, 4), L(8, 1), M(2, -3)$ **22.** $H(-2, -3), I(4, 0), J(3, 2), K(-3, -1)$

23. $W(-1, 1), X(0, 2), Y(1, 1), Z(0, -2)$ **24.** $D(-3, 1), E(-7, -3), F(6, -3), G(2, 1)$

© 25. Think About a Plan Do the triangles at the right have the same side lengths? How do you know?
- Which formula should you use?
- What are the corresponding sides?

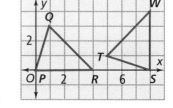

© 26. Reasoning A quadrilateral has opposite sides with equal slopes and consecutive sides with slopes that are negative reciprocals. What is the most precise classification of the quadrilateral? Explain.

Determine the most precise name for the quadrilateral with the given vertices. Then find its area.

27. $A(0, 2), B(4, 2), C(-3, -4), D(-7, -4)$ **28.** $J(1, -3), K(3, 1), L(7, -1), M(5, -5)$

29. Interior Design Interior designers often use grids to plan the placement of furniture in a room. The design at the right shows four chairs around a coffee table. The designer plans for cutouts of chairs on lattice points, where the grid lines intersect. She wants the chairs oriented at the vertices of a parallelogram. Does she need to fix her plan? If so, describe the change(s) she should make.

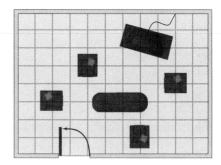

30. Use the diagram at the right.

  a. What is the most precise classification of *ABCD*?

  b. What is the most precise classification of *EFGH*?

  c. Do *ABCD* and *EFGH* have the same side lengths and angle measures? Explain.

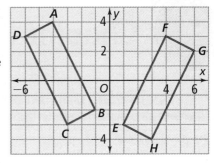

Ⓒ Challenge

31. Coordinate Geometry The diagonals of quadrilateral *EFGH* intersect at *D*(−1, 4). *EFGH* has vertices at *E*(2, 7) and *F*(−3, 5). What must be the coordinates of *G* and *H* to ensure that *EFGH* is a parallelogram?

The endpoints of $\overline{AB}$ are *A*(−3, 5) and *B*(9, 15). Find the coordinates of the points that divide $\overline{AB}$ into the given number of congruent segments.

32. 4   **33.** 6   **34.** 10   **35.** 50   **36.** *n*

9-1 Perimeter and Area in the Coordinate Plane

Quick Review

The perimeter P of a polygon is the sum of the lengths of its sides. Circles have a circumference C. The area A of a polygon or a circle is the number of square units it encloses.

    Square: $P = 4s$; $A = s^2$

    Rectangle: $P = 2b + 2h$; $A = bh$

    Triangle: $P = a + b + c$; $A = \frac{1}{2}bh$

    Circle: $C = \pi d$ or $C = 2\pi r$; $A = \pi r^2$

Example

Find the perimeter and area of a rectangle with $b = 12$ m and $h = 8$ m.

$$P = 2b + 2h \qquad\qquad A = bh$$
$$= 2(12) + 2(8) \qquad = 12 \cdot 8$$
$$= 40 \qquad\qquad\qquad = 96$$

The perimeter is 40 m and the area is 96 m².

Exercises

Find the perimeter and area of each figure.

1.
8 cm

2.
3 in.
5 in.

Find the circumference and the area for each circle in terms of π.

3. $r = 3$ in.

4. $d = 15$ m

9-2 Areas of Parallelograms and Triangles

Quick Review

You can find the area of a rectangle, a parallelogram, or a triangle if you know the **base** b and the **height** h.

h
b

The area of a rectangle or parallelogram is $A = bh$.

The area of a triangle is $A = \frac{1}{2}bh$.

Example

What is area of the parallelogram?

$A = bh$ Use the area formula.

$= (12)(8) = 96$ Substitute and simplify.

12 cm
8 cm

The area of the parallelogram is 96 cm².

Exercises

Find the area of each figure.

5.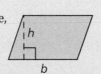
5 m
4 m

6.
10 in.
9 in.

7.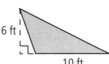
6 ft
10 ft

8.
10 ft
16 ft

9. A right triangle has legs measuring 5 ft and 12 ft, and hypotenuse measuring 13 ft. What is its area?

9-3 Areas of Trapezoids, Rhombuses, and Kites

Quick Review

The **height of a trapezoid** h is the perpendicular distance between the bases, b_1 and b_2.

The area of a trapezoid is $A = \frac{1}{2}h(b_1 + b_2)$.

The area of a rhombus or a kite is $A = \frac{1}{2}d_1d_2$, where d_1 and d_2 are the lengths of its diagonals.

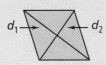

Example

What is the area of the trapezoid?

$A = \frac{1}{2}h(b_1 + b_2)$ Use the area formula.

$= \frac{1}{2}(8)(7 + 3)$ Substitute.

$= 40$ Simplify.

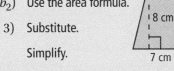

The area of the trapezoid is 40 cm².

Exercises

Find the area of each figure. If necessary, leave your answer in simplest radical form.

10.
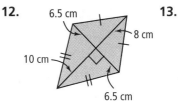

11.
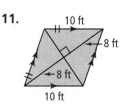

12.
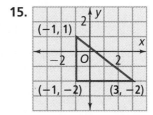

13.
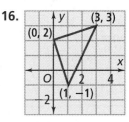

14. A trapezoid has a height of 6 m. The length of one base is three times the length of the other base. The sum of the base lengths is 18 m. What is the area of the trapezoid?

9-4 Polygons in the Coordinate Plane

Quick Review

To determine whether sides or diagonals are congruent, use the Distance Formula. To determine the coordinates of the midpoint of a side, or whether the diagonals bisect each other, use the Midpoint Formula. To determine whether opposite sides are parallel, or whether diagonals or sides are perpendicular, use the Slope Formula.

Example

$\triangle XYZ$ has vertices $X(1, 0)$, $Y(-2, -4)$, and $Z(4, -4)$. Is $\triangle XYZ$ *scalene*, *isosceles*, or *equilateral*?

To find the lengths of the legs, use the Distance Formula.

$XY = \sqrt{(-2 - 1)^2 + (-4 - 0)^2} = \sqrt{9 + 16} = 5$

$YZ = \sqrt{(4 - (-2))^2 + (-4 - (-4))^2} = \sqrt{36 + 0} = 6$

$XZ = \sqrt{(4 - 1)^2 + (-4 - 0)^2} = \sqrt{9 + 16} = 5$

Two side lengths are equal, so $\triangle XYZ$ is isosceles.

Exercises

Determine whether $\triangle ABC$ is *scalene*, *isosceles*, or *equilateral*.

15.

16.

What is the most precise classification of the quadrilateral with the given vertices?

17. $G(2, 5)$, $R(5, 8)$, $A(-2, 12)$, $D(-5, 9)$

18. $F(-13, 7)$, $I(1, 12)$, $N(15, 7)$, $E(1, -5)$

19. $Q(4, 5)$, $U(12, 14)$, $A(20, 5)$, $D(12, -4)$

20. $W(-11, 4)$, $H(-9, 10)$, $A(2, 10)$, $T(4, 4)$

Pull It **All Together**

Finding the Area of a Plot of Land

ASSESSMENT

A traveling carnival requires a plot of land with an area of at least 45 m² to set up one of their rides. The carnival's manager wants to know if the plot of land determined by quadrilateral *ABCD* on the coordinate plane below will work. Each unit of the coordinate plane represents one meter.

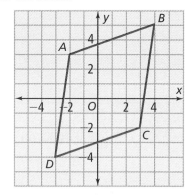

Task Description

Decide whether the plot of land determined by quadrilateral *ABCD* meets the carnival's requirements.

- How can you determine the type of quadrilateral formed by vertices *A*, *B*, *C*, and *D*?

- What lengths do you need to know in order to calculate the area of the quadrilateral?

Get Ready!

Evaluating Expressions

Evaluate each expression for the given value of *x*.

1. $9x - 13$ for $x = 7$ **2.** $90 - 3x$ for $x = 31$ **3.** $\frac{1}{2}x + 14$ for $x = 23$

Solving Equations

Solve each equation.

4. $2x - 17 = 4$ **5.** $3x + 8 = 53$

6. $(10x + 5) + (6x - 1) = 180$ **7.** $14x = 2(5x + 14)$

8. $2(x + 4) = x + 13$ **9.** $7x + 5 = 5x + 17$

10. $(x + 21) + (2x + 9) = 90$ **11.** $2(3x - 4) + 10 = 5(x + 4)$

Segments and Angles

Use the figure at the right.

12. Name $\angle 1$ in two other ways.

13. If D is the midpoint of $\overline{AB}$, find the value of x.

14. If $\angle ACB$ is a right angle, $m\angle 1 = 4y$, and $m\angle 2 = 2y + 18$, find $m\angle 1$ and $m\angle 2$.

15. Name a pair of angles that form a linear pair.

16. Name a pair of adjacent angles that are not supplementary.

17. If $m\angle ADC + m\angle BDC = 180$, name the straight angle.

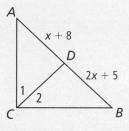

Looking Ahead Vocabulary

18. A scientist often makes an assumption, or *hypothesis*, about a scientific problem. Then the scientist uses experiments to test the *hypothesis* to see if it is true. How might a *hypothesis* in geometry be similar? How might it be different?

19. The *conclusion* of a novel answers questions raised by the story. How do you think the term *conclusion* applies in geometry?

20. A detective uses *deductive reasoning* to solve a case by gathering, combining, and analyzing clues. How might you use *deductive reasoning* in geometry?

Reasoning and Proof

Big Ideas

Reasoning and Proof
Essential Question How can you make a conjecture and prove that it is true?

Ⓒ Domains

- Congruence

Chapter Preview

Interactive Digital Path
Log in to **pearsonsuccessnet.com** and click on Interactive Digital Path to access the Solve Its and animated Problems.

 ## Vocabulary

English/Spanish Vocabulary Audio Online:

English	Spanish
biconditional, *p. 614*	bicondicional
conclusion, *p. 607*	conclusión
conditional, *p. 607*	condicional
conjecture, *p. 600*	conjetura
contrapositive, *p. 610*	contrapositivo
converse, *p. 610*	recíproco
deductive reasoning, *p. 622*	razonamiento deductivo
hypothesis, *p. 607*	hipótesis
inductive reasoning, *p. 599*	razonamiento inductivo
inverse, *p. 610*	inverso
negation, *p. 610*	negación
perpendicular bisector, *p. 593*	mediatriz
theorem, *p. 636*	teorema

Basic Constructions

G.CO.12 Make formal geometric constructions with a variety of tools and methods (compass and straightedge . . .).

Objective To make basic constructions using a straightedge and a compass

Solve It! Write your solution to the Solve It in the space below.

In this lesson, you will learn another way to construct figures like the one in the Solve It.

Essential Understanding You can use special geometric tools to make a figure that is congruent to an original figure without measuring. This method is more accurate than sketching and drawing.

A **straightedge** is a ruler with no markings on it. A **compass** is a geometric tool used to draw circles and parts of circles called *arcs*. A **construction** is a geometric figure drawn using a straightedge and a compass.

 **Problem 1** **Constructing Congruent Segments**

Got It? Use a straightedge to draw $\overline{XY}$. Then construct $\overline{RS}$ so that $RS = 2XY$.

1. Construct $\overline{XY}$ congruent to $\overline{AB}$.

A   B

2. Construct $\overline{QJ}$ so that $QJ = TR - PS$.

T   R P   S

Problem 2 **Constructing Congruent Angles**

Got It? **a.** Construct $\angle F$ so that $m\angle F = 2m\angle B$.

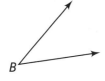

B

> **Think**
>
> Which postulate allows you to construct an angle with measure $2m\angle B$?

b. Reasoning How is constructing a congruent angle similar to constructing a congruent segment?

A Practice **3.** Construct $\angle D$ so that $\angle D \cong \angle C$.

4. Construct $\angle F$ so that $m\angle F = 2m\angle C$.

Perpendicular lines are two lines that intersect to form right angles. The symbol $\perp$ means "is perpendicular to." In the diagram at the right, $\overleftrightarrow{AB} \perp \overleftrightarrow{CD}$ and $\overleftrightarrow{CD} \perp \overleftrightarrow{AB}$.

A **perpendicular bisector** of a segment is a line, segment, or ray that is perpendicular to the segment at its midpoint. In the diagram at the right, $\overleftrightarrow{EF}$ is the perpendicular bisector of $\overline{GH}$. The perpendicular bisector bisects the segment into two congruent segments. The construction in Problem 3 will show you how this works. You will justify the steps for this construction in Chapter 12, as well as for the other constructions in this lesson.

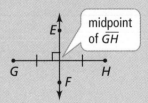

midpoint of $\overline{GH}$

Problem 3   **Constructing the Perpendicular Bisector**

Got It?   Draw $\overline{ST}$. Construct its perpendicular bisector.

Think

Why must the compass opening be greater than $\frac{1}{2}ST$?

 Practice   **5.** Construct the perpendicular bisector of $\overline{AB}$.

A

B

6. Construct the perpendicular bisector of $\overline{TR}$.

T

R

Problem 4 **Constructing the Angle Bisector**

Got It? Draw obtuse ∠*XYZ*. Then construct its bisector $\overrightarrow{YP}$.

Practice **7.** Draw acute ∠*PQR*. Then construct its bisector.

Lesson Check

Do you know HOW?

8. Construct a segment congruent to $\overline{PQ}$.

P ●————————● Q

9. Construct the perpendicular bisector of $\overline{PQ}$.

10. Draw an obtuse $\angle JKL$. Construct its bisector.

Do you UNDERSTAND?

11. Vocabulary What two tools do you use to make constructions?

12. Compare and Contrast Describe the difference in accuracy between sketching a figure, drawing a figure with a ruler and protractor, and constructing a figure. Explain.

13. Error Analysis Your friend constructs $\overleftrightarrow{XY}$ so that it is perpendicular to and contains the midpoint of $\overline{AB}$. He claims that $\overline{AB}$ is the perpendicular bisector of $\overleftrightarrow{XY}$. What is his error?

More Practice and Problem-Solving Exercises

B Apply

Sketch the figure described. Explain how to construct it. Then do the construction.

14. $\overleftrightarrow{XY} \perp \overleftrightarrow{YZ}$

15. $\overrightarrow{ST}$ bisects right $\angle PSQ$.

16. Compare and Contrast How is constructing an angle bisector similar to constructing a perpendicular bisector?

17. Think About a Plan Draw an $\angle A$. Construct an angle whose measure is $\frac{1}{4}m\angle A$.
- How is the angle you need to construct related to the angle bisector of $\angle A$?
- How can you use previous constructions to help you?

18. Answer the questions about a segment in a plane. Explain each answer.
  a. How many midpoints does the segment have?
  b. How many bisectors does it have?
  c. How many lines in the plane are its perpendicular bisectors?
  d. How many lines in space are its perpendicular bisectors?

For Exercises 19–21, copy $\angle 1$ and $\angle 2$. Construct each angle described.

19. $\angle B$; $m\angle B = m\angle 1 + m\angle 2$

20. $\angle C$; $m\angle C = m\angle 1 - m\angle 2$

21. $\angle D$; $m\angle D = 2m\angle 2$

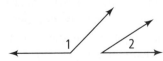

© 22. **Writing** Explain how to do each construction with a compass and straightedge.
  a. Draw a segment $\overline{PQ}$. Construct the midpoint of $\overline{PQ}$.
  b. Divide $\overline{PQ}$ into four congruent segments.

© 23. a. Draw a large triangle with three acute angles. Construct the bisectors of the three angles. What appears to be true about the three angle bisectors?
  b. Repeat the constructions with a triangle that has one obtuse angle.
  c. **Make a Conjecture** What appears to be true about the three angle bisectors of any triangle?

Use a ruler to draw segments of 2 cm, 4 cm, and 5 cm. Then construct each triangle with the given side measures, if possible. If it is not possible, explain why not.

24. 4 cm, 4 cm, and 5 cm

25. 2 cm, 5 cm, and 5 cm

26. 2 cm, 2 cm, and 5 cm

27. 2 cm, 2 cm, and 4 cm

© 28. a. Draw a segment, $\overline{XY}$. Construct a triangle with sides congruent to $\overline{XY}$.
  b. Measure the angles of the triangle.
  c. **Writing** Describe how to construct a 60° angle using what you know. Then describe how to construct a 30° angle.

29. Which steps best describe how to construct the pattern at the right?

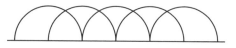

  Ⓐ Use a straightedge to draw the segment and then a compass to draw five half circles.
  Ⓑ Use a straightedge to draw the segment and then a compass to draw six half circles.
  Ⓒ Use a compass to draw five half circles and then a straightedge to join their ends.
  Ⓓ Use a compass to draw six half circles and then a straightedge to join their ends.

© **Challenge**

30. Study the figures. Complete the definition of a line perpendicular to a plane: A line is perpendicular to a plane if it is __?__ to every line in the plane that __?__.

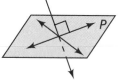

Line $r \perp$ plane M.   Line t is not $\perp$ plane P.

© 31. a. Use your compass to draw a circle. Locate three points A, B, and C on the circle.
  b. Draw $\overline{AB}$ and $\overline{BC}$. Then construct the perpendicular bisectors of $\overline{AB}$ and $\overline{BC}$.
  c. **Reasoning** Label the intersection of the two perpendicular bisectors as point O. What do you think is true about point O?

32. Two triangles are *congruent* if each side and each angle of one triangle is congruent to a side or angle of the other triangle. In Chapter 12, you will learn that if each side of one triangle is congruent to a side of the other triangle, then you can conclude that the triangles are congruent without finding the angles. Explain how you can use congruent triangles to justify the angle bisector construction.

10-2   Patterns and Inductive Reasoning

Prepares for **G.CO.9** Prove theorems about lines and angles . . . Also prepares for **G.CO.10, G.CO.11**

Objective   To use inductive reasoning to make conjectures

 Solve It!   Write your solution to the Solve It in the space below.

In the Solve It, you may have used inductive reasoning. **Inductive reasoning** is reasoning based on patterns you observe.

Essential Understanding   You can observe patterns in some number sequences and some sequences of geometric figures to discover relationships.

Problem 1   **Finding and Using a Pattern**

Got It?   What are the next two terms in each sequence?

a. 45, 40, 35, 30, . . .

b.

A Practice Find a pattern for each sequence. Use the pattern to show the next two terms.

1. $1, \frac{1}{2}, \frac{1}{4}, \frac{1}{8}, \ldots$

2.

> You may want to find the tenth or the one-hundredth term in a sequence. In this case, rather than find every previous term, you can look for a pattern and make a conjecture. A **conjecture** is a conclusion you reach using inductive reasoning.

Problem 2 Using Inductive Reasoning

Got It? What conjecture can you make about the twenty-first term in R, W, B, R, W, B, . . .?

Plan

> **Do you need to extend the sequence to 21 terms?**

A Practice Use the sequence and inductive reasoning to make a conjecture.

3. What is the color of the thirtieth figure?

4. What is the shape of the fortieth figure?

> It is important to gather enough data before you make a conjecture. For example, you do not have enough information about the sequence 1, 3, . . . to make a reasonable conjecture. The next term could be 3 • 3 = 9 or 3 + 2 = 5.

 **Problem 3** Collecting Information to Make a Conjecture

Plan

What's the first step?

Got It? What conjecture can you make about the sum of the first 30 odd numbers?

**Practice** Make a conjecture for each scenario. Show your work.

5. the sum of the first 100 positive even numbers

6. the product of two odd numbers

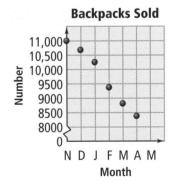 **Problem 4** Making a Prediction

Got It? **a.** Use the graph of the sales information from Problem 4. What conjecture can you make about backpack sales in June?

Backpacks Sold

b. Reasoning Is it reasonable to use this graph to make a conjecture about sales in August? Explain.

STEM **7.** Lightning travels much faster than thunder, so you see lightning before you hear thunder. If you count 5 s between the lightning and thunder, how far away is the storm?

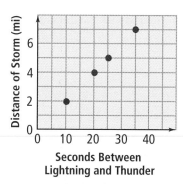

Seconds Between
Lightning and Thunder

8. The speed at which a cricket chirps is affected by the temperature. If you hear 20 cricket chirps in 14 s, what is the temperature?

Number of Chirps per 14 Seconds	Temperature (°F)
5	45
10	55
15	65

Not all conjectures turn out to be true. You should test your conjecture multiple times. You can prove that a conjecture is false by finding *one* counterexample. A **counterexample** is an example that shows that a conjecture is incorrect.

ONLINE PROBLEMS

Problem 5 **Finding a Counterexample**

Got It? What is a counterexample for each conjecture?

a. If a flower is red, it is a rose.

b. One and only one plane exists through any three points.

c. When you multiply a number by 3, the product is divisible by 6.

Ⓐ Practice Find one counterexample to show that each conjecture is false.

9. ∠1 and ∠2 are supplementary, so one of the angles is acute.

10. The sum of two numbers is greater than either number.

Lesson Check

Do you know HOW?

What are the next two terms in each sequence?

11. 7, 13, 19, 25, . . .

12.

13. What is a counterexample for the following conjecture?
All four-sided figures are squares.

Do you UNDERSTAND?

14. Vocabulary How does the word *counter* help you understand the term *counterexample*?

15. Compare and Contrast Clay thinks the next term in the sequence 2, 4, . . . is 6. Given the same pattern, Ott thinks the next term is 8, and Stacie thinks the next term is 7. What conjecture is each person making? Is there enough information to decide who is correct?

More Practice and Problem-Solving Exercises

B Apply

Find a pattern for each sequence. Use inductive reasoning to show the next two terms.

16. 1, 3, 7, 13, 21, . . .

17. 1, 2, 5, 6, 9, . . .

18. 0.1, 0.01, 0.001, . . .

19. 2, 6, 7, 21, 22, 66, 67, . . .

20. 1, 3, 7, 15, 31, . . .

21. $0, \frac{1}{2}, \frac{3}{4}, \frac{7}{8}, \frac{15}{16}, \ldots$

Predict the next term in each sequence. Use your calculator to verify your answer.

22. $12345679 \times 9 = 111111111$
$12345679 \times 18 = 222222222$
$12345679 \times 27 = 333333333$
$12345679 \times 36 = 444444444$
$12345679 \times 45 = \blacksquare$

23. $1 \times 1 = 1$
$11 \times 11 = 121$
$111 \times 111 = 12321$
$1111 \times 1111 = 1234321$
$11111 \times 11111 = \blacksquare$

24. Patterns Draw the next figure in the sequence. Make sure you think about color and shape.

Draw the next figure in each sequence.

25.

26.

27. **Reasoning** Find the perimeter when 100 triangles are put together in the pattern shown. Assume that all triangle sides are 1 cm long.

28. **Think About a Plan** Below are 15 points. Most of the points fit a pattern. Which does not? Explain.

$A(6, -2)$ $B(6, 5)$ $C(8, 0)$ $D(8, 7)$ $E(10, 2)$ $F(10, 6)$ $G(11, 4)$ $H(12, 3)$
$I(4, 0)$ $J(7, 6)$ $K(5, 6)$ $L(4, 7)$ $M(2, 2)$ $N(1, 4)$ $O(2, 6)$

- How can you draw a diagram to help you find a pattern?
- What pattern do the majority of the points fit?

29. **Language** Look for a pattern in the Chinese number system.
   a. What is the Chinese name for the numbers 43, 67, and 84?
   b. **Reasoning** Do you think that the Chinese number system is base 10? Explain.

30. **Open-Ended** Write two different number sequences that begin with the same two numbers.

31. **Error Analysis** For each of the past four years, Paulo has grown 2 in. every year. He is now 16 years old and is 5 ft 10 in. tall. He figures that when he is 22 years old he will be 6 ft 10 in. tall. What would you tell Paulo about his conjecture?

Chinese Number System

Number	Chinese Word	Number	Chinese Word
1	yī	9	jiǔ
2	èr	10	shí
3	sān	11	shí-yī
4	sì	12	shí-èr
5	wǔ	⋮	⋮
6	liù	20	èr-shí
7	qī	21	èr-shí-yī
8	bā	⋮	⋮
		30	sān-shí

32. **Bird Migration** During bird migration, volunteers get up early on Bird Day to record the number of bird species they observe in their community during a 24-h period. Results are posted online to help scientists and students track the migration.
   a. Make a graph of the data.
   b. Use the graph and inductive reasoning to make a conjecture about the number of bird species the volunteers in this community will observe in 2015.

33. **Writing** Describe a real-life situation in which you recently used inductive reasoning.

Bird Count

Year	Number of Species
2004	70
2005	83
2006	80
2007	85
2008	90

34. History When he was in the third grade, German mathematician Karl Gauss (1777–1855) took ten seconds to sum the integers from 1 to 100. Now it's your turn. Find a fast way to sum the integers from 1 to 100. Find a fast way to sum the integers from 1 to n. (*Hint:* Use patterns.)

35. Chess The small squares on a chessboard can be combined to form larger squares. For example, there are sixty-four 1×1 squares and one 8×8 square. Use inductive reasoning to determine how many 2×2 squares, 3×3 squares, and so on, are on a chessboard. What is the total number of squares on a chessboard?

36. a. Algebra Write the first six terms of the sequence that starts with 1, and for which the difference between consecutive terms is first 2, and then 3, 4, 5, and 6.

    b. Evaluate $\frac{n^2 + n}{2}$ for $n = 1, 2, 3, 4, 5$, and 6. Compare the sequence you get with your answer for part (a).

    c. Examine the diagram at the right and explain how it illustrates a value of $\frac{n^2 + n}{2}$.

    d. Draw a similar diagram to represent $\frac{n^2 + n}{2}$ for $n = 5$.

Conditional Statements

Prepares for **G.CO.10** Prove theorems about triangles . . . Also prepares for **G.CO.9, G.CO.11**

Objectives To recognize conditional statements and their parts
To write converses, inverses, and contrapositives of conditionals

 Solve It! Write your solution to the Solve It in the space below.

The study of *if-then* statements and their truth values is a foundation of reasoning.

Essential Understanding You can describe some mathematical relationships using a variety of *if-then* statements.

Key Concept Conditional Statements

Definition	Symbols	Diagram
A **conditional** is an *if-then* statement. The **hypothesis** is the part *p* following *if*. The **conclusion** is the part *q* following *then*.	$p \rightarrow q$ Read as "if *p* then *q*" or "*p* implies *q*."	

The Venn diagram above illustrates how the set of things that satisfy the hypothesis lies inside the set of things that satisfy the conclusion.

Problem 1 Identifying the Hypothesis and the Conclusion

Got It? What are the hypothesis and the conclusion of the conditional?
If an angle measures 130, then the angle is obtuse.

What would a Venn diagram of the statement look like?

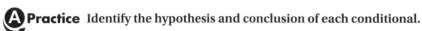

A Practice Identify the hypothesis and conclusion of each conditional.

1. If a figure is a rectangle, then it has four sides.

2. If you want to be healthy, then you should eat vegetables.

 Problem 2 **Writing a Conditional**

Got It? How can you write "Dolphins are mammals" as a conditional?

> Think
> **Which part of the statement is the hypothesis, (p)?**

A Practice **3. Algebra** Write the following sentence as a conditional.

$3x - 7 = 14$ implies that $3x = 21$.

4. Write a conditional statement that the Venn diagram illustrates.

The **truth value** of a conditional is either *true* or *false*. To show that a conditional is true, show that every time the hypothesis is true, the conclusion is also true. To show that a conditional is false, find *only one* counterexample for which the hypothesis is true and the conclusion is false.

Problem 3 Finding the Truth Value of a Conditional

Got It? Is the conditional *true* or *false*? If it is false, find a counterexample.

    a. If a month has 28 days, then it is February.

    b. If two angles form a linear pair, then they are supplementary.

Practice Determine if the conditional is *true* or *false*. If it is false, find a counterexample.

    5. If you live in a country that borders the United States, then you live in Canada.

    6. If an angle measures 80°, then it is acute.

The **negation** of a statement p is the opposite of the statement. The symbol is $\sim p$ and is read "not p." The negation of the statement "The sky is blue" is "The sky is *not* blue." You can use negations to write statements related to a conditional. Every conditional has three related conditional statements.

take note

Key Concept Related Conditional Statements

Statement	How to Write It	Example	Symbols	How to Read it
Conditional	Use the given hypothesis and conclusion.	If $m\angle A = 15$, then $\angle A$ is acute.	$p \rightarrow q$	If p, then q.
Converse	Exchange the hypothesis and the conclusion.	If $\angle A$ is acute, then $m\angle A = 15$.	$q \rightarrow p$	If q, then p.
Inverse	Negate both the hypothesis and the conclusion of the conditional.	If $m\angle A \neq 15$, then $\angle A$ is not acute.	$\sim p \rightarrow \sim q$	If not p, then not q.
Contrapositive	Negate both the hypothesis and the conclusion of the converse.	If $\angle A$ is not acute, then $m\angle A \neq 15$.	$\sim q \rightarrow \sim p$	If not q, then not p.

Below are the truth values of the related statements above. **Equivalent statements** have the same truth value.

Statement	Example	Truth Value
Conditional	If $m\angle A = 15$, then $\angle A$ is acute.	True
Converse	If $\angle A$ is acute, then $m\angle A = 15$.	False
Inverse	If $m\angle A \neq 15$, then $\angle A$ is not acute.	False
Contrapositive	If $\angle A$ is not acute, then $m\angle A \neq 15$.	True

A conditional and its contrapositive are equivalent statements. They are either both true or both false. The converse and inverse of a statement are also equivalent statements.

Got It? What are the converse, inverse, and contrapositive of the conditional statement below? What are the truth values of each? If a statement is false, give a counterexample.

If a vegetable is a carrot, then it contains beta carotene.

 Practice If the given statement is not in *if-then* form, rewrite it. Write the converse, inverse, and contrapositive of the given conditional statement. Determine the truth value of all four statements. If a statement is false, give a counterexample.

7. Algebra If $4x + 8 = 28$, then $x = 5$.

8. Pianists are musicians.

Lesson Check

Do you know HOW?

9. What are the hypothesis and the conclusion of the following statement? Write it as a conditional.

Residents of Key West live in Florida.

10. What are the converse, inverse, and contrapositive of the statement? Which statements are true?

If a figure is a rectangle with sides 2 cm and 3 cm, then it has a perimeter of 10 cm.

Do you UNDERSTAND?

11. Error Analysis Your classmate rewrote the statement "You jog every Sunday" as the conditional below. What is your classmate's error? Correct it.

If you jog, then it is Sunday.

12. Reasoning Suppose a conditional statement and its converse are both true. What are the truth values of the contrapositive and inverse? How do you know?

More Practice and Problem-Solving Exercises

 Apply

Write each statement as a conditional.

13. "We're half the people; we should be half the Congress." —Jeanette Rankin, former U.S. congresswoman, calling for more women in office

14. "Anyone who has never made a mistake has never tried anything new." —Albert Einstein

15. Probability An event with probability 1 is certain to occur.

16. Think About a Plan Your classmate claims that the conditional and contrapositive of the following statement are both true. Is he correct? Explain.

If $x = 2$, then $x^2 = 4$.

- Can you find a counterexample of the conditional?
- Do you need to find a counterexample of the contrapositive to know its truth value?

© 17. **Open-Ended** Write a true conditional that has a true converse, and write a true conditional that has a false converse.

© 18. **Multiple Representations** Write three separate conditional statements that the Venn diagram illustrates.

© 19. **Error Analysis** A given conditional is true. Natalie claims its contrapositive is also true. Sean claims its contrapositive is false. Who is correct and how do you know?

Draw a Venn diagram to illustrate each statement.

20. If an angle measures 100, then it is obtuse.

21. If you are the captain of your team, then you are a junior or senior.

22. Peace Corps volunteers want to help other people.

Algebra Write the converse of each statement. If the converse is true, write *true*. If it is not true, provide a counterexample.

23. If $x = -6$, then $|x| = 6$.

24. If y is negative, then $-y$ is positive.

25. If $x < 0$, then $x^3 < 0$.

26. If $x < 0$, then $x^2 > 0$.

27. **Advertising** Advertisements often suggest conditional statements. What conditional does the ad at the right imply?

Write each postulate as a conditional statement.

28. Two intersecting lines meet in exactly one point.

29. Two congruent figures have equal areas.

30. Through any two points there is exactly one line.

© **Challenge**

Write a statement beginning with *all*, *some*, or *no* to match each Venn diagram.

31.

32.
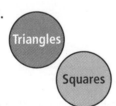

33.

34. Let a represent an integer. Consider the five statements r, s, t, u, and v.

$r: a$ is even. $s: a$ is odd. $t: 2a$ is even. $u: 2a$ is odd. $v: 2a + 1$ is odd.

How many statements of the form $p \rightarrow q$ can you make from these statements? Decide which are true, and provide a counterexample if they are false.

10-4 Biconditionals and Definitions

Prepares for **G.CO.11** Prove theorems about parallelograms . . . Also prepares for **G.CO.9**, **G.CO.10**

Objective To write biconditionals and recognize good definitions

 Solve It! Write your solution to the Solve It in the space below.

In the Solve It, you used conditional statements. A **biconditional** is a single true statement that combines a true conditional and its true converse. You can write a biconditional by joining the two parts of each conditional with the phrase *if and only if*.

Essential Understanding A definition is good if it can be written as a biconditional.

 **Problem 1** Writing a Biconditional

Got It? What is the converse of the following true conditional? If the converse is also true, rewrite the statements as a biconditional.

If two angles have equal measure, then the angles are congruent.

Think

How do you form the converse of a conditional?

(A) Practice Each conditional statement below is true. Write its converse. If the converse is also true, combine the statements as a biconditional.

1. Algebra If $x = 3$, then $|x| = 3$.

2. In the United States, if it is July 4, then it is Independence Day.

Key Concept Biconditional Statements

A biconditional combines $p \rightarrow q$ and $q \rightarrow p$ as $p \leftrightarrow q$.

Example	**Symbols**	**How to Read It**
A point is a midpoint if and only if it divides a segment into two congruent segments.	$p \leftrightarrow q$	"p if and only if q"

You can write a biconditional as two conditionals that are converses.

Problem 2 Identifying the Conditionals in a Biconditional

Got It? What are the two conditionals that form this biconditional?

Two numbers are reciprocals if and only if their product is 1.

(A) Practice Write the two statements that form each biconditional.

3. You live in Washington, D.C., if and only if you live in the capital of the United States.

4. Algebra $x^2 = 144$ if and only if $x = 12$ or $x = -12$.

Undefined terms such as *point*, *line*, and *plane* are the building blocks of geometry. You understand the meanings of these terms intuitively. Then you use them to define other terms such as *segment*.

A good definition is a statement that can help you identify or classify an object. A good definition has several important components.

✓ A good definition uses clearly understood terms. These terms should be commonly understood or already defined.

✓ A good definition is precise. Good definitions avoid words such as *large, sort of,* and *almost.*

✓ A good definition is reversible. That means you can write a good definition as a true biconditional.

 Problem 3 **Writing a Definition as a Biconditional**

Got It? Is this definition of *straight angle* reversible? If yes, write it as a true biconditional.

A straight angle is an angle that measures 180.

Think

How do you determine whether a definition is reversible?

Ⓐ Practice Test each statement below to see if it is reversible. If so, write it as a true biconditional. If not, write *not reversible.*

5. A perpendicular bisector of a segment is a line, segment, or ray that is perpendicular to a segment at its midpoint.

6. Two angles that form a linear pair are adjacent.

One way to show that a statement is *not* a good definition is to find a counterexample.

Problem 4 Identifying Good Definitions

Got It? **a.** Is the following statement a good definition? Explain.

A square is a figure with four right angles.

b. Reasoning How can you rewrite the statement "Obtuse angles have greater measures than acute angles" so that it is a good definition?

Practice Is each statement below a good definition? If not, explain.

7. A compass is a geometric tool.

8. Perpendicular lines are two lines that intersect to form right angles.

Lesson Check

Do you know HOW?

9. How can you write the following statement as two true conditionals?

Collinear points are points that lie on the same line.

10. How can you combine the following statements as a biconditional?

If this month is June, then next month is July.

If next month is July, then this month is June.

11. Write the following definition as a biconditional.

Vertical angles are two angles whose sides are opposite rays.

Do you UNDERSTAND?

@ **12. Vocabulary** Explain how the term *biconditional* is fitting for a statement composed of *two* conditionals.

13. **Error Analysis** Why is the following statement a poor definition?

> Elephants are gigantic animals.

14. **Compare and Contrast** Which of the following statements is a better definition of a linear pair? Explain.

> A linear pair is a pair of supplementary angles.
>
> A linear pair is a pair of adjacent angles with noncommon sides that are opposite rays.

More Practice and Problem-Solving Exercises

MATHEMATICAL PRACTICES

B Apply

15. **Think About a Plan** Is the following a good definition? Explain.
    A ligament is a band of tough tissue connecting bones or holding organs in place.
    - Can you write the statement as two true conditionals?
    - Are the two true conditionals converses of each other?

16. **Reasoning** Is the following a good definition? Explain.
    An obtuse angle is an angle with measure greater than 90.

17. **Open-Ended** Choose a definition from a dictionary or from a glossary. Explain what makes the statement a good definition.

18. **Error Analysis** Your friend defines a right angle as an angle that is greater than an acute angle. Use a biconditional to show that this is not a good definition.

19. Which conditional and its converse form a true biconditional?

    Ⓐ If $x > 0$, then $|x| > 0$.
    Ⓒ If $x^3 = 5$, then $x = 125$.
    Ⓑ If $x = 3$, then $x^2 = 9$.
    Ⓓ If $x = 19$, then $2x - 3 = 35$.

Write each statement as a biconditional.

20. Points in Quadrant III have two negative coordinates.

21. When the sum of the digits of an integer is divisible by 9, the integer is divisible by 9 and vice versa.

22. The whole numbers are the nonnegative integers.

23. A hexagon is a six-sided polygon.

Language For Exercises 24–27, use the chart below. Decide whether the description of each letter is a good definition. If not, provide a counterexample by giving another letter that could fit the definition.

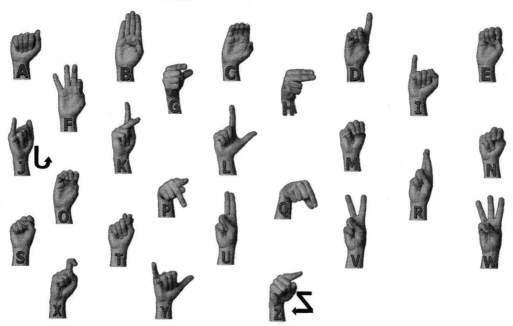

24. The letter *D* is formed by pointing straight up with the finger beside the thumb and folding the other fingers and the thumb so that they all touch.

25. The letter *K* is formed by making a *V* with the two fingers beside the thumb.

26. You have formed the letter *I* if and only if the smallest finger is sticking up and the other fingers are folded into the palm of your hand with your thumb folded over them and your hand is held still.

27. You form the letter *B* by holding all four fingers tightly together and pointing them straight up while your thumb is folded into the palm of your hand.

 **Reading Math** Let statements p, q, r, and s be as follows:

p : $\angle A$ and $\angle B$ are a linear pair.
q : $\angle A$ and $\angle B$ are supplementary angles.
r : $\angle A$ and $\angle B$ are adjacent angles.
s : $\angle A$ and $\angle B$ are adjacent and supplementary angles.

Substitute for p, q, r, and s, and write each statement the way you would read it.

28. $p \rightarrow q$ **29.** $p \rightarrow r$ **30.** $p \rightarrow s$ **31.** $p \leftrightarrow s$

Challenge

32. Writing Use the figures to write a good definition of a *line* in spherical geometry.

Lines   Not Lines

33. Multiple Representations You have illustrated true conditional statements with Venn diagrams. You can do the same thing with true biconditionals. Consider the following statement.

An integer is divisible by 10 if and only if its last digit is 0.

a. Write the two conditional statements that make up this biconditional.
b. Illustrate the first conditional from part (a) with a Venn diagram.
c. Illustrate the second conditional from part (a) with a Venn diagram.
d. Combine your two Venn diagrams from parts (b) and (c) to form a Venn diagram representing the biconditional statement.
e. What must be true of the Venn diagram for any true biconditional statement?
f. Reasoning How does your conclusion in part (e) help to explain why you can write a good definition as a biconditional?

Prepares for **G.CO.9** Prove theorems about lines and angles . . . Also prepares for **G.CO.10, G.CO.11**

Objective To use the Law of Detachment and the Law of Syllogism

Solve It! Write your solution to the Solve It in the space below.

In the Solve It, you drew a conclusion based on several facts. You used deductive reasoning. **Deductive reasoning** (sometimes called logical reasoning) is the process of reasoning logically from given statements or facts to a conclusion.

Essential Understanding Given true statements, you can use deductive reasoning to make a valid or true conclusion.

take note

Property Law of Detachment

Law	Symbols
If the hypothesis of a true conditional is true, then the conclusion is true.	If $\quad p \rightarrow q \quad$ is true
	And $\quad p \quad$ is true,
	Then $\quad q \quad$ is true.

To use the Law of Detachment, identify the hypothesis of the given true conditional. If the second given statement matches the hypothesis of the conditional, then you can make a valid conclusion.

 **Problem 1** Using the Law of Detachment

Got It? What can you conclude from the given information?

    a. If there is lightning, then it is not safe to be out in the open.
       Marla sees lightning from the soccer field.

Think

What conditions must be met for you to reach a valid conclusion?

    b. If a figure is a square, then its sides have equal length.
       Figure *ABCD* has sides of equal length.

Practice If possible, use the Law of Detachment to make a conclusion. If it is not possible to make a conclusion, tell why.

    1. If a doctor suspects her patient has a broken bone, then she should
       take an X-ray. Dr. Ngemba suspects Lilly has a broken arm.

    2. If three points are on the same line, then they are collinear. Points *X*,
       Y, and *Z* are on line *m*.

Another law of deductive reasoning is the Law of Syllogism. The **Law of Syllogism** allows you to state a conclusion from two true conditional statements when the conclusion of one statement is the hypothesis of the other statement.

take note

Property Law of Syllogism

Symbols			Example
If	$p \rightarrow q$	is true	If it is July, then you are on summer vacation.
and	$q \rightarrow r$	is true,	If you are on summer vacation, then you work at a smoothie shop.
then	$p \rightarrow$	r	is true.	**You conclude:** If it is July, then you work at a smoothie shop.

 **Problem 2** Using the Law of Syllogism

Got It? What can you conclude from the given information? What is your reasoning?

Think

What conditions must be met for you to reach a valid conclusion?

    a. If a whole number ends in 0, then it is divisible by 10. If a whole number is divisible by 10, then it is divisible by 5.

    b. If $\overrightarrow{AB}$ and $\overrightarrow{AD}$ are opposite rays, then the two rays form a straight angle. If two rays are opposite rays, then the two rays form a straight angle.

Practice If possible, use the Law of Syllogism to make a conclusion. If it is not possible to make a conclusion, tell why.

STEM **3. Ecology** If an animal is a Florida panther, then its scientific name is *Puma concolor coryi*.

If an animal is a *Puma concolor coryi*, then it is endangered.

4. If a line intersects a segment at its midpoint, then the line bisects the segment.

If a line bisects a segment, then it divides the segment into two congruent segments.

You can use the Law of Syllogism and the Law of Detachment together to make conclusions.

Problem 3 Using the Laws of Syllogism and Detachment

Got It?

a. What can you conclude from the given information? What is your reasoning?

If a river is more than 4000 mi long, then it is longer than the Amazon.

If a river is longer than the Amazon, then it is the longest river in the world. The Nile is 4132 mi long.

b. **Reasoning** In Problem 3, does it matter whether you use the Law of Syllogism or the Law of Detachment first? Explain.

Practice Use the Law of Detachment and the Law of Syllogism to make conclusions from the following statements. If it is not possible to make a conclusion, tell why.

5. If a mountain is the highest in Alaska, then it is the highest in the United States.

If an Alaskan mountain is more than 20,300 ft high, then it is the highest in Alaska.

Alaska's Mount McKinley is 20,320 ft high.

6. If you live in the Bronx, then you live in New York.

Tracy lives in the Bronx.

If you live in New York, then you live in the eleventh state to enter the Union.

Lesson Check

Do you know HOW?

If possible, make a conclusion from the given true statements. What reasoning did you use?

7. If it is Tuesday, then you will go bowling. You go bowling.

8. If a figure is a three-sided polygon, then it is a triangle. Figure *ABC* is a three-sided polygon.

9. If it is Saturday, then you walk to work. If you walk to work, then you wear sneakers.

Do you UNDERSTAND?

MATHEMATICAL PRACTICES

10. Error Analysis What is the error in the reasoning at the right?

Birds that weigh more than 50 pounds cannot fly. A kiwi cannot fly. So, a kiwi weighs more than 50 pounds.

11. Compare and Contrast How is deductive reasoning different from inductive reasoning?

More Practice and Problem-Solving Exercises

 **MATHEMATICAL PRACTICES**

B Apply

© 12. Think About a Plan If it is the night of your weekly basketball game, your family eats at your favorite restaurant. When your family eats at your favorite restaurant, you always get chicken fingers. If it is Tuesday, then it is the night of your weekly basketball game. How much do you pay for chicken fingers after your game? Use the specials board at the right to decide. Explain your reasoning.

- How can you reorder and rewrite the sentences to help you?
- How can you use the Law of Syllogism to answer the question?

Beverages For Exercises 13–18, assume that the following statements are true.

A. If Maria is drinking juice, then it is breakfast time.

B. If it is lunchtime, then Kira is drinking milk and nothing else.

C. If it is mealtime, then Curtis is drinking water and nothing else.

D. If it is breakfast time, then Julio is drinking juice and nothing else.

E. Maria is drinking juice.

Use only the information given above. For each statement, write *must be true,* *may be true,* **or** *is not true.* **Explain your reasoning.**

13. Julio is drinking juice.

14. Curtis is drinking water.

15. Kira is drinking milk.

16. Curtis is drinking juice.

17. Maria is drinking water.

18. Julio is drinking milk.

STEM 19. Physics Quarks are subatomic particles identified by electric charge and rest energy. The table shows how to categorize quarks by their flavors. Show how the Law of Detachment and the table are used to identify the flavor of a quark with a charge of $-\frac{1}{3}$ e and rest energy 540 MeV.

Rest Energy and Charge of Quarks						
Rest Energy (MeV)	360	360	1500	540	173,000	5000
Electric Charge (e)	$+\frac{2}{3}$	$-\frac{1}{3}$	$+\frac{2}{3}$	$-\frac{1}{3}$	$+\frac{2}{3}$	$-\frac{1}{3}$
Flavor	Up	Down	Charmed	Strange	Top	Bottom

Write the first statement as a conditional. If possible, use the Law of Detachment to make a conclusion. If it is not possible to make a conclusion, tell why.

20. All national parks are interesting. Mammoth Cave is a national park.

21. All squares are rectangles. *ABCD* is a square.

22. The temperature is always above 32°F in Key West, Florida. The temperature is 62°F.

23. Every high school student likes art. Ling likes art.

Ⓖ **24. Writing** Give an example of a rule used in your school that could be written as a conditional. Explain how the Law of Detachment is used in applying that rule.

Ⓒ Challenge

25. Reasoning Use the following algorithm: Choose an integer. Multiply the integer by 3. Add 6 to the product. Divide the sum by 3.

  a. Complete the algorithm for four different integers. Look for a pattern in the chosen integers and in the corresponding answers. Make a conjecture that relates the chosen integers to the answers.

  b. Let the variable x represent the chosen integer. Apply the algorithm to x. Simplify the resulting expression.

  c. How does your answer to part (b) confirm your conjecture in part (a)? Describe how inductive and deductive reasoning are exhibited in parts (a) and (b).

STEM **26. Biology** Consider the following given statements and conclusion.

Given: If an animal is a fish, then it has gills.
               A turtle does not have gills.

You conclude: A turtle is not a fish.

  a. Make a Venn diagram to illustrate the given information.

  b. Use the Venn diagram to help explain why the argument uses good reasoning.

10-6 Reasoning in Algebra and Geometry

Prepares for **G.CO.10** Prove theorems about triangles . . . Also prepares for **G.CO.9, G.CO.11**

Objective To connect reasoning in algebra and geometry

 Solve It! Write your solution to the Solve It in the space below.

In the Solve It, you logically examined a series of steps. In this lesson, you will apply logical reasoning to algebraic and geometric situations.

Essential Understanding Algebraic properties of equality are used in geometry. They will help you solve problems and justify each step you take.

In geometry you accept postulates and properties as true. Some of the properties that you accept as true are the properties of equality from algebra.

take note

Key Concept Properties of Equality

Let a, b, and c be any real numbers.

Addition Property   If $a = b$, then $a + c = b + c$.

Subtraction Property   If $a = b$, then $a - c = b - c$.

Multiplication Property   If $a = b$, then $a \cdot c = b \cdot c$.

Division Property   If $a = b$ and $c \neq 0$, then $\frac{a}{c} = \frac{b}{c}$.

Reflexive Property $a = a$

Symmetric Property   If $a = b$, then $b = a$.

Transitive Property   If $a = b$ and $b = c$, then $a = c$.

Substitution Property   If $a = b$, then b can replace a in any expression.

Key Concept The Distributive Property

Use multiplication to distribute *a* to each term of the sum or difference within the parentheses.

Sum:
$$a(b + c) = a(b + c) = ab + ac$$

Difference:
$$a(b - c) = a(b - c) = ab - ac$$

You use deductive reasoning when you solve an equation. You can justify each step with a postulate, a property, or a definition. For example, you can use the Distributive Property to justify combining like terms. If you think of the Distributive Property as $ab + ac = a(b + c)$ or $ab + ac = (b + c)a$, then $2x + x = (2 + 1)x = 3x$.

Problem 1 Justifying Steps When Solving an Equation

Got It? What is the value of *x*? Justify each step.

Given: $\overrightarrow{AB}$ bisects $\angle RAN$.

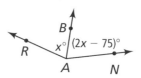

Plan

How can you use the given information?

Ⓐ Practice Algebra Fill in the reason that justifies each step.

1. $\frac{1}{2}x - 5 = 10$ Given

$2\left(\frac{1}{2}x - 5\right) = 20$ **a.** _____

$x - 10 = 20$ **b.** _____

$x = 30$ **c.** _____

2. $XY = 42$ Given

$\overset{3(n+4)}{\underset{X}{\bullet}} \quad \overset{3n}{\underset{Z}{\bullet}} \quad \underset{Y}{\bullet}$

$XZ + ZY = XY$ **a.** _____

$3(n + 4) + 3n = 42$ **b.** _____

$3n + 12 + 3n = 42$ **c.** _____

$6n + 12 = 42$ **d.** _____

$6n = 30$ **e.** _____

$n = 5$ **f.** _____

Some properties of equality have corresponding properties of congruence.

take note

Key Concept   Properties of Congruence

Reflexive Property	$\overline{AB} \cong \overline{AB}$ $\angle A \cong \angle A$
Symmetric Property	If $\overline{AB} \cong \overline{CD}$, then $\overline{CD} \cong \overline{AB}$. If $\angle A \cong \angle B$, then $\angle B \cong \angle A$.
Transitive Property	If $\overline{AB} \cong \overline{CD}$ and $\overline{CD} \cong \overline{EF}$, then $\overline{AB} \cong \overline{EF}$. If $\angle A \cong \angle B$ and $\angle B \cong \angle C$, then $\angle A \cong \angle C$. If $\angle B \cong \angle A$ and $\angle B \cong \angle C$, then $\angle A \cong \angle C$.

Problem 2   Using Properties of Equality and Congruence

Got It? For parts (a)–(c), what is the name of the property of equality or congruence that justifies going from the first statement to the second statement?

a. $\overline{AR} \cong \overline{TY}$
$\overline{TY} \cong \overline{AR}$

b. $3(x + 5) = 9$
$3x + 15 = 9$

c. $\frac{1}{4}x = 7$
$x = 28$

Ⓒ d. Reasoning What property justifies the statement $m\angle R = m\angle R$?

Think

How do you know if each justification is a property of equality or congruence?

Ⓐ Practice Name the property of equality or congruence that justifies going from the first statement to the second statement.

3. $\overline{ST} \cong \overline{QR}$
$\overline{QR} \cong \overline{ST}$

4. $AB - BC = 12$
$AB = 12 + BC$

A **proof** is a convincing argument that uses deductive reasoning. A proof logically shows why a conjecture is true. A **two-column proof** lists each statement on the left. The justification, or the reason for each statement, is on the right. Each statement must follow logically from the steps before it. The diagram below shows the setup for a two-column proof. You will find the complete proof in Problem 3.

Given: m∠1 = m∠3

Prove: m∠AEC = m∠DEB

Statements	Reasons
1) m∠1 = m∠3	1) Given
2) ‿‿‿‿	2) ‿‿‿‿
3) ‿‿‿‿	3) ‿‿‿‿
4) ‿‿‿‿	4) ‿‿‿‿
5) m∠AEC = m∠DEB	5) ‿‿‿‿

The first statement is usually the given statement.

Each statement should follow logically from the previous statements.

The last statement is what you want to prove.

Problem 3 Writing a Two-Column Proof

Got It? a. Write a two-column proof.

Given: $\overline{AB} \cong \overline{CD}$

Prove: $\overline{AC} \cong \overline{BD}$

A   B   C   D

b. **Reasoning** In Problem 3, why is Statement 2 necessary in the proof?

Practice

© **5. Developing Proof** Fill in the missing statements or reasons for the following two-column proof.

Given: C is the midpoint of $\overline{AD}$.

Prove: $x = 6$

$$\overset{\displaystyle 4x \qquad\qquad 2x + 12}{\underset{\displaystyle A \qquad\qquad C \qquad\qquad D}{\bullet\!\!-\!\!-\!\!-\!\!-\!\!\bullet\!\!-\!\!-\!\!-\!\!-\!\!\bullet}}$$

Statements	Reasons
1) C is the midpoint of $\overline{AD}$.	**1) a.** _____
2) $\overline{AC} \cong \overline{CD}$	**2) b.** _____
3) $AC = CD$	**3)** $\cong$ segments have equal length.
4) $4x = 2x + 12$	**4) c.** _____
5) d. _____	**5)** Subtraction Property of Equality
6) $x = 6$	**6) e.** _____

 ## Lesson Check

Do you know HOW?

Name the property of equality or congruence that justifies going from the first statement to the second statement.

6. $m\angle A = m\angle S$ and $m\angle S = m\angle K$
$m\angle A = m\angle K$

7. $3x + x + 7 = 23$
$4x + 7 = 23$

8. $4x + 5 = 17$
$4x = 12$

Do you UNDERSTAND?

9. **Developing Proof** Fill in the reasons for this algebraic proof.

Given: $5x + 1 = 21$

Prove: $x = 4$

Statements	Reasons
1) $5x + 1 = 21$	1) a. _____
2) $5x = 20$	2) b. _____
3) $x = 4$	3) c. _____

More Practice and Problem-Solving Exercises

B Apply

Use the given property to complete each statement.

10. Symmetric Property of Equality
If $AB = YU$, then __?__.

11. Symmetric Property of Congruence
If $\angle H \cong \angle K$, then __?__ $\cong \angle H$.

12. Reflexive Property of Congruence
$\angle POR \cong$ __?__

13. Distributive Property
$3(x - 1) = 3x -$ __?__

14. Substitution Property
If $LM = 7$ and $EF + LM = NP$,
then __?__ $= NP$.

15. Transitive Property of Congruence
If $\angle XYZ \cong \angle AOB$
and $\angle AOB \cong \angle WYT$, then __?__.

16. **Think About a Plan** A very important part in writing proofs is analyzing the diagram for key information. What true statements can you make based on the diagram at the right?
   - What theorems or definitions relate to the geometric figures in the diagram?
   - What types of markings show relationships between parts of geometric figures?

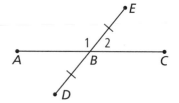

17. **Writing** Explain why the statements $\overline{LR} \cong \overline{RL}$ and $\angle CBA \cong \angle ABC$ are both true by the Reflexive Property of Congruence.

⊚ 18. Reasoning Complete the following statement. Describe the reasoning that supports your answer.

The Transitive Property of Falling Dominoes: If Domino A causes Domino B to fall, and Domino B causes Domino C to fall, then Domino A causes Domino ? to fall.

Write a two-column proof.

Proof 19. Given: $KM = 35$

Prove: $KL = 15$

$$\overset{2x-5 \quad\quad 2x}{\underset{K \quad\quad L \quad\quad M}{\bullet\!\!-\!\!-\!\!-\!\!\bullet\!\!-\!\!-\!\!-\!\!\bullet}}$$

Proof 20. Given: $m\angle GFI = 128$

Prove: $m\angle EFI = 40$

⒞ Challenge

21. Error Analysis The steps below "show" that $1 = 2$. Describe the error.

$a = b$	Given
$ab = b^2$	Multiplication Property of Equality
$ab - a^2 = b^2 - a^2$	Subtraction Property of Equality
$a(b - a) = (b + a)(b - a)$	Distributive Property
$a = b + a$	Division Property of Equality
$a = a + a$	Substitution Property
$a = 2a$	Simplify.
$1 = 2$	Division Property of Equality

Relationships Consider the following relationships among people. Tell whether each relationship is *reflexive, symmetric, transitive,* or *none of these.* Explain.

Sample: The relationship "is younger than" is not reflexive because Sue is not younger than herself. It is not symmetric because if Sue is younger than Fred, then Fred is not younger than Sue. It is transitive because if Sue is younger than Fred and Fred is younger than Alana, then Sue is younger than Alana.

22. has the same birthday as
23. is taller than
24. lives in a different state than

G.CO.9 Prove theorems about lines and angles . . . Theorems include: vertical angles are congruent . . .

Objective To prove and apply theorems about angles

 Solve It! Write your solution to the Solve It in the space below.

In the Solve It, you may have noticed a relationship between vertical angles. You can prove that this relationship is always true using deductive reasoning. A **theorem** is a conjecture or statement that you prove true.

Essential Understanding You can use given information, definitions, properties, postulates, and previously proven theorems as reasons in a proof.

take note

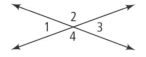 **Theorem 1** **Vertical Angles Theorem**

Vertical angles are congruent.

$\angle 1 \cong \angle 3$ and $\angle 2 \cong \angle 4$

When you are writing a geometric proof, it may help to separate the theorem you want to prove into a hypothesis and conclusion. Another way to write the Vertical Angles Theorem is "If two angles are vertical, then they are congruent." The hypothesis becomes the given statement, and the conclusion becomes what you want to prove. A two-column proof of the Vertical Angles Theorem follows.

Proof **Proof of Theorem 1: Vertical Angles Theorem**

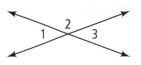

Given: ∠1 and ∠3 are vertical angles.

Prove: ∠1 ≅ ∠3

Statements	Reasons
1) ∠1 and ∠3 are vertical angles.	1) Given
2) ∠1 and ∠2 are supplementary. ∠2 and ∠3 are supplementary.	2) ⦞ that form a linear pair are supplementary.
3) $m\angle 1 + m\angle 2 = 180$ $m\angle 2 + m\angle 3 = 180$	3) The sum of the measures of supplementary ⦞ is 180.
4) $m\angle 1 + m\angle 2 = m\angle 2 + m\angle 3$	4) Transitive Property of Equality
5) $m\angle 1 = m\angle 3$	5) Subtraction Property of Equality
6) ∠1 ≅ ∠3	6) ⦞ with the same measure are ≅.

ONLINE PROBLEMS

Problem 1 Using the Vertical Angles Theorem

Think

How can you check that your value of x is correct?

Got It? What is the value of x?

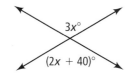

$3x°$

$(2x + 40)°$

 Practice **1.** Find the value of each variable.

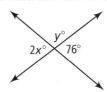

$y°$

$2x°$ $76°$

2. Find the measures of the labeled angles in Exercise 1.

Problem 2 Proof Using the Vertical Angles Theorem

Think

How can you use the given information?

Proof **Got It?**   **a.** Use the Vertical Angles Theorem to prove the following.

       Given: $\angle 1 \cong \angle 2$

       Prove: $\angle 1 \cong \angle 2 \cong \angle 3 \cong \angle 4$

     b. Reasoning How can you prove $\angle 1 \cong \angle 2 \cong \angle 3 \cong \angle 4$ without using the Vertical Angles Theorem?

Practice 3. **Developing Proof** Complete the following proof by filling in the blanks.

Given: $\angle 1 \cong \angle 3$

Prove: $\angle 6 \cong \angle 4$

Statements	Reasons
1) $\angle 1 \cong \angle 3$	1) Given
2) $\angle 3 \cong \angle 6$	2) a. _____
3) b. _____	3) Transitive Property of Congruence
4) $\angle 1 \cong \angle 4$	4) c. _____
5) $\angle 6 \cong \angle 4$	5) d. _____

The proof in Problem 2 is two-column, but there are many ways to display a proof.

A **paragraph proof** is written as sentences in a paragraph. Below is the proof from Problem 2 in paragraph form. Each statement in the Problem 2 proof is red in the paragraph proof.

Proof **Given:** $\angle 1 \cong \angle 4$

Prove: $\angle 2 \cong \angle 3$

Proof: $\angle 1 \cong \angle 4$ is given. $\angle 4 \cong \angle 2$ because vertical angles are congruent. By the Transitive Property of Congruence, $\angle 1 \cong \angle 2$. $\angle 1 \cong \angle 3$ because vertical angles are congruent. By the Transitive Property of Congruence, $\angle 2 \cong \angle 3$.

The Vertical Angles Theorem is a special case of the following theorem.

take note

Theorem 2 Congruent Supplements Theorem

Theorem	**If . . .**	**Then . . .**
If two angles are supplements of the same angle (or of congruent angles), then the two angles are congruent.	$\angle 1$ and $\angle 3$ are supplements and $\angle 2$ and $\angle 3$ are supplements.	$\angle 1 \cong \angle 2$

You will prove Theorem 2 in Problem 3.

Problem 3 Writing a Paragraph Proof

Proof **Got it?** Write a paragraph proof for the Vertical Angles Theorem.

(A) Practice

© **4. Developing Proof** Fill in the blanks to complete this proof of the Congruent Complements Theorem (Theorem 3).

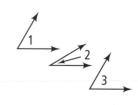

If two angles are complements of the same angle, then the two angles are congruent.

Given: ∠1 and ∠2 are complementary.
∠3 and ∠2 are complementary.

Prove: ∠1 ≅ ∠3

Proof: ∠1 and ∠2 are complementary and ∠3 and ∠2 are complementary

because it is given. By the definition of complementary angles,

$m\angle 1 + m\angle 2 =$ **a.** _____ and $m\angle 3 + m\angle 2 =$ **b.** _____.

Then $m\angle 1 + m\angle 2 = m\angle 3 + m\angle 2$ by the Transitive Property of

Equality. Subtract $m\angle 2$ from each side. By the Subtraction Property

of Equality, you get $m\angle 1 =$ **c.** _____. Angles with the same

measure are **d.** _____, so ∠1 ≅ ∠3.

The following theorems are similar to the Congruent Supplements Theorem.

Theorem 3   Congruent Complements Theorem

Theorem	If . . .	Then . . .
If two angles are complements of the same angle (or of congruent angles), then the two angles are congruent.	$\angle 1$ and $\angle 2$ are complements and $\angle 3$ and $\angle 2$ are complements	$\angle 1 \cong \angle 3$

Theorem 4

Theorem	If . . .	Then . . .
All right angles are congruent.	$\angle 1$ and $\angle 2$ are right angles	$\angle 1 \cong \angle 2$

You will prove Theorem 4 in Exercise 14.

Theorem 5

Theorem	If . . .	Then . . .
If two angles are congruent and supplementary, then each is a right angle.	$\angle 1 \cong \angle 2$, and $\angle 1$ and $\angle 2$ are supplements	$m\angle 1 = m\angle 2 = 90$

You will prove Theorem 5 in Exercise 19.

Lesson Check

Do you know HOW?

5. What are the measures of $\angle 1$, $\angle 2$, and $\angle 3$?

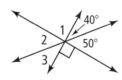

6. What is the value of x?

   (A) 12   (C) 120

   (B) 20   (D) 136

Do you UNDERSTAND?

MATHEMATICAL PRACTICES

7. Reasoning If $\angle A$ and $\angle B$ are supplements, and $\angle A$ and $\angle C$ are supplements, what can you conclude about $\angle B$ and $\angle C$? Explain.

8. Error Analysis Your friend knows that $\angle 1$ and $\angle 2$ are complementary and that $\angle 1$ and $\angle 3$ are complementary. He concludes that $\angle 2$ and $\angle 3$ must be complementary. What is his error in reasoning?

9. Compare and Contrast How is a theorem different from a postulate?

More Practice and Problem-Solving Exercises

Ⓑ **Apply**

ⓒ **10. Think About a Plan** What is the measure of the angle formed by Park St. and 116ᵗʰ St.?
- Can you make a connection between the angle you need to find and the labeled angle?
- How are angles that form a right angle related?

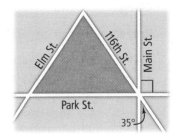

ⓒ **11. Open-Ended** Give an example of vertical angles in your home or classroom.

Algebra Find the value of each variable and the measure of each labeled angle.

12.

13.

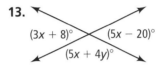

ⓒ **14. Developing Proof** Fill in the blanks to complete this proof of Theorem 4. All right angles are congruent.

Given: ∠X and ∠Y are right angles.

Prove: ∠X ≅ ∠Y

Proof: ∠X and **a.** __?__ are right angles because it is given.
By the definition of **b.** __?__, $m\angle X = 90$ and $m\angle Y = 90$.
By the Transitive Property of Equality, $m\angle X =$ **c.** __?__ .
Because angles of equal measure are congruent, **d.** __?__ .

15. Miniature Golf In the game of miniature golf, the ball bounces off the wall at the same angle it hit the wall. (This is the angle formed by the path of the ball and the line perpendicular to the wall at the point of contact.) In the diagram, the ball hits the wall at a 40° angle. Using Theorem 3, what are the values of x and y?

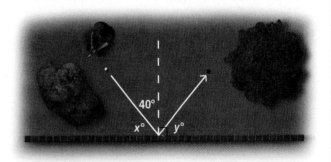

Name two pairs of congruent angles in each figure. Justify your answers.

16.

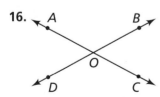

17.

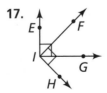

18.

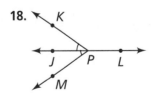

19. Developing Proof Fill in the blanks to complete this proof of Theorem 5. If two angles are congruent and supplementary, then each is a right angle.

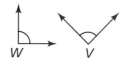

Given: ∠W and ∠V are congruent and supplementary.

Prove: ∠W and ∠V are right angles.

Proof: ∠W and ∠V are congruent because **a.** _____. Because congruent angles have the same measure, $m\angle W =$ **b.** _____. ∠W and ∠V are supplementary because it is given. By the definition of supplementary angles, $m\angle W + m\angle V =$ **c.** _____. Substituting $m\angle W$ for $m\angle V$, you get $m\angle W + m\angle W = 180$, or $2m\angle W = 180$. By the **d.** _____ Property of Equality, $m\angle W = 90$. Since $m\angle W = m\angle V$, $m\angle V = 90$ by the Transitive Property of Equality. Both angles are **e.** _____ angles by the definition of right angles.

20. Design In the photograph, the legs of the table are constructed so that ∠1 ≅ ∠2. What theorem can you use to justify the statement that ∠3 ≅ ∠4?

21. Reasoning Explain why this statement is true:
If $m\angle ABC + m\angle XYZ = 180$ and $\angle ABC \cong \angle XYZ$, then ∠ABC and ∠XYZ are right angles.

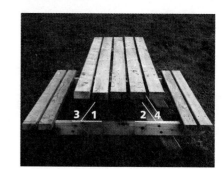

Algebra Find the measure of each angle.

22. ∠A is twice as large as its complement, ∠B.

23. ∠A is half as large as its complement, ∠B.

24. ∠A is twice as large as its supplement, ∠B.

25. ∠A is half as large as twice its supplement, ∠B.

Proof 26. Write a proof for this form of Theorem 2. If two angles are supplements of congruent angles, then the two angles are congruent.

Given: ∠1 and ∠2 are supplementary.
∠3 and ∠4 are supplementary.
∠2 ≅ ∠4

Prove: ∠1 ≅ ∠3

Challenge

27. Coordinate Geometry $\angle DOE$ contains points $D(2, 3)$, $O(0, 0)$, and $E(5, 1)$. Find the coordinates of a point F so that $\overrightarrow{OF}$ is a side of an angle that is adjacent and supplementary to $\angle DOE$.

28. Coordinate Geometry $\angle AOX$ contains points $A(1, 3)$, $O(0, 0)$, and $X(4, 0)$.
   a. Find the coordinates of a point B so that $\angle BOA$ and $\angle AOX$ are adjacent complementary angles.
   b. Find the coordinates of a point C so that $\overrightarrow{OC}$ is a side of a different angle that is adjacent and complementary to $\angle AOX$.

Algebra Find the value of each variable and the measure of each angle.

29.

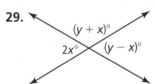

30.

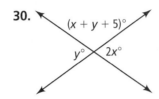

31.

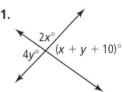

10 Chapter Review

10-1 Basic Constructions

Quick Review

Construction is the process of making geometric figures using a **compass** and a **straightedge**. Four basic constructions involve congruent segments, congruent angles, and bisectors of segments and angles.

Example

Construct $\overline{AB}$ **congruent to** $\overline{EF}$.

Step 1

Draw a ray with endpoint A.

Step 2

Open the compass to the length of $\overline{EF}$. Keep that compass setting and put the compass point on point A. Draw an arc that intersects the ray. Label the point of intersection B.

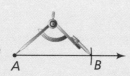

Exercises

1. Use a protractor to draw a 73° angle. Then construct an angle congruent to it.

2. Use a protractor to draw a 60° angle. Then construct the bisector of the angle.

3. Sketch $\overline{LM}$ on paper. Construct a line segment congruent to $\overline{LM}$. Then construct the perpendicular bisector of your line segment.

4. **a.** Sketch $\angle B$ on paper. Construct an angle congruent to $\angle B$.
   b. Construct the bisector of your angle from part (a).

10-2 Patterns and Inductive Reasoning

Quick Review

You use **inductive reasoning** when you make conclusions based on patterns you observe. A **conjecture** is a conclusion you reach using inductive reasoning. A **counterexample** is an example that shows a conjecture is incorrect.

Example

Describe the pattern. What are the next two terms in the sequence?

$$1, -3, 9, -27, \ldots$$

Each term is -3 times the previous term. The next two terms are $-27 \times (-3) = 81$ and $81 \times (-3) = -243$.

Exercises

Find a pattern for each sequence. Describe the pattern and use it to show the next two terms.

5. 1000, 100, 10, . . .

6. 5, −5, 5, −5, . . .

7. 34, 27, 20, 13, . . .

8. 6, 24, 96, 384, . . .

Find a counterexample to show that each conjecture is false.

9. The product of any integer and 2 is greater than 2.

10. The city of Portland is in Oregon.

10-3 Conditional Statements

Quick Review

A **conditional** is an *if-then* statement. The symbolic form of a conditional is $p \rightarrow q$, where p is the **hypothesis** and q is the **conclusion**.

- To find the **converse**, switch the hypothesis and conclusion of the conditional ($q \rightarrow p$).
- To find the **inverse**, negate the hypothesis and the conclusion of the conditional ($\sim p \rightarrow \sim q$).
- To find the **contrapositive**, negate the hypothesis and the conclusion of the converse ($\sim q \rightarrow \sim p$).

Example

What is the converse of the conditional statement below? What is its truth value?

> **If you are a teenager, then you are younger than 20.**

Converse: If you are younger than 20, then you are a teenager.

A 7-year-old is not a teenager. The converse is false.

Exercises

Rewrite each sentence as a conditional statement.

11. All motorcyclists wear helmets.

12. Two nonparallel lines intersect in one point.

13. Angles that form a linear pair are supplementary.

14. School is closed on certain holidays.

Write the converse, inverse, and contrapositive of the given conditional. Then determine the truth value of each statement.

15. If an angle is obtuse, then its measure is greater than 90 and less than 180.

16. If a figure is a square, then it has four sides.

17. If you play the tuba, then you play an instrument.

18. If you baby-sit, then you are busy on Saturday night.

10-4 Biconditionals and Definitions

Quick Review

When a conditional and its converse are true, you can combine them as a true **biconditional** using the phrase *if and only if*. The symbolic form of a biconditional is $p \leftrightarrow q$. You can write a good **definition** as a true biconditional.

Example

Is the following definition reversible? If yes, write it as a true biconditional.

> **A hexagon is a polygon with exactly six sides.**

Yes. The conditional is true: If a figure is a hexagon, then it is a polygon with exactly six sides. Its converse is also true: If a figure is a polygon with exactly six sides, then it is a hexagon.

Biconditional: A figure is a hexagon *if and only if* it is a polygon with exactly six sides.

Exercises

Determine whether each statement is a good definition. If not, explain.

19. A newspaper has articles you read.

20. A linear pair is a pair of adjacent angles whose noncommon sides are opposite rays.

21. An angle is a geometric figure.

22. Write the following definition as a biconditional. An oxymoron is a phrase that contains contradictory terms.

23. Write the following biconditional as two statements, a conditional and its converse. Two angles are complementary if and only if the sum of their measures is 90.

10-5 Deductive Reasoning

Quick Review

Deductive reasoning is the process of reasoning logically from given statements to a conclusion.

Law of Detachment: If $p \rightarrow q$ is true and p is true, then q is true.

Law of Syllogism: If $p \rightarrow q$ and $q \rightarrow r$ are true, then $p \rightarrow r$ is true.

Example

What can you conclude from the given information?

Given: **If you play hockey, then you are on the team. If you are on the team, then you are a varsity athlete.**

The conclusion of the first statement matches the hypothesis of the second statement. Use the Law of Syllogism to conclude: If you play hockey, then you are a varsity athlete.

Exercises

Use the Law of Detachment to make a conclusion.

24. If you practice tennis every day, then you will become a better player. Colin practices tennis every day.

25. $\angle 1$ and $\angle 2$ are supplementary. If two angles are supplementary, then the sum of their measures is 180.

Use the Law of Syllogism to make a conclusion.

26. If two angles are vertical, then they are congruent. If two angles are congruent, then their measures are equal.

27. If your father buys new gardening gloves, then he will work in his garden. If he works in his garden, then he will plant tomatoes.

10-6 Reasoning in Algebra and Geometry

Quick Review

You use deductive reasoning and properties to solve equations and justify your reasoning. A **proof** is a convincing argument that uses deductive reasoning. A **two-column proof** lists each statement on the left and the justification for each statement on the right.

Example

What is the name of the property that justifies going from the first line to the second line?

$\angle A \cong \angle B$ and $\angle B \cong \angle C$
$\angle A \cong \angle C$

Transitive Property of Congruence

Exercises

28. Algebra Fill in the reason that justifies each step.

Given: $QS = 42$
Prove: $x = 13$

Statements	Reasons
1) $QS = 42$	1) a. ?
2) $QR + RS = QS$	2) b. ?
3) $(x + 3) + 2x = 42$	3) c. ?
4) $3x + 3 = 42$	4) d. ?
5) $3x = 39$	5) e. ?
6) $x = 13$	6) f. ?

Use the given property to complete the statement.

29. Division Property of Equality

If $2(AX) = 2(BY)$, then $AX = $? .

30. Distributive Property: $3p - 6q = 3(\underline{\ ?\ })$

10-7 Proving Angles Congruent

Quick Review

A statement that you prove true is a **theorem**. A proof written as a paragraph is a **paragraph proof**. In geometry, each statement in a proof is justified by given information, a property, postulate, definition, or theorem.

Example

Write a paragraph proof.

Given: $\angle 1 \cong \angle 4$

Prove: $\angle 2 \cong \angle 3$

$\angle 1 \cong \angle 4$ because it is given. $\angle 1 \cong \angle 2$ because vertical angles are congruent. $\angle 4 \cong \angle 2$ by the Transitive Property of Congruence. $\angle 4 \cong \angle 3$ because vertical angles are congruent. $\angle 2 \cong \angle 3$ by the Transitive Property of Congruence.

Exercises

Use the diagram for Exercises 31–34.

31. Find the value of y.

32. Find $m\angle AEC$.

33. Find $m\angle BED$.

34. Find $m\angle AEB$.

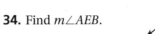

35. Given: $\angle 1$ and $\angle 2$ are complementary.
$\angle 3$ and $\angle 4$ are complementary.
$\angle 2 \cong \angle 4$

   Prove: $\angle 1 \cong \angle 3$

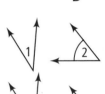

Pull It All Together

Analyzing a Calendar Pattern

 ASSESSMENT

The figure shows a page from a calendar. Choose any four numbers from the calendar that lie inside a 2-by-2 square. One such set of numbers is shown below. Find the sum of the pair of numbers that lie on each diagonal of the square. What do you notice about the sums? Try this using other squares on the calendar and using calendar pages for different months.

MARCH						
SUN	**MON**	**TUE**	**WED**	**THU**	**FRI**	**SAT**
				1	2	3
4	5	6	7	8	9	10
11	12	13	14	15	16	17
18	19	20	21	22	23	24
25	26	27	28	29	30	31

Task Description

Use inductive reasoning to make a conjecture about the calendar pattern you observed. Then use deductive reasoning to prove your conjecture.

- How can you write your conjecture as a conditional statement?

- How can you use algebraic expressions to represent the four numbers that lie inside any 2-by-2 square on any calendar page?

Get Ready!

Identifying Angle Pairs

Identify all pairs of each type of angles in the diagram.

1. linear pair

2. complementary angles

3. vertical angles

4. supplementary angles

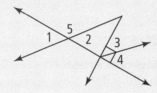

Justifying Statements

Name the property that justifies each statement.

5. If $3x = 6$, then $x = 2$.

6. If $\angle 1 \cong \angle 2$ and $\angle 2 \cong \angle 3$, then $\angle 1 \cong \angle 3$.

Solving Equations

Algebra Solve each equation.

7. $3x + 11 = 7x - 5$
8. $(x - 4) + 52 = 109$
9. $(2x + 5) + (3x - 10) = 70$

 Looking Ahead Vocabulary

10. The core of an apple is in the *interior* of the apple. The peel is on the *exterior*. How can the terms *interior* and *exterior* apply to geometric figures?

11. A ship sailing from the United States to Europe makes a transatlantic voyage. What does the prefix *trans-* mean in this situation? A *transversal* is a special type of line in geometry. What might a *transversal* do? Explain.

12. People in many jobs use *flow*charts to describe the logical steps of a particular process. How do you think you can use a *flow proof* in geometry?

CHAPTER 11

Proving Theorems About Lines and Angles

Big Ideas

1 Reasoning and Proof
Essential Question How do you prove that two lines are parallel?

2 Measurement
Essential Question What is the sum of the measures of the angles of a triangle?

©Domains

• Congruence
• Modeling with Geometry

Chapter Preview

Interactive Digital Path

Log in to **pearsonsuccessnet.com** and click on Interactive Digital Path to access the Solve Its and animated Problems.

 **Vocabulary**

English/Spanish Vocabulary Audio Online:

English	Spanish
alternate exterior angles, *p. 655*	ángulos alternos externos
alternate interior angles, *p. 655*	ángulos alternos internos
corresponding angles, *p. 655*	ángulos correspondientes
exterior angle of a polygon, *p. 689*	ángulo exterior de un polígono
parallel lines, *p. 653*	rectas paralelas
same-side interior angles, *p. 655*	ángulos internos del mismo lado
skew lines, *p. 653*	rectas cruzadas
transversal, *p. 655*	transversal

11-1 Lines and Angles

G.CO.1 Know precise definitions of . . . perpendicular line, parallel line . . . based on the undefined notions of point, line . . . Also prepares for **G.CO.9**

Objectives To identify relationships between figures in space
To identify angles formed by two lines and a transversal

Solve It! Write your solution to the Solve It in the space below.

In the Solve It, you used relationships among planes in space to write the instructions. In this lesson, you will explore relationships of nonintersecting lines and planes.

Essential Understanding Not all lines and not all planes intersect.

take note Key Concept Parallel and Skew

Definition	Symbols	Diagram
Parallel lines are coplanar lines that do not intersect. The symbol ∥ means "is parallel to."	$\overleftrightarrow{AE} \parallel \overleftrightarrow{BF}$ $\overleftrightarrow{AD} \parallel \overleftrightarrow{BC}$	
Skew lines are noncoplanar; they are not parallel and do not intersect.	$\overleftrightarrow{AB}$ and $\overleftrightarrow{CG}$ are skew.	
Parallel planes are planes that do not intersect.	plane *ABCD* ∥ plane *EFGH*	

Use arrows to show
$\overleftrightarrow{AE} \parallel \overleftrightarrow{BF}$ and $\overleftrightarrow{AD} \parallel \overleftrightarrow{BC}$.

A line and a plane that do not intersect are parallel. Segments and rays can also be parallel or skew. They are parallel if they lie in parallel lines and skew if they lie in skew lines.

Problem 1 Identifying Nonintersecting Lines and Planes

Got It? Use the figure in Problem 1, shown at the right.

    a. Which segments are parallel to $\overline{AD}$?

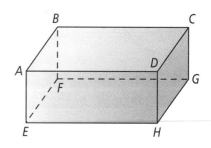

    © **b. Reasoning** Explain why $\overline{FE}$ and $\overline{CD}$ are *not* skew.

    c. What is another pair of parallel planes?

    d. What are two segments parallel to plane *DCGH*?

 Practice Use the diagram to name each of the following. Assume that lines and planes that appear to be parallel are parallel.

    1. two lines that are skew to $\overleftrightarrow{EJ}$

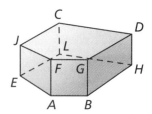

    2. all lines that are parallel to plane *JFAE*

Essential Understanding When a line intersects two or more lines, the angles formed at the intersection points create special angle pairs.

A **transversal** is a line that intersects two or more coplanar lines at distinct points. The diagram below shows the eight angles formed by a transversal t and two lines ℓ and m.

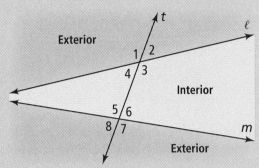

Notice that angles 3, 4, 5, and 6 lie between ℓ and m. They are *interior* angles. Angles 1, 2, 7, and 8 lie outside of ℓ and m. They are *exterior* angles.

Pairs of the eight angles have special names as suggested by their positions.

take note

Key Concept Angle Pairs Formed by Transversals

Definition	Example	
Alternate interior angles are nonadjacent interior angles that lie on opposite sides of the transversal.	$\angle 4$ and $\angle 6$ $\angle 3$ and $\angle 5$	
Same-side interior angles are interior angles that lie on the same side of the transversal.	$\angle 4$ and $\angle 5$ $\angle 3$ and $\angle 6$	
Corresponding angles lie on the same side of the transversal t and in corresponding positions.	$\angle 1$ and $\angle 5$ $\angle 4$ and $\angle 8$ $\angle 2$ and $\angle 6$ $\angle 3$ and $\angle 7$	
Alternate exterior angles are nonadjacent exterior angles that lie on opposite sides of the transversal.	$\angle 1$ and $\angle 7$ $\angle 2$ and $\angle 8$	

Problem 2 **Identifying an Angle Pair**

Got It? Use the figure at the right. What are three pairs of corresponding angles?

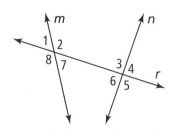

Ⓐ Practice Identify all pairs of each type of angles in the diagram. Name the two lines and the transversal that form each pair.

3. same-side interior angles

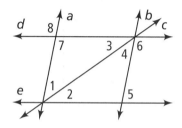

4. alternate exterior angles

Problem 3 **Classifying an Angle Pair**

Got It? In Problem 3, are angles 1 and 3 *alternate interior angles, same-side interior angles, corresponding angles,* or *alternate exterior angles*?

Think
How do the positions of ∠1 and ∠3 compare?

5. Are the angles labeled in the same color *alternate interior angles, same-side interior angles, corresponding angles,* or *alternate exterior angles?*

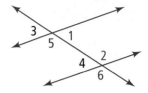

6. Aviation The photo shows an overhead view of airport runways. Are ∠1 and ∠2 *alternate interior angles, same-side interior angles, corresponding angles,* or *alternate exterior angles?*

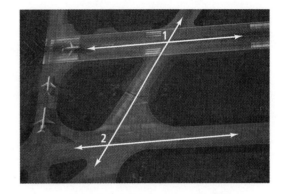

Lesson Check

Do you know HOW?

Name one pair each of the segments, planes, or angles. Lines and planes that appear to be parallel are parallel.

7. parallel segments

8. skew segments

9. parallel planes

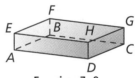

Exercises 7–9

10. alternate interior angles

11. same-side interior angles

12. corresponding angles

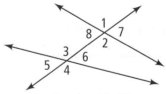

Exercises 10–13

13. alternate exterior angles

Do you UNDERSTAND?

14. Vocabulary Why is the word *coplanar* included in the definition for parallel lines?

15. Vocabulary How does the phrase *alternate interior angles* describe the positions of the two angles?

16. Error Analysis In the figure at the right, lines and planes that appear to be parallel are parallel. Carly says $\overline{AB} \parallel \overline{HG}$. Juan says $\overline{AB}$ and $\overline{HG}$ are skew. Who is correct? Explain.

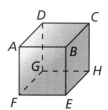

More Practice and Problem-Solving Exercises

 Apply

How many pairs of each type of angles do two lines and a transversal form?

17. alternate interior angles

18. corresponding angles

19. alternate exterior angles

20. vertical angles

21. Recreation You and a friend are driving go-karts on two different tracks. As you drive on a straight section heading east, your friend passes above you on a straight section heading south. Are these sections of the two tracks *parallel, skew,* or *neither*? Explain.

In Exercises 22–27, describe the statement as *true* or *false*. If false, explain. Assume that lines and planes that appear to be parallel are parallel.

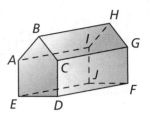

22. $\overleftrightarrow{CB} \parallel \overleftrightarrow{HG}$

23. $\overleftrightarrow{ED} \parallel \overleftrightarrow{HG}$

24. plane *AED* $\parallel$ plane *FGH*

25. plane *ABH* $\parallel$ plane *CDF*

26. $\overleftrightarrow{AB}$ and $\overleftrightarrow{HG}$ are skew lines.

27. $\overleftrightarrow{AE}$ and $\overleftrightarrow{BC}$ are skew lines.

© 28. Think About a Plan A rectangular rug covers the floor in a living room. One of the walls in the same living room is painted blue. Are the rug and the blue wall parallel? Explain.
  • Can you visualize the rug and the wall as geometric figures?
  • What must be true for these geometric figures to be parallel?

In Exercises 29–34, determine whether each statement is *always, sometimes,* or *never* true.

29. Two parallel lines are coplanar.

30. Two planes that do not intersect are parallel.

31. Two skew lines are coplanar.

32. Two lines that lie in parallel planes are parallel.

33. Two lines in intersecting planes are skew.

34. A line and a plane that do not intersect are skew.

© 35. a. Writing Describe the three ways in which two lines may be related.
  b. Give examples from the real world to illustrate each of the relationships you described in part (a).

© 36. Open-Ended The letter Z illustrates alternate interior angles. Find at least two other letters that illustrate pairs of angles presented in this lesson. Draw the letters. Then mark and describe the angles.

© 37. a. Reasoning Suppose two parallel planes *A* and *B* are each intersected by a third plane *C*. Make a conjecture about the intersection of planes *A* and *C* and the intersection of planes *B* and *C*.
  b. Find examples in your classroom to illustrate your conjecture in part (a).

Use the figure at the right for Exercises 38 and 39.

38. Do planes *A* and *B* have other lines in common that are parallel to $\overleftrightarrow{CD}$? Explain.

© 39. Visualization Are there planes that intersect planes *A* and *B* in lines parallel to $\overleftrightarrow{CD}$? Draw a sketch to support your answer.

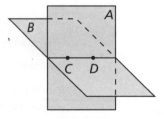

© 40. Draw a Diagram A transversal *r* intersects lines ℓ and *m*. If ℓ and *r* form ∠1 and ∠2 and *m* and *r* form ∠3 and ∠4, sketch a diagram that meets the following conditions.
  • ∠1 ≅ ∠2
  • ∠3 is an interior angle.
  • ∠4 is an exterior angle.
  • ∠2 and ∠4 lie on opposite sides of *r*.
  • ∠3 and ∠4 are supplementary.

11-2 Properties of Parallel Lines

G.CO.9 Prove theorems about lines and angles. Theorems include: . . . when a transversal crosses parallel lines, alternate interior angles are congruent . . .

Objectives To prove theorems about parallel lines
To use properties of parallel lines to find angle measures

Solve It! Write your solution to the Solve It in the space below.

In the Solve It, you identified several pairs of angles that appear congruent. You already know the relationship between vertical angles. In this lesson, you will explore the relationships between the angles you learned about in Lesson 11-1 when they are formed by *parallel* lines and a transversal.

Essential Understanding The special angle pairs formed by parallel lines and a transversal are congruent, supplementary, or both.

take note

Postulate 11   Same-Side Interior Angles Postulate

Postulate	If . . .	Then . . .
If a transversal intersects two parallel lines, then same-side interior angles are supplementary.	$\ell \parallel m$	$m\angle 4 + m\angle 5 = 180$ $m\angle 3 + m\angle 6 = 180$

ⓒGot It? **Reasoning** If you know the measure of one of the angles, can you always find the measures of all 8 angles when two parallel lines are cut by a transversal? Explain.

ⒶPractice Identify all the numbered angles that are congruent to the given angle. Justify your answers.

1.

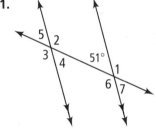

2.

You can use the Same-Side Interior Angles Postulate to prove other angle relationships.

take note

Theorem 6   Alternate Interior Angles Theorem

Theorem	If . . .	Then . . .
If a transversal intersects two parallel lines, then alternate interior angles are congruent.	$\ell \parallel m$	$\angle 4 \cong \angle 6$ $\angle 3 \cong \angle 5$

Theorem 7   Corresponding Angles Theorem

Theorem	If . . .	Then . . .
If a transversal intersects two parallel lines, then corresponding angles are congruent.	$\ell \parallel m$	$\angle 1 \cong \angle 5$ $\angle 2 \cong \angle 6$ $\angle 3 \cong \angle 7$ $\angle 4 \cong \angle 8$

You will prove Theorem 7 in Exercise 22.

Proof Proof of Theorem 6: Alternate Interior Angles Theorem

Given: $\ell \parallel m$

Prove: $\angle 4 \cong \angle 6$

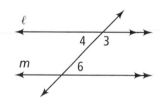

Statement	Reasons
1) $\ell \parallel m$	1) Given
2) $m\angle 3 + m\angle 4 = 180$	2) Supplementary Angles
3) $m\angle 3 + m\angle 6 = 180$	3) Same-Side Interior Angles Postulate
4) $m\angle 3 + m\angle 4 = m\angle 3 + m\angle 6$	4) Transitive Property of Equality
5) $m\angle 4 = m\angle 6$	5) Subtraction Property of Equality
6) $\angle 4 \cong \angle 6$	6) Definition of Congruence

 **Problem 2** **Proving an Angle Relationship**

Got It? Let $a \parallel b$. Prove that $\angle 1 \cong \angle 7$.

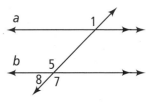

Ⓐ Practice **3. Developing Proof** Supply the missing reasons in the two-column proof.

Given: $a \parallel b, c \parallel d$

Prove: $\angle 1 \cong \angle 3$

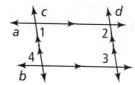

Statements	Reasons
1) $a \parallel b$	**1)** Given
2) $\angle 3$ and $\angle 2$ are supplementary.	**2) a.** _____
3) $c \parallel d$	**3)** Given
4) $\angle 1$ and $\angle 2$ are supplementary.	**4) b.** _____
5) $\angle 1 \cong \angle 3$	**5) c.** _____

Proof **4.** Write a two-column proof for Exercise 3 that does not use ∠2.

In the diagram for Problem 2, ∠1 and ∠7 are alternate exterior angles. In Got It 2, you proved the following theorem.

take note

Theorem 8   Alternate Exterior Angles Theorem

Theorem	If . . .	Then . . .
If a transversal intersects two parallel lines, then alternate exterior angles are congruent.	$\ell \parallel m$ 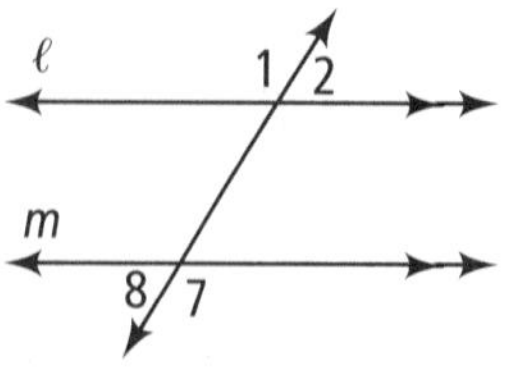	$\angle 1 \cong \angle 7$ $\angle 2 \cong \angle 8$

If you know the measure of one of the angles formed by two parallel lines and a transversal, you can use theorems and postulates to find the measures of the other angles.

Problem 3 **Finding Measures of Angles**

How does ∠4
relate to ∠1?

Think

Got It? Use the diagram in Problem 3. What is the measure of each angle?
Justify each answer.

    a. ∠1   **b.** ∠2

    c. ∠5   **d.** ∠6

    e. ∠7   **f.** ∠8

Ⓐ Practice Find $m\angle 1$ and $m\angle 2$. Justify each answer.

5.

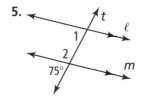

6.

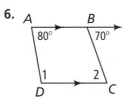

You can combine theorems and postulates with your knowledge of algebra to find angle measures.

Problem 4 **Finding an Angle Measure**

Got It? **a.** In the figure below, what are the values of x and y?

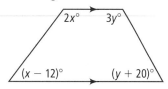

Think

What is the relationship between the two angles on the left side of the figure?

b. What are the measures of the four angles in the figure?

A **Practice** **Algebra** Find the value of x. Then find the measure of each labeled angle.

7.

8.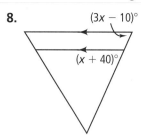

Lesson Check

Do you know HOW?

Use the diagram for Exercises 9–12.

9. Identify four pairs of congruent angles. (Exclude vertical angle pairs.)

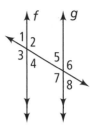

10. Identify two pairs of supplementary angles. (Exclude linear pairs.)

11. If $m\angle 1 = 70$, what is $m\angle 8$?

12. If $m\angle 4 = 70$ and $m\angle 7 = 2x$, what is the value of x?

Do you UNDERSTAND?

13. Compare and Contrast How are the Alternate Interior Angles Theorem and the Alternate Exterior Angles Theorem alike? How are they different?

14. In Problem 2, you proved that $\angle 1$ and $\angle 8$, in the diagram at the right, are supplementary. What is a good name for this pair of angles? Explain.

More Practice and Problem-Solving Exercises

B Apply

Algebra Find the values of the variables.

15.

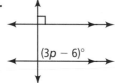

16.

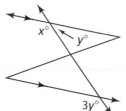

17.

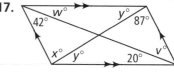

18. Think About a Plan People in ancient Rome played a game called *terni lapilli*. The exact rules of this game are not known. Etchings on floors and walls in Rome suggest that the game required a grid of two intersecting pairs of parallel lines, similar to the modern game tick-tack-toe. The measure of one of the angles formed by the intersecting lines is 90°. Find the measure of each of the other 15 angles. Justify your answers.
- How can you use a diagram to help?
- You know the measure of one angle. How does the position of that angle relate to the position of each of the other angles?
- Which angles formed by two parallel lines and a transversal are congruent? Which angles are supplementary?

19. Error Analysis Which solution for the value of x in the figure at the right is incorrect? Explain.

A.

$2x = x + 75$

$x = 75$

B.

$2x + (x + 75) = 180$

$3x + 75 = 180$

$3x = 105$

$x = 35$

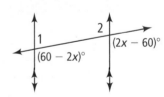

20. Outdoor Recreation Campers often use a "bear bag" at night to avoid attracting animals to their food supply. In the bear bag system at the right, a camper pulls or releases one end of the rope to raise or lower the food bag.

  a. Suppose a camper pulls the rope taut between the two parallel trees, as shown. What is $m\angle 1$?

  b. Are $\angle 1$ and the given angle *alternate interior angles, same-side interior angles,* or *corresponding angles*?

21. Writing Are same-side interior angles ever congruent? Explain.

Proof **22.** Write a two-column proof to prove the Corresponding Angles Theorem (Theorem 7).

  Given: $\ell \parallel m$

  Prove: $\angle 2$ and $\angle 6$ are congruent.

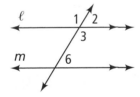

Proof **23.** Write a two-column proof.

  Given: $a \parallel b$, $\angle 1 \cong \angle 4$

  Prove: $\angle 2 \cong \angle 3$

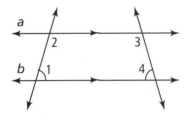

Challenge

Use the diagram at the right for Exercises 24 and 25.

24. Algebra Suppose the measures of $\angle 1$ and $\angle 2$ are in a 4 : 11 ratio. Find their measures. (Diagram is not to scale.)

25. Error Analysis The diagram at the right contains contradictory information. What is it? Why is it contradictory?

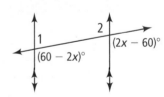

11-3 Proving Lines Parallel

G.CO.9 Prove theorems about lines and angles. Theorems include: . . . when a transversal crosses parallel lines, alternate interior angles are congruent and corresponding angles are congruent . . .

Objective To determine whether two lines are parallel

 Solve It! Write your solution to the Solve It in the space below.

In the Solve It, you used parallel lines to find congruent and supplementary relationships of special angle pairs. In this lesson you will do the converse. You will use the congruent and supplementary relationships of the special angle pairs to prove lines parallel.

Essential Understanding You can use certain angle pairs to decide whether two lines are parallel.

take note

Theorem 9 Converse of the Corresponding Angles Theorem

Theorem	**If . . .**	**Then . . .**
If two lines and a transversal form corresponding angles that are congruent, then the lines are parallel.	$\angle 2 \cong \angle 6$	$\ell \parallel m$

You will prove Theorem 9 in Lesson 13-5.

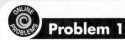 **Problem 1** Identifying Parallel Lines

Think

Which line is the transversal for ∠6 and ∠7?

Got It? Which lines are parallel if ∠6 ≅ ∠7? Justify your answer.

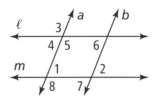

 Practice Which lines or segments are parallel? Justify your answer.

1.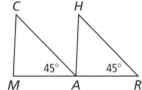

2.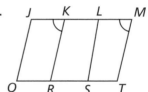

In the last lesson you proved theorems based on the Corresponding Angles Theorem. You can use the Converse of the Corresponding Angles Theorem to prove converses of the theorems and postulate you learned in the last lesson.

take note

Theorem 10 Converse of the Alternate Interior Angles Theorem

Theorem	If . . .	Then . . .
If two lines and a transversal form alternate interior angles that are congruent, then the two lines are parallel.	∠4 ≅ ∠6	ℓ ∥ m

Theorem 11 Converse of the Same-Side Interior Angles Postulate

Theorem	If . . .	Then . . .
If two lines and a transversal form same-side interior angles that are supplementary, then the two lines are parallel.	$m\angle 3 + m\angle 6 = 180$ 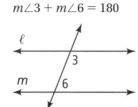	$\ell \parallel m$

Theorem 12 Converse of the Alternate Exterior Angles Theorem

Theorem	If . . .	Then . . .
If two lines and a transversal form alternate exterior angles that are congruent, then the two lines are parallel.	$\angle 1 \cong \angle 7$ 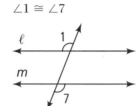	$\ell \parallel m$

The proof of the Converse of the Alternate Interior Angles Theorem below looks different than any proof you have seen so far in this course. You know two forms of proof—paragraph and two-column. In a third form, called **flow proof**, arrows show the logical connections between the statements. Reasons are written below the statements.

Proof Proof of Theorem 10: Converse of the Alternate Interior Angles Theorem

Given: $\angle 4 \cong \angle 6$

Prove: $\ell \parallel m$

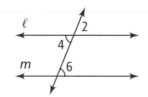

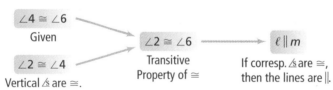

Got It? Use the same diagram used to prove Theorem 12 in Problem 2 to Prove Theorem 11.

Given: $m\angle 3 + m\angle 6 = 180$

Prove: $\ell \parallel m$

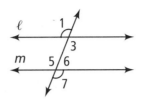

Ⓐ Practice **3. Developing Proof** Complete the flow proof below.

Given: $\angle 1$ and $\angle 3$ are supplementary.

Prove: $a \parallel b$

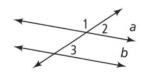

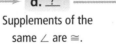

a. _____

b. _____

c. _____

d. _____

e. _____

The four theorems you have just learned provide you with four ways to determine if two lines are parallel.

 Problem 3 Determining Whether Lines are Parallel

Got It? In Problem 3, what is another way to explain why $r \parallel s$? Justify your answer.

Ⓐ **Practice** 4. **Parking** Two workers paint lines for angled parking spaces. One worker paints a line so that $m\angle 1 = 65$. The other worker paints a line so that $m\angle 2 = 65$. Are their lines parallel? Explain.

You can use algebra along with the postulates and theorems from the last lesson and this lesson to help you solve problems involving parallel lines.

 Problem 4 Using Algebra

Got It? What is the value of w for which $c \parallel d$?

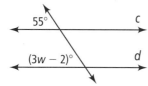

Think

What must be true of the given angles for lines c and d to be parallel?

Algebra Find the value of *x* for which ℓ ∥ *m*.

5.

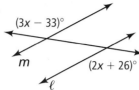

(3x − 33)°

m

(2x + 26)°

ℓ

6.

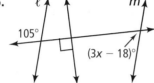

ℓ   *m*

105°

(3x − 18)°

Lesson Check

Do you know HOW?

State the theorem or postulate that proves *a* ∥ *b*.

7.

a

b

8.

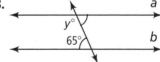

a

y°

65°

b

9. What is the value of y for which $a \parallel b$ in Exercise 8?

Do you UNDERSTAND?

10. Explain how you know when to use the Alternate Interior Angles Theorem and when to use the Converse of the Alternate Interior Angles Theorem.

Ⓒ 11. Compare and Contrast How are flow proofs and two-column proofs alike? How are they different?

Ⓒ 12. Error Analysis A classmate says that $\overleftrightarrow{AB} \parallel \overleftrightarrow{DC}$ based on the diagram at the right. Explain your classmate's error.

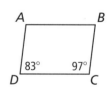

More Practice and Problem-Solving Exercises

B Apply

Ⓖ Developing Proof Use the given information to determine which lines, if any, are parallel. Justify each conclusion with a theorem or postulate.

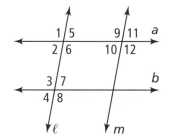

13. $\angle 2$ is supplementary to $\angle 3$.

14. $\angle 1 \cong \angle 3$

15. $\angle 6$ is supplementary to $\angle 7$.

16. $\angle 9 \cong \angle 12$

17. $m\angle 7 = 65$, $m\angle 9 = 115$

18. $\angle 2 \cong \angle 10$

19. $\angle 1 \cong \angle 8$

20. $\angle 8 \cong \angle 6$

21. $\angle 11 \cong \angle 7$

22. $\angle 5 \cong \angle 10$

Algebra Find the value of x for which $\ell \parallel m$.

23.

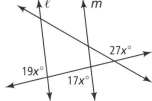

24.

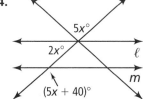

Ⓖ 25. Think About a Plan If the rowing crew at the right strokes in unison, the oars sweep out angles of equal measure. Explain why the oars on each side of the shell stay parallel.

- What type of information do you need to prove lines parallel?
- How do the positions of the angles of equal measure relate?

Algebra Determine the value of x for which $r \parallel s$. Then find $m\angle 1$ and $m\angle 2$.

26. $m\angle 1 = 80 - x$, $m\angle 2 = 90 - 2x$

27. $m\angle 1 = 60 - 2x$, $m\angle 2 = 70 - 4x$

28. $m\angle 1 = 40 - 4x$, $m\angle 2 = 50 - 8x$

29. $m\angle 1 = 20 - 8x$, $m\angle 2 = 30 - 16x$

Use the diagram at the right below for Exercises 30–36.

Ⓒ Open-Ended Use the given information. State another fact about one of the given angles that will guarantee two lines are parallel. Tell which lines will be parallel and why.

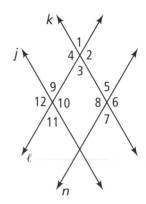

30. $\angle 1 \cong \angle 3$

31. $m\angle 8 = 110,\ m\angle 9 = 70$

32. $\angle 5 \cong \angle 11$

33. $\angle 11$ and $\angle 12$ are supplementary.

Ⓒ 34. Reasoning If $\angle 1 \cong \angle 7$, what theorem or postulate can you use to show that $\ell \parallel n$?

Write a flow proof.

 **35. Given:** $\ell \parallel n,\ \angle 12 \cong \angle 8$

    Prove: $j \parallel k$

Proof 36. Given: $j \parallel k,\ m\angle 8 + m\angle 9 = 180$

    Prove: $\ell \parallel n$

Ⓒ Challenge

Which sides of quadrilateral *PLAN* must be parallel? Explain.

37. $m\angle P = 72,\ m\angle L = 108,\ m\angle A = 72,\ m\angle N = 108$

38. $m\angle P = 59,\ m\angle L = 37,\ m\angle A = 143,\ m\angle N = 121$

39. $m\angle P = 67,\ m\angle L = 120,\ m\angle A = 73,\ m\angle N = 100$

40. $m\angle P = 56,\ m\angle L = 124,\ m\angle A = 124,\ m\angle N = 56$

Proof 41. Write a two-column proof to prove the following: If a transversal intersects two parallel lines, then the bisectors of two corresponding angles are parallel. (*Hint:* Start by drawing and marking a diagram.)

11-4   Parallel and Perpendicular Lines

G.CO.9 Prove theorems about lines and angles. Theorems include: . . . when a transversal crosses parallel lines . . .

Objective   To relate parallel and perpendicular lines

Solve It!   Write your solution to the Solve It in the space below.

In the Solve It, you likely made your conjecture about Oak Street and Court Road based on their relationships to Schoolhouse Road. In this lesson you will use similar reasoning to prove that lines are parallel or perpendicular.

Essential Understanding You can use the relationships of two lines to a third line to decide whether the two lines are parallel or perpendicular to each other.

Theorem 13

Theorem	If . . .	Then . . .
If two lines are parallel to the same line, then they are parallel to each other.	$a \parallel b$ and $b \parallel c$	$a \parallel c$

You will prove Theorem 13 in Exercise 2.

Theorem 14

Theorem	If . . .	Then . . .
In a plane, if two lines are perpendicular to the same line, then they are parallel to each other.	$m \perp t$ and $n \perp t$ 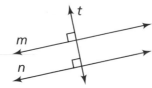	$m \parallel n$

Notice that Theorem 14 includes the phrase *in a plane*. In Exercise 17, you will consider why this phrase is necessary.

Proof **Proof of Theorem 14**

Given: In a plane, $r \perp t$ and $s \perp t$.

Prove: $r \parallel s$

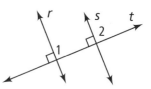

Proof: $\angle 1$ and $\angle 2$ are right angles by the definition of perpendicular. So, $\angle 1 \cong \angle 2$. Since corresponding angles are congruent, $r \parallel s$.

Problem 1   Solving a Problem With Parallel Lines

Got It?   Can you assemble the pieces below to form a picture frame with opposite sides parallel? Explain.

60°	60°
60°	60°

← 30° →

← 30° →

Think

How can a sketch help you visualize how to assemble the pieces?

1. A carpenter is building a trellis for vines to grow on. The completed trellis will have two sets of diagonal pieces of wood that overlap each other.

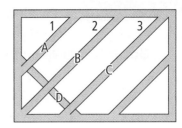

a. If pieces A, B, and C must be parallel, what must be true of ∠1, ∠2, and ∠3?

b. The carpenter attaches piece D so that it is perpendicular to piece A. If he wants to place more pieces parallel to piece D, how can he do so? Justify your answer using theorems from this lesson.

Theorems 13 and 14 give conditions that allow you to conclude that lines are parallel. The Perpendicular Transversal Theorem below provides a way for you to conclude that lines are perpendicular.

take note

Theorem 15 Perpendicular Transversal Theorem

Theorem	**If . . .**	**Then . . .**
In a plane, if a line is perpendicular to one of two parallel lines, then it is also perpendicular to the other.	$n \perp \ell$ and $\ell \parallel m$	$n \perp m$

You will prove Theorem 15 in Exercise 10.

The Perpendicular Transversal Theorem states that the lines must be *in a plane*. The diagram at the right shows why. In the rectangular solid, $\overleftrightarrow{AC}$ and $\overleftrightarrow{BD}$ are parallel. $\overleftrightarrow{EC}$ is perpendicular to $\overleftrightarrow{AC}$, but it is not perpendicular to $\overleftrightarrow{BD}$. In fact, $\overleftrightarrow{EC}$ and $\overleftrightarrow{BD}$ are skew because they are not in the same plane.

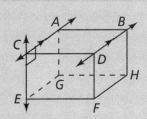

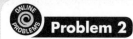 **Problem 2** **Proving a Relationship Between Two Lines**

Got It? In Problem 2, could you also conclude $a \parallel b$? Explain.

Think

How do lines *a* and *b* relate to line *d*?

A Practice 2. **Developing Proof** Copy and complete this paragraph proof of Theorem 13 for three coplanar lines.

Given: $\ell \parallel k$ and $m \parallel k$

Prove: $\ell \parallel m$

Proof: Since $\ell \parallel k$, $\angle 2 \cong \angle 1$ by the

    a. __?__ Theorem. Since $m \parallel k$, **b.** __?__ $\cong$
    c. __?__ for the same reason. By the Transitive Property of Congruence, $\angle 2 \cong \angle 3$. By the
    d. __?__ Theorem, $\ell \parallel m$.

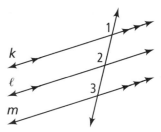

a. _____

b. _____

c. _____

d. _____

Proof 3. Write a paragraph proof.

Given: In a plane, $a \perp b$, $b \perp c$, and $c \parallel d$.

Prove: $a \parallel d$

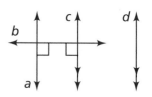

Lesson Check

Do you know HOW?

4. Main Street intersects Avenue A and Avenue B. Avenue A is parallel to Avenue B. Avenue A is also perpendicular to Main Street. How are Avenue B and Main Street related? Explain.

5. In the diagram at the right, lines *a, b,* and *c* are coplanar. What conclusion can you make about lines *a* and *b*? Explain.

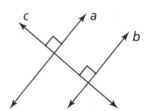

Do you UNDERSTAND?

6. Explain why the phrase *in a plane* is not necessary in Theorem 13.

7. Which theorem or postulate from earlier in the chapter supports the conclusion in Theorem 14? In the Perpendicular Transversal Theorem? Explain.

8. Error Analysis Shiro sketched coplanar lines *m, n,* and *r* on his homework paper. He claims that it shows that lines *m* and *n* are parallel. What other information do you need about line *r* in order for Shiro's claim to be true? Explain.

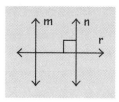

More Practice and Problem-Solving Exercises

B Apply

9. Think About a Plan One traditional type of log cabin is a single rectangular room. Suppose you begin building a log cabin by placing four logs in the shape of a rectangle. What should you measure to guarantee that the logs on opposite walls are parallel? Explain.

- What type of information do you need to prove lines parallel?
- How can you use a diagram to help you?
- What do you know about the angles of the geometric shape?

Proof 10. Prove the Perpendicular Transversal Theorem (Theorem 15): In a plane, if a line is perpendicular to one of two parallel lines, then it is also perpendicular to the other.

Given: In a plane, $a \perp b$ and $b \parallel c$.

Prove: $a \perp c$

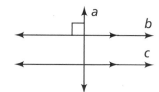

The following statements describe a ladder. Based only on the statement, make a conclusion about the rungs, one side, or both sides of the ladder. Explain.

11. The rungs are each perpendicular to one side.

12. The rungs are parallel and the top rung is perpendicular to one side.

13. The sides are parallel. The rungs are perpendicular to one side.

14. Each side is perpendicular to the top rung.

15. The rungs are perpendicular to one side. The sides are not parallel.

16. Public Transportation The map at the right is a section of a subway map. The light blue line is perpendicular to the red line, the red line is perpendicular to the black line, and the black line is perpendicular to the orange line. What conclusion can you make about the light blue line and the orange line? Explain.

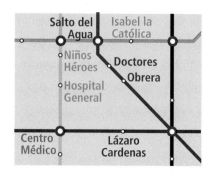

◎ 17. Writing Theorem 14 states that in a plane, two lines perpendicular to the same line are parallel. Explain why the phrase *in a plane* is needed. (*Hint:* Refer to a rectangular solid to help you visualize the situation.)

18. Quilting You plan to sew two triangles of fabric together to make a square for a quilting project. The triangles are both right triangles and have the same side and angle measures. What must also be true about the triangles in order to guarantee that the opposite sides of the fabric square are parallel? Explain.

ⓒ Challenge

For Exercises 19–24, *a, b, c,* and *d* are distinct lines in the same plane. For each combination of relationships, tell how *a* and *d* relate. Justify your answer.

19. $a \parallel b, b \parallel c, c \parallel d$

20. $a \parallel b, b \parallel c, c \perp d$

21. $a \parallel b, b \perp c, c \parallel d$

22. $a \perp b, b \parallel c, c \parallel d$

23. $a \parallel b, b \perp c, c \perp d$

24. $a \perp b, b \parallel c, c \perp d$

◎ 25. Reasoning Review the reflexive, symmetric, and transitive properties for congruence in Lesson 10-6. Write reflexive, symmetric, and transitive statements for "is parallel to" ($\parallel$). Tell whether each statement is *true* or *false*. Justify your answer.

◎ 26. Reasoning Repeat Exercise 25 for "is perpendicular to" ($\perp$).

G.CO.10 Prove theorems about triangles . . . measures of interior angles of a triangle sum to 180°. Also **G.CO.9**

Objectives To use parallel lines to prove a theorem about triangles
To find measures of angles of triangles

Solve It! Write your solution to the Solve It in the space below.

In the Solve It, you may have discovered that you can rearrange the corners of the triangle to form a straight angle. You can do this for any triangle.

Essential Understanding The sum of the angle measures of a triangle is always the same.

The Solve It suggests an important theorem about triangles. To prove this theorem, you will need to use parallel lines.

Postulate 12   Parallel Postulate

Through a point not on a line, there is one and only one line parallel to the given line.

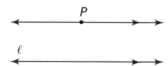

There is exactly one line through P parallel to ℓ.

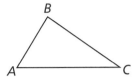

Theorem 16   Triangle Angle-Sum Theorem

The sum of the measures of the angles of a triangle is 180.

$$m\angle A + m\angle B + m\angle C = 180$$

The proof of the Triangle Angle-Sum Theorem requires an *auxiliary line*. An **auxiliary line** is a line that you add to a diagram to help explain relationships in proofs. The red line in the diagram below is an auxiliary line.

Proof Proof of Theorem 16: Triangle Angle-Sum Theorem

Given: $\triangle ABC$

Prove: $m\angle A + m\angle 2 + m\angle C = 180$

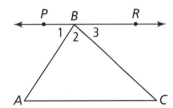

Statements	Reasons
1) Draw $\overleftrightarrow{PR}$ through B, parallel to $\overleftrightarrow{AC}$.	1) Parallel Postulate
2) $\angle PBC$ and $\angle 3$ are supplementary.	2) $\angle\!\!\angle$ that form a linear pair are suppl.
3) $m\angle PBC + m\angle 3 = 180$	3) Definition of suppl. $\angle\!\!\angle$
4) $m\angle PBC = m\angle 1 + m\angle 2$	4) Angle Addition Postulate
5) $m\angle 1 + m\angle 2 + m\angle 3 = 180$	5) Substitution Property
6) $\angle 1 \cong \angle A$ and $\angle 3 \cong \angle C$	6) If lines are $\parallel$, then alternate interior $\angle\!\!\angle$ are $\cong$.
7) $m\angle 1 = m\angle A$ and $m\angle 3 = m\angle C$	7) Congruent $\angle\!\!\angle$ have equal measure.
8) $m\angle A + m\angle 2 + m\angle C = 180$	8) Substitution Property

When you know the measures of two angles of a triangle, you can use the Triangle Angle-Sum Theorem to find the measure of the third angle.

Problem 1   Using the Triangle Angle-Sum Theorem

Plan

Got It?   Use the diagram below. What is the value of *z*?

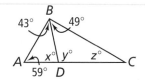

Which triangle will you use to find the value of *z*?

Ⓐ **Practice**   **1.** Find $m\angle 1$.

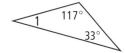

2. Algebra Find the value of each variable.

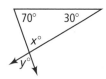

An **exterior angle of a polygon** is an angle formed by a side and an extension of an adjacent side. For each exterior angle of a triangle, the two nonadjacent interior angles are its **remote interior angles**. In each triangle below, ∠1 is an exterior angle and ∠2 and ∠3 are its remote interior angles.

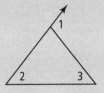 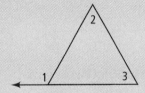 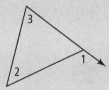

The theorem below states the relationship between an exterior angle and its two remote interior angles.

take note

Theorem 17 Triangle Exterior Angle Theorem

The measure of each exterior angle of a triangle equals the sum of the measures of its two remote interior angles.

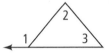

$$m\angle 1 = m\angle 2 + m\angle 3$$

You will prove Theorem 17 in Exercise 26.

You can use the Triangle Exterior Angle Theorem to find angle measures.

Problem 2 Using the Triangle Exterior Angle Theorem

Think

How can you draw a diagram to represent the given information?

Got It? Two angles of a triangle measure 53. What is the measure of an exterior angle at each vertex of the triangle?

Ⓐ Practice **3. a.** Which of the numbered angles are exterior angles?

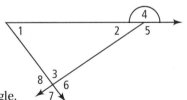

b. Name the remote interior angles for each exterior angle.

c. How are exterior angles 6 and 8 related?

4. Algebra Find the measure of ∠2.

Problem 3   **Applying the Triangle Theorems**

© **Got It?**   **Reasoning** In Problem 3, can you find $m\angle A$ without using the Triangle Exterior Angle Theorem? Explain.

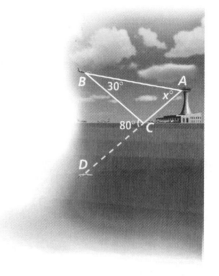

A Practice   **5.** A ramp forms the angles shown at the right. What are the values of a and b?

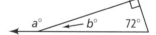

6. A lounge chair has different settings that change the angles formed by its parts. Suppose $m\angle 2 = 71$ and $m\angle 3 = 43$. Find $m\angle 1$.

Lesson Check

Do you know HOW?

Find the measure of the third angle of a triangle given the measures of two angles.

7. 34 and 88

8. 45 and 90

9. 10 and 102

10. x and 50

In a triangle, $\angle 1$ is an exterior angle and $\angle 2$ and $\angle 3$ are its remote interior angles. Find the missing angle measure.

11. $m\angle 2 = 24$ and $m\angle 3 = 106$

12. $m\angle 1 = 70$ and $m\angle 2 = 32$

Do you UNDERSTAND?

13. Explain how the Triangle Exterior Angle Theorem makes sense based on the Triangle Angle-Sum Theorem.

14. Error Analysis The measures of the interior angles of a triangle are 30, x, and $3x$. Which of the following methods for solving for x is incorrect? Explain.

A.
$$x + 3x = 30$$
$$4x = 30$$
$$x = 7.5$$

B.
$$x + 3x + 30 = 180$$
$$4x + 30 = 180$$
$$4x = 150$$
$$x = 37.5$$

More Practice and Problem-Solving Exercises

MATHEMATICAL
PRACTICES

 Apply

Algebra Use the given information to find the unknown angle measures in the triangle.

15. The ratio of the angle measures of the acute angles in a right triangle is 1 : 2.

16. The measure of one angle of a triangle is 40. The measures of the other two angles are in a ratio of 3 : 4.

17. The measure of one angle of a triangle is 108. The measures of the other two angles are in a ratio of 1 : 5.

18. Think About a Plan The angle measures of $\triangle RST$ are represented by $2x$, $x + 14$, and $x - 38$. What are the angle measures of $\triangle RST$?
- How can you use the Triangle Angle-Sum Theorem to write an equation?
- How can you check your answer?

Proof 19. Prove the following theorem: The acute angles of a right triangle are complementary.

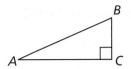

Given: $\triangle ABC$ with right angle C

Prove: $\angle A$ and $\angle B$ are complementary.

20. Reasoning What is the measure of each angle of an equiangular triangle? Explain.

21. Draw a Diagram Which diagram below correctly represents the following description? Explain your reasoning.

Draw any triangle. Label it $\triangle ABC$. Extend two sides of the triangle to form two exterior angles at vertex A.

I.
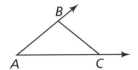

II.
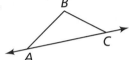

III.
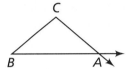

Find the values of the variables and the measures of the angles.

22.
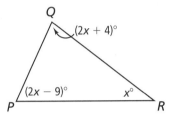

23.
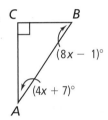

24.
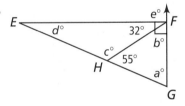

25.
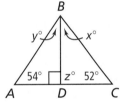

Proof 26. Prove the Triangle Exterior Angle Theorem (Theorem 17). The measure of each exterior angle of a triangle equals the sum of the measures of its two remote interior angles.

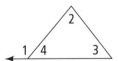

Given: $\angle 1$ is an exterior angle of the triangle.

Prove: $m\angle 1 = m\angle 2 + m\angle 3$

27. Reasoning Two angles of a triangle measure 64 and 48. What is the measure of the largest exterior angle of the triangle? Explain.

28. Algebra A right triangle has exterior angles at each of its acute angles with measures in the ratio 13 : 14. Find the measures of the two acute angles of the right triangle.

Probability In Exercises 29–33, you know only the given information about the measures of the angles of a triangle. Find the probability that the triangle is equiangular.

29. Each is a multiple of 30.

30. Each is a multiple of 20.

31. Each is a multiple of 60.

32. Each is a multiple of 12.

33. One angle is obtuse.

34. In the figure at the right, $\overline{CD} \perp \overline{AB}$ and $\overline{CD}$ bisects $\angle ACB$. Find $m\angle DBF$.

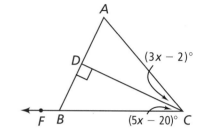

35. If the remote interior angles of an exterior angle of a triangle are congruent, what can you conclude about the bisector of the exterior angle? Justify your answer.

11-6 Constructing Parallel and Perpendicular Lines

G.CO.12 Make formal geometric constructions with a variety of tools and methods . . . constructing perpendicular lines . . . and constructing a line parallel to a given line through a point not on the line. Also **G.CO.13**

Objective To construct parallel and perpendicular lines

 Solve It! Write your solution to the Solve It in the space below.

In the Solve It, you used paper-folding to construct lines.

Essential Understanding You can also use a straightedge and a compass to construct parallel and perpendicular lines.

In Lesson 11-5, you learned that through a point not on a line, there is a unique line parallel to the given line. Problem 1 shows the construction of this line.

Problem 1 Constructing Parallel Lines

Got It? **Reasoning** In Problem 1, why must lines ℓ and m be parallel?

Practice Construct the line through point *J* that is parallel to $\overleftrightarrow{AB}$.

1.

• *J*

A ——————————— B

2.

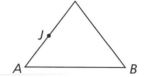

 **Problem 2** **Constructing a Special Quadrilateral**

Got It? **a.** Draw a segment. Label its length *m*. Construct quadrilateral *ABCD* with $\overleftrightarrow{AB} \parallel \overleftrightarrow{CD}$, so that $AB = m$ and $CD = 2m$.

b. Reasoning Suppose you and a friend both use the steps in Problem 2 to construct *ABYZ* independently. Will your quadrilaterals necessarily have the same angle measures and side lengths? Explain.

> **Think**
> How can you test whether your answer to part (b) is correct?

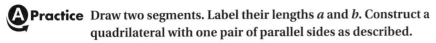

A Practice Draw two segments. Label their lengths *a* and *b*. Construct a quadrilateral with one pair of parallel sides as described.

3. The sides have length 2*a* and *b*.

4. The sides have length *a* and $\frac{1}{2}b$.

Problem 3 **Perpendicular at a Point on a Line**

Got It? Use a straightedge to draw $\overleftrightarrow{EF}$. Construct $\overleftrightarrow{FG}$ so that $\overleftrightarrow{FG} \perp \overleftrightarrow{EF}$ at point *F*.

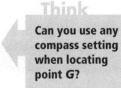

Think

Can you use any compass setting when locating point *G*?

Practice Construct the line that is perpendicular to ℓ at point *P*.

5.

6.

You can also construct a perpendicular line from a point to a line. This perpendicular line is unique according to the Perpendicular Postulate. You will prove in Chapter 13 that the shortest path from any point to a line is along this unique perpendicular line.

take note

Postulate 13   Perpendicular Postulate

Through a point not on a line, there is one and only one line perpendicular to the given line.

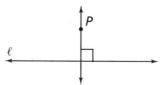

There is exactly one line through *P* perpendicular to ℓ.

Problem 4 **Perpendicular From a Point to a Line**

Got It? Draw $\overleftrightarrow{CX}$ and a point Z not on $\overleftrightarrow{CX}$. Construct $\overleftrightarrow{ZB}$ so that $\overleftrightarrow{ZB} \perp \overleftrightarrow{CX}$.

A Practice Construct the line through point P that is perpendicular to $\overleftrightarrow{RS}$.

7.

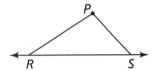

8.

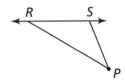

Lesson Check

Do you know HOW?

9. Draw a line ℓ and a point P not on the line. Construct the line through P parallel to line ℓ.

10. Draw $\overleftrightarrow{QR}$ and a point S on the line. Construct the line perpendicular to $\overleftrightarrow{QR}$ at point S.

11. Draw a line w and a point X not on the line. Construct the line perpendicular to line w at point X.

Do you UNDERSTAND?

12. In Problem 3, is $\overline{AC}$ congruent to $\overline{BC}$? Explain.

13. Suppose you use a wider compass setting in Step 1 of Problem 4. Will you construct a different perpendicular line? Explain.

14. Compare and Contrast How are the constructions in Problems 3 and 4 similar? How are they different?

More Practice and Problem-Solving Exercises

B Apply

15. Think About a Plan Draw an acute angle. Construct an angle congruent to your angle so that the two angles are alternate interior angles.
  • What does a sketch of the angle look like?
  • Which construction(s) should you use?

16. Constructions Construct a square with side length p.

17. Writing Explain how to use the Converse of the Alternate Interior Angles Theorem to construct a line parallel to the given line through a point not on the line. (*Hint:* See Exercise 15.)

For Exercises 18–24, use the segments at the right.

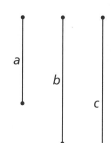

18. Draw a line m. Construct a segment of length b that is perpendicular to line m.

19. Construct a rectangle with base b and height c.

20. Construct a square with sides of length a.

21. Construct a rectangle with one side of length a and a diagonal of length b.

Ⓒ **22. a.** Construct a quadrilateral with a pair of parallel sides of length c.
    b. Make a Conjecture What appears to be true about the other pair of sides in the quadrilateral you constructed?
    c. Use a protractor, a ruler, or both to check the conjecture you made in part (b).

23. Construct a right triangle with legs of lengths a and b.

Ⓒ **24. a.** Construct a triangle with sides of lengths a, b, and c.
    b. Construct the midpoint of each side of the triangle.
    c. Form a new triangle by connecting the midpoints.
    d. Make a Conjecture How do the sides of the smaller triangle and the sides of the larger triangle appear to be related?
    e. Use a protractor, ruler, or both to check the conjecture you made in part (d).

25. Constructions The diagrams below show steps for a parallel line construction.

    I. 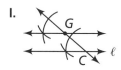   **II.**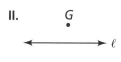

    III. 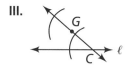   **IV.**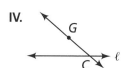

    a. List the construction steps in the correct order.
    b. For the steps that use a compass, describe the location(s) of the compass point.

Ⓒ Challenge

Draw $\overline{DG}$. Construct a quadrilateral with diagonals that are congruent to $\overline{DG}$, bisect each other, and meet the given conditions. Describe the figure.

26. The diagonals are not perpendicular.   **27.** The diagonals are perpendicular.

Construct a rectangle with side lengths a and b that meets the given condition.

28. $b = 2a$ **29.** $b = \frac{1}{2}a$ **30.** $b = \frac{1}{3}a$ **31.** $b = \frac{2}{3}a$

Construct a triangle with side lengths a, b, and c that meets the given conditions. If such a triangle is not possible, explain.

32. $a = b = c$ **33.** $a = b = 2c$ **34.** $a = 2b = 2c$ **35.** $a = b + c$

11-1 Lines and Angles

Quick Review

A **transversal** is a line that intersects two or more coplanar lines at distinct points.

∠1 and ∠3 are **corresponding angles.**

∠2 and ∠6 are **alternate interior angles.**

∠2 and ∠3 are **same-side interior angles.**

∠4 and ∠8 are **alternate exterior angles.**

Example

Name two other pairs of corresponding angles in the diagram above.

∠5 and ∠7

∠2 and ∠4

Exercises

Identify all numbered angle pairs that form the given type of angle pair. Then name the two lines and transversal that form each pair.

1. alternate interior angles

2. same-side interior angles

3. corresponding angles

4. alternate exterior angles

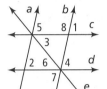

Classify the angle pair formed by ∠1 and ∠2.

5. 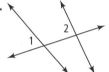   **6.**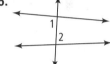

11-2 Properties of Parallel Lines

Quick Review

If two parallel lines are cut by a transversal, then

- corresponding angles, alternate interior angles, and alternate exterior angles are congruent
- same-side interior angles are supplementary

Example

Which other angles measure 110?

∠6 (corresponding angles)

∠3 (alternate interior angles)

∠8 (vertical angles)

Exercises

Find *m*∠1 and *m*∠2. Justify your answers.

7. 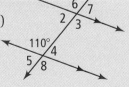   **8.**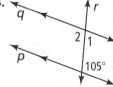

9. Find the values of *x* and *y* in the diagram below.

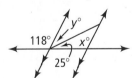

11-3 Proving Lines Parallel

Quick Review

If two lines and a transversal form

- congruent corresponding angles,
- congruent alternate interior angles,
- congruent alternate exterior angles, or
- supplementary same-side interior angles,

then the two lines are parallel.

Example

What is the value of x for which $\ell \parallel m$?

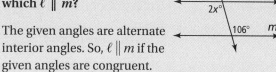

The given angles are alternate interior angles. So, $\ell \parallel m$ if the given angles are congruent.

$2x = 106$ Congruent $\angle$ have equal measures.

$x = 53$ Divide each side by 2.

Exercises

Find the value of x for which $\ell \parallel m$.

10.

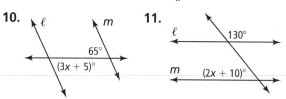

65°
$(3x + 5)°$

11.

130°
$(2x + 10)°$

Use the given information to decide which lines, if any, are parallel. Justify your conclusion.

12. $\angle 1 \cong \angle 9$

13. $m\angle 3 + m\angle 6 = 180$

14. $m\angle 2 + m\angle 3 = 180$

15. $\angle 5 \cong \angle 11$

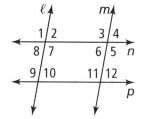

11-4 Parallel and Perpendicular Lines

Quick Review

- Two lines $\parallel$ to the same line are $\parallel$ to each other.
- In a plane, two lines $\perp$ to the same line are $\parallel$.
- In a plane, if one line is $\perp$ to one of two $\parallel$ lines, then it is $\perp$ to both $\parallel$ lines.

Example

What are the pairs of parallel and perpendicular lines in the diagram?

$\ell \parallel n$, $\ell \parallel m$, and $m \parallel n$.

$a \perp \ell$, $a \perp m$, and $a \perp n$.

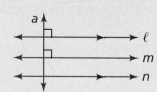

Exercises

Use the diagram at the right to complete each statement.

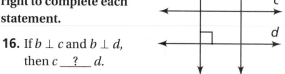

16. If $b \perp c$ and $b \perp d$, then c __?__ d.

17. If $c \parallel d$, then __?__ $\perp c$.

18. Maps Morris Avenue intersects both 1st Street and 3rd Street at right angles. 3rd Street is parallel to 5th Street. How are 1st Street and 5th Street related? Explain.

11-5 Parallel Lines and Triangles

Quick Review

The sum of the measures of the angles of a triangle is 180.

The measure of each **exterior angle** of a triangle equals the sum of the measures of its two **remote interior angles**.

Example

What are the values of *x* and *y*?

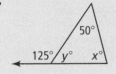

$x + 50 = 125$	Exterior Angle Theorem
$x = 75$	Simplify.
$x + y + 50 = 180$	Triangle Angle-Sum Theorem
$75 + y + 50 = 180$	Substitute 75 for *x*.
$y = 55$	Simplify.

Exercises

Find the values of the variables.

19.
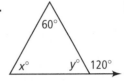

20.
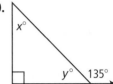

The measures of the three angles of a triangle are given. Find the value of *x*.

21. $x, 2x, 3x$

22. $x + 10, x - 20, x + 25$

23. $20x + 10, 30x - 2, 7x + 1$

11-6 Constructing Parallel and Perpendicular Lines

Quick Review

You can use a compass and a straightedge to construct

- a line parallel to a given line through a point not on the line
- a line perpendicular to a given line through a point on the line, or through a point not on the line

Example

Which step of the parallel lines construction guarantees the lines are parallel?

The parallel lines construction involves constructing a pair of congruent angles. Since the congruent angles are corresponding angles, the lines are parallel.

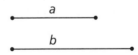

Exercises

24. Draw a line *m* and point *Q* not on *m*. Construct a line perpendicular to *m* through *Q*.

Use the segments below.

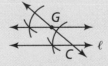

25. Construct a rectangle with side lengths *a* and *b*.

26. Construct a rectangle with side lengths *a* and 2*b*.

27. Construct a quadrilateral with one pair of parallel opposite sides, each side of length 2*a*.

Pull It All Together

Planning the Paths for a Park

Kiana works for a city's planning department. The city is developing a new park, and Kiana is reviewing the plans for the builders. The park is rectangular with two sets of parallel walkways that go through the park, as shown in the blueprint below.

Kiana notices that only a few angle measures are provided in the blueprint. She would like to add additional angle measures to make it easier for the builders to create the correct paths.

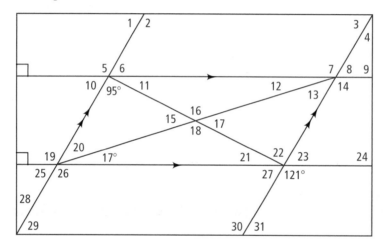

Task Description

Determine the measure of each numbered angle in the blueprint.

- Which postulates theorems can you use to help you find the angle measures?
- Which angles in the blueprint must be congruent to the 121° angle?

Get Ready!

The Distance Formula
Find the side lengths of △ABC.

1. $A(3, 1), B(-1, 1), C(-1, -2)$

2. $A(-3, 2), B(-3, -6), C(8, 6)$

3. $A(-1, -2), B(6, 1), C(2, 5)$

Proving Angles Congruent
Draw a conclusion based on the information given.

4. $\angle J$ is supplementary to $\angle K$;
$\angle L$ is supplementary to $\angle K$.

5. $\angle M$ is supplementary to $\angle N$;
$\angle M \cong \angle N$.

6. $\angle 1$ is complementary to $\angle 2$.

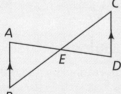

7. $\overrightarrow{FA} \perp \overrightarrow{FC}, \overrightarrow{FB} \perp \overrightarrow{FD}$

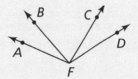

Parallel Lines and the Triangle Angle-Sum Theorem
What can you conclude about the angles in each diagram?

8.

9.

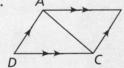

10.

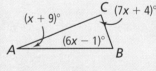

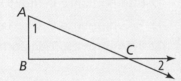

Looking Ahead Vocabulary

11. The foundation of a building is the *base* of the building. How would you describe the *base of an isosceles triangle* in geometry?

12. The *legs* of a table support the tabletop and are equal in length. How might they be similar to the *legs of an isosceles triangle*?

13. A postal worker delivers each piece of mail to the mailbox that *corresponds* to the address on the envelope. What might the term *corresponding parts* of geometric figures mean?

CHAPTER 12

Congruent Triangles

Big Ideas

1 Visualization

Essential Question: How do you identify corresponding parts of congruent triangles?

2 Reasoning and Proof

Essential Question: How do you show that two triangles are congruent?

3 Reasoning and Proof

Essential Question: How can you tell whether a triangle is isosceles or equilateral?

Ⓒ Domains

- Congruence
- Mathematical Practice: Construct viable arguments
- Modeling with Geometry

Log in to **pearsonsuccessnet.com** and click on Interactive Digital Path to access the Solve Its and animated Problems.

Chapter Preview

  ## Vocabulary

English/Spanish Vocabulary Audio Online:

English	Spanish
base angles of an isosceles triangle, *p. 744*	ángulos de base de un triángulo isósceles
base of an isosceles triangle, *p. 744*	base de un triángulo isósceles
congruence transformation, *p. 774*	transformación de congruencia
congruent polygons, *p. 709*	polígonos congruentes
corollary, *p. 747*	corolario
hypotenuse, *p. 753*	hipotenusa
legs of an isosceles triangle, *p. 744*	catetos de un triángulo isósceles
legs of a right triangle, *p. 753*	catetos de un triángulo rectángulo
vertex angle of an isosceles triangle, *p. 744*	ángulo en vértice de un triángulo isósceles

12-1 Congruent Figures

Prepares for **G.CO.7** . . . Show that two triangles are congruent if and only if corresponding pairs of sides and corresponding pairs of angles are congruent. Also prepares for **G.SRT.5**

Objective To recognize congruent figures and their corresponding parts

Solve It! Write your solution to the Solve It in the space below.

Congruent figures have the same size and shape. When two figures are congruent, you can slide, flip, or turn one so that it fits exactly on the other one, as shown below. In this lesson, you will learn how to determine if geometric figures are congruent.

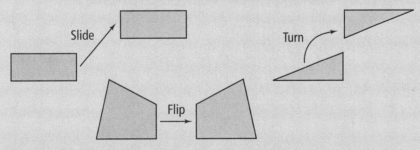

Essential Understanding You can determine whether two figures are congruent by comparing their corresponding parts.

take note

Key Concept Congruent Figures

Definition

Congruent polygons have congruent corresponding parts—their matching sides and angles. When you name congruent polygons, you must list corresponding vertices in the same order.

Example

A B F E
D C G H

$ABCD \cong EFGH$

$\overline{AB} \cong \overline{EF}$ $\overline{BC} \cong \overline{FG}$
$\overline{CD} \cong \overline{GH}$ $\overline{DA} \cong \overline{HE}$

$\angle A \cong \angle E$ $\angle B \cong \angle F$
$\angle C \cong \angle G$ $\angle D \cong \angle H$

Problem 1 Finding Congruent Parts

Got It?   If $\triangle WYS \cong \triangle MKV$, what are the congruent corresponding parts?

Practice   1. **Construction** Builders use the king post truss for the top of a simple structure. In this truss, $\triangle ABC \cong \triangle ABD$. List the congruent corresponding parts.

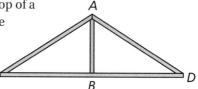

2. The attic frame truss provides open space in the center for storage. In this truss, $\triangle EFG \cong \triangle HIJ$. List the congruent corresponding parts.

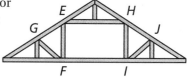

Problem 2 Using Congruent Parts

Got It?   Suppose that $\triangle WYS \cong \triangle MKV$. If $m\angle W = 62$ and $m\angle Y = 35$, what is $m\angle V$? Explain.

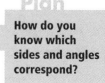

Plan

How do you know which sides and angles correspond?

A Practice At an archaeological site, the remains of two ancient step pyramids are congruent. If $ABCD \cong EFGH$, find each of the following. (Diagrams are not to scale.)

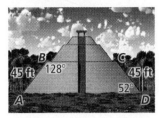 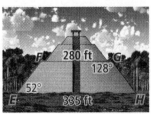

3. AD **4.** $m\angle DCB$

ONLINE PROBLEMS **Problem 3** **Finding Congruent Triangles**

Got It? Is $\triangle ABD \cong \triangle CBD$? Justify your answer.

A Practice For Exercises 5 and 6, can you conclude that the triangles are congruent? Justify your answers.

5. $\triangle TRK$ and $\triangle TUK$

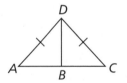 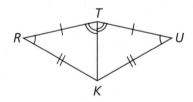

6. $\triangle SPQ$ and $\triangle TUV$

Recall the Triangle Angle-Sum Theorem: The sum of the measures of the angles in a triangle is 180. The next theorem follows from the Triangle Angle-Sum Theorem.

take note

Theorem 18   Third Angles Theorem

Theorem	**If . . .**	**Then . . .**
If two angles of one triangle are congruent to two angles of another triangle, then the third angles are congruent.	$\angle A \cong \angle D$ and $\angle B \cong \angle E$	$\angle C \cong \angle F$

Proof **Proof of Theorem 18: Third Angles Theorem**

Given: $\angle A \cong \angle D, \angle B \cong \angle E$
Prove: $\angle C \cong \angle F$

Statements	**Reasons**
1) $\angle A \cong \angle D, \angle B \cong \angle E$	**1)** Given
2) $m\angle A = m\angle D, m\angle B = m\angle E$	**2)** Def. of $\cong$ $\angle$s
3) $m\angle A + m\angle B + m\angle C = 180,$ $m\angle D + m\angle E + m\angle F = 180$	**3)** $\triangle$ Angle-Sum Thm.
4) $m\angle A + m\angle B + m\angle C = m\angle D + m\angle E + m\angle F$	**4)** Subst. Prop.
5) $m\angle D + m\angle E + m\angle C = m\angle D + m\angle E + m\angle F$	**5)** Subst. Prop.
6) $m\angle C = m\angle F$	**6)** Subtraction Prop. of $=$
7) $\angle C \cong \angle F$	**7)** Def. of $\cong$ $\angle$s

Problem 4 **Proving Triangles Congruent**

Got It? **Given:** $\angle A \cong \angle D, \overline{AE} \cong \overline{DC},$
$\overline{EB} \cong \overline{CB}, \overline{BA} \cong \overline{BD}$

Prove: $\triangle AEB \cong \triangle DCB$

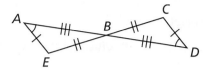

Plan

What else do you need to prove that the triangles are congruent?

Ⓐ Practice **7. Given:** $\overline{AB} \parallel \overline{DC}, \angle B \cong \angle D,$
Proof $\overline{AB} \cong \overline{DC}, \overline{BC} \cong \overline{AD}$

Prove: $\triangle ABC \cong \triangle CDA$

Lesson Check

Do you know HOW?

Complete the following statements.

8. Given: $\triangle QXR \cong \triangle NYC$

   a. $\overline{QX} \cong$ _____

   b. $\angle Y \cong$ _____

9. Given: $\triangle BAT \cong \triangle FOR$

   a. $\overline{TA} \cong$ _____

   b. $\angle R \cong$ _____

10. Given: $BAND \cong LUCK$

   a. $\angle U \cong$ _____

   b. $\overline{DB} \cong$ _____

   c. $NDBA \cong$ _____

11. In $\triangle MAP$ and $\triangle TIE$, $\angle A \cong \angle I$ and $\angle P \cong \angle E$.

   a. What is the relationship between $\angle M$ and $\angle T$?

   b. If $m\angle A = 52$ and $m\angle P = 36$, what is $m\angle T$?

Do you UNDERSTAND?

12. Open-Ended When do you think you might need to know that things are congruent in your everyday life?

13. If each angle in one triangle is congruent to its corresponding angle in another triangle, are the two triangles congruent? Explain.

©14. Error Analysis Walter sketched the diagram at the right. He claims it shows that the two polygons are congruent. What information is missing to support his claim?

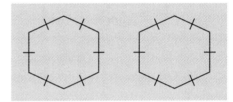

More Practice and Problem-Solving Exercises

Ⓑ Apply

15. If $\triangle DEF \cong \triangle LMN$, which of the following must be a correct congruence statement?

  Ⓐ $\overline{DE} \cong \overline{LN}$ Ⓒ $\angle N \cong \angle F$

  Ⓑ $\overline{FE} \cong \overline{NL}$ Ⓓ $\angle M \cong \angle F$

©16. Reasoning Randall says he can use the information in the figure to prove $\triangle BCD \cong \triangle DAB$. Is he correct? Explain.

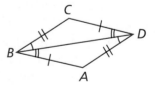

Algebra $\triangle ABC \cong \triangle DEF$. **Find the measures of the given angles or the lengths of the given sides.**

17. $m\angle A = x + 10$, $m\angle D = 2x$ **18.** $m\angle B = 3y$, $m\angle E = 6y - 12$

19. $BC = 3z + 2$, $EF = z + 6$ **20.** $AC = 7a + 5$, $DF = 5a + 9$

21. Think About a Plan $\triangle ABC \cong \triangle DBE$. Find the value of x.

- What does it mean for two triangles to be congruent?
- Which angle measures do you already know?
- How can you find the missing angle measure in a triangle?

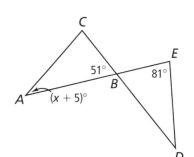

Algebra Find the values of the variables.

22.

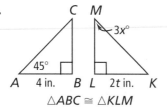

$\triangle ABC \cong \triangle KLM$

23.

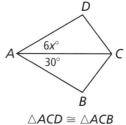

$\triangle ACD \cong \triangle ACB$

24. Complete in two different ways: $\triangle JLM \cong$ __?__ .

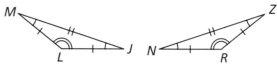

25. Open-Ended Write a congruence statement for two triangles. List the congruent sides and angles.

Proof **26. Given:** $\overline{AB} \perp \overline{AD}, \overline{BC} \perp \overline{CD}, \overline{AB} \cong \overline{CD}$
$\overline{AD} \cong \overline{CB}, \overline{AB} \parallel \overline{CD}$
Prove: $\triangle ABD \cong \triangle CDB$

Proof **27. Given:** $\overline{PR} \parallel \overline{TQ}, \overline{PR} \cong \overline{TQ}, \overline{PS} \cong \overline{QS}, \overline{PQ}$ bisects $\overline{RT}$
Prove: $\triangle PRS \cong \triangle QTS$

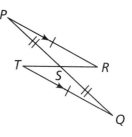

28. Writing The 225 cards in Tracy's sports card collection are rectangles of three different sizes. How could Tracy quickly sort the cards?

Challenge

Coordinate Geometry The vertices of $\triangle GHJ$ are $G(-2, -1)$, $H(-2, 3)$, and $J(1, 3)$.

29. $\triangle KLM \cong \triangle GHJ$. Find KL, LM, and KM.

30. If L and M have coordinates $L(3, -3)$ and $M(6, -3)$, how many pairs of coordinates are possible for K? Find one such pair.

31. **a.** A polygon is called *convex* if it has no diagonals with points outside the polygon. A polygon is called *concave* if it has at least one diagonal with points outside the polygon. How many quadrilaterals (convex and concave) with different shapes or sizes can you make on a three-by-three geoboard? Sketch them. One is shown at the right.
    b. How many quadrilaterals of each type are there?

12-2 Triangle Congruence by SSS and SAS

G.SRT.5 Use congruence . . . criteria for triangles to solve problems and to prove relationships in geometric figures. Also prepares for **G.CO.8**

Objective   To prove two triangles congruent using the SSS and SAS Postulates

 Solve It!   Write your solution to the Solve It in the space below.

In the Solve It, you looked for relationships between corresponding sides and angles. In Lesson 12-1, you learned that if two triangles have three pairs of congruent corresponding angles and three pairs of congruent corresponding sides, then the triangles are congruent.

If you know . . .

$\angle F \cong \angle J$	$\overline{FG} \cong \overline{JK}$
$\angle G \cong \angle K$	$\overline{GH} \cong \overline{KL}$
$\angle H \cong \angle L$	$\overline{FH} \cong \overline{JL}$

. . . then you know $\triangle FGH \cong \triangle JKL$.

However, this is more information about the corresponding parts than you need to prove triangles congruent.

Essential Understanding   You can prove that two triangles are congruent without having to show that *all* corresponding parts are congruent. In this lesson, you will prove triangles congruent by using (1) three pairs of corresponding sides and (2) two pairs of corresponding sides and one pair of corresponding angles.

Postulate 14 Side-Side-Side (SSS) Postulate

Postulate	If . . .	Then . . .
If the three sides of one triangle are congruent to the three sides of another triangle, then the two triangles are congruent.	$\overline{AB} \cong \overline{DE}, \overline{BC} \cong \overline{EF}, \overline{AC} \cong \overline{DF}$ 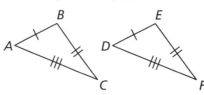	$\triangle ABC \cong \triangle DEF$

A postulate is an accepted statement of fact. The Side-Side-Side Postulate is perhaps the most logical fact about triangles. It agrees with the notion that triangles are rigid figures; their shape does not change until pressure on their sides forces them to break. This rigidity property is important to architects and engineers when they build things such as bicycle frames and steel bridges.

Problem 1 Using SSS

Got It? **Given:** $\overline{BC} \cong \overline{BF}, \overline{CD} \cong \overline{FD}$

Prove: $\triangle BCD \cong \triangle BFD$

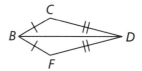

Plan

What else do you need to prove that the triangles are congruent?

Practice **1. Developing Proof** Complete the flow proof.

Given: $\overline{JK} \cong \overline{LM}, \overline{JM} \cong \overline{LK}$

Prove: $\triangle JKM \cong \triangle LMK$

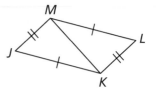

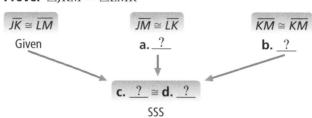

a. _____

b. _____

c. _____

d. _____

Proof **2. Given:** $\overline{IE} \cong \overline{GH}$, $\overline{EF} \cong \overline{HF}$,
F is the midpoint of $\overline{GI}$

Prove: $\triangle EFI \cong \triangle HFG$

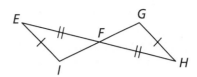

You can also show relationships between a pair of corresponding sides and an *included* angle.

The word *included* refers to the angles and the sides of a triangle, as shown at the right.

$\angle A$ is included between $\overline{BA}$ and $\overline{AC}$.

$\overline{BC}$ is included between $\angle B$ and $\angle C$.

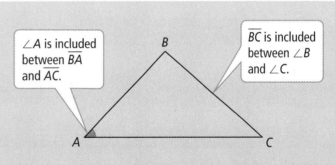

take note

Postulate 15   Side-Angle-Side (SAS) Postulate

Postulate	If . . .	Then . . .
If two sides and the included angle of one triangle are congruent to two sides and the included angle of another triangle, then the two triangles are congruent.	$\overline{AB} \cong \overline{DE}$, $\angle A \cong \angle D$, $\overline{AC} \cong \overline{DF}$	$\triangle ABC \cong \triangle DEF$

You likely have used the properties of the Side-Angle-Side Postulate before. For example, SAS can help you determine whether a box will fit through a doorway.

Suppose you keep your arms at a fixed angle as you move from the box to the doorway. The triangle you form with the box is congruent to the triangle you form with the doorway. The two triangles are congruent because two sides and the included angle of one triangle are congruent to the two sides and the included angle of the other triangle.

Problem 2 Using SAS

Got It? What other information do you need to prove △*LEB* ≅ △*BNL* by SAS?

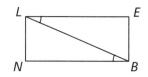

Practice What other information, if any, do you need to prove the two triangles congruent by SAS? Explain.

3.

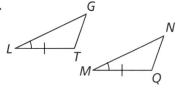

4.

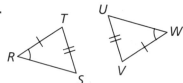

Recall that, in Lesson 10-1, you learned to construct segments using a compass open to a fixed angle. Now you can show that it works. Similar to the situation with the box and the doorway, the Side-Angle-Side Postulate tells you that the triangles outlined at the right are congruent. So, $\overline{AB} \cong \overline{CD}$.

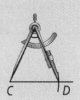

 **Problem 3** **Identifying Congruent Triangles**

Got It? Would you use SSS or SAS to prove the triangles below congruent? Explain.

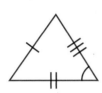

~~Plan~~

What should you look for first, congruent sides or congruent angles?

Ⓐ Practice Would you use SSS or SAS to prove the triangles congruent? If there is not enough information to prove the triangles congruent by SSS or SAS, write *not enough information*. Explain your answer.

5.
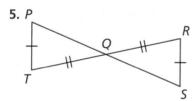

6.
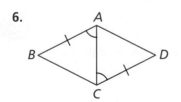

Lesson Check

Do you know HOW?

7. In △*PEN*, name the angle that is included between the given sides.

    a. $\overline{PE}$ and $\overline{EN}$ **b.** $\overline{NP}$ and $\overline{PE}$

8. In △*HAT*, between which sides is the given angle included?

    a. ∠*H*   **b.** ∠*T*

Name the postulate you would use to prove the triangles congruent.

  9.   **10.**

Do you UNDERSTAND?

11. Compare and Contrast How are the SSS Postulate and the SAS Postulate alike? How are they different?

12. Error Analysis Your friend thinks that the triangles shown at the right are congruent by SAS. Is your friend correct? Explain.

13. Reasoning A carpenter trims a triangular peak of a house with three 7-ft pieces of molding. The carpenter uses 21 ft of molding to trim a second triangular peak. Are the two triangles formed congruent? Explain.

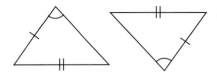

More Practice and Problem-Solving Exercises

B Apply

14. Think About a Plan You and a friend are cutting triangles out of felt for an art project. You want all the triangles to be congruent. Your friend tells you that each triangle should have two 5-in. sides and a 40° angle. If you follow this rule, will all your felt triangles be congruent? Explain.
- How can you use diagrams to help you?
- Which postulate, SSS or SAS, are you likely to apply to the given situation?

Proof **15. Given:** $\overline{BC} \cong \overline{DA}$, $\angle CBD \cong \angle ADB$

Prove: $\triangle BCD \cong \triangle DAB$

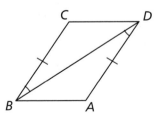

Proof **16. Given:** X is the midpoint of $\overline{AG}$ and $\overline{NR}$.

Prove: $\triangle ANX \cong \triangle GRX$

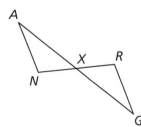

Use the Distance Formula to determine whether $\triangle ABC$ and $\triangle DEF$ are congruent. Justify your answer.

17. $A(1, 4)$, $B(5, 5)$, $C(2, 2)$;
$D(-5, 1)$, $E(-1, 0)$, $F(-4, 3)$

18. $A(3, 8)$, $B(8, 12)$, $C(10, 5)$;
$D(3, -1)$, $E(7, -7)$, $F(12, -2)$

19. $A(2, 9)$, $B(2, 4)$, $C(5, 4)$;
$D(1, -3)$, $E(1, 2)$, $F(-2, 2)$

© 20. Writing List three real-life uses of congruent triangles. For each real-life use, describe why you think congruence is necessary.

21. Sierpinski's Triangle Sierpinski's triangle is a famous geometric pattern. To draw Sierpinski's triangle, start with a single triangle and connect the midpoints of the sides to draw a smaller triangle. If you repeat this pattern over and over, you will form a figure like the one shown. This particular figure started with an isosceles triangle. Are the triangles outlined in red congruent? Explain.

22. Constructions Use a straightedge to draw any triangle JKL. Then construct $\triangle MNP \cong \triangle JKL$ using the given postulate.
 a. SSS
 b. SAS

Can you prove the triangles congruent? If so, write the congruence statement and name the postulate you would use. If not, write *not enough information* and tell what other information you would need.

23.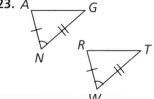

24.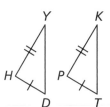

25.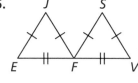

© 26. Reasoning Suppose $\overline{GH} \cong \overline{JK}$, $\overline{HI} \cong \overline{KL}$, and $\angle I \cong \angle L$. Is $\triangle GHI$ congruent to $\triangle JKL$? Explain.

Proof 27. Given: $\overline{GK}$ bisects $\angle JGM$, $\overline{GJ} \cong \overline{GM}$

Prove: $\triangle GJK \cong \triangle GMK$

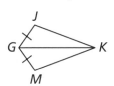

Proof 28. Given: $\overline{AE}$ and $\overline{BD}$ bisect each other.

Prove: $\triangle ACB \cong \triangle ECD$

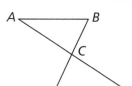

29. Given: $\overline{FG} \parallel \overline{KL}, \overline{FG} \cong \overline{KL}$

Proof

 Prove: $\triangle FGK \cong \triangle KLF$

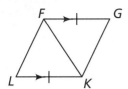

30. Given: $\overline{AB} \perp \overline{CM}, \overline{AB} \perp \overline{DB}, \overline{CM} \cong \overline{DB},$

Proof M is the midpoint of $\overline{AB}$.

 Prove: $\triangle AMC \cong \triangle MBD$

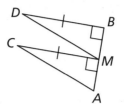

Challenge

31. Given: $\overline{HK} \cong \overline{LG}, \overline{HF} \cong \overline{LJ}, \overline{FG} \cong \overline{JK}$

Proof

 Prove: $\triangle FGH \cong \triangle JKL$

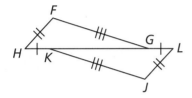

32. Given: $\angle N \cong \angle L, \overline{MN} \cong \overline{OL}, \overline{NO} \cong \overline{LM}$

Proof

 Prove: $\overline{MN} \parallel \overline{OL}$

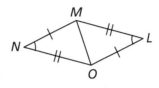

33. Reasoning Four sides of polygon *ABCD* are congruent, respectively, to the four sides of polygon *EFGH*. Are *ABCD* and *EFGH* congruent? Is a quadrilateral a rigid figure? If not, what could you add to make it a rigid figure? Explain.

12-3 Triangle Congruence by ASA and AAS

G.SRT.5 Use congruence . . . criteria for triangles to solve problems and to prove relationships in geometric figures. Also prepares for **G.CO.8**

Objective To prove two triangles congruent using the ASA Postulate and the AAS Theorem

 Solve It! Write your solution to the Solve It in the space below.

You already know that triangles are congruent if two pairs of sides and the included angles are congruent (SAS). You can also prove triangles congruent using other groupings of angles and sides.

Essential Understanding You can prove that two triangles are congruent without having to show that *all* corresponding parts are congruent. In this lesson, you will prove triangles congruent by using one pair of corresponding sides and two pairs of corresponding angles.

take note

Postulate 16 Angle-Side-Angle (ASA) Postulate

Postulate	If . . .	Then . . .
If two angles and the included side of one triangle are congruent to two angles and the included side of another triangle, then the two triangles are congruent.	$\angle A \cong \angle D$, $\overline{AC} \cong \overline{DF}$, $\angle C \cong \angle F$	$\triangle ABC \cong \triangle DEF$

Problem 1 Using ASA

Got It? Which two triangles are congruent by ASA? Explain.

Think

When you use ASA, what must be true about the corresponding sides?

Practice Name two triangles that are congruent by ASA.

1.

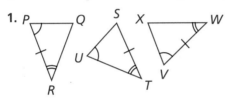

2.

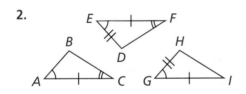

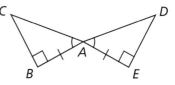

Problem 2 Writing a Proof Using ASA

Got It? **Given:** $\angle CAB \cong \angle DAE$, $\overline{BA} \cong \overline{EA}$, $\angle B$ and $\angle E$ are right angles

Prove: $\triangle ABC \cong \triangle AED$

Ⓐ Practice **3. Developing Proof** Complete the paragraph proof by filling in the blanks.

Given: $\angle LKM \cong \angle JKM$, $\angle LMK \cong \angle JMK$

Prove: $\triangle LKM \cong \triangle JKM$

Proof: $\angle LKM \cong \angle JKM$ and $\angle LMK \cong \angle JMK$ are given.

$\overline{KM} \cong \overline{KM}$ by the **a.** _____ Property of Congruence.

So, $\triangle LKM \cong \triangle JKM$ by **b.** _____.

Proof 4. Given: $\overline{QR} \cong \overline{TS}$, $\overline{QR} \parallel \overline{TS}$

Prove: $\triangle QRT \cong \triangle TSQ$

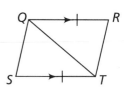

You can also prove triangles congruent by using two angles and a nonincluded side, as stated in the theorem below.

Theorem 19   Angle-Angle-Side (AAS) Theorem

Theorem	If . . .	Then . . .
If two angles and a nonincluded side of one triangle are congruent to two angles and the corresponding nonincluded side of another triangle, then the triangles are congruent.	$\angle A \cong \angle D$, $\angle B \cong \angle E$, $\overline{AC} \cong \overline{DF}$	$\triangle ABC \cong \triangle DEF$

Proof   Proof of Theorem 19: Angle-Angle-Side Theorem

Given: $\angle A \cong \angle D$, $\angle B \cong \angle E$, $\overline{AC} \cong \overline{DF}$

Prove: $\triangle ABC \cong \triangle DEF$

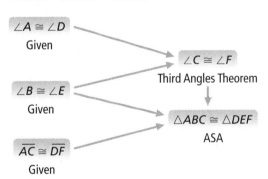

You have seen and used three methods of proof in this book—two-column, paragraph, and flow proof. Each method is equally as valid as the others. Unless told otherwise, you can choose any of the three methods to write a proof. Just be sure your proof always presents logical reasoning with justification.

Problem 3 Writing a Proof Using AAS

Think

How can you show on a diagram that $\overline{RP}$ bisects $\angle SRQ$?

Got It? **a. Given:** $\angle S \cong \angle Q$, $\overline{RP}$ bisects $\angle SRQ$

Prove: $\triangle SRP \cong \triangle QRP$

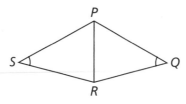

b. Reasoning In Problem 3, how could you prove that $\triangle WMR \cong \triangle RKW$ by ASA? Explain.

Practice **5. Developing Proof** Complete the two-column proof by filling in the blanks.

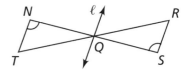

Given: $\angle N \cong \angle S$, line ℓ bisects $\overline{TR}$ at Q

Prove: $\triangle NQT \cong \triangle SQR$

Statements	Reasons
1) $\angle N \cong \angle S$	**1)** Given
2) $\angle NQT \cong \angle SQR$	**2) a.** _____
3) Line ℓ bisects $\overline{TR}$ at Q.	**3) b.** _____
4) c. _____	**4)** Definition of bisect
5) $\triangle NQT \cong \triangle SQR$	**5) d.** _____

Proof 6. Given: $\overline{PQ} \perp \overline{QS}$, $\overline{RS} \perp \overline{SQ}$, T is the midpoint of $\overline{PR}$

Prove: $\triangle PQT \cong \triangle RST$

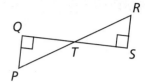

Problem 4 Determining Whether Triangles Are Congruent

Got It? Are $\triangle PAR$ and $\triangle SIR$ congruent? Explain.

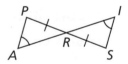

Practice Determine whether the triangles must be congruent. If so, name the postulate or theorem that justifies your answer. If not, explain.

7.

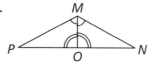

8.

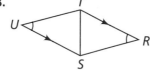

 Lesson Check

Do you know HOW?

9. In $\triangle RST$, which side is included between $\angle R$ and $\angle S$?

10. In $\triangle NOM$, $\overline{NO}$ is included between which angles?

Which postulate or theorem could you use to prove △*ABC* ≅ △*DEF*?

11.

12. A B E D
C F

Do you UNDERSTAND?

MATHEMATICAL
PRACTICES

🅒 **13. Compare and Contrast** How are the ASA Postulate and the SAS Postulate alike? How are they different?

🅒 **14. Error Analysis** Your friend asks you for help on a geometry exercise. To the right is your friend's paper. What error did your friend make? Explain.

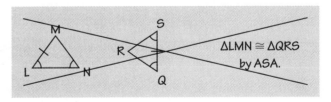

© **15. Reasoning** Suppose $\angle E \cong \angle I$ and $\overline{FE} \cong \overline{GI}$. What else must you know in order to prove $\triangle FDE \cong \triangle GHI$ by ASA? By AAS?

More Practice and Problem-Solving Exercises

B Apply

Proof **16. Given:** $\angle N \cong \angle P, \overline{MO} \cong \overline{QO}$

Prove: $\triangle MON \cong \triangle QOP$

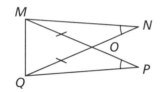

Proof **17. Given:** $\angle FJG \cong \angle HGJ, \overline{FG} \parallel \overline{JH}$

Prove: $\triangle FGJ \cong \triangle HJG$

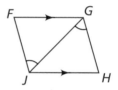

© **18. Think About a Plan** While helping your family clean out the attic, you find the piece of paper shown at the right. The paper contains clues to locate a time capsule buried in your backyard. The maple tree is due east of the oak tree in your backyard. Will the clues always lead you to the correct spot? Explain.

- How can you use a diagram to help you?
- What type of geometric figure do the paths and the marked line form?
- How does the position of the marked line relate to the positions of the angles?

Mark a line on the ground from the oak tree to the maple tree. From the oak tree, walk along a path that forms a 70° angle with the marked line, keeping the maple tree to your right. From the maple tree, walk along a path that forms a 40° angle with the marked line. The time capsule is buried where the paths meet.

19. Constructions Use a straightedge to draw a triangle. Label it $\triangle JKL$. Construct $\triangle MNP$ so that $\triangle MNP \cong \triangle JKL$ by ASA.

© **20. Reasoning** Can you prove that the triangles at the right are congruent? Justify your answer.

© **21. Writing** Anita says that you can rewrite any proof that uses the AAS Theorem as a proof that uses the ASA Postulate. Do you agree with Anita? Explain.

Proof **22. Given:** $\overline{AE} \parallel \overline{BD}$, $\overline{AE} \cong \overline{BD}$, $\angle E \cong \angle D$

Prove: $\triangle AEB \cong \triangle BDC$

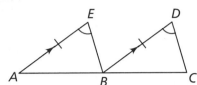

Proof **23. Given:** $\angle 1 \cong \angle 2$, and $\overline{DH}$ bisects $\angle BDF$.

Prove: $\triangle BDH \cong \triangle FDH$

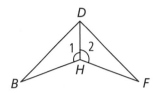

24. Draw a Diagram Draw two noncongruent triangles that have two pairs of congruent angles and one pair of congruent sides.

Proof **25. Given:** $\overline{AB} \parallel \overline{DC}$, $\overline{DA} \parallel \overline{BC}$

Prove: $\triangle ABC \cong \triangle CDA$

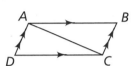

Challenge

26. Given $\overline{AD} \parallel \overline{BC}$ and $\overline{AB} \parallel \overline{DC}$, name as many pairs of congruent triangles as you can.

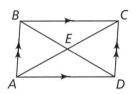

27. Constructions In $\triangle RST$ at the right, $RS = 5$, $RT = 9$, and $m\angle T = 30$. Show that there is no SSA congruence rule by constructing $\triangle UVW$ with $UV = RS$, $UW = RT$, and $m\angle W = m\angle T$, but with $\triangle UVW \not\cong \triangle RST$.

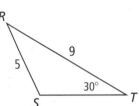

28. Probability Below are six statements about the triangles.

$\angle A \cong \angle X$ $\angle B \cong \angle Y$ $\angle C \cong \angle Z$
$\overline{AB} \cong \overline{XY}$ $\overline{AC} \cong \overline{XZ}$ $\overline{BC} \cong \overline{YZ}$

There are 20 ways to choose a group of three statements from these six. What is the probability that three statements chosen at random from the six will guarantee that the triangles are congruent?

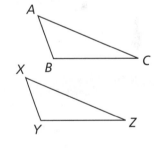

12-4 Using Corresponding Parts of Congruent Triangles

G.SRT.5 Use congruence . . . criteria for triangles to solve problems and to prove relationships in geometric figures. Also **G.CO.12**, prepares for **G.CO.7**

Objective   To use triangle congruence and corresponding parts of congruent triangles to prove that parts of two triangles are congruent

Solve It!   Write your solution to the Solve It in the space below.

With SSS, SAS, ASA, and AAS, you know how to use three congruent parts of two triangles to show that the triangles are congruent. Once you know that two triangles are congruent, you can make conclusions about their other corresponding parts because, by definition, corresponding parts of congruent triangles are congruent.

Essential Understanding   If you know two triangles are congruent, then you know that every pair of their corresponding parts is also congruent.

 **Problem 1**   **Proving Parts of Triangles Congruent**

Got It?   **Given:** $\overline{BA} \cong \overline{DA}$, $\overline{CA} \cong \overline{EA}$

Prove: $\angle C \cong \angle E$

Think

In the diagram, which congruent pair is not marked?

1. Developing Proof Tell why the two triangles are congruent. Give the congruence statement. Then list all the other corresponding parts of the triangles that are congruent.

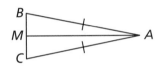 **Problem 2** **Proving Triangle Parts Congruent to Measure Distance**

Plan

Which congruency rule can you use?

Got It?   **a. Given:** $\overline{AB} \cong \overline{AC}$, M is the midpoint of $\overline{BC}$

Prove: $\angle AMB \cong \angle AMC$

© **b. Reasoning** If the landmark in Problem 2 were not at sea level, would the method in Problem 2 work? Explain.

2. Given: $\overline{OM} \cong \overline{ER}$, $\overline{ME} \cong \overline{RO}$
Prove: $\angle M \cong \angle R$

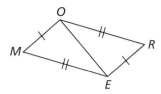

Ⓒ **3. Developing Proof** A balalaika is a stringed instrument. Prove that the bases of the balalaikas are congruent.

Given: $\overline{RA} \cong \overline{NY}$, $\angle KRA \cong \angle JNY$,
$\angle KAR \cong \angle JYN$

Prove: $\overline{KA} \cong \overline{JY}$

Proof: It is given that two angles and the included side of one triangle are congruent to two angles and the included side of the other.

So, **a.** _____ $\cong \triangle JNY$ by **b.** _____.

$\overline{KA} \cong \overline{JY}$ because **c.** _____.

Lesson Check

Do you know HOW?

Name the postulate or theorem that you can use to show the triangles are congruent. Then explain why the statement is true.

4. $\overline{EA} \cong \overline{MA}$

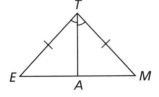

5. $\angle U \cong \angle E$

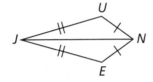

Do you UNDERSTAND?

6. Reasoning How does the fact that corresponding parts of congruent triangles are congruent relate to the definition of congruent triangles?

7. Error Analysis Find and correct the error(s) in the proof.

Given: $\overline{KH} \cong \overline{NH}$, $\angle L \cong \angle M$

Prove: H is the midpoint of $\overline{LM}$.

Proof: $\overline{KH} \cong \overline{NH}$ because it is given. $\angle L \cong \angle M$ because it is given. $\angle KHL \cong \angle NHM$ because vertical angles are congruent. So, $\triangle KHL \cong \triangle MHN$ by ASA Postulate. Since corresponding parts of congruent triangles are congruent, $\overline{LH} \cong \overline{MH}$. By the definition of midpoint, H is the midpoint of $\overline{LM}$.

More Practice and Problem-Solving Exercises

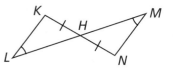

Ⓑ Apply

Proof 8. Given: $\angle SPT \cong \angle OPT$, $\overline{SP} \cong \overline{OP}$

  Prove: $\angle S \cong \angle O$

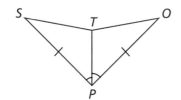

Proof 9. Given: $\overline{YT} \cong \overline{YP}$, $\angle C \cong \angle R$, $\angle T \cong \angle P$

  Prove: $\overline{CT} \cong \overline{RP}$

Ⓒ Reasoning Copy and mark the figure to show the given information. Explain how you would prove $\angle P \cong \angle Q$.

10. Given: $\overline{PK} \cong \overline{QK}$, $\overline{KL}$ bisects $\angle PKQ$

11. Given: $\overline{KL}$ is the perpendicular bisector of $\overline{PQ}$.

12. Given: $\overline{KL} \perp \overline{PQ}$, $\overline{KL}$ bisects $\angle PKQ$

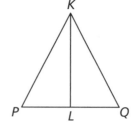

© 13. Think About a Plan The construction of a line perpendicular to line ℓ through point P on line ℓ is shown. Explain why you can conclude that $\overleftrightarrow{CP}$ is perpendicular to ℓ.

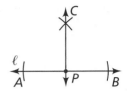

- How can you use congruent triangles to justify the construction?
- Which lengths or distances are equal by construction?

Proof 14. Given: $\overline{BA} \cong \overline{BC}$, $\overline{BD}$ bisects $\angle ABC$

Prove: $\overline{BD} \perp \overline{AC}$, $\overline{BD}$ bisects $\overline{AC}$

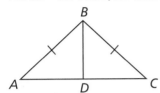

Proof 15. Given: $\ell \perp \overline{AB}$, ℓ bisects $\overline{AB}$ at C, P is on ℓ

Prove: $PA = PB$

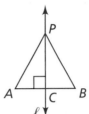

16. Constructions The construction of $\angle B$ congruent to given $\angle A$ is shown. $\overline{AD} \cong \overline{BF}$ because they are congruent radii. $\overset{\frown}{DC} \cong \overset{\frown}{FE}$ because both arcs have the same compass settings. Explain why you can conclude that $\angle A \cong \angle B$.

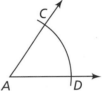
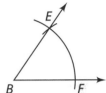

Proof 17. Given: $\overline{BE} \perp \overline{AC}$, $\overline{DF} \perp \overline{AC}$

$\overline{BE} \cong \overline{DF}$, $\overline{AF} \cong \overline{CE}$

Prove: $\overline{AB} \cong \overline{CD}$

Proof 18. Given: $\overline{JK} \parallel \overline{QP}$, $\overline{JK} \cong \overline{PQ}$

Prove: $\overline{KQ}$ bisects $\overline{JP}$.

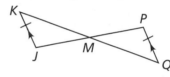

19. Designs Rangoli is a colorful design pattern drawn outside houses in India, especially during festivals. Vina plans to use the pattern at the right as the base of her design. In this pattern, $\overline{RU}$, $\overline{SV}$, and $\overline{QT}$ bisect each other at O. $RS = 6$, $\overline{RU} = 12$, $\overline{RU} \cong \overline{SV}$, $\overline{ST} \parallel \overline{RU}$, and $\overline{RS} \parallel \overline{QT}$. What is the perimeter of the hexagon?

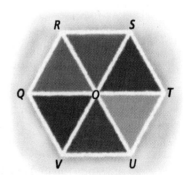

© Challenge

In the diagram below, $\overline{BA} \cong \overline{KA}$ and $\overline{BE} \cong \overline{KE}$.

Proof 20. Prove: S is the midpoint of $\overline{BK}$.

Proof 21. Prove: $\overline{BK} \perp \overline{AE}$

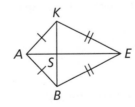

ACTIVITY LAB

Use With Lesson 12-5

Paper-Folding Conjectures

G.CO.12 Make formal geometric constructions with a variety of tools and methods (. . . paper folding . . .). Also prepares for **G.CO.10**

Isosceles triangles have two congruent sides. Folding one of the sides onto the other will suggest another important property of isosceles triangles.

Activity 1

Step 1   Construct an isosceles △*ABC* on tracing paper, with $\overline{AC} \cong \overline{BC}$.

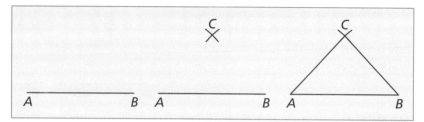

Step 2   Fold the paper so the two congruent sides fit exactly one on top of the other. Crease the paper. Label the intersection of the fold line and $\overline{AB}$ as point *D*.

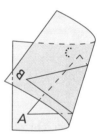

1. What do you notice about ∠*A* and ∠*B*? Compare your results with others. Make a conjecture about the angles opposite the congruent sides in an isosceles triangle.

2. **a.** Study the fold line $\overline{CD}$ and the base $\overline{AB}$. What type of angles are ∠*CDA* and ∠*CDB*? How do $\overline{AD}$ and $\overline{BD}$ seem to be related?

   b. Use your answers to part (a) to complete the conjecture: The fold line $\overline{CD}$ is

   the _____ of the base $\overline{AB}$ of isosceles △*ABC*.

Activity 2

In Activity 1, you made a conjecture about angles opposite the congruent sides of a triangle. You can also fold paper to study whether the converse is true.

Step 1 On tracing paper, draw acute angle F and one side $\overline{FG}$. Construct $\angle G$ as shown, so that $\angle G \cong \angle F$.

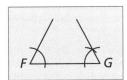

Step 2 Fold the paper so $\angle F$ and $\angle G$ fit exactly one on top of the other.

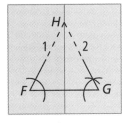

3. Why do sides 1 and 2 meet at point H on the fold line? Make a conjecture about sides $\overline{FH}$ and $\overline{GH}$ opposite congruent angles in a triangle.

4. Write your conjectures from Questions 1 and 3 as a biconditional.

12-5 Isosceles and Equilateral Triangles

G.CO.10 Prove theorems about triangles . . . base angles of isosceles triangles are congruent . . . Also **G.CO.13, G.SRT.5**

Objective To use and apply properties of isosceles and equilateral triangles

 Solve It! Write your solution to the Solve It in the space below.

In the Solve It, you classified a triangle based on the lengths of its sides. You can also identify certain triangles based on information about their angles. In this lesson, you will learn how to use and apply properties of isosceles and equilateral triangles.

Essential Understanding The angles and sides of isosceles and equilateral triangles have special relationships.

Isosceles triangles are common in the real world. You can frequently see them in structures such as bridges and buildings, as well as in art and design. The congruent sides of an isosceles triangle are its **legs**. The third side is the **base**. The two congruent legs form the **vertex angle**. The other two angles are the **base angles**.

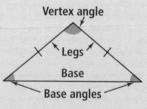

take note

Theorem 20 Isosceles Triangle Theorem

Theorem	If . . .	Then . . .
If two sides of a triangle are congruent, then the angles opposite those sides are congruent.	$\overline{AC} \cong \overline{BC}$	$\angle A \cong \angle B$

The proof of the Isosceles Triangle Theorem requires an auxiliary line.

Proof **Proof of Theorem 20: Isosceles Triangle Theorem**

Begin with isosceles $\triangle XYZ$ with $\overline{XY} \cong \overline{XZ}$. Draw $\overline{XB}$, the bisector of the vertex angle $\angle YXZ$.

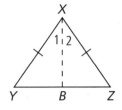

Given: $\overline{XY} \cong \overline{XZ}$, $\overline{XB}$ bisects $\angle YXZ$

Prove: $\angle Y \cong \angle Z$

Proof: $\overline{XY} \cong \overline{XZ}$ is given. By the definition of angle bisector, $\angle 1 \cong \angle 2$. By the Reflexive Property of Congruence, $\overline{XB} \cong \overline{XB}$. So by the SAS Postulate, $\triangle XYB \cong \triangle XZB$. $\angle Y \cong \angle Z$ since corresponding parts of congruent triangles are congruent.

take note

Theorem 21   Converse of the Isosceles Triangle Theorem

Theorem	If . . .	Then . . .
If two angles of a triangle are congruent, then the sides opposite those angles are congruent.	$\angle A \cong \angle B$	$\overline{AC} \cong \overline{BC}$

You will prove Theorem 21 in Exercise 22.

ONLINE PROBLEMS

Problem 1   Using the Isosceles Triangle Theorems

Got It?   **a.** Is $\angle WVS$ congruent to $\angle S$? Is $\overline{TR}$ congruent to $\overline{TS}$? Explain.

Think

What are you looking for in the diagram?

b. Reasoning Can you conclude that $\triangle RUV$ is isosceles? Explain.

Practice Complete each statement. Explain why it is true.

1. $\overline{VT} \cong$ _____

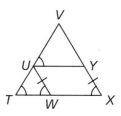

2. $\overline{UT} \cong$ _____ $\cong \overline{YX}$

3. $\overline{VU} \cong$ _____

4. $\angle VYU \cong$ _____

An isosceles triangle has a certain type of symmetry about a line through its vertex angle.

---

take note

Theorem 22

Theorem	**If . . .**	**Then . . .**
If a line bisects the vertex angle of an isosceles triangle, then the line is also the perpendicular bisector of the base.	$\overline{AC} \cong \overline{BC}$ and $\angle ACD \cong \angle BCD$	$\overline{CD} \perp \overline{AB}$ and $\overline{AD} \cong \overline{BD}$ *You will prove Theorem 22 in Exercise 25.*

 **Problem 2** **Using Algebra**

Got It? Suppose $m\angle A = 27$. What is the value of x?

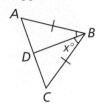

Think

How can you determine the measure of $\angle C$?

 Practice **Algebra** Find the values of x and y.

5.

6.

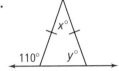

A **corollary** is a theorem that can be proved easily using another theorem. Since a corollary is a theorem, you can use it as a reason in a proof.

take note

Corollary to Theorem 20

Corollary

If a triangle is equilateral, then the triangle is equiangular.

If . . .

$\overline{XY} \cong \overline{YZ} \cong \overline{ZX}$

Then . . .

$\angle X \cong \angle Y \cong \angle Z$

Corollary to Theorem 21

Corollary

If a triangle is equiangular, then the triangle is equilateral.

If . . .

$\angle X \cong \angle Y \cong \angle Z$

Then . . .

$\overline{XY} \cong \overline{YZ} \cong \overline{ZX}$

Got It? Suppose the triangles in Problem 3 are isosceles triangles, where ∠ADE, ∠DEC, and ∠ECB are vertex angles. If the vertex angles each have a measure of 58, what are $m\angle A$ and $m\angle BCD$?

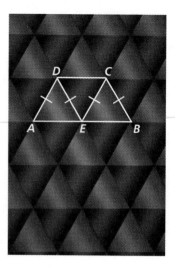

Practice

7. The equilateral triangle and the isosceles triangle shown here share a common side. What is the measure of ∠ABC?

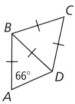

Lesson Check

Do you know HOW?

8. What is $m\angle A$?

a.

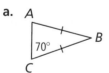

b.

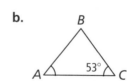

9. What is the value of x?

a.

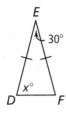

b.

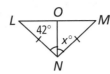

10. The measure of one base angle of an isosceles triangle is 23. What are the measures of the other two angles?

Do you UNDERSTAND?

11. What is the relationship between sides and angles for each type of triangle?

a. isosceles

b. equilateral

12. Error Analysis Claudia drew an isosceles triangle. She asked Sue to mark it. Explain why the marking of the diagram is incorrect.

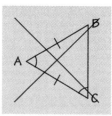

More Practice and Problem-Solving Exercises

B Apply

STEM **13. Architecture** Each face of the Great Pyramid at Giza is an isosceles triangle with a 76° vertex angle. What are the measures of the base angles?

14. Reasoning What are the measures of the base angles of a right isosceles triangle? Explain.

Given isosceles △*JKL* with base $\overline{JL}$, find each value.

15. If $m\angle L = 58$, then $m\angle LKJ = $ _?_.

16. If $\overline{JL} = 5$, then $\overline{ML} = $ _?_.

17. If $m\angle JKM = 48$, then $m\angle J = $ _?_.

18. If $m\angle J = 55$, then $m\angle JKM = $ _?_.

19. Think About a Plan A triangle has angle measures $x + 15$, $3x - 35$, and $4x$. What type of triangle is it? Be as specific as possible. Justify your answer.
- What do you know about the sum of the angle measures of a triangle?
- What do you need to know to classify a triangle?
- What type of triangle has no congruent angles? Two congruent angles? Three congruent angles?

20. Reasoning An exterior angle of an isosceles triangle has measure 100. Find two possible sets of measures for the angles of the triangle.

21. Developing Proof Here is another way to prove the Isosceles Triangle Theorem. Supply the missing information.

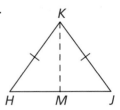

Begin with isosceles △HKJ with $\overline{KH} \cong \overline{KJ}$.

Draw **a.** ?, a bisector of the base $\overline{HJ}$.

Given: $\overline{KH} \cong \overline{KJ}$, **b.** ? bisects $\overline{HJ}$

Prove: $\angle H \cong \angle J$

Statements	Reasons
1) $\overline{KM}$ bisects $\overline{HJ}$.	1) **c.** ?
2) $\overline{HM} \cong \overline{JM}$	2) **d.** ?
3) $\overline{KH} \cong \overline{KJ}$	3) Given
4) $\overline{KM} \cong \overline{KM}$	4) **e.** ?
5) △KHM ≅ △KJM	5) **f.** ?
6) $\angle H \cong \angle J$	6) **g.** ?

Proof 22. Supply the missing information in this statement of the Converse of the Isosceles Triangle Theorem. Then write a proof.

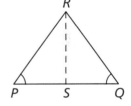

Begin with △PRQ with $\angle P \cong \angle Q$.

Draw **a.** ?, a bisector of $\angle PRQ$.

Given: $\angle P \cong \angle Q$, **b.** ? bisects $\angle PRQ$

Prove: $\overline{PR} \cong \overline{QR}$

23. Writing Explain how the corollaries to the Isosceles Triangle Theorem and its converse follow from the theorems.

Proof 24. Given: $\overline{AE} \cong \overline{DE}$, $\overline{AB} \cong \overline{DC}$

Prove: △ABE ≅ △DCE

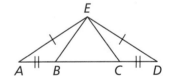

Proof 25. Prove Theorem 22. Use the diagram given in the statement of the theorem.

STEM 26. a. Communications In the diagram at the right, what type of triangle is formed by the cables of the same height and the ground?
b. What are the two different base lengths of the triangles?
c. How is the tower related to each of the triangles?

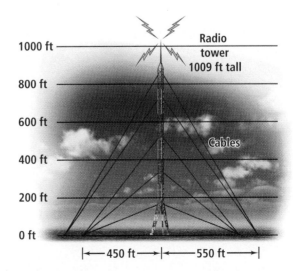

27. Algebra The length of the base of an isosceles triangle is x. The length of a leg is $2x - 5$. The perimeter of the triangle is 20. Find x.

28. Constructions Construct equiangular triangle ABC. Justify your method.

Algebra Find the values of m and n.

29.

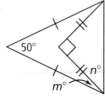

30.

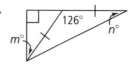

31.

32. Constructions A polygon is *inscribed in* a circle if the vertices of the polygon are on the circle. Given a circle and its center, construct a square inscribed in the circle. Justify your method by showing that the figure you inscribed is a quadrilateral with four right angles and four congruent sides.

33. Constructions Use a compass to draw a circle.
  a. Using the same compass setting, place the point of the compass on the circle and draw two arcs that intersect the circle.
  b. Again using the same compass setting, place the point of the compass on one of the two points of intersection from part (a) and draw two more arcs that intersect the original circle. Continue in this way until you have gone entirely around the original circle.
  c. Connect points of intersection of the arcs and the original circle. What regular polygon have you constructed? Explain.
  d. Use the construction from parts (a)–(c) to construct an equilateral triangle inscribed in a circle. Justify your construction.

Ⓒ Challenge

Coordinate Geometry For each pair of points, there are six points that could be the third vertex of an isosceles right triangle. Find the coordinates of each point.

34. $(4, 0)$ and $(0, 4)$ **35.** $(0, 0)$ and $(5, 5)$ **36.** $(2, 3)$ and $(5, 6)$

◎ 37. Reasoning What measures are possible for the base angles of an acute isosceles triangle?

12-6 Congruence in Right Triangles

G.SRT.5 Use congruence . . . criteria . . . to solve problems and to prove relationships in geometric figures.
Also **G.CO.10**

Objective   To prove right triangles congruent using the Hypotenuse-Leg Theorem

 Solve It!   Write your solution to the Solve It in the space below.

In the diagram below, two sides and a nonincluded angle of one triangle are congruent to two sides and the nonincluded angle of another triangle.

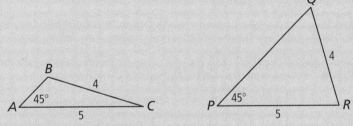

Notice that the triangles are not congruent. So, you can conclude that Side-Side-Angle is *not* a valid method for proving two triangles congruent. This method, however, works in the special case of right triangles, where the right angles are the nonincluded angles.

In a right triangle, the side opposite the right angle is called the **hypotenuse.** It is the longest side in the triangle. The other two sides are called **legs.**

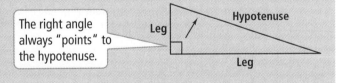

The right angle always "points" to the hypotenuse.

Essential Understanding   You can prove that two triangles are congruent without having to show that *all* corresponding parts are congruent. In this lesson, you will prove right triangles congruent by using one pair of right angles, a pair of hypotenuses, and a pair of legs.

Theorem 23   Hypotenuse-Leg (HL) Theorem

Theorem	**If . . .**	**Then . . .**
If the hypotenuse and a leg of one right triangle are congruent to the hypotenuse and a leg of another right triangle, then the triangles are congruent.	$\triangle PQR$ and $\triangle XYZ$ are right $\triangle$, $\overline{PR} \cong \overline{XZ}$, and $\overline{PQ} \cong \overline{XY}$	$\triangle PQR \cong \triangle XYZ$

To prove the HL Theorem you will need to draw auxiliary lines to make a third triangle.

Proof **Proof of Theorem 23: Hypotenuse-Leg Theorem**

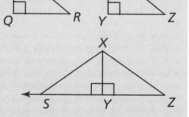

Given: $\triangle PQR$ and $\triangle XYZ$ are right triangles, with right angles Q and Y. $\overline{PR} \cong \overline{XZ}$ and $\overline{PQ} \cong \overline{XY}$.

Prove: $\triangle PQR \cong \triangle XYZ$

Proof: On $\triangle XYZ$, draw $\overrightarrow{ZY}$.

Mark point S so that $YS = QR$. Then, $\triangle PQR \cong \triangle XYS$ by SAS.

Since corresponding parts of congruent triangles are congruent, $\overline{PR} \cong \overline{XS}$. It is given that $\overline{PR} \cong \overline{XZ}$, so $\overline{XS} \cong \overline{XZ}$ by the Transitive Property of Congruence. By the Isosceles Triangle Theorem, $\angle S \cong \angle Z$, so $\triangle XYS \cong \triangle XYZ$ by AAS. Therefore, $\triangle PQR \cong \triangle XYZ$ by the Transitive Property of Congruence.

Key Concept   Conditions for HL Theorem

To use the HL Theorem, the triangles must meet three conditions.

Conditions

- There are two right triangles.
- The triangles have congruent hypotenuses.
- There is one pair of congruent legs.

Problem 1 **Using the HL Theorem**

Got It? **a. Given:** $\angle PRS$ and $\angle RPQ$ are right angles, $\overline{SP} \cong \overline{QR}$

Prove: $\triangle PRS \cong \triangle RPQ$

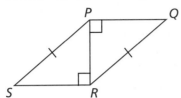

Think

What do you need to know if you want to use the HL Theorem?

b. Reasoning Your friend says, "Suppose you have two right triangles with congruent hypotenuses and one pair of congruent legs. It does not matter which leg in the first triangle is congruent to which leg in the second triangle. The triangles will be congruent." Is your friend correct? Explain.

A Practice **1. Developing Proof** Complete the flow proof.

Given: $\overline{PS} \cong \overline{PT}$, $\angle PRS \cong \angle PRT$

Prove: $\triangle PRS \cong \triangle PRT$

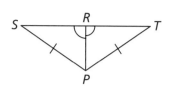

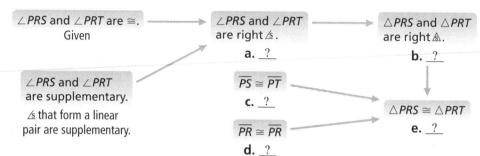

a. _____

b. _____

c. _____

d. _____

e. _____

2. Developing Proof Complete the paragraph proof.

Given: $\angle A$ and $\angle D$ are right angles, $\overline{AB} \cong \overline{DE}$

Prove: $\triangle ABE \cong \triangle DEB$

Proof: It is given that $\angle A$ and $\angle D$ are right angles.

So, **a.** _____ by the definition of right

triangles. **b.** _____, because of the

Reflexive Property of Congruence. It is also given

that **c.** _____.

So, $\triangle ABE \cong \triangle DEB$ by **d.** _____.

 Problem 2 **Writing a Proof Using the HL Theorem**

Got It? **Given:** $\overline{CD} \cong \overline{EA}$, $\overline{AD}$ is the
perpendicular bisector of $\overline{CE}$

Prove: $\triangle CBD \cong \triangle EBA$

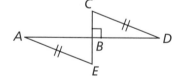

Think

**What can you
conclude if
$\overline{AD}$ is the
perpendicular
bisector of $\overline{CE}$?**

3. Given: $\overline{HV} \perp \overline{GT}$, $\overline{GH} \cong \overline{TV}$, I is the midpoint of $\overline{HV}$

Prove: $\triangle IGH \cong \triangle ITV$

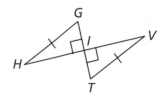

Proof **4. Given:** $\overline{PM} \cong \overline{RJ}$, $\overline{PT} \perp \overline{TJ}$, $\overline{RM} \perp \overline{TJ}$, M is the midpoint of $\overline{TJ}$.

Prove: $\triangle PTM \cong \triangle RMJ$

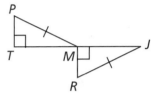

Lesson Check

Do you know HOW?

For Exercises 5–8, determine whether the two triangles are congruent. If so, write the congruence statement.

5.

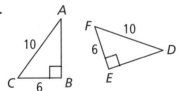

6.

7.

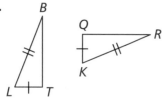

8.

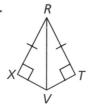

Do you UNDERSTAND?

MATHEMATICAL
PRACTICES

9. Vocabulary A right triangle has side lengths of 5 cm, 12 cm, and 13 cm. What is the length of the hypotenuse? How do you know?

10. Compare and Contrast How do the HL Theorem and the SAS Postulate compare? How are they different? Explain.

11. Error Analysis Your classmate says that there is not enough information to determine whether the two triangles at the right are congruent. Is your classmate correct? Explain.

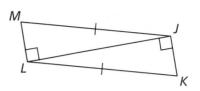

More Practice and Problem-Solving Exercises

B Apply

Algebra For what values of *x* and *y* are the triangles congruent by HL?

12.

13.

14. Study Exercise 1. Can you prove that $\triangle PRS \cong \triangle PRT$ without using the HL Theorem? Explain.

15. Think About a Plan $\triangle ABC$ and $\triangle PQR$ are right triangular sections of a fire escape, as shown. Is each story of the building the same height? Explain.
- What can you tell from the diagram?
- How can you use congruent triangles here?

16. Writing "A HA!" exclaims your classmate. "There must be an HA Theorem, sort of like the HL Theorem!" Is your classmate correct? Explain.

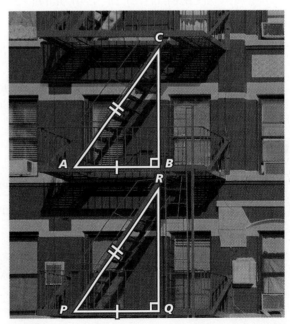

Proof 17. Given: $\overline{RS} \cong \overline{TU}$, $\overline{RS} \perp \overline{ST}$, $\overline{TU} \perp \overline{UV}$, T is the midpoint of $\overline{RV}$

Prove: $\triangle RST \cong \triangle TUV$

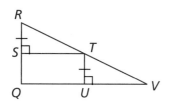

Proof 18. Given: $\triangle LNP$ is isosceles with base $\overline{NP}$, $\overline{MN} \perp \overline{NL}$, $\overline{QP} \perp \overline{PL}$, $\overline{ML} \cong \overline{QL}$

Prove: $\triangle MNL \cong \triangle QPL$

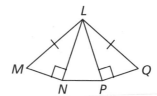

Constructions Copy the triangle and construct a triangle congruent to it using the given method.

19. SAS

20. HL

21. ASA

22. SSS

Proof 23. Given: $\triangle GKE$ is isosceles with base $\overline{GE}$, $\angle L$ and $\angle D$ are right angles, and K is the midpoint of $\overline{LD}$.

Prove: $\overline{LG} \cong \overline{DE}$

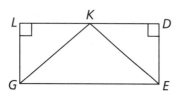

Proof 24. Given: $\overline{LO}$ bisects $\angle MLN$, $\overline{OM} \perp \overline{LM}$, $\overline{ON} \perp \overline{LN}$

Prove: $\triangle LMO \cong \triangle LNO$

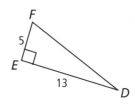

ⓒ 25. Reasoning Are the triangles to the right congruent? Explain.

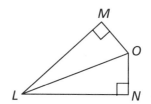

26. a. Coordinate Geometry Graph the points $A(-5, 6)$, $B(1, 3)$, $D(-8, 0)$, and $E(-2, -3)$. Draw $\overline{AB}$, $\overline{AE}$, $\overline{BD}$, and $\overline{DE}$. Label point C, the intersection of $\overline{AE}$ and $\overline{BD}$.

  b. Find the slopes of $\overline{AE}$ and $\overline{BD}$. How would you describe $\angle ACB$ and $\angle ECD$?

  c. Algebra Write equations for $\overleftrightarrow{AE}$ and $\overleftrightarrow{BD}$. What are the coordinates of C?

  d. Use the Distance Formula to find AB, BC, DC, and DE.

  e. Write a paragraph to prove that $\triangle ABC \cong \triangle EDC$.

ⓒ Challenge

Geometry in 3 Dimensions For Exercises 27 and 28, use the figure at the right.

Proof 27. Given: $\overline{BE} \perp \overline{EA}$, $\overline{BE} \perp \overline{EC}$, $\triangle ABC$ is equilateral

  Prove: $\triangle AEB \cong \triangle CEB$

28. Given: $\triangle AEB \cong \triangle CEB$, $\overline{BE} \perp \overline{EA}$, $\overline{BE} \perp \overline{EC}$
  Can you prove that $\triangle ABC$ is equilateral? Explain.

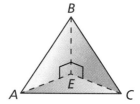

12-7 Congruence in Overlapping Triangles

G.SRT.5 Use congruence . . . criteria . . . to solve problems and to prove relationships in geometric figures.
Also **G.CO.10**

Objectives To identify congruent overlapping triangles
To prove two triangles congruent using other congruent triangles

Solve It! Write your solution to the Solve It in the space below.

In the Solve It, you located individual triangles among a jumble of triangles. Some triangle relationships are difficult to see because the triangles overlap.

Essential Understanding You can sometimes use the congruent corresponding parts of one pair of congruent triangles to prove another pair of triangles congruent. This often involves overlapping triangles.

Overlapping triangles may have a common side or angle. You can simplify your work with overlapping triangles by separating and redrawing the triangles.

Problem 1   Identifying Common Parts

Got It?   **a.** What is the common side in $\triangle ABD$ and $\triangle DCA$?

b. What is the common side in $\triangle ABD$ and $\triangle BAC$?

1. In the diagram, the red and blue triangles are congruent. Identify the common side or angle.

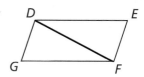

2. Separate and redraw $\triangle JKL$ and $\triangle MLK$. Identify any common angles or sides.

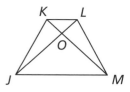

Problem 2 Using Common Parts

Got It? **Given:** $\triangle CAB \cong \triangle BDC$

Prove: $\overline{CE} \cong \overline{BE}$

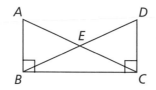

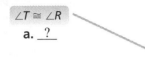 **Practice** **3. Developing Proof** Complete the flow proof.

Given: $\angle T \cong \angle R$, $\overline{PQ} \cong \overline{PV}$

Prove: $\angle PQT \cong \angle PVR$

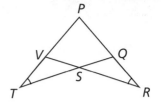

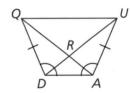

| $\angle T \cong \angle R$ |
| a. __?__ |

| $\angle TPQ \cong \angle RPV$ | → | $\triangle TPQ \cong \triangle RPV$ | → | $\angle PQT \cong \angle PVR$ |
| b. __?__ | | d. __?__ | | e. __?__ |

| $\overline{PQ} \cong \overline{PV}$ |
| c. __?__ |

a. _____

b. _____

c. _____

d. _____

e. _____

Proof **4. Given:** $\overline{QD} \cong \overline{UA}$, $\angle QDA \cong \angle UAD$

Prove: $\triangle QDA \cong \triangle UAD$

Problem 3 Using Two Pairs of Triangles

Got It? **Given:** $\overline{PS} \cong \overline{RS}$, $\angle PSQ \cong \angle RSQ$

Prove: $\triangle QPT \cong \triangle QRT$

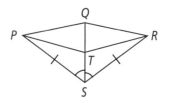

Plan

How do you choose another pair of triangles to help in your proof?

Ⓐ**Practice** **5. Given:** $\overline{AD} \cong \overline{ED}$, D is the midpoint of $\overline{BF}$

Proof **Prove:** $\triangle ADC \cong \triangle EDG$

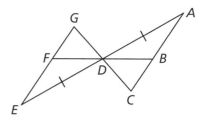

When several triangles overlap and you need to use one pair of congruent triangles to prove another pair congruent, you may find it helpful to draw a diagram of each pair of triangles.

Problem 4 **Separating Overlapping Triangles**

Plan

Which triangles are useful here?

Got It? **Given:** $\angle CAD \cong \angle EAD$, $\angle C \cong \angle E$

Prove: $\overline{BD} \cong \overline{FD}$

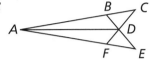

Practice **6. Given:** $\angle 1 \cong \angle 2$, $\angle 3 \cong \angle 4$

Proof **Prove:** $\triangle QET \cong \triangle QEU$

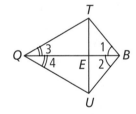

Lesson Check

Do you know HOW?

Identify any common angles or sides.

7. △*MKJ* and △*LJK*

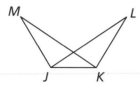

8. △*DEH* and △*DFG*

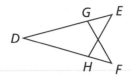

Separate and redraw the overlapping triangles. Label the vertices.

9.

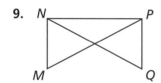

10.

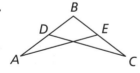

Do you UNDERSTAND?

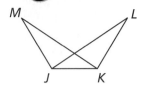

11. Reasoning In Exercise 7, both triangles have vertices J and K. Are $\angle J$ and $\angle K$ common angles for $\triangle MKJ$ and $\triangle LJK$? Explain.

12. Error Analysis In the diagram, $\triangle PSY \cong \triangle SPL$. Based on that fact, your friend claims that $\triangle PRL$ is not congruent to $\triangle SRY$. Explain why your friend is incorrect.

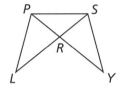

13. In the figure at the right, which pair of triangles could you prove congruent first in order to prove that $\triangle ACD \cong \triangle CAB$? Explain.

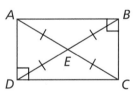

More Practice and Problem-Solving Exercises

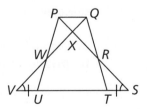

B Apply

14. Think About a Plan In the diagram at the right, $\angle V \cong \angle S$, $\overline{VU} \cong \overline{ST}$, and $\overline{PS} \cong \overline{QV}$. Which two triangles are congruent by SAS? Explain.
- How can you use a new diagram to help you identify the triangles?
- What do you need to prove triangles congruent by SAS?

STEM **15. Clothing Design** The figure at the right is part of a clothing design pattern, and it has the following relationships.

- $\overline{GC} \perp \overline{AC}$
- $\overline{AB} \perp \overline{BC}$
- $\overline{AB} \parallel \overline{DE} \parallel \overline{FG}$
- $m\angle A = 50$
- $\triangle DEC$ is isosceles with base $\overline{DC}$.

a. Find the measures of all the numbered angles in the figure.
b. Suppose $\overline{AB} \cong \overline{FC}$. Name two congruent triangles and explain how you can prove them congruent.

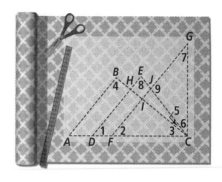

Proof **16. Given:** $\overline{AC} \cong \overline{EC}$, $\overline{CB} \cong \overline{CD}$

Prove: $\angle A \cong \angle E$

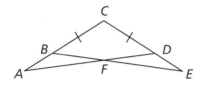

Proof **17. Given:** $\overline{QT} \perp \overline{PR}$, $\overline{QT}$ bisects $\overline{PR}$, $\overline{QT}$ bisects $\angle VQS$

Prove: $\overline{VQ} \cong \overline{SQ}$

Open-Ended Draw the diagram described.

18. Draw a vertical segment on your paper. On the right side of the segment draw two triangles that share the vertical segment as a common side.

19. Draw two triangles that have a common angle.

Proof **20. Given:** $\overline{TE} \cong \overline{RI}$, $\overline{TI} \cong \overline{RE}$, $\angle TDI$ and $\angle ROE$ are right $\angle s$

Prove: $\overline{TD} \cong \overline{RO}$

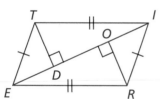

Proof **21. Given:** $\overline{AB} \perp \overline{BC}$, $\overline{DC} \perp \overline{BC}$, $\overline{AC} \cong \overline{DB}$

Prove: $\overline{AE} \cong \overline{DE}$

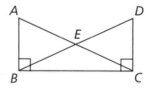

Challenge

22. Identify a pair of overlapping congruent triangles in the diagram at the right. Then use the given information to write a proof to show that the triangles are congruent.

Given: $\overline{AC} \cong \overline{BC}$, $\angle A \cong \angle B$

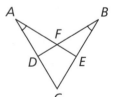

23. Reasoning Draw a quadrilateral $ABCD$ with $\overline{AB} \parallel \overline{DC}$, $\overline{AD} \parallel \overline{BC}$, and diagonals $\overline{AC}$ and $\overline{DB}$ intersecting at E. Label your diagram to indicate the parallel sides.
a. List all the pairs of congruent segments in your diagram.
b. **Writing** Explain how you know that the segments you listed are congruent.

LESSON LAB

Use With Lesson 12-8

Review of Transformations

G.CO.6 Use geometric descriptions of rigid motions to transform figures . . .

Recall that a transformation of a geometric figure is a function, or *mapping*, that results in a change in the position, shape, or size of the figure. The original figure is called the *preimage* and the result of the transformation is the *image*. A special kind of transformation that preserves distance is a *rigid motion*, or *isometry*. Translations, reflections, and rotations are examples of rigid motions.

Example 1

What is a rule that describes the transformation that maps $\triangle ABC$ onto $\triangle A'B'C'$?

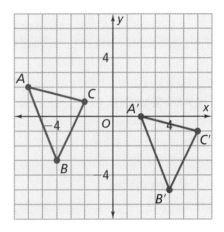

Find the vertices of the preimage $\triangle ABC$ and the image $\triangle A'B'C'$.

Preimage:		Image:	
$A(-6, 2)$		$A'(2, 0)$	
$B(-4, -3)$		$B'(4, -5)$	
$C(-2, 1)$		$C'(6, -1)$	

If you add 8 to each x-coordinate of the preimage and subtract 2 from each y-coordinate, the results are of the vertices of the image. This is an example of a translation. A translation is a transformation that maps all points of a figure the same distance in the same direction.

This translation is written using the function notation $T_{<8, -2>}(\triangle ABC) = \triangle A'B'C'$.

Example 2

What is a rule that describes the transformation that maps trapezoid *STUV* onto trapezoid $S'T'U'V'$?

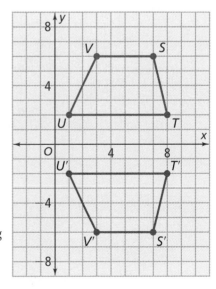

Find the vertices of the preimage *STUV* and the image $S'T'U'V'$.

Preimage:		Image:	
$S(7, 6)$		$S'(7, -6)$	
$T(8, 2)$		$T'(8, -2)$	
$U(1, 2)$		$U'(1, -2)$	
$V(3, 6)$		$V'(3, -6)$	

The vertices of the preimage and image have the same x-coordinates and opposite y-coordinates. Each vertex of the preimage is the same distance from the x-axis as the corresponding vertex of the image. This is an example of a reflection.

This reflection is written using function notation as $R_{x\text{-axis}}(STUV) = S'T'U'V'$.

Example 3

What is a rule that describes the transformation that maps △MNP onto △M′N′P′?

Find the vertices of the preimage △MNP and the image △M′N′P′.

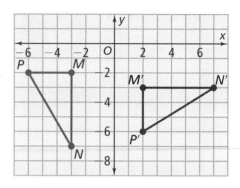

Preimage:	$M(-3, -2)$	Image:	$M'(2, -3)$
	$N(-3, -7)$		$N'(7, -3)$
	$P(-6, -2)$		$P'(2, -6)$

Each vertex (x, y) of the preimage is mapped to $(-y, x)$. Notice that the distance from the origin to each vertex of the preimage and each corresponding vertex of the image is the same. △MNP has been *turned* about the origin to form △M′N′P′. A rotation is a transformation that turns the preimage about a fixed point, called the center of rotation, to form the image.

In this Example, △MNP has been rotated 90° counterclockwise about the origin to form △M′N′P′. This rotation is written using function notation as $r_{(90°,O)}(\triangle MNP) = \triangle M'N'P'$.

Exercises

What is a rule that describes the transformation from each preimage onto each image?

1.

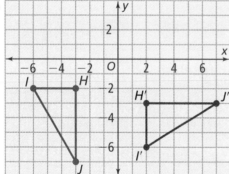

2.

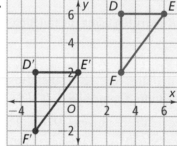

Sketch each preimage and image.

3. $\triangle ABC$ has vertices $A(3, -6)$, $B(1, 0)$, $C(5, 2)$;
$T_{<-5, 4>}(\triangle ABC)$

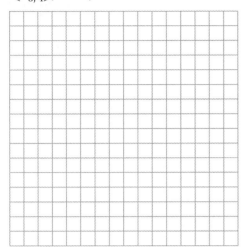

4. $\triangle DEF$ has vertices $D(-7, 2)$, $E(-2, 5)$,
$F(-3, -3)$; $R_{y\text{-axis}}(\triangle DEF)$

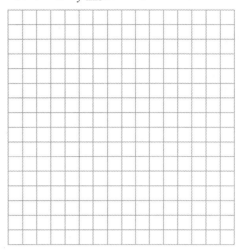

5. $\triangle GHI$ has vertices $G(2, -4)$, $H(4, -3)$, $I(7, -6)$; $r_{(270°, O)}(\triangle GHI)$

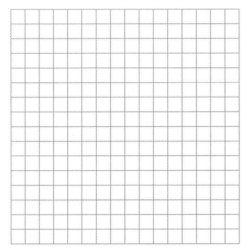

6. Recall that you can write the composition of rigid motions that describes a translation of quadrilateral $GHJK$ 2 units left and 3 units up, followed by a reflection across the x-axis as $(R_{x\text{-axis}} \circ T_{<-2,3>})(GHJK)$. $GHJK$ has vertices $G(0, 2)$, $H(1, -1)$, $J(3, -3)$, and $K(3, 1)$. Sketch $GHJK$ and $(R_{x\text{-axis}} \circ T_{<-2,3>})(GHJK)$.

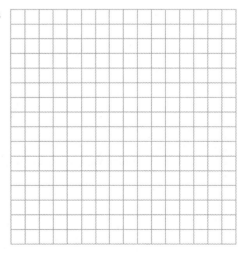

12-8 Congruence Transformations

G.CO.7 Use the definition of congruence in terms of rigid motions to show that two triangles are congruent . . . Also **G.CO.6, G.CO.8**

Objectives To identify congruence transformations
To prove triangle congruence using isometries

Solve It! Write your solution to the Solve It in the space below.

In the Solve It, you may have used the properties of rigid motions to describe why the wings are identical.

Essential Understanding You can use compositions of rigid motions to understand congruence.

Problem 1 Identifying Equal Measures

Got It? The composition $(R_t \circ T_{<2,\, 3>})(\triangle ABC) = \triangle XYZ$. List all of the pairs of angles and sides with equal measures.

Practice **1.** The composition $(r_{(180°,O)} \circ T_{<-4,\,-6>})(\triangle HJK) = \triangle PRS$. List all of the pairs of angles and sides with equal measures.

In Problem 1 you saw that compositions of rigid motions preserve corresponding side lengths and angle measures. This suggests another way to define congruence.

take note

Key Concept   Congruent Figures

Two figures are **congruent** if and only if there is a sequence of one or more rigid motions that maps one figure onto the other.

Problem 2   **Identifying Congruent Figures**

Got It?   Which pairs of figures in the grid are congruent? For each pair, what is a sequence of rigid motions that maps one figure to the other?

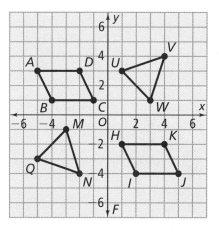

Practice   For each coordinate grid, identify a pair of congruent figures. Then determine a congruence transformation that maps the preimage to the congruent image.

2.

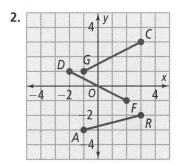

3.

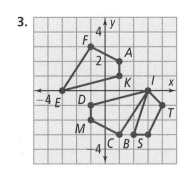

Because compositions of rigid motions take figures to congruent figures, they are also called **congruence transformations**.

Problem 3 Identifying Congruence Transformations

Think

What does the orientation of the triangles tell you?

Got It? What is a congruence transformation that maps △NAV to △BCY?

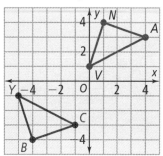

Practice In Exercises 4 and 5, find a congruence transformation that maps △LMN to △RST.

4.

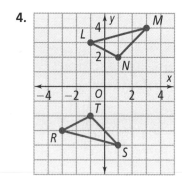

5.

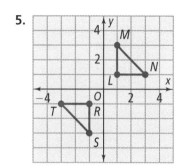

Earlier in this chapter, you studied triangle congruence postulates and theorems. You can use congruence transformations to justify criteria for determining triangle congruence.

Problem 4 **Verifying the SAS Postulate**

Think

How do you show that the two triangles are congruent?

Got It? Verify the SSS postulate.

Given: $\overline{TD} = \overline{EN}$, $\overline{YT} = \overline{SE}$, $\overline{YD} = \overline{SN}$
Prove: $\triangle YDT \cong \triangle SNE$

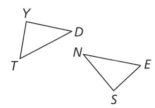

Ⓐ Practice 6. Verify the ASA Postulate for triangle congruence by using congruence
Proof transformations.

Given: $\overline{EK} \cong \overline{LH}$
$\angle E \cong \angle H$
$\angle K \cong \angle L$

Prove: $\triangle EKS \cong \triangle HLA$

Proof 7. Verify the AAS Postulate for triangle congruence by using congruence transformations.

Given: $\angle I \cong \angle V$
$\angle C \cong \angle N$
$\overline{QC} \cong \overline{NZ}$

Prove: $\triangle NVZ \cong \triangle CIQ$

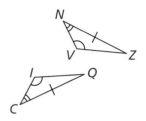

In Problem 4, you used the transformational approach to prove triangle congruence. Because this approach is more general, you can use what you know about congruence transformations to determine whether any two figures are congruent.

Problem 5 **Determining Congruence**

Got It? Are the figures shown at the right congruent? Explain.

Practice In Exercises 8 and 9, determine whether the figures are congruent. If so, describe a congruence transformation that maps one to the other. If not, explain.

8.

9.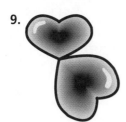

 Lesson Check

Do you know HOW?

Use the graph for Exercises 10 and 11.

10. Identify a pair of congruent figures and write a congruence statement.

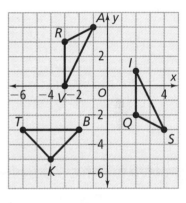

11. What is a congruence transformation that relates two congruent figures?

Do you UNDERSTAND?

 MATHEMATICAL PRACTICES

12. How can the definition of congruence in terms of rigid motions be more useful than a definition of congruence that relies on corresponding angles and sides?

13. Reasoning Is a composition of a rotation followed by a glide reflection a congruence transformation? Explain.

14. Open-Ended What is an example of a board game in which a game piece is moved by using a congruence transformation?

More Practice and Problem-Solving Exercises

B Apply

Construction The figure at the right shows a roof truss of a new building. Identify an isometry or composition of isometries to justify each of the following statements.

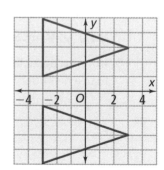

15. Triangle 1 is congruent to triangle 3.

16. Triangle 1 is congruent to triangle 4.

17. Triangle 2 is congruent to triangle 5.

18. Vocabulary If two figures are ___?___, then there is an isometry that maps one figure onto the other.

19. Think About a Plan The figure at the right shows two congruent, isosceles triangles. What are four different isometries that map the top triangle onto the bottom triangle?
- How can you use the three basic rigid motions to map the top triangle onto the bottom triangle?
- What other isometries can you use?

20. **Graphic Design** Most companies have a logo that is used on company letterhead and signs. A graphic designer sketched the logo at the right. What congruence transformations might she have used to draw this logo?

21. **Art** Artists frequently use congruence transformations in their work. The artworks shown below are called *tessellations*. What types of congruence transformations can you identify in the tessellations?

a.

b.

22. In the footprints shown below, what congruence transformations can you use to extend the footsteps?

Proof 23. Prove the statements in parts (a) and (b) to show congruence in terms of transformations is equivalent to the criteria for triangle congruence you learned earlier in this chapter.

a. If there is a congruence transformation that maps $\triangle ABC$ to $\triangle DEF$ then corresponding pairs of sides and corresponding pairs of angles are congruent.

b. In $\triangle ABC$ and $\triangle DEF$, if corresponding pairs of sides and corresponding pairs of angles are congruent, then there is a congruence transformation that maps $\triangle ABC$ to $\triangle DEF$.

24. **Baking** Cookie makers often use a cookie press so that the cookies all look the same. The baker fills a cookie sheet for baking in the pattern shown. What types of congruence transformations are being used to set each cookie on the sheet?

Proof 25. Use congruence transformations to prove the Isosceles Triangle Theorem.
Given: $\overline{FG} \cong \overline{FH}$
Prove: $\angle G \cong \angle H$

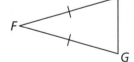

© **Challenge**

26. **Reasoning** You project an image for viewing in a large classroom. Is the projection of the image an example of a congruence transformation? Explain your reasoning.

12-1 Congruent Figures

Quick Review

Congruent polygons have congruent corresponding parts. When you name congruent polygons, always list corresponding vertices in the same order.

Example

HIJK ≅ *PQRS*. Write all possible congruence statements.

The order of the parts in the congruence statement tells you which parts correspond.

Sides: $\overline{HI} \cong \overline{PQ}$, $\overline{IJ} \cong \overline{QR}$, $\overline{JK} \cong \overline{RS}$, $\overline{KH} \cong \overline{SP}$

Angles: $\angle H \cong \angle P$, $\angle I \cong \angle Q$, $\angle J \cong \angle R$, $\angle K \cong \angle S$

Exercises

RSTUV ≅ *KLMNO*. Complete the congruence statements.

1. $\overline{TS} \cong$ __?__   **2.** $\angle N \cong$ __?__

3. $\overline{LM} \cong$ __?__   **4.** *VUTSR* ≅ __?__

WXYZ ≅ *PQRS*. Find each measure or length.

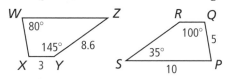

5. $m\angle P$ **6.** QR **7.** WX

8. $m\angle Z$ **9.** $m\angle X$ **10.** $m\angle R$

12-2 and 12-3 Triangle Congruence by SSS, SAS, ASA, and AAS

Quick Review

You can prove triangles congruent with limited information about their congruent sides and angles.

Postulate or Theorem	You Need
Side-Side-Side (SSS)	three sides
Side-Angle-Side (SAS)	two sides and an included angle
Angle-Side-Angle (ASA)	two angles and an included side
Angle-Angle-Side (AAS)	two angles and a nonincluded side

Example

What postulate would you use to prove the triangles congruent?

You know that three pairs of sides are congruent. Use SSS.

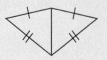

Exercises

11. In △*HFD*, what angle is included between $\overline{DH}$ and $\overline{DF}$?

12. In △*OMR*, what side is included between $\angle M$ and $\angle R$?

Which postulate or theorem, if any, could you use to prove the two triangles congruent? If there is not enough information to prove the triangles congruent, write *not enough information*.

13.   **14.**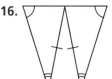

15.    **16.**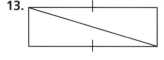

12-4 Using Corresponding Parts of Congruent Triangles

Quick Review

Once you know that triangles are congruent, you can make conclusions about corresponding sides and angles because, by definition, corresponding parts of congruent triangles are congruent. You can use congruent triangles in the proofs of many theorems.

Example

How can you use congruent triangles to prove $\angle Q \cong \angle D$?

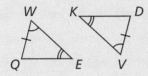

Since $\triangle QWE \cong \triangle DVK$ by AAS, you know that $\angle Q \cong \angle D$ because corresponding parts of congruent triangles are congruent.

Exercises

How can you use congruent triangles to prove the statement true?

17. $\overline{TV} \cong \overline{YW}$

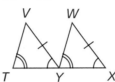

18. $\overline{BE} \cong \overline{DE}$

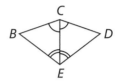

19. $\angle B \cong \angle D$

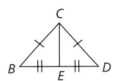

20. $\overline{KN} \cong \overline{ML}$

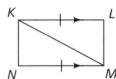

12-5 Isosceles and Equilateral Triangles

Quick Review

If two sides of a triangle are congruent, then the angles opposite those sides are also congruent by the **Isosceles Triangle Theorem.** If two angles of a triangle are congruent, then the sides opposite the angle are congruent by the **Converse of the Isosceles Triangle Theorem.**

Equilateral triangles are also equiangular.

Example

What is $m\angle G$?

Since $\overline{EF} \cong \overline{EG}$, $\angle F \cong \angle G$ by the Isosceles Triangle Theorem. So $m\angle G = 30$.

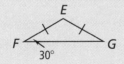

Exercises

Algebra Find the values of x and y.

21.

22.

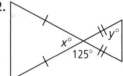

23.

24.

12-6 Congruence in Right Triangles

Quick Review

If the hypotenuse and a leg of one right triangle are congruent to the hypotenuse and a leg of another right triangle, then the triangles are congruent by the **Hypotenuse-Leg (HL) Theorem.**

Example

Which two triangles are congruent? Explain.

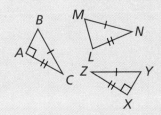

Since $\triangle ABC$ and $\triangle XYZ$ are right triangles with congruent legs, and $\overline{BC} \cong \overline{YZ}$, $\triangle ABC \cong \triangle XYZ$ by HL.

Exercises

Write a proof for each of the following.

25. Given: $\overline{LN} \perp \overline{KM}, \overline{KL} \cong \overline{ML}$

    Prove: $\triangle KLN \cong \triangle MLN$

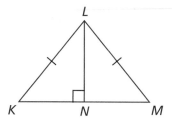

26. Given: $\overline{PS} \perp \overline{SQ}, \overline{RQ} \perp \overline{QS},$
              $\overline{PQ} \cong \overline{RS}$

    Prove: $\triangle PSQ \cong \triangle RQS$

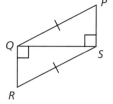

12-7 Congruence in Overlapping Triangles

Quick Review

To prove overlapping triangles congruent, you look for the common or shared sides and angles.

Example

Separate and redraw the overlapping triangles. Label the vertices.

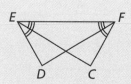

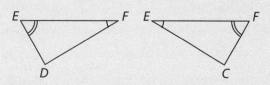

Exercises

Name a pair of overlapping congruent triangles in each diagram. State whether the triangles are congruent by SSS, SAS, ASA, AAS, or HL.

27.

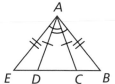

28.

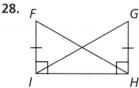

29.

12-8 Congruence Transformations

Quick Review

Two figures are congruent if and only if there is a sequence of rigid motions that maps one figure onto the other.

Example

$R_{y\text{-axis}} (TGMB) = KWAV$. What are all of the congruent angles and all of the congruent sides?

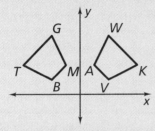

A reflection is a congruence transformation, so $TGMB \cong KWAV$, and corresponding angles and corresponding sides are congruent.

$\angle T \cong \angle K$, $\angle G \cong \angle W$, $\angle M \cong \angle A$, and $\angle B \cong \angle V$
$TG = KW$, $GM = WA$, $MB = AV$, and $TB = KV$

Exercises

30. In the diagram below, $\triangle LMN \cong \triangle XYZ$. Identify a congruence transformation that maps $\triangle LMN$ onto $\triangle XYZ$.

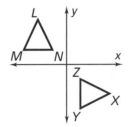

31. Fonts Graphic designers use some fonts because they have pleasing proportions or are easy to read from far away. The letters p and d above are used on a sign using a special font. Are the letters congruent? If so, describe a congruence transformation that maps one onto the other. If not, explain why not.

Pull It **All Together**

Applying Indirect Measurement

ASSESSMENT

Jamal wants to estimate the distance across a canyon, shown below. He locates a tree directly opposite his position at point *Y* and labels it point *X*. He then walks west along the canyon 500 feet and marks point *A*. After walking another 500 feet in the same direction, he turns 90° and walks south, perpendicular to the canyon. He stops when his location appears to form a straight line with points *A* and *X*. He measures the distance *BC* as 327 feet.

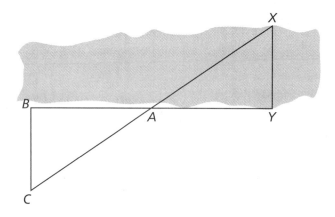

Task Description

Label the diagram above using the information given. Then estimate the distance across the canyon. Justify your answer.

- What part of the diagram represents the distance across the canyon?

- How are triangles *ABC* and *AYX* related?

Get Ready!

Basic Constructions

Use a compass and straightedge for each construction.

1. Construct the perpendicular bisector of a segment.

2. Construct the bisector of an angle.

The Midpoint Formula and Distance Formula

Find the coordinates of the midpoints of the sides of $\triangle ABC$. Then find the lengths of the three sides of the triangle.

3. $A(5, 1), B(-3, 3), C(1, -7)$

4. $A(-1, 2), B(9, 2), C(-1, 8)$

5. $A(-2, -3), B(2, -3), C(0, 3)$

Finding the Negation

Write the negation of each statement.

6. The team won.

7. It is not too late.

8. $m\angle R > 60$

Slope

Find the slope of the line passing through the given points.

9. $A(9, 6), B(8, 12)$

10. $C(3, -2), D(0, 6)$

11. $E(-3, 7), F(-3, 12)$

 Looking Ahead Vocabulary

12. The *distance* between your home and your school is the length of the shortest path connecting them. How might you define the *distance between a point and a line* in geometry?

13. Consider the *midpoint* of a segment. What do you think a *midsegment* of a triangle is?

14. If two parties are happening at the same time, they are *concurrent*. What would it mean for three lines to be *concurrent*?

CHAPTER 13

Proving Theorems About Triangles

Big Ideas

1 Coordinate Geometry
Essential Question How do you use coordinate geometry to find relationships within triangles?

2 Measurement
Essential Question How do you solve problems that involve measurements of triangles?

3 Reasoning and Proof
Essential Question How do you write indirect proofs?

ⓒ Domains

- Congruence
- Similarity, Right Triangles, and Trigonometry
- Mathematical Practice: Construct viable arguments

Interactive Digital Path

Log in to **pearsonsuccessnet.com** and click on Interactive Digital Path to access the Solve Its and animated Problems.

Chapter Preview

Vocabulary

English/Spanish Vocabulary Audio Online:

English	Spanish
altitude of a triangle, *p. 813*	altura de un triángulo
centroid, *p. 811*	centroid
circumcenter, *p. 803*	circuncentro
concurrent, *p. 803*	concurrente
equidistant, *p. 795*	equidistante
incenter, *p. 806*	incentro
indirect proof, *p. 820*	prueba indirecta
median, *p. 811*	mediana
midsegment of a triangle, *p. 787*	segmento medio de un triángulo
orthocenter, *p. 814*	ortocentro

G.CO.10 Prove theorems about triangles . . . the segment joining midpoints of two sides of a triangle is parallel to the third side and half the length . . . Also **G.SRT.5**

Objective   To use properties of midsegments to solve problems

Solve It!   Write your solution to the Solve It in the space below.

In the Solve It, $\overline{LN}$ is a midsegment of $\triangle ABC$. A **midsegment of a triangle** is a segment connecting the midpoints of two sides of the triangle.

Essential Understanding   There are two special relationships between a midsegment of a triangle and the third side of the triangle.

take note

Theorem 24   Triangle Midsegment Theorem

Theorem	If . . .	Then . . .
If a segment joins the midpoints of two sides of a triangle, then the segment is parallel to the third side and is half as long.	D is the midpoint of $\overline{CA}$ and E is the midpoint of $\overline{CB}$	$\overline{DE} \parallel \overline{AB}$ and $DE = \frac{1}{2}AB$

You will prove Theorem 24 in Lesson 14-8.

Here's Why It Works You can verify that the Triangle Midsegment Theorem works for a particular triangle. Use the following steps to show that $\overline{DE} \parallel \overline{AB}$ and that $DE = \frac{1}{2}AB$ for a triangle with vertices at $A(4, 6)$, $B(6, 0)$, and $C(0, 0)$, where D and E are the midpoints of $\overline{CA}$ and $\overline{CB}$.

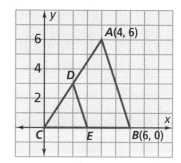

Step 1 Use the Midpoint Formula, $M = \left(\frac{x_1 + x_2}{2}, \frac{y_1 + y_2}{2}\right)$, to find the coordinates of D and E.

The midpoint of $\overline{CA}$ is $D\left(\frac{0 + 4}{2}, \frac{0 + 6}{2}\right) = D(2, 3)$.

The midpoint of $\overline{CB}$ is $E\left(\frac{0 + 6}{2}, \frac{0 + 0}{2}\right) = E(3, 0)$.

Step 2 To show that the midsegment $\overline{DE}$ is parallel to the side $\overline{AB}$, find the slope, $m = \frac{y_2 - y_1}{x_2 - x_1}$, of each segment.

slope of $\overline{DE} = \frac{0 - 3}{3 - 2}$ slope of $\overline{AB} = \frac{0 - 6}{6 - 4}$

$= \frac{-3}{1}$ $= \frac{-6}{2}$

$= -3$ $= -3$

The slopes of $\overline{DE}$ and $\overline{AB}$ are equal, so $\overline{DE}$ and $\overline{AB}$ are parallel.

Step 3 To show $DE = \frac{1}{2}AB$, use the Distance Formula, $d = \sqrt{(x_2 - x_1)^2 + (y_2 - y_1)^2}$, to find DE and AB.

$DE = \sqrt{(3 - 2)^2 + (0 - 3)^2}$ $AB = \sqrt{(6 - 4)^2 + (0 - 6)^2}$

$= \sqrt{1 + 9}$ $= \sqrt{4 + 36}$

$= \sqrt{10}$ $= \sqrt{40}$

             $= 2\sqrt{10}$

Since $\sqrt{10} = \frac{1}{2}(2\sqrt{10})$, you know that $DE = \frac{1}{2}AB$.

Problem 1   **Identifying Parallel Segments**

Got It?   **a.** In $\triangle XYZ$, A is the midpoint of $\overline{XY}$, B is the midpoint of $\overline{YZ}$, and C is the midpoint of $\overline{ZX}$. What are the three pairs of parallel segments?

b. Reasoning What is $m\angle VUO$ in the figure below? Explain your reasoning.

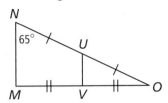

Think

What is the relationship between the 65° angle and $\angle VUO$?

Practice   1. Identify three pairs of parallel segments in the diagram.

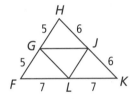

2. Name the segment that is parallel to $\overline{GE}$.

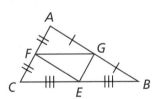

Problem 2 **Finding Lengths**

Got It? In the figure at the right, $AD = 6$ and $DE = 7.5$.
What are the lengths of $\overline{DC}$, $\overline{AC}$, $\overline{EF}$, and $\overline{AB}$?

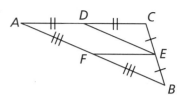

 Practice Algebra Find the value of x.

3.

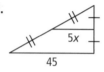

4.

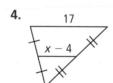

You can use the Triangle Midsegment Theorem to find lengths of segments that might be difficult to measure directly.

Problem 3 Using a Midsegment of a Triangle

Got It? $\overline{CD}$ is a bridge being built over a lake, as shown in the figure below. What is the length of the bridge?

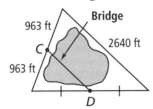

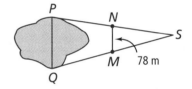

Think
Which theorem will help you solve this problem?

A Practice 5. **Surveying** A surveyor needs to measure the distance PQ across the lake. Beginning at point S, she locates the midpoints of $\overline{SQ}$ and $\overline{SP}$ at M and N. She then measures $\overline{NM}$. What is PQ?

 Lesson Check

Do you know HOW?

Use the figure at the right for Exercises 6–8.

6. Which segment is parallel to $\overline{JK}$?

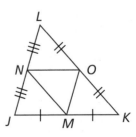

7. If $LK = 46$, what is NM?

8. If $JK = 5x + 20$ and $NO = 20$, what is the value of x?

Do you UNDERSTAND?

9. Vocabulary How does the term *midsegment* describe the segments discussed in this lesson?

10. Reasoning If two noncollinear segments in the coordinate plane have slope 3, what can you conclude?

11. Error Analysis A student sees this figure and concludes that $\overline{PL} \parallel \overline{NO}$. What is the error in the student's reasoning?

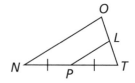

More Practice and Problem-Solving Exercises

B Apply

12. **Kayaking** You want to paddle your kayak across a lake. To determine how far you must paddle, you pace out a triangle, counting the number of strides, as shown.
    a. If your strides average 3.5 ft, what is the length of the longest side of the triangle?
    b. What distance must you paddle across the lake?

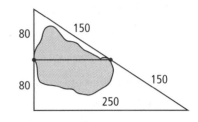

13. **Architecture** The triangular face of the Rock and Roll Hall of Fame in Cleveland, Ohio, is isosceles. The length of the base is 229 ft 6 in. Each leg is divided into four congruent parts by the red segments. What is the length of the white segment? Explain your reasoning.

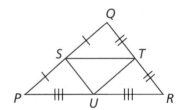

14. **Think About a Plan** Draw △ABC. Construct another triangle so that the three sides of △ABC are the midsegments of the new triangle.
    • Can you visualize or sketch the final figure?
    • Which segments in your final construction will be parallel?

15. **Writing** In the figure at the right, $m\angle QST = 40$. What is $m\angle QPR$? Explain how you know.

16. **Coordinate Geometry** The coordinates of the vertices of a triangle are $E(1, 2)$, $F(5, 6)$, and $G(3, -2)$.
    a. Find the coordinates of H, the midpoint of $\overline{EG}$, and J, the midpoint of $\overline{FG}$.
    b. Show that $\overline{HJ} \parallel \overline{EF}$.
    c. Show that $HJ = \frac{1}{2}EF$.

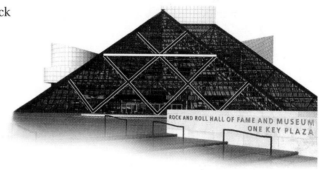

X is the midpoint of $\overline{UV}$. Y is the midpoint of $\overline{UW}$.

17. If $m\angle UXY = 60$, find $m\angle V$.

18. If $m\angle W = 45$, find $m\angle UYX$.

19. If $XY = 50$, find VW.

20. If $VW = 110$, find XY.

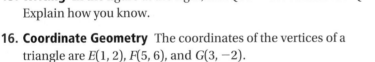

$\overline{IJ}$ is a midsegment of △FGH. $IJ = 7$, $FH = 10$, and $GH = 13$. Find the perimeter of each triangle.

21. △IJH

22. △FGH

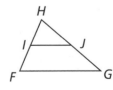

23. **Kite Design** You design a kite to look like the one at the right. Its diagonals measure 64 cm and 90 cm. You plan to use ribbon, represented by the rectangle, to connect the midpoints of its sides. How much ribbon do you need?

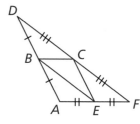

  (A) 77 cm

  (B) 122 cm

  (C) 154 cm

  (D) 308 cm

Algebra Find the value of each variable.

24.

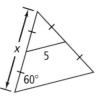

25.

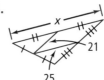

26.

27.

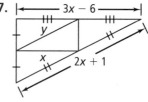

Use the figure at the right for Exercises 28–30.

28. $DF = 24$, $BC = 6$, and $DB = 8$. Find the perimeter of $\triangle ADF$.

29. **Algebra** If $BE = 2x + 6$ and $DF = 5x + 9$, find DF.

30. **Algebra** If $EC = 3x - 1$ and $AD = 5x + 7$, find EC.

© 31. **Open-Ended** Explain how you could use the Triangle Midsegment Theorem as the basis for this construction: Draw $\overline{CD}$. Draw point A not on $\overline{CD}$. Construct $\overline{AB}$ so that $\overline{AB} \parallel \overline{CD}$ and $AB = \frac{1}{2}CD$.

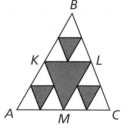

© **Challenge**

© 32. **Reasoning** In the diagram at the right, K, L, and M are the midpoints of the sides of $\triangle ABC$. The vertices of the three small red triangles are the midpoints of the sides of $\triangle KBL$, $\triangle AKM$, and $\triangle MLC$. The perimeter of $\triangle ABC$ is 24 cm. What is the perimeter of the shaded region?

33. **Coordinate Geometry** In $\triangle GHJ$, $K(2, 3)$ is the midpoint of $\overline{GH}$, $L(4, 1)$ is the midpoint of $\overline{HJ}$, and $M(6, 2)$ is the midpoint of $\overline{GJ}$. Find the coordinates of G, H, and J.

Proof 34. Complete the Prove statement and then write a proof.

  Given: In $\triangle VYZ$, S, T, and U are midpoints.

  Prove: $\triangle YST \cong \triangle TUZ \cong \triangle SVU \cong$ __?__

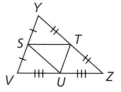

13-2 Perpendicular and Angle Bisectors

G.CO.9 Prove theorems about lines and angles . . . points on a perpendicular bisector of a line segment are exactly those equidistant from the segment's endpoints. Also **G.CO.12, G.SRT.5**

Objective To use properties of perpendicular bisectors and angle bisectors

 Solve It! Write your solution to the Solve It in the space below.

In the Solve It, you thought about the relationships that must exist in order for a bulletin board to hang straight. You will explore these relationships in this lesson.

Essential Understanding There is a special relationship between the points on the perpendicular bisector of a segment and the endpoints of the segment.

In the diagram below, $\overleftrightarrow{CD}$ is the perpendicular bisector of $\overline{AB}$. $\overleftrightarrow{CD}$ is perpendicular to $\overline{AB}$ at its midpoint. In the diagram on the right, $\overline{CA}$ and $\overline{CB}$ are drawn to complete $\triangle CAD$ and $\triangle CBD$.

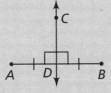 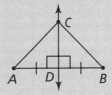

You should recognize from your work in Chapter 12 that $\triangle CAD \cong \triangle CBD$. So you can conclude that $\overline{CA} \cong \overline{CB}$, or that $CA = CB$. A point is **equidistant** from two objects if it is the same distance from the objects. So point C is equidistant from points A and B.

This suggests a proof of Theorem 25, the Perpendicular Bisector Theorem. Its converse is also true and is stated as Theorem 26.

Theorem 25 Perpendicular Bisector Theorem

Theorem

If a point is on the perpendicular bisector of a segment, then it is equidistant from the endpoints of the segment.

If . . .

$\overleftrightarrow{PM} \perp \overline{AB}$ and $MA = MB$

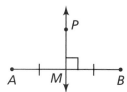

Then . . .

$PA = PB$

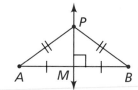

You will prove Theorem 25 in Exercise 26.

Theorem 26 Converse of the Perpendicular Bisector Theorem

Theorem

If a point is equidistant from the endpoints of a segment, then it is on the perpendicular bisector of the segment.

If . . .

$PA = PB$

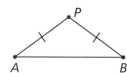

Then . . .

$\overleftrightarrow{PM} \perp \overline{AB}$ and $MA = MB$

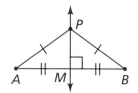

You will prove Theorem 26 in Exercise 27.

Problem 1 Using the Perpendicular Bisector Theorem

Got It? What is the length of $\overline{QR}$?

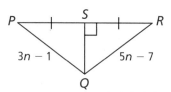

Ⓐ **Practice** Use the figure at the right for Exercises 1 and 2.

1. What is the relationship between $\overline{MB}$ and $\overline{JK}$?

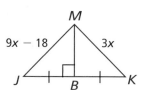

2. Find JM.

Problem 2 **Using a Perpendicular Bisector**

Got It? **a.** Suppose the director from Problem 2 wants the T-shirt stand to be equidistant from the paddle boats and the Spaceship Shoot. What are the possible locations?

Plan

How do you find points that are equidistant from two given points?

© **b. Reasoning** Can you place the T-shirt stand so that it is equidistant from the paddle boats, the Spaceship Shoot, and the Rollin' Coaster? Explain.

ⒶPractice **3. Reading Maps** Use the map of a part of Manhattan. Is St. Vincent's Hospital equidistant from Village Kids Nursery School and Legacy School? How do you know?

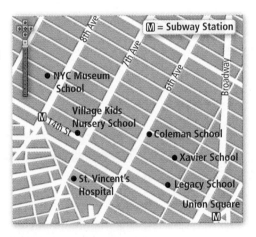

© **4. Writing** On a piece of paper, mark a point *H* for home and a point *S* for school. Describe how to find the set of points equidistant from *H* and *S*.

Essential Understanding There is a special relationship between the points on the bisector of an angle and the sides of the angle.

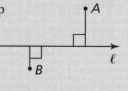

The **distance from a point to a line** is the length of the perpendicular segment from the point to the line. This distance is also the length of the shortest segment from the point to the line. You will prove this in Lesson 13-6. In the figure at the right, the distances from A to ℓ and from B to ℓ are represented by the red segments.

In the diagram, $\overrightarrow{AD}$ is the bisector of $\angle CAB$. If you measure the lengths of the perpendicular segments from D to the two sides of the angle, you will find that the lengths are equal. Point D is equidistant from the sides of the angle.

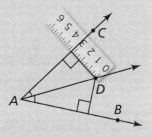

take note

Theorem 27 Angle Bisector Theorem

Theorem

If a point is on the bisector of an angle, then the point is equidistant from the sides of the angle.

If . . .

$\overrightarrow{QS}$ bisects $\angle PQR$, $\overline{SP} \perp \overrightarrow{QP}$, and $\overline{SR} \perp \overrightarrow{QR}$

Then . . .

$SP = SR$

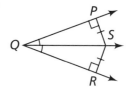

You will prove Theorem 27 in Exercise 28.

Theorem 28 Converse of the Angle Bisector Theorem

Theorem

If a point in the interior of an angle is equidistant from the sides of the angle, then the point is on the angle bisector.

If . . .

$\overline{SP} \perp \overrightarrow{QP}$, $\overline{SR} \perp \overrightarrow{QR}$, and $SP = SR$

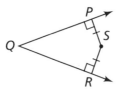

Then . . .

$\overrightarrow{QS}$ bisects $\angle PQR$

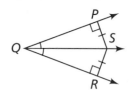

You will prove Theorem 28 in Exercise 29.

Problem 3 **Using the Angle Bisector Theorem**

Got It? What is the length of $\overline{FB}$?

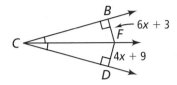

Think

How can you use the expression for **FD** to check your answer?

Ⓐ **Practice** **5.** Find $m\angle KHL$ and $m\angle FHL$.

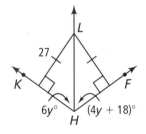

6. Algebra Find x, JK, and JM.

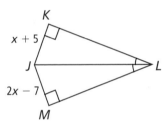

Lesson Check

Do you know HOW?

Use the figure at the right for Exercises 7–9.

7. What is the relationship between $\overline{AC}$ and $\overline{BD}$?

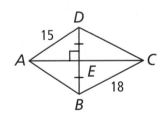

8. What is the length of $\overline{AB}$?

9. What is the length of $\overline{DC}$?

Do you UNDERSTAND?

10. Vocabulary Draw a line and a point not on the line. Draw the segment that represents the distance from the point to the line.

11. Writing Point P is in the interior of $\angle LOX$. Describe how you can determine whether P is on the bisector of $\angle LOX$ without drawing the angle bisector.

More Practice and Problem-Solving Exercises

MATHEMATICAL
PRACTICES

ⓑ Apply

Algebra Use the figure at the right for Exercises 12–16.

12. Find the value of x.

13. Find TW.

14. Find WZ.

15. What kind of triangle is $\triangle TWZ$? Explain.

16. If R is on the perpendicular bisector of $\overline{TZ}$, then R is ____?____ from T and Z, or ____?____ = ____?____.

Ⓒ **17. Think About a Plan** In the diagram at the right, the soccer goalie will prepare for a shot from the player at point P by moving out to a point on $\overline{XY}$. To have the best chance of stopping the ball, should the goalie stand at the point on $\overline{XY}$ that lies on the perpendicular bisector of $\overline{GL}$ or at the point on $\overline{XY}$ that lies on the bisector of $\angle GPL$? Explain your reasoning.

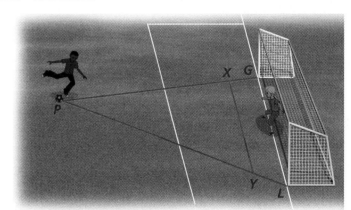

* How can you draw a diagram to help?
* Would the goalie want to be the same distance from G and L or from $\overline{PG}$ and $\overline{PL}$?

Ⓒ **18. a. Constructions** Draw $\angle CDE$. Construct the angle bisector of the angle.
   b. Reasoning Use the converse of the Angle Bisector Theorem to justify your construction.

Ⓒ **19. a. Constructions** Draw $\overline{QR}$. Construct the perpendicular bisector of $\overline{QR}$ to construct $\triangle PQR$.
   b. Reasoning Use the Perpendicular Bisector Theorem to justify that your construction is an isosceles triangle.

20. Write Theorems 25 and 26 as a single biconditional statement.

21. Write Theorems 27 and 28 as a single biconditional statement.

Ⓒ **22. Error Analysis** To prove that $\triangle PQR$ is isosceles, a student began by stating that since Q is on the segment perpendicular to $\overline{PR}$, Q is equidistant from the endpoints of $\overline{PR}$. What is the error in the student's reasoning?

Ⓔ Writing Determine whether A must be on the bisector of $\angle TXR$. Explain.

23.
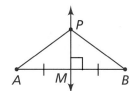

24.
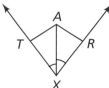

25.
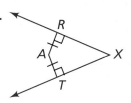

Proof 26. Prove the Perpendicular Bisector Theorem.

    Given: $\overleftrightarrow{PM} \perp \overline{AB}$, $\overleftrightarrow{PM}$ bisects $\overline{AB}$

    Prove: $AP = BP$

Proof 27. Prove the Converse of the Perpendicular Bisector Theorem.

    Given: $PA = PB$, with $\overline{PM} \perp \overline{AB}$ at M.

    Prove: P is on the perpendicular bisector of $\overline{AB}$.

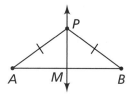

Proof 28. Prove the Angle Bisector Theorem.

    Given: $\overrightarrow{QS}$ bisects $\angle PQR$, $\overline{SP} \perp \overrightarrow{QP}$, $\overline{SR} \perp \overrightarrow{QR}$

    Prove: $SP = SR$

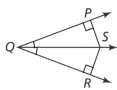

Proof 29. Prove the Converse of the Angle Bisector Theorem.

    Given: $\overline{SP} \perp \overrightarrow{QP}$, $\overline{SR} \perp \overrightarrow{QR}$, $SP = SR$

    Prove: $\overrightarrow{QS}$ bisects $\angle PQR$.

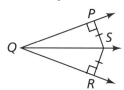

30. **Coordinate Geometry** Use points $A(6, 8)$, $O(0, 0)$, and $B(10, 0)$.
    a. Write equations of lines ℓ and m such that $\ell \perp \overleftrightarrow{OA}$ at A and $m \perp \overleftrightarrow{OB}$ at B.
    b. Find the intersection C of lines ℓ and m.
    c. Show that $CA = CB$.
    d. Explain why C is on the bisector of $\angle AOB$.

Ⓒ Challenge

31. A, B, and C are three noncollinear points. Describe and sketch a line in plane ABC such that points A, B, and C are equidistant from the line. Justify your response.

Ⓔ 32. **Reasoning** M is the intersection of the perpendicular bisectors of two sides of $\triangle ABC$. Line ℓ is perpendicular to plane ABC at M. Explain why a point E on ℓ is equidistant from A, B, and C. (*Hint:* See Lesson 10-1, Exercise 30. Explain why $\triangle EAM \cong \triangle EBM \cong \triangle ECM$.)

13-3 Bisectors in Triangles

G.CO.10 Prove theorems about triangles . . . Also **G.C.3**

Objective To identify properties of perpendicular bisectors and angle bisectors

 Solve It! Write your solution to the Solve It in the space below.

In the Solve It, the three lines you drew intersect at one point, the center of the circle. When three or more lines intersect at one point, they are **concurrent.** The point at which they intersect is the **point of concurrency.**

Essential Understanding For any triangle, certain sets of lines are always concurrent. Two of these sets of lines are the perpendicular bisectors of the triangle's three sides and the bisectors of the triangle's three angles.

take note

Theorem 29 Concurrency of Perpendicular Bisectors Theorem

Theorem

The perpendicular bisectors of the sides of a triangle are concurrent at a point equidistant from the vertices.

Diagram

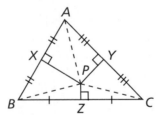

Symbols

Perpendicular bisectors $\overline{PX}$, $\overline{PY}$, and $\overline{PZ}$ are concurrent at P.

$PA = PB = PC$

The point of concurrency of the perpendicular bisectors of a triangle is called the **circumcenter of the triangle.**

Since the circumcenter is equidistant from the vertices, you can use the circumcenter as the center of the circle that contains each vertex of the triangle. You say the circle is **circumscribed about** the triangle.

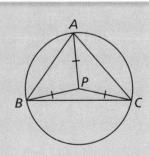

Proof **Proof of Theorem 29**

Given: Lines ℓ, m, and n are the perpendicular bisectors of the sides of $\triangle ABC$. P is the intersection of lines ℓ and m.

Prove: Line n contains point P, and $PA = PB = PC$.

Proof: A point on the perpendicular bisector of a segment is equidistant from the endpoints of the segment. Point P is on ℓ, which is the perpendicular bisector of $\overline{AB}$, so $PA = PB$. Using the same reasoning, since P is on m, and m is the perpendicular bisector of $\overline{BC}$, $PB = PC$. Thus, $PA = PC$ by the Transitive Property. Since $PA = PC$, P is equidistant from the endpoints of $\overline{AC}$. Then, by the Converse of the Perpendicular Bisector Theorem, P is on line n, the perpendicular bisector of $\overline{AC}$.

The circumcenter of a triangle can be inside, on, or outside a triangle.

Acute triangle

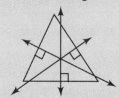

Right triangle

Obtuse triangle

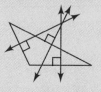

 **Problem 1** **Finding the Circumcenter of a Triangle**

Got It? What are the coordinates of the circumcenter of the triangle with vertices $A(2, 7)$, $B(10, 7)$, and $C(10, 3)$?

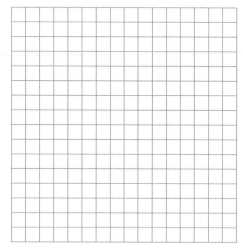

Ⓐ Practice   1. **Coordinate Geometry**   Find the coordinates of the circumcenter of the triangle.

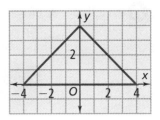

2. **Coordinate Geometry**   Find the coordinates of the circumcenter of the triangle with vertices $A(-4, 5)$, $B(-2, 5)$, and $C(-2, -2)$.

Problem 2   **Using a Circumcenter**

Got It?   In Problem 2, the town planner wants to place a bench equidistant from the three trees in the park. Where should he place the bench?

Think

How do you find a point equidistant from three points?

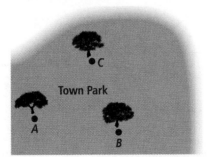

Town Park

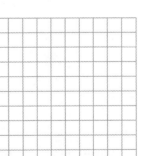

3. City Planning Show where town officials should place a recycling barrel so that it is equidistant from the lifeguard chair, the snack bar, and the volleyball court. Explain.

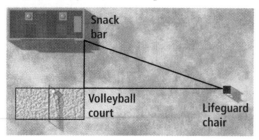

Theorem 30   Concurrency of Angle Bisectors Theorem

Theorem	Diagram	Symbols
The bisectors of the angles of a triangle are concurrent at a point equidistant from the sides of the triangle.	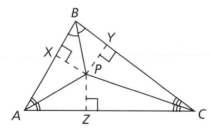	Angle bisectors $\overline{AP}$, $\overline{BP}$, and $\overline{CP}$ are concurrent at P. $PX = PY = PZ$ *You will prove Theorem 30 in Exercise 17.*

The point of concurrency of the angle bisectors of a triangle is called the **incenter of the triangle**. For any triangle, the incenter is always inside the triangle. In the diagram, points X, Y, and Z are equidistant from P, the incenter of $\triangle ABC$. P is the center of the circle that is **inscribed in** the triangle.

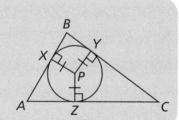

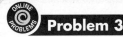

Problem 3 **Identifying and Using the Incenter of a Triangle**

Got It?   **a.** $QN = 5x + 36$ and $QM = 2x + 51$. What is QO?

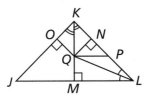

© **b. Reasoning** Is it possible for QP to equal 50? Explain.

 Practice   **4.** Name the point of concurrency of the angle bisectors.

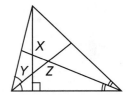

5. Find the value of x.

$RS = 4(x - 3) + 6$ and $RT = 5(2x - 6)$.

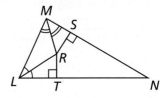

Lesson Check

Do you know HOW?

6. What are the coordinates of the circumcenter of the triangle at the right?

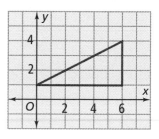

7. In the figure at the right, $TV = 3x - 12$ and $TU = 5x - 24$. What is the value of x?

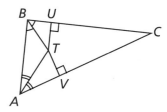

Do you UNDERSTAND?

MATHEMATICAL PRACTICES

© 8. Vocabulary A triangle's circumcenter is outside the triangle. What type of triangle is it?

© 9. Reasoning You want to find the circumcenter of a triangle. Why do you only need to find the intersection of two of the triangle's perpendicular bisectors, instead of all three?

10. Error Analysis Your friend sees the triangle at the right and concludes that $CT = CP$. What is the error in your friend's reasoning?

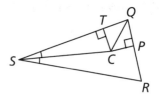

11. Compare and Contrast How are the circumcenter and incenter of a triangle alike? How are they different?

More Practice and Problem-Solving Exercises

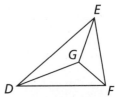

B Apply

12. Think About a Plan In the figure at the right, P is the incenter of isosceles $\triangle RST$. What type of triangle is $\triangle RPT$? Explain.
- What segments determine the incenter of a triangle?
- What do you know about the base angles of an isosceles triangle?

Constructions Draw a triangle that fits the given description. Then construct the inscribed circle and the circumscribed circle. Describe your method.

13. right triangle, $\triangle DEF$

14. obtuse triangle, $\triangle STU$

15. Algebra In the diagram at the right, G is the incenter of $\triangle DEF$, $m\angle DEF = 60$, and $m\angle EFD = 2 \cdot m\angle EDF$. What are $m\angle DGE$, $m\angle DGF$, and $m\angle EGF$?

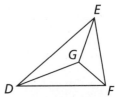

© 16. Writing Ivars found an old piece of paper inside an antique book.

It read,

From the spot I buried Olaf's treasure, equal sets of paces did I measure; each of three directions in a line, there to plant a seedling Norway pine. I could not return for failing health; now the hounds of Haiti guard my wealth. —*Karl*

After searching Caribbean islands for five years, Ivars found an island with three tall Norway pines. How might Ivars find where Karl buried Olaf's treasure?

Proof 17. Use the diagram at the right to prove the Concurrrency of Angle Bisectors Theorem.

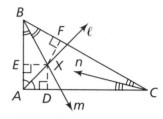

Given: Rays ℓ, m, and n are bisectors of the angles of $\triangle ABC$. X is the intersection of rays ℓ and m, $\overline{XD} \perp \overline{AC}$, $\overline{XE} \perp \overline{AB}$, and $\overline{XF} \perp \overline{BC}$.

Prove: Ray n contains point X, and $XD = XE = XF$.

18. Noise Control You are trying to talk to a friend on the phone in a busy bus station. The buses are so loud that you can hardly hear. Referring to the figure at the right, should you stand at P or C to be as far as possible from all the buses? Explain.

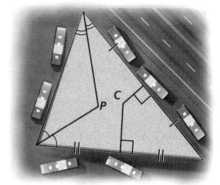

© Reasoning Determine whether each statement is *true* or *false*. If the statement is false, give a counterexample.

19. The incenter of a triangle is equidistant from all three vertices.

20. The incenter of a triangle always lies inside the triangle.

21. You can circumscribe a circle about any three points in a plane.

22. If point C is the circumcenter of $\triangle PQR$ and the circumcenter of $\triangle PQS$, then R and S must be the same point.

© Challenge

© 23. Reasoning Explain why the circumcenter of a right triangle is on one of the triangle's sides.

Determine whether each statement is *always*, *sometimes*, or *never* true. Explain.

24. It is possible to find a point equidistant from three parallel lines in a plane.

25. The circles inscribed in and circumscribed about an isosceles triangle have the same center.

13-4 Medians and Altitudes

G.CO.10 Prove theorems about triangles . . . the medians of a triangle meet at a point. Also **G.SRT.5**

Objective To identify properties of medians and altitudes of a triangle

 Solve It! Write your solution to the Solve It in the space below.

In the Solve It, the last set of segments you drew are the triangle's medians. A **median of a triangle** is a segment whose endpoints are a vertex and the midpoint of the opposite side.

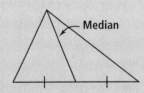

Essential Understanding A triangle's three medians are always concurrent.

take note Theorem 31 Concurrency of Medians Theorem

The medians of a triangle are concurrent at a point that is two thirds the distance from each vertex to the midpoint of the opposite side.

$$DC = \tfrac{2}{3}DJ \qquad EC = \tfrac{2}{3}EG \qquad FC = \tfrac{2}{3}FH$$

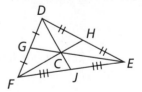

You will prove Theorem 31 in Lesson 14–8.

In a triangle, the point of concurrency of the medians is the **centroid of the triangle**. The point is also called the *center of gravity* of a triangle because it is the point where a triangular shape will balance. For any triangle, the centroid is always inside the triangle.

Problem 1   **Finding the Length of a Median**

Got It?   **a.** If $ZA = 9$, what is the length of $\overline{ZC}$?

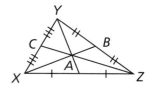

ⓒ b. Reasoning   What is the ratio of ZA to AC? Explain.

 Practice   In $\triangle TUV$, Y is the centroid.

     1. If $YU = 3.6$, find ZY and ZU.

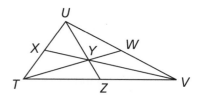

     2. If $VX = 9$, find VY and YX.

An **altitude of a triangle** is the perpendicular segment from a vertex of the triangle to the line containing the opposite side. An altitude of a triangle can be inside or outside the triangle, or it can be a side of the triangle.

Problem 2 Identifying Medians and Altitudes

Plan

How do you determine whether a segment is an altitude or a median?

Got It? For △ABC, is each segment a *median*, an *altitude*, or *neither*? Explain.

a. $\overline{AD}$

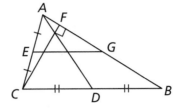

b. $\overline{EG}$

c. $\overline{CF}$

Practice For △ABC, is the red segment a *median*, an *altitude*, or *neither*? Explain.

3.

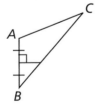

4.

take note

Theorem 32 Concurrency of Altitudes Theorem

The lines that contain the altitudes of a triangle are concurrent.

You will prove Theorem 32 in Lesson 14–8.

The lines that contain the altitudes of a triangle are concurrent at the **orthocenter of the triangle**. The orthocenter of a triangle can be inside, on, or outside the triangle.

Acute triangle   **Right triangle**   **Obtuse triangle**

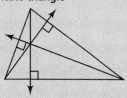 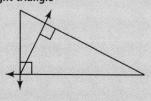 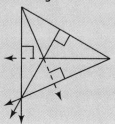

 Problem 3   **Finding the Orthocenter**

Got It? $\triangle DEF$ has vertices $D(1, 2)$, $E(1, 6)$, and $F(4, 2)$. What are the coordinates of the orthocenter of $\triangle DEF$?

Think

Which two altitudes of $\triangle DEF$ should you choose?

A **Practice**   **Coordinate Geometry**   In Exercises 5 and 6, find the coordinates of the orthocenter of $\triangle ABC$ with the given vertices.

5. $A(0, 0)$, $B(4, 0)$, and $C(4, 2)$

6. $A(0, -2)$, $B(4, -2)$, and $C(-2, -8)$

Concept Summary   Special Segments and Lines in Triangles

Perpendicular Bisectors   **Angle Bisectors**

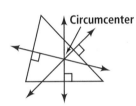
Circumcenter

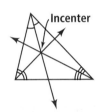
Incenter

Medians

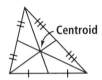
Centroid

Altitudes

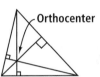
Orthocenter

Lesson Check

Do you know HOW?

Use $\triangle ABC$ for Exercises 7–10.

7. Is $\overline{AP}$ a *median* or an *altitude*?

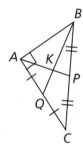

8. If $AP = 18$, what is KP?

9. If $BK = 15$, what is KQ?

10. Which two segments are altitudes?

Do you UNDERSTAND?

11. Error Analysis Your classmate says she drew $\overline{HJ}$ as an altitude of $\triangle ABC$. What error did she make?

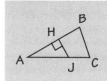

12. Reasoning Does it matter which two altitudes you use to locate the orthocenter of a triangle? Explain.

13. Reasoning The orthocenter of △ABC lies at vertex A. What can you conclude about $\overline{BA}$ and $\overline{AC}$? Explain.

More Practice and Problem-Solving Exercises

B Apply

Name the centroid.

14.

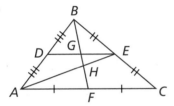

15.

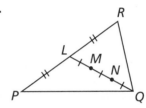

Name the orthocenter of △XYZ.

16.

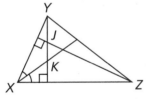

17.

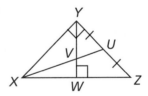

18. Think About a Plan In the diagram at the right, $\overline{QS}$ and $\overline{PT}$ are altitudes and $m\angle R = 55$. What is $m\angle POQ$?

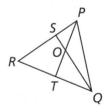

- What does it mean for a segment to be an altitude?
- What do you know about the sum of the angle measures in a triangle?
- How do you sketch overlapping triangles separately?

Constructions Draw a triangle that fits the given description. Then construct the centroid and the orthocenter.

19. acute scalene triangle, △LMN

20. obtuse isosceles triangle, △RST

In Exercises 21–24, name each segment.

21. a median in △ABC

22. an altitude in △ABC

23. a median in △BDC

24. an altitude in △AOC

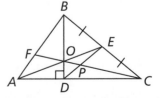

© **25. Reasoning** A centroid separates a median into two segments. What is the ratio of the length of the shorter segment to the length of the longer segment?

Paper Folding The figures below show how to construct altitudes and medians by paper folding. Refer to them for Exercises 26 and 27.

Folding an Altitude   **Folding a Median**

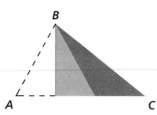 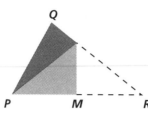 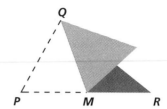

Fold the triangle so that a side $\overline{AC}$ overlaps itself and the fold contains the opposite vertex *B*.

Fold one vertex *R* to another vertex *P*. This locates the midpoint *M* of a side.

Unfold the triangle. Then fold it so that the fold contains the midpoint *M* and the opposite vertex *Q*.

26. Cut out a large triangle. Fold the paper carefully to construct the three medians of the triangle and demonstrate the Concurrency of Medians Theorem. Use a ruler to measure the length of each median and the distance of each vertex from the centroid.

27. Cut out a large acute triangle. Fold the paper carefully to construct the three altitudes of the triangle and demonstrate the Concurrency of Altitudes Theorem.

28. In the figure at the right, *C* is the centroid of $\triangle DEF$. If $GF = 12x^2 + 6y$, which expression represents *CF*?

Ⓐ $6x^2 + 3y$ Ⓒ $4x^2 + 2y$

Ⓑ $8x^2 + 4y$ Ⓓ $8x^2 + 3y$

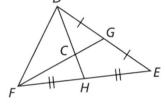

© **29. Reasoning** What type of triangle has its orthocenter on the exterior of the triangle? Draw a sketch to support your answer.

© **30. Writing** Explain why the median to the base of an isosceles triangle is also an altitude.

31. Coordinate Geometry $\triangle ABC$ has vertices $A(0, 0)$, $B(2, 6)$, and $C(8, 0)$. Complete the following steps to verify the Concurrency of Medians Theorem for $\triangle ABC$.
  a. Find the coordinates of midpoints *L*, *M*, and *N*.
  b. Find equations of $\overleftrightarrow{AM}$, $\overleftrightarrow{BN}$, and $\overleftrightarrow{CL}$.
  c. Find the coordinates of *P*, the intersection of $\overleftrightarrow{AM}$ and $\overleftrightarrow{BN}$. This point is the centroid.
  d. Show that point *P* is on $\overleftrightarrow{CL}$.
  e. Use the Distance Formula to show that point *P* is two-thirds of the distance from each vertex to the midpoint of the opposite side.

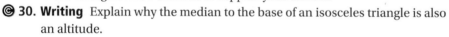
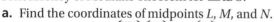
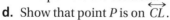

32. Constructions *A*, *B*, and *O* are three noncollinear points. Construct point *C* such that *O* is the orthocenter of △*ABC*. Describe your method.

© 33. Reasoning In an isosceles triangle, show that the circumcenter, incenter, centroid, and orthocenter can be four different points, but all four must be collinear.

A, B, C, and *D* are points of concurrency for the triangle. Determine whether each point is a *circumcenter, incenter, centroid,* or *orthocenter*. Explain.

34.

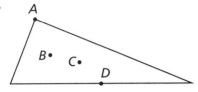

35.

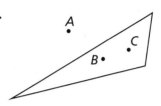

36. History In 1765, Leonhard Euler proved that, for any triangle, three of the four points of concurrency are collinear. The line that contains these three points is known as Euler's Line. Use Exercises 34 and 35 to determine which point of concurrency does not necessarily lie on Euler's Line.

13-5 Indirect Proof

G.CO.10 Prove theorems about triangles . . .

Objective To use indirect reasoning to write proofs

 Solve It! Write your solution to the Solve It in the space below.

In the Solve It, you can conclude that a square must contain a certain number if you can eliminate the other three numbers as possibilities. This type of reasoning is called indirect reasoning. In **indirect reasoning,** all possibilities are considered and then all but one are proved false. The remaining possibility must be true.

Essential Understanding You can use indirect reasoning as another method of proof.

A proof involving indirect reasoning is an **indirect proof.** Often in an indirect proof, a statement and its negation are the only possibilities. When you see that one of these possibilities leads to a conclusion that contradicts a fact you know to be true, you can eliminate that possibility. For this reason, indirect proof is sometimes called *proof by contradiction.*

take note

Key Concept   Writing an Indirect Proof

Step 1   State as a temporary assumption the opposite (negation) of what you want to prove.

Step 2   Show that this temporary assumption leads to a contradiction.

Step 3   Conclude that the temporary assumption must be false and that what you want to prove must be true.

In the first step of an indirect proof you assume as true the opposite of what you want to prove.

Got It? Suppose you want to write an indirect proof of each statement. As the first step of the proof, what would you assume?

    a. $\triangle BOX$ is not acute.

    b. At least one pair of shoes you bought cost more than $25.

Ⓐ Practice Write the first step of an indirect proof of the given statement.

    1. At least one angle is obtuse.

    2. $m\angle 2 > 90$

To write an indirect proof, you have to be able to identify a contradiction.

Problem 2 **Identifying Contradictions**

Got It? **a.** Which two statements contradict each other?

    I. $\triangle XYZ$ is acute.

    II. $\triangle XYZ$ is scalene.

    III. $\triangle XYZ$ is equiangular.

Think

How do you know that two statements contradict each other?

b. Reasoning Statements I and II below contradict each other. Statement III is the negation of Statement I. Are Statements II and III equivalent? Explain your reasoning.

    I. $\triangle ABC$ is scalene.

    II. $\triangle ABC$ is equilateral.

    III. $\triangle ABC$ is not scalene.

Practice Identify the two statements that contradict each other.

3. **I.** Each of the two items that Val bought costs more than $10.

    II. Val spent $34 for the two items.

    III. Neither of the two items that Val bought costs more than $15.

4. **I.** In right $\triangle ABC$, $m\angle A = 60$.

    II. In right $\triangle ABC$, $\angle A \cong \angle C$.

    III. In right $\triangle ABC$, $m\angle B = 90$.

Got It?   **Given:** $7(x + y) = 70$ and $x \neq 4$.

Prove: $y \neq 6$

Plan

What statement should be negated to begin the proof?

 Practice   5. **Developing Proof** Fill in the blanks to prove the following statement. If the Yoga Club and Go Green Club together have fewer than 20 members and the Go Green Club has 10 members, then the Yoga Club has fewer than 10 members.

Given: The total membership of the Yoga Club and the Go Green Club is fewer than 20. The Go Green Club has 10 members.

Prove: The Yoga Club has fewer than 10 members.

Proof: Assume temporarily that the Yoga Club has 10 or more members.

This means that together the two clubs have

a. _____ members. This contradicts the given

information that b. _____.

The temporary assumption is false. Therefore, it is true that

c. _____.

6. **Developing Proof** Fill in the blanks to prove the following statement. In a given triangle, $\triangle LMN$, there is at most one right angle.

Given: $\triangle LMN$

Prove: $\triangle LMN$ has at most one right angle.

Proof: Assume temporarily that $\triangle LMN$ has more than one

a. _____. That is, assume that both $\angle M$ and

$\angle N$ are b. _____. If $\angle M$ and $\angle N$ are both right

angles, then $m\angle M = m\angle N =$ c. _____. By

the Triangle Angle-Sum Theorem, $m\angle L + m\angle M + m\angle N =$

d. _____. Use substitution to write the equation

$m\angle L +$ e. _____ + f. _____ = 180. When you solve

for $m\angle L$, you find that $m\angle L =$ g. _____. This means

that there is no $\triangle LMN$, which contradicts the given

statement. So the temporary assumption that $\triangle LMN$ has

h. _____ must be false. Therefore, $\triangle LMN$ has

i. _____.

Lesson Check

Do you know HOW?

7. Suppose you want to write an indirect proof of the following statement. As the first step of the proof, what would you assume?

Quadrilateral $ABCD$ has four right angles.

8. Write a statement that contradicts the following statement. Draw a diagram to support your answer.

Lines a and b are parallel.

Do you UNDERSTAND?

9. Error Analysis A classmate began an indirect proof as shown at the right. Explain and correct your classmate's error.

Given: △ABC
Prove: ∠A is obtuse.
~~Assume temporarily that ∠A is acute.~~

More Practice and Problem-Solving Exercises

B Apply

10. History Use indirect reasoning to eliminate all but one of the following answers. In what year was George Washington born?

Ⓐ 1492   Ⓑ 1732   Ⓒ 1902   Ⓓ 2002

11. Think About a Plan Write an indirect proof.

Given: ∠1 ≇ ∠2

Prove: $\ell \not\parallel p$

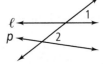

• What assumption should be the first step of your proof?
• In the figure, what type of angle pair do ∠1 and ∠2 form?

Write the first step of an indirect proof of the given statement.

12. If a number n ends in 5, then it is not divisible by 2.

13. If point X is on the perpendicular bisector of $\overline{AB}$, then $\overline{XB} \cong \overline{XA}$.

14. If a transversal intersects two parallel lines, then alternate exterior angles are congruent.

15. Reasoning Identify the two statements that contradict each other.

   I. The orthocenter of △JRK is on the triangle.

   II. The centroid of △JRK is inside the triangle.

   III. △JRK is an obtuse triangle.

Write an indirect proof.

Proof **16.** Use the figure at the right.

   Given: $\triangle ABC$ with $BC > AC$

   Prove: $\angle A \not\cong \angle B$

Proof **17. Given:** $\triangle XYZ$ is isosceles.

   Prove: Neither base angle is a right angle.

© **Writing** For Exercises 18 and 19, write a convincing argument that uses indirect reasoning.

STEM **18. Chemistry** Ice is forming on the sidewalk in front of Toni's house. Show that the temperature of the sidewalk surface must be 32°F or lower.

19. Show that an obtuse triangle cannot contain a right angle.

© **20. Error Analysis** Your friend wants to prove indirectly that $\triangle ABC$ is equilateral. For a first step, he writes, "Assume temporarily that $\triangle ABC$ is scalene." What is wrong with your friend's statement? How can he correct himself?

21. Literature In Arthur Conan Doyle's story "The Sign of the Four," Sherlock Holmes talks to his friend Watson about how a culprit enters a room that has only four entrances: a door, a window, a chimney, and a hole in the roof.

> "You will not apply my precept," he said, shaking his head. "How often have I said to you that when you have eliminated the impossible, whatever remains, however improbable, must be the truth? We know that he did not come through the door, the window, or the chimney. We also know that he could not have been concealed in the room, as there is no concealment possible. Whence, then, did he come?"

How did the culprit enter the room? Explain.

Proof **22.** Prove Theorem 9, the Converse of the Corresponding Angles Theorem. (*Hint:* Use the Triangle Angle-Sum Theorem.)

© **Challenge**

Use the figure at the right for Exercises 23 and 24.

Proof **23. Given:** $\triangle ABC$ is scalene, $m\angle ABX = 36$, $m\angle CBX = 36$
   Prove: $\overline{XB}$ is not perpendicular to $\overline{AC}$.

Proof **24. Given:** $\triangle ABC$ is scalene, $m\angle ABX = 36$, $m\angle CBX = 36$
   Prove: $\overline{AX} \not\cong \overline{XC}$

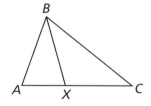

13-6 Inequalities in One Triangle

G.CO.10 Prove theorems about triangles . . .

Objective To use inequalities involving angles and sides of triangles

 Solve It! Write your solution to the Solve It in the space below.

In the Solve It, you explored triangles formed by various lengths of board. You may have noticed that changing the angle formed by two sides of the sandbox changes the length of the third side.

Essential Understanding The angles and sides of a triangle have special relationships that involve inequalities.

take note

Property   Comparison Property of Inequality

If $a = b + c$ and $c > 0$, then $a > b$.

Proof **Proof of the Comparison Property of Inequality**

Given: $a = b + c, c > 0$
Prove: $a > b$

Statements	Reasons
1) $c > 0$	1) Given
2) $b + c > b + 0$	2) Addition Property of Inequality
3) $b + c > b$	3) Identity Property of Addition
4) $a = b + c$	4) Given
5) $a > b$	5) Substitution

The Comparison Property of Inequality allows you to prove the following corollary to the Triangle Exterior Angle Theorem (Theorem 17).

take note

Corollary   Corollary to the Triangle Exterior Angle Theorem

Corollary	If . . .	Then . . .
The measure of an exterior angle of a triangle is greater than the measure of each of its remote interior angles.	$\angle 1$ is an exterior angle. 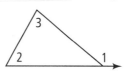	$m\angle 1 > m\angle 2$ and $m\angle 1 > m\angle 3$

Proof **Proof of the Corollary**

Given: $\angle 1$ is an exterior angle of the triangle.
Prove: $m\angle 1 > m\angle 2$ and $m\angle 1 > m\angle 3$.

Proof: By the Triangle Exterior Angle Theorem, $m\angle 1 = m\angle 2 + m\angle 3$.
Since $m\angle 2 > 0$ and $m\angle 3 > 0$, you can apply the Comparison Property of Inequality and conclude that $m\angle 1 > m\angle 2$ and $m\angle 1 > m\angle 3$.

 Problem 1   **Applying the Corollary**

Got It?   Why is $m\angle 5 > m\angle C$?

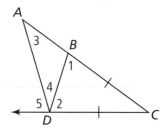

 Practice   Explain why $m\angle 1 > m\angle 2$.

1.

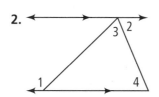

2.

You can use the corollary to Theorem 17 to prove the following theorem.

take note

Theorem 33

Theorem	If . . .	Then . . .
If two sides of a triangle are not congruent, then the larger angle lies opposite the longer side.	$XZ > XY$	$m\angle Y > m\angle Z$

You will prove Theorem 33 in Exercise 23.

Problem 2 **Using Theorem 33**

Got It?   Suppose the landscape architect from Problem 2 wants to place a drinking fountain at the corner with the second-largest angle. Which two streets form the corner with the second-largest angle?

A Practice   For Exercises 3 and 4, list the angles of each triangle in order from smallest to largest.

3.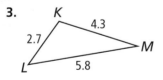

4. $\triangle ABC$, where $AB = 8$, $BC = 5$, and $CA = 7$

Theorem 34 below is the converse of Theorem 33. The proof of Theorem 34 relies on indirect reasoning.

take note

Theorem 34

Theorem	If . . .	Then . . .
If two angles of a triangle are not congruent, then the longer side lies opposite the larger angle.	$m\angle A > m\angle B$ 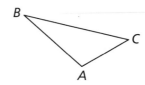	$BC > AC$

Proof Indirect Proof of Theorem 34

Given: $m\angle A > m\angle B$
Prove: $BC > AC$

Step 1 Assume temporarily that BC is not greater than AC. That is, assume temporarily that either $BC < AC$ or $BC = AC$.

Step 2 If $BC < AC$, then $m\angle A < m\angle B$ (Theorem 33). This contradicts the given fact that $m\angle A > m\angle B$. Therefore, $BC < AC$ must be false.

If $BC = AC$, then $m\angle A = m\angle B$ (Isosceles Triangle Theorem). This also contradicts $m\angle A > m\angle B$. Therefore, $BC = AC$ must be false.

Step 3 The temporary assumption $BC \not> AC$ is false, so $BC > AC$.

Problem 3 Using Theorem 34

Ⓒ Got It? **Reasoning** In the figure below, $m\angle S = 24$ and $m\angle O = 130$. Which side of $\triangle SOX$ is the shortest side? Explain your reasoning.

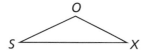

Plan

How do you use the angle measures to order the side lengths?

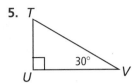 **Practice** For Exercises 5 and 6, list the sides of each triangle in order from shortest to longest.

5. T

30°

U   V

6. △DEF, with m∠D = 20, m∠E = 120, and m∠F = 40

For three segments to form a triangle, their lengths must be related in a certain way. Notice that only one of the sets of segments below can form a triangle. The sum of the smallest two lengths must be greater than the greatest length.

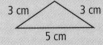
3 cm   3 cm
5 cm

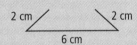
2 cm   2 cm
6 cm

take note

Theorem 35   Triangle Inequality Theorem

The sum of the lengths of any two sides of a triangle is greater than the length of the third side.

$XY + YZ > XZ$ $YZ + XZ > XY$ $XZ + XY > YZ$

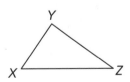
Y

X   Z

You will prove Theorem 35 in Exercise 28.

Problem 4 Using the Triangle Inequality Theorem

Got It? Can a triangle have sides with the given lengths? Explain.

    a. 2 m, 6 m, and 9 m

Think

How can you determine if the lengths can form a triangle?

    b. 4 yd, 6 yd, and 9 yd

Ⓐ Practice Can a triangle have sides with the given lengths? Explain.

    7. 2 in., 3 in., 6 in.

    8. 11 cm, 12 cm, 15 cm

Problem 5 **Finding Possible Side Lengths**

Got It? A triangle has side lengths of 4 in. and 7 in. What is the range of possible lengths for the third side?

Ⓐ Practice **Algebra** The lengths of two sides of a triangle are given. Find the range of possible lengths for the third side.

9. 18 m, 23 m

10. 20 km, 35 km

Lesson Check

Do you know HOW?

Use $\triangle ABC$ for Exercises 11 and 12.

11. Which side is the longest?

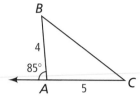

12. Which angle is the smallest?

13. Can a triangle have sides of lengths 4, 5, and 10? Explain.

Do you UNDERSTAND?

MATHEMATICAL PRACTICES

14. Error Analysis A friend tells you that she drew a triangle with perimeter 16 and one side of length 8. How do you know she made an error in her drawing?

15. Reasoning Is it possible to draw a right triangle with an exterior angle measuring 88? Explain your reasoning.

More Practice and Problem-Solving Exercises

MATHEMATICAL PRACTICES

Ⓑ Apply

Ⓒ 16. Think About a Plan You are setting up a study area where you will do your homework each evening. It is triangular with an entrance on one side. You want to put your computer in the corner with the largest angle and a bookshelf on the longest side. Where should you place your computer? On which side should you place the bookshelf? Explain.

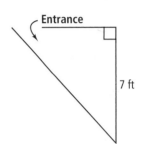

- What type of triangle is shown in the figure?
- Once you find the largest angle of a triangle, how do you find the longest side?

17. Algebra Find the longest side of $\triangle ABC$, with $m\angle A = 70$, $m\angle B = 2x - 10$, and $m\angle C = 3x + 20$.

Ⓒ 18. Writing You and a friend compete in a scavenger hunt at a museum. The two of you walk from the Picasso exhibit to the Native American gallery along the dashed red line. When he sees that another team is ahead of you, your friend says, "They must have cut through the courtyard." Explain what your friend means.

Ⓒ 19. Error Analysis Your family drives across Kansas on Interstate 70. A sign reads, "Wichita 90 mi, Topeka 110 mi." Your little brother says, "I didn't know that it was only 20 miles from Wichita to Topeka." Explain why the distance between the two cities does not have to be 20 mi.

Ⓒ Reasoning Determine which segment is shortest in each diagram.

20.

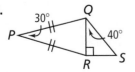

21.

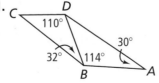

22.

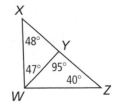

23. Developing Proof Fill in the blanks for a proof of Theorem 33: If two sides of a triangle are not congruent, then the larger angle lies opposite the longer side.

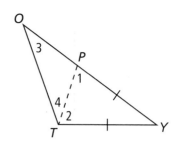

Given: $\triangle TOY$, with $YO > YT$
Prove: a. __?__ > b. __?__

Mark P on $\overline{YO}$ so that $\overline{YP} \cong \overline{YT}$. Draw $\overline{TP}$.

Statements	Reasons
1) $\overline{YP} \cong \overline{YT}$	**1)** Ruler Postulate
2) $m\angle 1 = m\angle 2$	**2) c.** __?__
3) $m\angle OTY = m\angle 4 + m\angle 2$	**3) d.** __?__
4) $m\angle OTY > m\angle 2$	**4) e.** __?__
5) $m\angle OTY > m\angle 1$	**5) f.** __?__
6) $m\angle 1 > m\angle 3$	**6) g.** __?__
7) $m\angle OTY > m\angle 3$	**7) h.** __?__

Proof 24. Prove this corollary to Theorem 34: The perpendicular segment from a point to a line is the shortest segment from the point to the line.

Given: $\overline{PT} \perp \overline{TA}$

Prove: $PA > PT$

ⓒ Challenge

25. Probability A student has two straws. One is 6 cm long and the other is 9 cm long. She picks a third straw at random from a group of four straws whose lengths are 3 cm, 5 cm, 11 cm, and 15 cm. What is the probability that the straw she picks will allow her to form a triangle? Justify your answer.

For Exercises 26 and 27, x and y are integers such that $1 < x < 5$ and $2 < y < 9$.

26. The sides of a triangle are 5 cm, x cm, and y cm. List all possible (x, y) pairs.

27. Probability What is the probability that you can draw an isosceles triangle that has sides 5 cm, x cm, and y cm, with x and y chosen at random?

Proof 28. Prove the Triangle Inequality Theorem: The sum of the lengths of any two sides of a triangle is greater than the length of the third side.

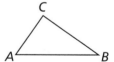

Given: $\triangle ABC$

Prove: $AC + CB > AB$

(*Hint:* On $\overrightarrow{BC}$, mark a point D not on $\overline{BC}$, so that $DC = AC$. Draw $\overline{DA}$ and use Theorem 34 with $\triangle ABD$.)

Inequalities in Two Triangles

G.CO.10 Prove theorems about triangles . . .

Objective To apply inequalities in two triangles

 Solve It! Write your solution to the Solve It in the space below.

In the Solve It, the hands of the clock and the segment labeled *x* form a triangle. As the time changes, the shape of the triangle changes, but the lengths of two of its sides do not change.

Essential Understanding In triangles that have two pairs of congruent sides, there is a relationship between the included angles and the third pair of sides.

When you close a door, the angle between the door and the frame (at the hinge) gets smaller. The relationship between the measure of the hinge angle and the length of the opposite side is the basis for the SAS Inequality Theorem, also known as the Hinge Theorem.

 Theorem 36 The Hinge Theorem (SAS Inequality Theorem)

Theorem	**If . . .**	**Then . . .**
If two sides of one triangle are congruent to two sides of another triangle, and the included angles are not congruent, then the longer third side is opposite the larger included angle.	$m\angle A > m\angle X$ 	$BC > YZ$ *You will prove Theorem 36 in Exercise 21.*

Problem 1 Using the Hinge Theorem

Got It? **a.** What inequality relates *LN* and *OQ* in the figure at the right?

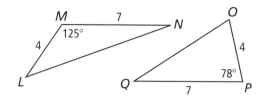

© b. Reasoning In △*ABC*, *AB* = 3, *BC* = 4, and *CA* = 6. In △*PQR*, *PQ* = 3, *QR* = 5, and *RP* = 6. How can you use indirect reasoning to explain why *m*∠*P* > *m*∠*A*?

A Practice Write an inequality relating the given side lengths. If there is not enough information to reach a conclusion, write *no conclusion*.

1. *LM* and *KL*

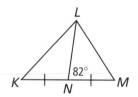

2. *YZ* and *UV*

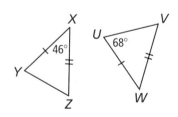

 **Problem 2** **Applying the Hinge Theorem**

What does not change about both pairs of scissors in the diagram?

Got It? The diagram below shows a pair of scissors in two different positions. In which position is the distance between the tips of the two blades greater? Use the Hinge Theorem to justify your answer.

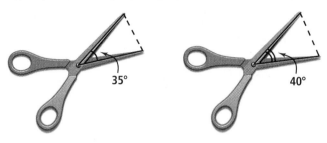

Practice **3.** The diagram below shows a robotic arm in two different positions. In which position is the tip of the robotic arm closer to the base? Use the Hinge Theorem to justify your answer.

The Converse of the Hinge Theorem is also true. The proof of the converse is an indirect proof.

take note

Theorem 37   Converse of the Hinge Theorem (SSS Inequality)

Theorem	**If . . .**	**Then . . .**
If two sides of one triangle are congruent to two sides of another triangle, and the third sides are not congruent, then the larger included angle is opposite the longer third side.	$BC > YZ$	$m\angle A > m\angle X$

Proof **Indirect Proof of the Converse of the Hinge Theorem (SSS Inequality)**

Given: $\overline{AB} \cong \overline{XY}$, $\overline{AC} \cong \overline{XZ}$, $BC > YZ$
Prove: $m\angle A > m\angle X$

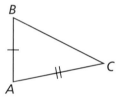 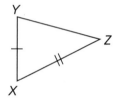

Step 1 Assume temporarily that $m\angle A \not> m\angle X$. This means either $m\angle A < m\angle X$ or $m\angle A = m\angle X$.

Step 2 If $m\angle A < m\angle X$, then $BC < YZ$ by the Hinge Theorem. This contradicts the given information that $BC > YZ$. Therefore, the assumption that $m\angle A < m\angle X$ must be false.

If $m\angle A = m\angle X$, then $\triangle ABC \cong \triangle XYZ$ by SAS. If the two triangles are congruent, then $BC = YZ$ because corresponding parts of congruent triangles are congruent. This contradicts the given information that $BC > YZ$. Therefore, the assumption that $m\angle A = m\angle X$ must be false.

Step 3 The temporary assumption that $m\angle A \not> m\angle X$ is false. Therefore, $m\angle A > m\angle X$.

ONLINE PROBLEMS

Problem 3   **Using the Converse of the Hinge Theorem**

Got It? What is the range of possible values for x in the figure at the right?

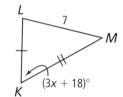 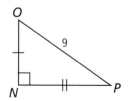

Ⓐ Practice **Algebra** Find the range of possible values for each variable.

4.

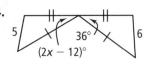

5   36°   6

$(2x - 12)°$

5.

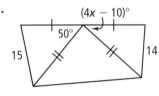

$(4x - 10)°$

50°

15   14

Problem 4 **Proving Relationships in Triangles**

Got It? **Given:** $m\angle MON = 80$, O is the midpoint of $\overline{LN}$

Prove: $LM > MN$

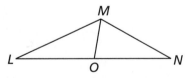

Think

How can you find the measure of $\angle MOL$?

© 6. **Developing Proof** Complete the following proof.

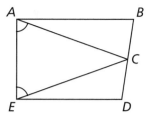

Given: *C* is the midpoint of $\overline{BD}$,
$m\angle EAC = m\angle AEC$,
$m\angle BCA > m\angle DCE$

Prove: $AB > ED$

Statements	Reasons
1) $m\angle EAC = m\angle AEC$	1) Given
2) $AC = EC$	2) a. _____
3) *C* is the midpoint of $\overline{BD}$.	3) b. _____
4) $\overline{BC} \cong \overline{CD}$	4) c. _____
5) d. _____	5) ≅ segments have = length.
6) $m\angle BCA > m\angle DCE$	6) e. _____
7) $AB > ED$	7) f. _____

 Lesson Check

Do you know HOW?

Write an inequality relating the given side lengths or angle measures.

7. *FD* and *BC*

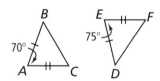

8. $m\angle UST$ and $m\angle VST$

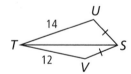

Do you UNDERSTAND?

© **9. Vocabulary** Explain why *Hinge Theorem* is an appropriate name for Theorem 36.

© **10. Error Analysis** From the figure at the right, your friend concludes that $m\angle BAD > m\angle BCD$. How would you correct your friend's mistake?

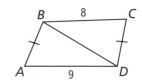

© **11. Compare and Contrast** How are the Hinge Theorem and the SAS Congruence Postulate similar?

More Practice and Problem-Solving Exercises

Ⓑ **Apply**

Copy and complete with $>$ or $<$. Explain your reasoning.

12. PT ▨ QR **13.** $m\angle QTR$ ▨ $m\angle RTS$

14. PT ▨ RS

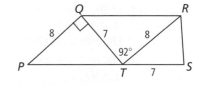

© **15. a. Error Analysis** Your classmate draws the figure at the right. Explain why the figure cannot have the labeled dimensions.

    b. Open-Ended Describe a way you could change the dimensions to make the figure possible.

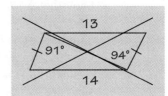

16. Reasoning The legs of a right isosceles triangle are congruent to the legs of an isosceles triangle with an 80° vertex angle. Which triangle has a greater perimeter? How do you know?

17. Think About a Plan Ship A and Ship B leave from the same point in the ocean. Ship A travels 150 mi due west, turns 65° toward north, and then travels another 100 mi. Ship B travels 150 mi due east, turns 70° toward south, and then travels another 100 mi. Which ship is farther from the starting point? Explain.

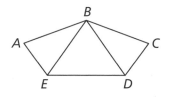

- How can you use the given angle measures?
- How does the Hinge Theorem help you to solve this problem?

18. Which of the following lists the segment lengths in order from least to greatest?

Ⓐ *CD, AB, DE, BC, EF*   Ⓒ *BC, DE, EF, AB, CD*

Ⓑ *EF, DE, AB, BC, CD*   Ⓓ *EF, BC, DE, AB, CD*

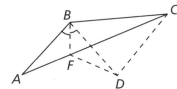

Proof 19. Use the figure at the right.

> **Given:** △*ABE* is isosceles with vertex ∠*B*,
> △*ABE* ≅ △*CBD*,
> *m*∠*EBD* > *m*∠*ABE*
>
> **Prove:** *ED* > *AE*

ⓒ Challenge

20. Coordinate Geometry △*ABC* has vertices *A*(0, 7), *B*(−1, −2), *C*(2, −1), and *O*(0, 0). Show that *m*∠*AOB* > *m*∠*AOC*.

Proof 21. Use the plan below to complete a proof of the Hinge Theorem: If two sides of one triangle are congruent to two sides of another triangle and the included angles are not congruent, then the longer third side is opposite the larger included angle.

> **Given:** $\overline{AB} \cong \overline{XY}$, $\overline{BC} \cong \overline{YZ}$, *m*∠*B* > *m*∠*Y*
> **Prove:** *AC* > *XZ*

Plan for proof:
- Copy △*ABC*. Locate point *D* outside △*ABC* so that *m*∠*CBD* = *m*∠*ZYX* and *BD* = *YX*. Show that △*DBC* ≅ △*XYZ*.
- Locate point *F* on $\overline{AC}$, so that $\overline{BF}$ bisects ∠*ABD*.
- Show that △*ABF* ≅ △*DBF* and that $\overline{AF} \cong \overline{DF}$.
- Show that *AC* = *FC* + *DF*.
- Use the Triangle Inequality Theorem to write an inequality that relates *DC* to the lengths of the other sides of △*FCD*.
- Relate *DC* and *XZ*.

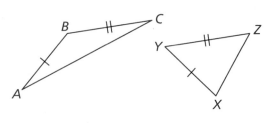

13 Chapter Review

13-1 Midsegments of Triangles

Quick Review

A **midsegment of a triangle** is a segment that connects the midpoints of two sides. A midsegment is parallel to the third side and is half as long.

Example

Algebra Find the value of x.

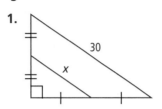

$\overline{DE}$ is a midsegment because D and E are midpoints.

$$DE = \tfrac{1}{2}BC \qquad \triangle \text{ Midsegment Theorem}$$

$$2x = \tfrac{1}{2}(x + 12) \qquad \text{Substitute.}$$

$$4x = x + 12 \qquad \text{Multiply each side by 2.}$$

$$3x = 12 \qquad \text{Subtract } x \text{ from each side.}$$

$$x = 4 \qquad \text{Divide each side by 3.}$$

Exercises

Algebra Find the value of x.

1.
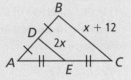

2.
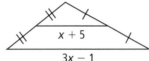

3. $\triangle ABC$ has vertices $A(0, 0)$, $B(2, 2)$, and $C(5, -1)$. Find the coordinates of L, the midpoint of $\overline{AC}$, and M, the midpoint of $\overline{BC}$. Verify that $\overline{LM} \parallel \overline{AB}$ and $LM = \tfrac{1}{2}AB$.

13-2 Perpendicular and Angle Bisectors

Quick Review

The **Perpendicular Bisector Theorem** together with its converse states that P is equidistant from A and B if and only if P is on the perpendicular bisector of $\overline{AB}$.

The **distance from a point to a line** is the length of the perpendicular segment from the point to the line.

The **Angle Bisector Theorem** together with its converse states that P is equidistant from the sides of an angle if and only if P is on the angle bisector.

Example

In the figure, $QP = 4$ and $AB = 8$. Find QR and CB.

Q is on the bisector of $\angle ABC$, so $QR = QP = 4$.
B is on the perpendicular bisector of $\overline{AC}$, so
$CB = AB = 8$.

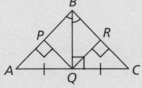

Exercises

4. **Writing** Describe how to find all the points on a baseball field that are equidistant from second base and third base.

In the figure, $m\angle DBE = 50$. Find each of the following.

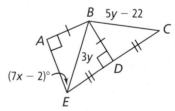

5. $m\angle BED$ 6. $m\angle BEA$ 7. x

8. y 9. BE 10. BC

13-3 Bisectors in Triangles

Quick Review

When three or more lines intersect in one point, they are **concurrent**.

- The point of concurrency of the perpendicular bisectors of a triangle is the **circumcenter of the triangle.**
- The point of concurrency of the angle bisectors of a triangle is the **incenter of the triangle.**

Example

Identify the incenter of the triangle.

The incenter of a triangle is the point of concurrency of the angle bisectors. $\overline{MR}$ and $\overline{LQ}$ are angle bisectors that intersect at Z. So, Z is the incenter.

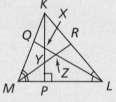

Exercises

Find the coordinates of the circumcenter of $\triangle DEF$.

11. $D(6, 0)$, $E(0, 6)$, $F(-6, 0)$

12. $D(0, 0)$, $E(6, 0)$, $F(0, 4)$

13. $D(5, -1)$, $E(-1, 3)$, $F(3, -1)$

14. $D(2, 3)$, $E(8, 3)$, $F(8, -1)$

P is the incenter of $\triangle XYZ$. Find the indicated angle measure.

15. $m\angle PXY$

16. $m\angle XYZ$

17. $m\angle PZX$

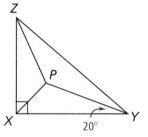

13-4 Medians and Altitudes

Quick Review

A **median of a triangle** is a segment from a vertex to the midpoint of the opposite side. An **altitude of a triangle** is a perpendicular segment from a vertex to the line containing the opposite side.

- The point of concurrency of the medians of a triangle is the **centroid of the triangle.** The centroid is two thirds the distance from each vertex to the midpoint of the opposite side.
- The point of concurrency of the altitudes of a triangle is the **orthocenter of the triangle.**

Example

If $PB = 6$, what is SB?

S is the centroid because $\overline{AQ}$ and $\overline{CR}$ are medians. So, $SB = \frac{2}{3}PB = \frac{2}{3}(6) = 4$.

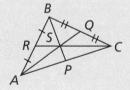

Exercises

Determine whether $\overline{AB}$ is a *median*, an *altitude*, or *neither*. Explain.

18. 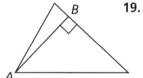   **19.**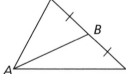

20. $\triangle PQR$ has medians $\overline{QM}$ and $\overline{PN}$ that intersect at Z. If $ZM = 4$, find QZ and QM.

$\triangle ABC$ has vertices $A(2, 3)$, $B(-4, -3)$, and $C(2, -3)$. Find the coordinates of each point of concurrency.

21. centroid   **22.** orthocenter

13-5 Indirect Proof

Quick Review

In an **indirect proof**, you first assume temporarily the opposite of what you want to prove. Then you show that this temporary assumption leads to a contradiction.

Example

Which two statements contradict each other?

  I. The perimeter of $\triangle ABC$ is 14.
  II. $\triangle ABC$ is isosceles.
  III. The side lengths of $\triangle ABC$ are 3, 5, and 6.

An isosceles triangle can have a perimeter of 14.

The perimeter of a triangle with side lengths 3, 5, and 6 is 14.

An isosceles triangle must have two sides of equal length. Statements II and III contradict each other.

Exercises

Write a convincing argument that uses indirect reasoning.

23. The product of two numbers is even. Show that at least one of the numbers must be even.

24. Two lines in the same plane are not parallel. Show that a third line in the plane must intersect at least one of the two lines.

25. Show that a triangle can have at most one obtuse angle.

26. Show that an equilateral triangle cannot have an obtuse angle.

27. The sum of three integers is greater than 9. Show that one of the integers must be greater than 3.

13-6 and 13-7 Inequalities in Triangles

Quick Review

For any triangle,

- the measure of an exterior angle is greater than the measure of each of its remote interior angles
- if two sides are not congruent, then the larger angle lies opposite the longer side
- if two angles are not congruent, then the longer side lies opposite the larger angle
- the sum of any two side lengths is greater than the third

The **Hinge Theorem** states that if two sides of one triangle are congruent to two sides of another triangle, and the included angles are not congruent, then the longer third side is opposite the larger included angle.

Example

Which is greater, BC or AD?

$\overline{BA} \cong \overline{CD}$ and $\overline{BD} \cong \overline{DB}$, so $\triangle ABD$ and $\triangle CDB$ have two pairs of congruent corresponding sides. Since $60 > 45$, you know $BC > AD$ by the Hinge Theorem.

Exercises

28. In $\triangle RST$, $m\angle R = 70$ and $m\angle S = 80$. List the sides of $\triangle RST$ in order from shortest to longest.

Is it possible for a triangle to have sides with the given lengths? Explain.

29. 5 in., 8 in., 15 in.

30. 10 cm, 12 cm, 20 cm

31. The lengths of two sides of a triangle are 12 ft and 13 ft. Find the range of possible lengths for the third side.

Use the figure below. Complete each statement with $>$, $<$, or $=$.

32. $m\angle BAD$ ▧ $m\angle ABD$

33. $m\angle CBD$ ▧ $m\angle BCD$

34. $m\angle ABD$ ▧ $m\angle CBD$

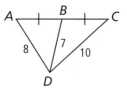

Pull It All Together

Estimating the Length of a Hiking Trail

 ASSESSMENT

A group of hikers plan to hike from the campground lookout tower to the hut. To challenge the group, the leader gives them the diagram below. (All distances are given in kilometers.) The dashed line shows the trail they will take, but the distances along the trail are unknown.

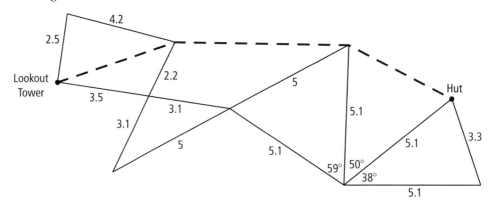

The group must determine the best lower bound and the best upper bound for the length of the trail. To do this, they are allowed to use the Triangle Inequality Theorem and the Hinge Theorem.

Task Description

Find a range in kilometers for the length of the trail.

- Do you need to draw any additional segments in the diagram to help you estimate the length of the trail?

- The trail from the lookout tower to the hut includes three segments. How can you find a range for each segment? How do these ranges lead you to determine the lower and upper bounds for the length of the trail?

Get Ready!

Properties of Parallel Lines

Algebra Use properties of parallel lines to find the value of *x*.

1.
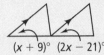
$(x + 9)°$ $(2x − 21)°$

2.
$(3x − 14)°$
$(2x − 16)°$

3.
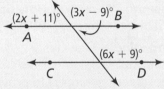
$5x°$
$(176 − 3x)°$

Proving Lines Parallel

Algebra Determine whether $\overline{AB}$ is parallel to $\overline{CD}$.

4.
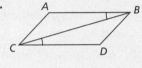

5.
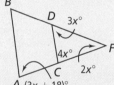
B, D, $3x°$, F, $4x°$, C, $2x°$, A $(3x + 18)°$

6.
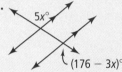
$(2x + 11)°$ $(3x − 9)°$ B
A
$(6x + 9)°$
C D

Using Slope to Determine Parallel and Perpendicular Lines

Algebra Determine whether each pair of lines is *parallel*, *perpendicular*, or *neither*.

7. $y = -2x; y = -2x + 4$ **8.** $y = -\frac{3}{5}x + 1; y = \frac{5}{3}x − 3$ **9.** $2x − 3y = 1; 3x − 2y = 8$

Proving Triangles Congruent

Determine the postulate or theorem that makes each pair of triangles congruent.

10.
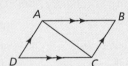

11.

12.
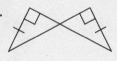

 Looking Ahead Vocabulary

13. You know the meaning of *equilateral*. What do you think an *equiangular* polygon is?

14. When a team wins two *consecutive* gold medals, it means they have won two gold medals in a row. What do you think two *consecutive* angles in a quadrilateral means?

CHAPTER 14

Proving Theorems About Quadrilaterals

Big Ideas

1 Measurement
Essential Question How can you find the sum of the measures of polygon angles?

2 Reasoning and Proof
Essential Question How can you classify quadrilaterals?

3 Coordinate Geometry
Essential Question How can you use coordinate geometry to prove general relationships?

Ⓔ Domains

- Congruence
- Similarity, Right Triangles, and Trigonometry
- Expressing Geometric Properties with Equations

Interactive Digital Path

Log in to **pearsonsuccessnet.com** and click on Interactive Digital Path to access the Solve Its and animated Problems.

Chapter Preview

Vocabulary

English/Spanish Vocabulary Audio Online:

English	Spanish
coordinate proof, *p. 907*	prueba de coordenadas
equiangular polygon, *p. 852*	polígono equiángulo
equilateral polygon, *p. 852*	polígono equilátero
isosceles trapezoid, *p. 894*	trapecio isósceles
kite, *p. 898*	cometa
midsegment of a trapezoid, *p. 896*	segmento medio de un trapecio
parallelogram, *p. 858*	paralelogramo
rectangle, *p. 877*	rectángulo
regular polygon, *p. 852*	polígono regular
rhombus, *p. 877*	rombo
trapezoid, *p. 894*	trapecio

14-1 The Polygon Angle-Sum Theorems

G.CO.9 Prove theorems about lines and angles . . . Also G.SRT.5

Objectives To find the sum of the measures of the interior angles of a polygon
To find the sum of the measures of the exterior angles of a polygon

Solve It! Write your solution to the Solve It in the space below.

The Solve It is related to a formula for the sum of the interior angle measures of a polygon. (In this textbook, a polygon is convex unless otherwise stated.)

Essential Understanding The sum of the interior angle measures of a polygon depends on the number of sides the polygon has.

By dividing a polygon with n sides into $(n-2)$ triangles, you can show that the sum of the interior angle measures of any polygon is a multiple of 180.

take note

Theorem 38 Polygon Angle-Sum Theorem

The sum of the measures of the interior angles of an n-gon is $(n-2)180$.

Problem 1 Finding a Polygon Angle Sum

Got It? **a.** What is the sum of the interior angle measures of a 17-gon?

ⓒ **b. Reasoning** The sum of the interior angle measures of a polygon
is 1980. How can you find the number of sides in the polygon?

 Practice Find the sum of the interior angle measures of each polygon.

1. 35-gon

2. 20-gon

An **equilateral polygon** is a polygon with all sides congruent.

An **equiangular polygon** is a polygon with all angles congruent.

A **regular polygon** is a polygon that is both equilateral and equiangular.

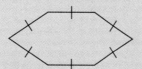

 take note

Corollary to the Polygon Angle-Sum Theorem

The measure of each interior angle of a regular n-gon is $\frac{(n-2)180}{n}$.

You will prove the Corollary to the Polygon Angle-Sum Theorem in Exercise 36.

Problem 2 Using the Polygon Angle-Sum Theorem

Got It? What is the measure of each interior angle in a regular nonagon?

Think
How does the word *regular* help you answer the question?

Ⓐ Practice Find the measure of one interior angle in each regular polygon.

3.

4.

 Problem 3 Using the Polygon Angle-Sum Theorem

Got It? What is $m\angle G$ in quadrilateral *EFGH*?

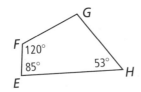

F 120°
85°
E
G
53°
H

Think

What is the sum of the measures of the angles of a quadrilateral?

Ⓐ Practice **Algebra** In Exercises 5 and 6, find the missing angle measures.

5.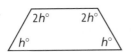

2h°   2h°
h°   h°

6.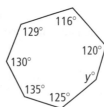

129°   116°
120°
130°
y°
135° 125°

You can draw exterior angles at any vertex of a polygon. The figures below show that the sum of the measures of the exterior angles, one at each vertex, is 360.

80°
100°
50° 30° 150°
130°

80 + 150 + 130 = 360

115° 105° 75°
65°   81°
71°   109° 99°

115 + 75 + 99 + 71 = 360

Theorem 39 Polygon Exterior Angle-Sum Theorem

The sum of the measures of the exterior angles of a polygon, one at each vertex, is 360.

For the pentagon, $m\angle 1 + m\angle 2 + m\angle 3 + m\angle 4 + m\angle 5 = 360$.

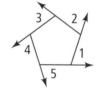

You will prove Theorem 39 in Exercise 32.

Problem 4   **Finding an Exterior Angle Measure**

Got It?   What is the measure of an exterior angle of a regular nonagon?

Practice Find the measure of an exterior angle of each regular polygon.

7. 36-gon

8. 100-gon

Lesson Check

Do you know HOW?

9. What is the sum of the interior angle measures of an 11-gon?

10. What is the sum of the measures of the exterior angles of a 15-gon?

11. Find the measures of an interior angle and an exterior angle of a regular decagon.

Do you UNDERSTAND?

@ **12. Vocabulary** Can you draw an equiangular polygon that is not equilateral? Explain.

© **13. Reasoning** Which angles are the exterior angles for ∠1? What do you know about their measures? Explain.

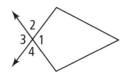

© **14. Error Analysis** Your friend says that she measured an interior angle of a regular polygon as 130. Explain why this result is impossible.

More Practice and Problem-Solving Exercises

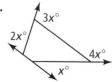

(B) **Apply**

The sum of the interior angle measures of a polygon with *n* sides is given. Find *n*.

15. 180   **16.** 1080   **17.** 1980   **18.** 2880

© **19. Open-Ended** Sketch an equilateral polygon that is not equiangular.

20. Stage Design A theater-in-the-round allows for a play to have an audience on all sides. The diagram at the right shows a platform constructed for a theater-in-the-round stage. What type of regular polygon is the largest platform? Find the measure of each numbered angle.

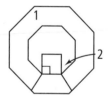

© **21. Think About a Plan** A triangle has two congruent interior angles and an exterior angle that measures 100. Find two possible sets of interior angle measures for the triangle.
   • How can a diagram help you?
   • What is the sum of the angle measures in a triangle?

Algebra Find the value of each variable.

22.
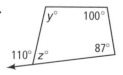

23.
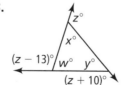

24.

The measure of an exterior angle of a regular polygon is given. Find the measure of an interior angle. Then find the number of sides.

25. 72 **26.** 36 **27.** 18 **28.** 30 **29.** x

Packaging The gift package at the right contains fruit and cheese. The fruit is in a container that has the shape of a regular octagon. The fruit container fits in a square box. A triangular cheese wedge fills each corner of the box.

30. Find the measure of each interior angle of a cheese wedge.

🌐 **31. Reasoning** Show how to rearrange the four pieces of cheese to make a regular polygon. What is the measure of each interior angle of the polygon?

32. Algebra A polygon has *n* sides. An interior angle of the polygon and an adjacent exterior angle form a straight angle.
  a. What is the sum of the measures of the *n* straight angles?
  b. What is the sum of the measures of the *n* interior angles?
  c. Using your answers above, what is the sum of the measures of the *n* exterior angles?
  d. What theorem do the steps above prove?

🌐 **33. Reasoning** Your friend says she has another way to find the sum of the interior angle measures of a polygon. She picks a point inside the polygon, draws a segment to each vertex, and counts the number of triangles. She multiplies the total by 180, and then subtracts 360 from the product. Does her method work? Explain.

34. Algebra The measure of an interior angle of a regular polygon is three times the measure of an exterior angle of the same polygon. What is the name of the polygon?

© Challenge

35. Probability Find the probability that the measure of an interior angle of a regular *n*-gon is a positive integer when *n* is an integer and $3 \le n \le 12$.

36. a. In the Corollary to the Polygon Angle-Sum Theorem, explain why the measure of an interior angle of a regular *n*-gon is given by the formulas $\frac{180(n-2)}{n}$ and $180 - \frac{360}{n}$.
  b. Use the second formula to explain what happens to the measures of the interior angles of regular *n*-gons as *n* becomes a large number. Explain also what happens to the polygons.

37. *ABCDEFGHJK* is a regular decagon. A ray bisects ∠*C*, and another ray bisects ∠*D*. The two rays intersect in the decagon's interior. Find the measure of the acute angles formed by the intersecting rays.

Properties of Parallelograms

G.CO.11 Prove theorems about parallelograms. Theorems include: opposite sides are congruent, opposite angles are congruent, the diagonals of a parallelogram bisect each other . . . Also **G.SRT.5**

Objectives To use relationships among sides and angles of parallelograms
To use relationships among diagonals of parallelograms

Solve It! Write your solution to the Solve It in the space below.

A **parallelogram** is a quadrilateral with both pairs of opposite sides parallel. In the Solve It, you made some conjectures about the characteristics of a parallelogram. In this lesson, you will verify whether your conjectures are correct.

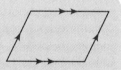

Essential Understanding Parallelograms have special properties regarding their sides, angles, and diagonals.

In a quadrilateral, **opposite sides** do not share a vertex and **opposite angles** do not share a side.

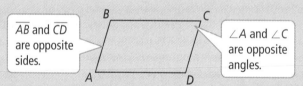

$\overline{AB}$ and $\overline{CD}$ are opposite sides.

$\angle A$ and $\angle C$ are opposite angles.

You can abbreviate *parallelogram* with the symbol ▱ and *parallelograms* with the symbol ▱. You can use what you know about parallel lines and transversals to prove some theorems about parallelograms.

take note

Theorem 40

Theorem	If . . .	Then . . .
If a quadrilateral is a parallelogram, then its opposite sides are congruent.	$ABCD$ is a ▱	$\overline{AB} \cong \overline{CD}$ and $\overline{BC} \cong \overline{DA}$

Proof **Proof of Theorem 40**

Given: ▱*ABCD*
Prove: $\overline{AB} \cong \overline{CD}$ and $\overline{BC} \cong \overline{DA}$

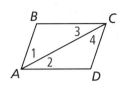

Statements	Reasons
1) *ABCD* is a parallelogram.	1) Given
2) $\overline{AB} \parallel \overline{CD}$ and $\overline{BC} \parallel \overline{DA}$	2) Definition of parallelogram
3) $\angle 1 \cong \angle 4$ and $\angle 3 \cong \angle 2$	3) If lines are ∥, then alt. int. ∡ are ≅.
4) $\overline{AC} \cong \overline{AC}$	4) Reflexive Property of ≅
5) $\triangle ABC \cong \triangle CDA$	5) ASA
6) $\overline{AB} \cong \overline{CD}$ and $\overline{BC} \cong \overline{DA}$	6) Corresp. parts of ≅ ▵ are ≅.

Angles of a polygon that share a side are **consecutive angles**. In the diagram, $\angle A$ and $\angle B$ are consecutive angles because they share side $\overline{AB}$.

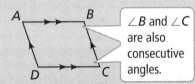

∠B and ∠C are also consecutive angles.

The theorem below uses the fact that consecutive angles of a parallelogram are same-side interior angles of parallel lines.

take note

Theorem 41

Theorem	If . . .	Then . . .
If a quadrilateral is a parallelogram, then its consecutive angles are supplementary.	*ABCD* is a ▱	$m\angle A + m\angle B = 180$ $m\angle B + m\angle C = 180$ $m\angle C + m\angle D = 180$ $m\angle D + m\angle A = 180$

You will prove Theorem 41 in Exercise 23.

ONLINE PROBLEMS

Problem 1 **Using Consecutive Angles**

Got It? Suppose you adjust the lamp in Problem 1 so that $m\angle S = 86$. What is $m\angle R$ in ▱*PQRS*?

Think

What is the relationship between $\angle R$ and $\angle S$?

1.

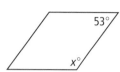

2.

Parallelograms have some other special properties.

take note

Theorem 42

Theorem	**If . . .**	**Then . . .**
If a quadrilateral is a parallelogram, then its opposite angles are congruent.	*ABCD* is a ▱ B →→ C A →→ D	∠*A* ≅ ∠*C* and ∠*B* ≅ ∠*D* B)) C A D

Theorem 43

Theorem	**If . . .**	**Then . . .**
If a quadrilateral is a parallelogram, then its diagonals bisect each other.	*ABCD* is a ▱ B → C A → D	$\overline{AE} \cong \overline{CE}$ and $\overline{BE} \cong \overline{DE}$ B C A E D

You will prove Theorem 43 in Exercise 3.

A proof of Theorem 42 in Problem 2 uses the consecutive angles of a parallelogram and the fact that supplements of the same angle are congruent.

Problem 2 **Using Properties of Parallelograms in a Proof**

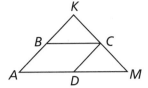

Think

What kind
of triangle is
△*AKM*?

Got It?   Use the diagram at the right.

    Given: □*ABCD*, $\overline{AK} \cong \overline{MK}$
    Prove: ∠*BCD* ≅ ∠*CMD*

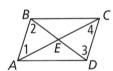

Practice   **3. Developing Proof** Complete this two-column proof of Theorem 43.

    Given: □*ABCD*
    Prove: $\overline{AC}$ and $\overline{BD}$ bisect each other at *E*.

Statements	Reasons
1) *ABCD* is a parallelogram.	**1)** Given
2) $\overline{AB} \parallel \overline{DC}$	**2) a.** _____
3) ∠1 ≅ ∠4; ∠2 ≅ ∠3	**3) b.** _____
4) $\overline{AB} \cong \overline{DC}$	**4) c.** _____
5) d. _____	**5)** ASA
6) $\overline{AE} \cong \overline{CE}; \overline{BE} \cong \overline{DE}$	**6) e.** _____
7) f. _____	**7)** Definition of bisector

You can use Theorem 43 to find unknown lengths in parallelograms.

 Problem 3 **Using Algebra to Find Lengths**

Got It? **a.** Find the values of x and y in $\square PQRS$ at the right. What are PR and SQ?

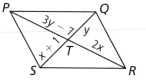

ⓖ b. Reasoning In Problem 3, does it matter which variable you solve for first? Explain.

ⒶPractice **Algebra** Find the values of x and y in $\square PQRS$.

4. $PT = 2x$, $TR = y + 4$, $QT = x + 2$, $TS = y$

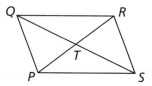

5. $PT = x + 2$, $TR = y$, $QT = 2x$, $TS = y + 3$

You will use parallelograms to prove the following theorem.

take note

Theorem 44

Theorem	If . . .	Then . . .
If three (or more) parallel lines cut off congruent segments on one transversal, then they cut off congruent segments on every transversal.	$\overleftrightarrow{AB} \parallel \overleftrightarrow{CD} \parallel \overleftrightarrow{EF}$ and $\overline{AC} \cong \overline{CE}$ 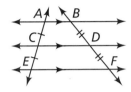	$\overline{BD} \cong \overline{DF}$

You will prove Theorem 44 in Exercise 34.

Problem 4 **Using Parallel Lines and Transversals**

Got It? Use the figure in Problem 4, shown at the right.
If $EF = FG = GH = 6$ and $AD = 15$, what is CD?

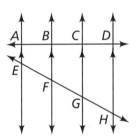

A Practice In the figure, $PQ = QR = RS$. Find each length.

6. ZU

7. WV

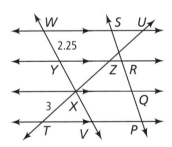

Lesson Check

Do you know HOW?

For Exercises 8–11, use the diagram of $\square ABCD$ to find each value.

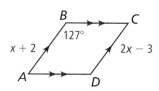

8. $m\angle A$

9. $m\angle D$

10. x

11. AB

12. What are ED and FD in the figure at the right?

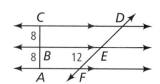

Do you UNDERSTAND?

13. Reasoning If you know one angle measure of a parallelogram, how do you find the other three angle measures? Explain.

14. Compare and Contrast What is the difference between a quadrilateral and a parallelogram?

15. Error Analysis Your classmate says that $QV = 10$. Explain why the statement may not be correct.

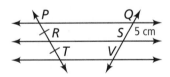

More Practice and Problem-Solving Exercises

B Apply

Algebra Find the value(s) of the variable(s) in each parallelogram.

16.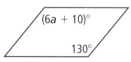

$(6a + 10)°$

$130°$

17.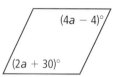

$(4a - 4)°$

$(2a + 30)°$

18.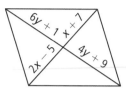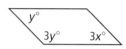

$6y + 1$ $x + 7$

$2x - 5$ $4y + 9$

19. Think About a Plan What are the values of x and y in the parallelogram?
- How are the angles related?
- Which variable should you solve for first?

$y°$

$3y°$ $3x°$

Algebra Find the value of a. Then find each side length or angle measure.

20.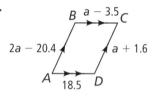

B $a - 3.5$ C

$2a - 20.4$ $a + 1.6$

A 18.5 D

21.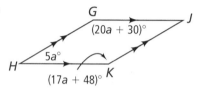

G $(20a + 30)°$ J

H $5a°$

$(17a + 48)°$ K

22. Studio Lighting A pantograph is an expandable device shown at the right. Pantographs are used in the television industry in positioning lighting and other equipment. In the photo, points D, E, F, and G are the vertices of a parallelogram. $\square DEFG$ is one of many parallelograms that change shape as the pantograph extends and retracts.
- **a.** If $DE = 2.5$ ft, what is FG?
- **b.** If $m\angle E = 129$, what is $m\angle G$?
- **c.** What happens to $m\angle D$ as $m\angle E$ increases or decreases? Explain.

Proof 23. Prove Theorem 41.

Given: $\square ABCD$
Prove: $\angle A$ is supplementary to $\angle B$.
$\angle A$ is supplementary to $\angle D$.

B C

A D

Proof In the figure at the right, $\overline{GS}$ and $\overline{EH}$ intersect at point N. Use the diagram at the right to complete Exercises 24–26.

24. Given: $\square LENS$ and $\square NGTH$
Prove: $\angle L \cong \angle T$

25. Given: $\square LENS$ and $\square NGTH$
Prove: $\overline{LS} \parallel \overline{GT}$

26. Given: $\square LENS$ and $\square NGTH$
Prove: $\angle E$ is supplementary to $\angle T$.

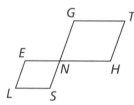

G T

E

N H

L S

Proof In the figure at the right, points *S*, *Y*, and *T* are collinear, and points *T*, *Z*, and *W* are collinear. Use the figure for Exercises 27 and 28.

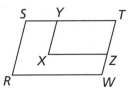

27. Given: □*RSTW* and □*XYTZ*
Prove: ∠*R* ≅ ∠*X*

28. Given: □*RSTW* and □*XYTZ*
Prove: $\overline{XY} \parallel \overline{RS}$

Find the measures of the numbered angles for each parallelogram.

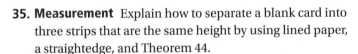

29.

30.

31.

32. Algebra The perimeter of □*ABCD* is 92 cm. *AD* is 7 cm more than twice *AB*. Find the lengths of all four sides of □*ABCD*.

⊙ Challenge

◎ 33. Writing Is there an SSSS congruence theorem for parallelograms? Explain.

Proof 34. Prove Theorem 44. Use the diagram at the right.

Given: $\overleftrightarrow{AB} \parallel \overleftrightarrow{CD} \parallel \overleftrightarrow{EF}$, $\overline{AC} \cong \overline{CE}$
Prove: $\overline{BD} \cong \overline{DF}$
(*Hint:* Draw lines through *B* and *D* parallel to $\overleftrightarrow{AE}$ and intersecting $\overleftrightarrow{CD}$ at *G* and $\overleftrightarrow{EF}$ at *H*.)

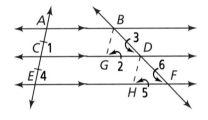

35. Measurement Explain how to separate a blank card into three strips that are the same height by using lined paper, a straightedge, and Theorem 44.

14-3 Proving That a Quadrilateral Is a Parallelogram

G.CO.11 Prove theorems about parallelograms ... the diagonals of a parallelogram bisect each other ... Also **G.SRT.5**

Objective To determine whether a quadrilateral is a parallelogram

Solve It! Write your solution to the Solve It in the space below.

In the Solve It, you used angle properties to show that lines are parallel. In this lesson, you will apply the same properties to show that a quadrilateral is a parallelogram.

Essential Understanding You can decide whether a quadrilateral is a parallelogram if its sides, angles, and diagonals have certain properties.

In Lesson 14-2, you learned theorems about the properties of parallelograms. In this lesson, you will learn the converses of those theorems. That is, if a quadrilateral has certain properties, then it must be a parallelogram. Theorem 45 is the converse of Theorem 40.

take note

Theorem 45

Theorem	**If . . .**	**Then . . .**
If both pairs of opposite sides of a quadrilateral are congruent, then the quadrilateral is a parallelogram.	$\overline{AB} \cong \overline{CD}$ $\overline{BC} \cong \overline{DA}$	$ABCD$ is a $\square$

You will prove Theorem 45 in Exercise 15.

Theorems 46 and 47 are the converses of Theorems 41 and 42, respectively. They use angle relationships to conclude that a quadrilateral is a parallelogram.

Theorem 46

Theorem	**If . . .**	**Then . . .**
If an angle of a quadrilateral is supplementary to both of its consecutive angles, then the quadrilateral is a parallelogram.	$m\angle A + m\angle B = 180$ $m\angle A + m\angle D = 180$	$ABCD$ is a $\square$

You will prove Theorem 46 in Exercise 16.

Theorem 47

Theorem	**If . . .**	**Then . . .**
If both pairs of opposite angles of a quadrilateral are congruent, then the quadrilateral is a parallelogram.	$\angle A \cong \angle C$ $\angle B \cong \angle D$	$ABCD$ is a $\square$

You will prove Theorem 47 in Exercise 13.

You can use algebra together with Theorems 45, 46, and 47 to find segment lengths and angle measures that assume that a quadrilateral is a parallelogram.

Problem 1 **Finding Values for Parallelograms**

Got It?   Use the diagram below. For what values of x and y must *EFGH* be a parallelogram?

E $(3y - 2)°$ F
$(4x + 13)°$
$(y + 10)°$
H $(12x + 7)°$ G

Practice Algebra In Exercises 1 and 2, for what values of *x* and *y* must *ABCD* be a parallelogram?

1.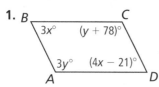

2.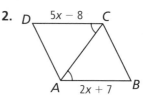

You know that the converses of Theorems 40, 41, and 42 are true. Using what you have learned, you can show that the converse of Theorem 43 is also true.

take note

Theorem 48

Theorem	**If . . .**	**Then . . .**
If the diagonals of a quadrilateral bisect each other, then the quadrilateral is a parallelogram.	$\overline{AE} = \overline{CE}$ $\overline{BE} = \overline{DE}$	*ABCD* is a ▱

Proof **Proof of Theorem 48**

Given: $\overline{AC}$ and $\overline{BD}$ bisect each other at *E*.

Prove: *ABCD* is a parallelogram.

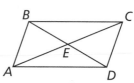

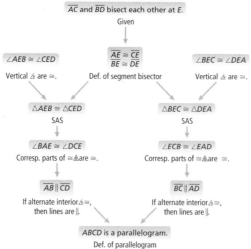

Theorem 49 suggests that if you keep two objects of the same length parallel, such as cross-country skis, then the quadrilateral formed by connecting their endpoints is always a parallelogram.

Theorem 49

Theorem	If . . .	Then . . .

If one pair of opposite sides of a quadrilateral is both congruent and parallel, then the quadrilateral is a parallelogram.

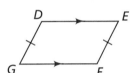

$\overline{BC} \cong \overline{DA}$
$\overline{BC} \parallel \overline{DA}$

$ABCD$ is a ▱

You will prove Theorem 49 in Exercise 14.

Problem 2 Deciding Whether a Quadrilateral Is a Parallelogram

Got It? Can you prove that the quadrilateral is a parallelogram based on the given information? Explain.

Think

How do you decide if you have enough information?

a. **Given:** $\overline{EF} \cong \overline{GD}, \overline{DE} \parallel \overline{FG}$

Prove: $DEFG$ is a parallelogram.

b. **Given:** $\angle ALN \cong \angle DNL, \angle ANL \cong \angle DLN$

Prove: $LAND$ is a parallelogram.

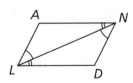

3.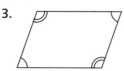

4.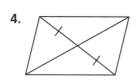

Problem 3 **Identifying Parallelograms**

Ⓒ Got It? **Reasoning** What is the maximum height that the vehicle lift can elevate the truck? Explain.

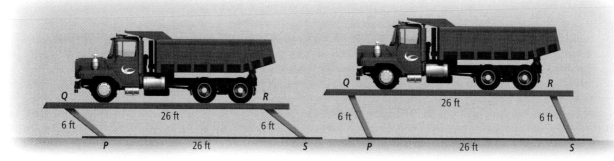

Practice   **5. Fishing** Quadrilaterals are formed on the side of this fishing tackle box by the adjustable shelves and connecting pieces. Explain why the shelves are always parallel to each other no matter what their position is.

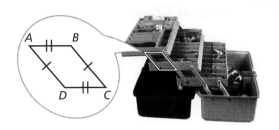

<take note>

Concept Summary   Proving That a Quadrilateral Is a Parallelogram

Method	Source	Diagram
Prove that both pairs of opposite sides are parallel.	Definition of parallelogram	
Prove that both pairs of opposite sides are congruent.	Theorem 45	
Prove that an angle is supplementary to both of its consecutive angles.	Theorem 46	75° 75° 105°
Prove that both pairs of opposite angles are congruent.	Theorem 47	
Prove that the diagonals bisect each other.	Theorem 48	
Prove that one pair of opposite sides is congruent and parallel.	Theorem 49	

Lesson Check

Do you know HOW?

6. For what value of *y* must *LMNP* be a parallelogram?

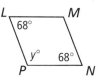

For Exercises 7 and 8, is the given information enough to prove that *ABCD* is a parallelogram? Explain.

7.

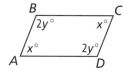

8.

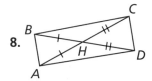

Do you UNDERSTAND?

9. Vocabulary Explain why you can now write a biconditional statement regarding opposite sides of a parallelogram.

10. **Compare and Contrast** How is Theorem 48 in this lesson different from Theorem 43 in the previous lesson? In what situations should you use each theorem? Explain.

11. **Error Analysis** Your friend says, "If a quadrilateral has a pair of opposite sides that are congruent and a pair of opposite sides that are parallel, then it is a parallelogram." What is your friend's error? Explain.

More Practice and Problem-Solving Exercises

 MATHEMATICAL PRACTICES

B Apply

12. **Writing** Combine each of Theorems 40, 41, 42, and 43 with its converse from this lesson into biconditional statements.

13. **Developing Proof** Complete this two-column proof of Theorem 47.

Given: $\angle A \cong \angle C, \angle B \cong \angle D$

Prove: $ABCD$ is a parallelogram.

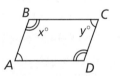

Statements	Reasons
1) $x + y + x + y = 360$	1) The sum of the measures of the angles of a quadrilateral is 360.
2) $2(x + y) = 360$	2) a. ___?___
3) $x + y = 180$	3) b. ___?___
4) $\angle A$ and $\angle B$ are supplementary. $\angle A$ and $\angle D$ are supplementary.	4) Definition of supplementary
5) c. ___?___ ‖ ___?___ , ___?___ ‖ ___?___	5) d. ___?___
6) $ABCD$ is a parallelogram.	6) e. ___?___

14. Think About a Plan Prove Theorem 49.

Proof

Given: $\overline{BC} \parallel \overline{DA}$, $\overline{BC} \cong \overline{DA}$

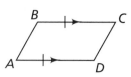

Prove: *ABCD* is a parallelogram.
- How can drawing diagonals help you?
- How can you use triangles in this proof?

Proof 15. Prove Theorem 45.

Given: $\overline{AB} \cong \overline{CD}$, $\overline{BC} \cong \overline{DA}$

Prove: *ABCD* is a parallelogram.

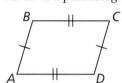

Proof 16. Prove Theorem 46.

Given: $\angle A$ is supplementary to $\angle B$.
$\angle A$ is supplementary to $\angle D$.

Prove: *ABCD* is a parallelogram.

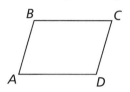

Algebra For what values of the variables must *ABCD* be a parallelogram?

17.

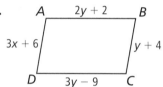

18.

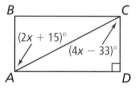

19.

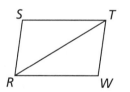

Proof 20. Given: $\triangle TRS \cong \triangle RTW$

Prove: *RSTW* is a parallelogram.

21. Open-Ended Sketch two noncongruent parallelograms *ABCD* and *EFGH* such that $\overline{AC} \cong \overline{EG}$ and $\overline{BD} \cong \overline{FH}$.

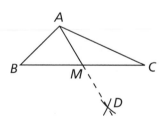

Challenge

Proof 22. Construction In the figure at the right, point *D* is constructed by drawing two arcs. One has center *C* and radius *AB*. The other has center *B* and radius *AC*. Prove that $\overline{AM}$ is a median of $\triangle ABC$.

23. Probability If two opposite angles of a quadrilateral measure 120 and the measures of the other angles are multiples of 10, what is the probability that the quadrilateral is a parallelogram?

14-4 Properties of Rhombuses, Rectangles, and Squares

G.CO.11 Prove theorems about parallelograms . . . rectangles are parallelograms with congruent diagonals.
Also **G.SRT.5**

Objectives To define and classify special types of parallelograms
To use properties of diagonals of rhombuses and rectangles

 Solve It! Write your solution to the Solve It in the space below.

In the Solve It, you formed a special type of parallelogram with characteristics that you will study in this lesson.

Essential Understanding The parallelograms in the Take Note box below have basic properties about their sides and angles that help identify them. The diagonals of these parallelograms also have certain properties.

take note

Key Concept Special Parallelograms

Definition	Diagram
A **rhombus** is a parallelogram with four congruent sides.	
A **rectangle** is a parallelogram with four right angles.	
A **square** is a parallelogram with four congruent sides and four right angles.	

The Venn diagram at the right shows the relationships among special parallelograms.

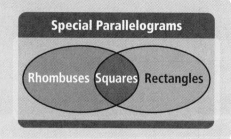

Special Parallelograms

Rhombuses Squares Rectangles

Problem 1 Classifying Special Parallelograms

Got It? Is □*EFGH* in Problem 1 a rhombus, a rectangle, or a square? Explain.

Think

How do you decide whether *EFGH* is a rhombus, rectangle, or square?

Practice Decide whether the parallelogram is a rhombus, a rectangle, or a square. Explain.

1.

2.

Theorem 50

Theorem	If . . .	Then . . .
If a parallelogram is a rhombus, then its diagonals are perpendicular.	*ABCD* is a rhombus 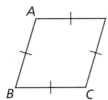	$\overline{AC} \perp \overline{BD}$ 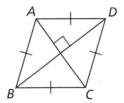

Theorem 51

Theorem	If . . .	Then . . .
If a parallelogram is a rhombus, then each diagonal bisects a pair of opposite angles.	*ABCD* is a rhombus 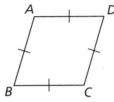	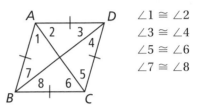

You will prove Theorem 51 in Exercise 34.

Proof **Proof of Theorem 50**

Given: *ABCD* is a rhombus.

Prove: The diagonals of *ABCD* are perpendicular.

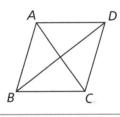

Statements	Reasons
1) *A* and *C* are equidistant from *B* and *D*; *B* and *D* are equidistant from *A* and *C*.	1) All sides of a rhombus are ≅.
2) *A* and *C* are on the perpendicular bisector of $\overline{BD}$; *B* and *D* are on the perpendicular bisector of $\overline{AC}$.	2) Converse of the Perpendicular Bisector Theorem
3) $\overline{AC} \perp \overline{BD}$	3) Through two points, there is one unique line perpendicular to a given line.

You can use Theorems 50 and 51 to find angle measures in a rhombus.

Problem 2 Finding Angle Measures

Think

What type of triangle is △PQR?

Got It? What are the measures of the numbered angles in rhombus *PQRS*?

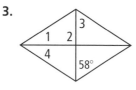

Practice Find the measures of the numbered angles in each rhombus.

3.

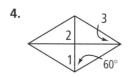

4.

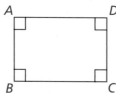

The diagonals of a rectangle also have a special property.

take note

Theorem 52

Theorem	**If . . .**	**Then . . .**
If a parallelogram is a rectangle, then its diagonals are congruent.	*ABCD* is a rectangle	$\overline{AC} \cong \overline{BD}$

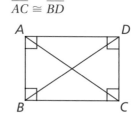

You will prove Theorem 52 in Exercise 30.

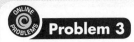
Got It?   **a.** If $LN = 4x - 17$ and $MO = 2x + 13$, what are the lengths of the diagonals of rectangle $LMNO$?

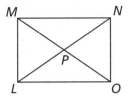

b. Reasoning What type of triangle is $\triangle PMN$? Explain.

Practice **Algebra** $LMNP$ is a rectangle. Find the value of x and the length of each diagonal.

5. $LN = 5x - 8$ and $MP = 2x + 1$

6. $LN = 3x + 1$ and $MP = 8x - 4$

Lesson Check

Do you know HOW?

Is each parallelogram a rhombus, rectangle, or square? Explain.

7.

8.

9. What are the measures of the numbered angles in the rhombus?

10. Algebra *JKLM* is a rectangle. If $JL = 4x - 12$ and $MK = x$, what is the value of x? What is the length of each diagonal?

Do you UNDERSTAND?

© 11. Vocabulary Which special parallelograms are equiangular? Which special parallelograms are equilateral?

© 12. Error Analysis Your class needs to find the value of *x* for which ▱*DEFG* is a rectangle. A classmate's work is shown at the right. What is the error? Explain.

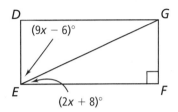

$$2x + 8 = 9x - 6$$
$$14 = 7x$$
$$2 = x$$

More Practice and Problem-Solving Exercises

B Apply

Determine the most precise name for each quadrilateral.

13.

14.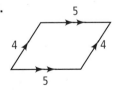

15.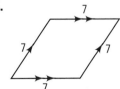

16.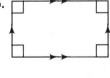

List the quadrilaterals that have the given property. Choose among *parallelogram, rhombus, rectangle,* **and** *square.*

17. All sides are ≅.

18. Opposite sides are ≅.

19. Opposite sides are ∥.

20. Opposite ⦞ are ≅.

21. All ⦞ are right ⦞.

22. Consecutive ⦞ are supplementary.

23. Diagonals bisect each other.

24. Diagonals are ≅.

25. Diagonals are ⊥.

26. Each diagonal bisects opposite ⦞.

Algebra **Find the values of the variables. Then find the side lengths.**

27. rhombus

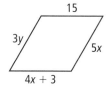

15
3y
5x
4x + 3

28. square

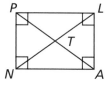

2x − 7
y − 1
2y − 5
3y − 9

© **29. Think About a Plan** Write a proof.

Proof

Given: Rectangle *PLAN*

Prove: △*LTP* ≅ △*NTA*

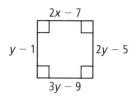

- What do you know about the diagonals of rectangles?
- Which triangle congruence postulate or theorem can you use?

© **30. Developing Proof** Complete the flow proof of Theorem 52.

Given: *ABCD* is a rectangle.

Prove: $\overline{AC} \cong \overline{BD}$

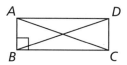

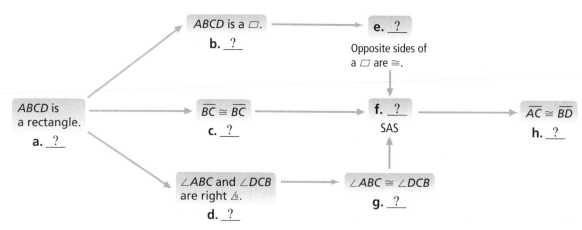

ABCD is a ▱.
b. ? → **e.** ?
Opposite sides of a ▱ are ≅.

ABCD is a rectangle.
a. ?

$\overline{BC} \cong \overline{BC}$
c. ? → **f.** ? SAS → $\overline{AC} \cong \overline{BD}$
h. ?

∠*ABC* and ∠*DCB* are right ⦞.
d. ? → ∠*ABC* ≅ ∠*DCB*
g. ?

Algebra Find the value(s) of the variable(s) for each parallelogram.

31. $RZ = 2x + 5$,
$SW = 5x - 20$

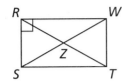

32. $m\angle 1 = 3y - 6$

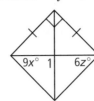

33. $BD = 4x - y + 1$

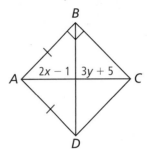

34. Prove Theorem 51.

Proof

Given: *ABCD* is a rhombus.

Prove: $\overline{AC}$ bisects $\angle BAD$ and $\angle BCD$.

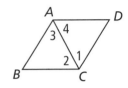

ⓒ **35. Writing** Summarize the properties of squares that follow from a square being (a) a parallelogram, (b) a rhombus, and (c) a rectangle.

36. Algebra Find the angle measures and the side lengths of the rhombus at the right.

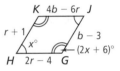

ⓒ **37. Open-Ended** On graph paper, draw a parallelogram that is neither a rectangle nor a rhombus.

Algebra *ABCD* is a rectangle. Find the length of each diagonal.

38. $AC = 2(x - 3)$ and $BD = x + 5$

39. $AC = 2(5a + 1)$ and $BD = 2(a + 1)$

40. $AC = \dfrac{3y}{5}$ and $BD = 3y - 4$

41. $AC = \dfrac{3c}{9}$ and $BD = 4 - c$

Ⓒ **Challenge**

Algebra Find the value of *x* in the rhombus.

42.

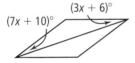

43.

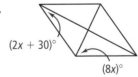

14-5 Conditions for Rhombuses, Rectangles, and Squares

G.CO.11 Prove theorems about parallelograms . . . rectangles are parallelograms with congruent diagonals. Also **G.SRT.5**

Objective To determine whether a parallelogram is a rhombus or rectangle

Solve It! Write your solution to the Solve It in the space below.

Essential Understanding You can determine whether a parallelogram is a rhombus or a rectangle based on the properties of its diagonals.

take note

Theorem 53

Theorem	**If . . .**	**Then . . .**
If the diagonals of a parallelogram are perpendicular, then the parallelogram is a rhombus.	$ABCD$ is a $\square$ and $\overline{AC} \perp \overline{BD}$ 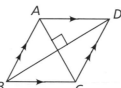	$ABCD$ is a rhombus 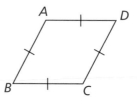

Proof **Proof of Theorem 53**

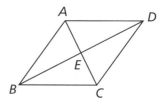

Given: $ABCD$ is a parallelogram, $\overline{AC} \perp \overline{BD}$
Prove: $ABCD$ is a rhombus.

Since $ABCD$ is a parallelogram, $\overline{AC}$ and $\overline{BD}$ bisect each other, so $\overline{BE} \cong \overline{DE}$. Since $\overline{AC} \perp \overline{BD}$, $\angle AED$ and $\angle AEB$ are congruent right angles. By the Reflexive Property of Congruence, $\overline{AE} \cong \overline{AE}$.

So $\triangle AEB \cong \triangle AED$ by SAS. Corresponding parts of congruent triangles are congruent, so $\overline{AB} \cong \overline{AD}$. Since opposite sides of a parallelogram are congruent, $\overline{AB} \cong \overline{DC} \cong \overline{BC} \cong \overline{AD}$. By definition, $ABCD$ is a rhombus.

Theorem 54

Theorem	**If . . .**	**Then . . .**
If one diagonal of a parallelogram bisects a pair of opposite angles, then the parallelogram is a rhombus.	$ABCD$ is a $\square$, $\angle 1 \cong \angle 2$, and $\angle 3 \cong \angle 4$ 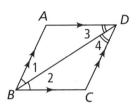	$ABCD$ is a rhombus 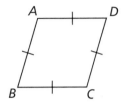

You will prove Theorem 54 in Exercise 21.

Theorem 55

Theorem	**If . . .**	**Then . . .**
If the diagonals of a parallelogram are congruent, then the parallelogram is a rectangle.	$ABCD$ is a $\square$, and $\overline{AC} \cong \overline{BD}$ 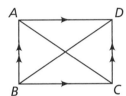	$ABCD$ is a rectangle 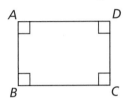

You will prove Theorem 55 in Exercise 22.

You can use Theorems 53, 54, and 55 to classify parallelograms. Notice that if a parallelogram is both a rectangle and a rhombus, then it is a square.

Problem 1 Identifying Special Parallelograms

Got It?   **a.** A parallelogram has angle measures of 20, 160, 20, and 160. Can you conclude that it is a rhombus, a rectangle, or a square? Explain.

Think

How can you determine whether a figure is a special parallelogram?

b. Reasoning Suppose the diagonals of a quadrilateral bisect each other. Can you conclude that it is a rhombus, a rectangle, or a square? Explain.

Practice Can you conclude that the parallelogram is a rhombus, a rectangle, or a square? Explain.

1.

2.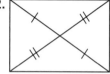

Problem 2 **Using Properties of Special Parallelograms**

Got It? For what value of y is $\square DEFG$ a rectangle?

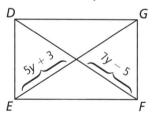

Think

What do you know about the diagonals of a rectangle?

Ⓐ Practice For what value of *x* is the figure the given special parallelogram?

3. rhombus

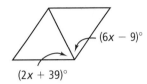

4. rectangle

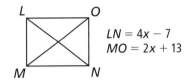

$LN = 4x - 7$
$MO = 2x + 13$

Problem 3 Using Properties of Parallelograms

Got It? Can you adapt the method described in Problem 3 to stake off a square play area? Explain.

Ⓐ Practice **5. Carpentry** A carpenter is building a bookcase. How can the carpenter use a tape measure to check that the bookshelf is rectangular? Justify your answer and name any theorems used.

Lesson Check

Do you know HOW?

Can you conclude that the parallelogram is a rhombus, a rectangle, or a square? Explain.

6.
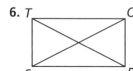
$\overline{SO} \cong \overline{TP}$

7.
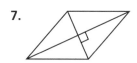

For what value of x is the figure the given special parallelogram?

8. rhombus

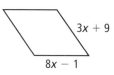
$3x + 9$

$8x - 1$

9. rectangle

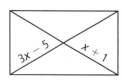
$3x - 5$ $x + 1$

Do you UNDERSTAND?

10. Name all of the special parallelograms that have each property.

a. Diagonals are perpendicular.

b. Diagonals are congruent.

c. Diagonals are angle bisectors.

d. Diagonals bisect each other.

e. Diagonals are perpendicular bisectors of each other.

11. Error Analysis Your friend says, "A parallelogram with perpendicular diagonals is a rectangle." What is your friend's error? Explain.

12. Reasoning When you draw a circle and two of its diameters and connect the endpoints of the diameters, what quadrilateral do you get? Explain.

More Practice and Problem-Solving Exercises

B) Apply

13. **Hardware** You can use a simple device called a turnbuckle to "square up" structures that are parallelograms. For the gate pictured at the right, you tighten or loosen the turnbuckle on the diagonal cable so that the rectangular frame will keep the shape of a parallelogram when it sags. What are two ways you can make sure that the turnbuckle works? Explain.

14. **Reasoning** Suppose the diagonals of a parallelogram are both perpendicular and congruent. What type of special quadrilateral is it? Explain your reasoning.

Algebra For what value of x is the figure the given special parallelogram?

15. rectangle

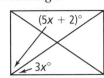
(5x + 2)°
3x°

16. rhombus

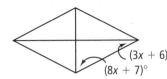
(3x + 6)°
(8x + 7)°

17. rectangle

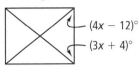
(4x − 12)°
(3x + 4)°

◎ **Open-Ended** Given two segments with lengths a and b ($a \neq b$), what special parallelograms meet the given conditions? Show each sketch.

18. Both diagonals have length a.

19. The two diagonals have lengths a and b.

20. One diagonal has length a, and one side of the quadrilateral has length b.

Proof 21. Prove Theorem 54.

    Given: $ABCD$ is a parallelogram.
          $\overline{AC}$ bisects $\angle BAD$ and $\angle BCD$.

    Prove: $ABCD$ is a rhombus.

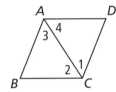

Proof 22. Prove Theorem 55.

    Given: $\square ABCD$, $\overline{AC} \cong \overline{BD}$

    Prove: $ABCD$ is a rectangle.

◎ **Think About a Plan** Explain how to construct each figure given its diagonals.
- What do you know about the diagonals of each figure?
- How can you apply constructions to what you know about the diagonals?

23. parallelogram   **24.** rectangle   **25.** rhombus

ⓒ Challenge

Determine whether the quadrilateral can be a parallelogram. Explain.

26. The diagonals are congruent, but the quadrilateral has no right angles.

27. Each diagonal is 3 cm long and two opposite sides are 2 cm long.

28. Two opposite angles are right angles, but the quadrilateral is not a rectangle.

Proof 29. In Theorem 54, replace "a pair of opposite angles" with "one angle." Write a paragraph that proves this new statement to be true, or give a counterexample to prove it to be false.

14-6 Trapezoids and Kites

G.SRT.5 Use congruence . . . criteria . . . to solve problems and to prove relationships in geometric figures. Also G.CO.9

Objective To verify and use properties of trapezoids and kites

 Solve It! Write your solution to the Solve It in the space below.

In the Solve It, the orange and green regions are trapezoids. The entire figure is a kite. In this lesson, you will learn about these special quadrilaterals that are not parallelograms.

Essential Understanding The angles, sides, and diagonals of a trapezoid have certain properties.

A **trapezoid** is a quadrilateral with exactly one pair of parallel sides. The parallel sides of a trapezoid are called **bases**. The nonparallel sides are called **legs**. The two angles that share a base of a trapezoid are called **base angles**. A trapezoid has two pairs of base angles.

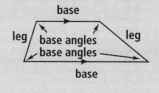

An **isosceles trapezoid** is a trapezoid with legs that are congruent. *ABCD* at the right is an isosceles trapezoid. The angles of an isosceles trapezoid have some unique properties.

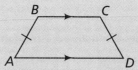

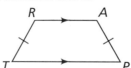 **Theorem 56**

Theorem	**If . . .**	**Then . . .**
If a quadrilateral is an isosceles trapezoid, then each pair of base angles is congruent.	*TRAP* is an isosceles trapezoid with bases $\overline{RA}$ and $\overline{TP}$	$\angle T \cong \angle P, \angle R \cong \angle A$

You will prove Theorem 56 in Exercise 35.

 **Problem 1** **Finding Angle Measures in Trapezoids**

Got It?   **a.** In the diagram, *PQRS* is an isosceles trapezoid and $m\angle R = 106$. What are $m\angle P$, $m\angle Q$, and $m\angle S$?

Think
What do you know about the angles of an isosceles trapezoid?

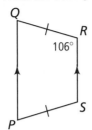

b. Reasoning In Problem 1, if *CDEF* were not an isosceles trapezoid, would $\angle C$ and $\angle D$ still be supplementary? Explain.

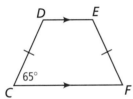

A Practice Find the measures of the numbered angles in each isosceles trapezoid.

1.

2.

Problem 2   **Finding Angle Measures in Isosceles Trapezoids**

Got It?   A fan like the one in Problem 2 has 15 angles meeting at the center. What
are the measures of the base angles of the trapezoids in its second ring?

 Practice   **Find the measures of the numbered angles in each isosceles trapezoid.**

3.

4.
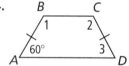

take note **Theorem 57**

Theorem	**If . . .**	**Then . . .**
If a quadrilateral is an isosceles trapezoid, then its diagonals are congruent.	*ABCD* is an isosceles trapezoid	$\overline{AC} \cong \overline{BD}$

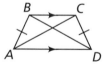

You will prove Theorem 57 in Exercise 43.

In Lesson 13-1, you learned about midsegments of triangles. Trapezoids also
have midsegments. The **midsegment of a trapezoid** is the segment that joins the
midpoints of its legs. The midsegment has two unique properties.

Theorem 58 Trapezoid Midsegment Theorem

Theorem	If . . .	Then . . .

Theorem

If a quadrilateral is a trapezoid, then
(1) the midsegment is parallel to the bases, and
(2) the length of the midsegment is half the sum of the lengths of the bases.

If . . .

TRAP is a trapezoid with midsegment $\overline{MN}$

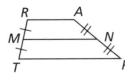

Then . . .

(1) $\overline{MN} \parallel \overline{TP}$, $\overline{MN} \parallel \overline{RA}$, and
(2) $MN = \frac{1}{2}\left(TP + RA\right)$

You will prove Theorem 58 in Lesson 14-8.

Problem 3 **Using the Midsegment of a Trapezoid**

Got It? **a. Algebra** $\overline{MN}$ is the midsegment of trapezoid *PQRS*. What is *x*? What is *MN*?

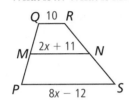

> **Think**
> **How can you check your answer?**

b. Reasoning How many midsegments can a triangle have? How many midsegments can a trapezoid have? Explain.

A Practice Find *EF* in each trapezoid.

5.

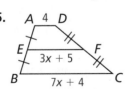

6.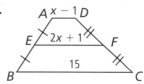

A **kite** is a quadrilateral with two pairs of consecutive sides congruent and no opposite sides congruent.

Essential Understanding The angles, sides, and diagonals of a kite have certain properties.

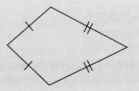

Theorem 59

Theorem	If . . .	Then . . .
If a quadrilateral is a kite, then its diagonals are perpendicular.	*ABCD* is a kite	$\overline{AC} \perp \overline{BD}$

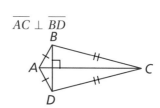

Proof **Proof of Theorem 59**

Given: Kite *ABCD* with $\overline{AB} \cong \overline{AD}$ and $\overline{CB} \cong \overline{CD}$

Prove: $\overline{AC} \perp \overline{BD}$

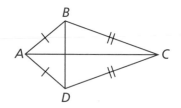

Statements	Reasons
1) Kite *ABCD* with $\overline{AB} \cong \overline{AD}$ and $\overline{CB} \cong \overline{CD}$	**1)** Given
2) *A* and *C* lie on the perpendicular bisector of $\overline{BD}$.	**2)** Converse of Perpendicular Bisector Theorem
3) $\overline{AC}$ is the perpendicular bisector of $\overline{BD}$.	**3)** Two points determine a line.
4) $\overline{AC} \perp \overline{BD}$	**4)** Definition of perpendicular bisector

Problem 4 **Finding Angle Measures in Kites**

Got It? Quadrilateral *KLMN* is a kite. What are $m\angle 1$, $m\angle 2$, and $m\angle 3$?

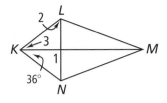

 Practice Find the measures of the numbered angles in each kite.

7.

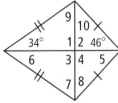

8.

Concept Summary Relationships Among Quadrilaterals

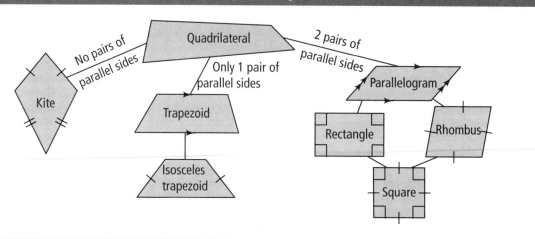

Lesson Check

Do you know HOW?

What are the measures of the numbered angles?

9.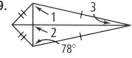

10.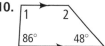

11. What is the length of the midsegment of a trapezoid with bases of lengths 14 and 26?

Do you UNDERSTAND?

Ⓒ **12. Vocabulary** Is a kite a parallelogram? Explain.

Ⓒ **13. Compare and Contrast** How is a kite similar to a rhombus? How is it different? Explain.

Ⓒ **14. Error Analysis** Since a parallelogram has two pairs of parallel sides, it certainly has one pair of parallel sides. Therefore, a parallelogram must also be a trapezoid. What is the error in this reasoning? Explain.

More Practice and Problem-Solving Exercises

Ⓑ Apply

Ⓒ **15. Open-Ended** Sketch two noncongruent kites such that the diagonals of one are congruent to the diagonals of the other.

Ⓒ **16. Think About a Plan** The perimeter of a kite is 66 cm. The length of one of its sides is 3 cm less than twice the length of another. Find the length of each side of the kite.
- Can you draw a diagram?
- How can you write algebraic expressions for the lengths of the sides?

Ⓒ **17. Reasoning** If $KLMN$ is an isosceles trapezoid, is it possible for $\overline{KM}$ to bisect $\angle LMN$ and $\angle LKN$? Explain.

Algebra Find the value of the variable in each isosceles trapezoid.

18.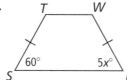

19.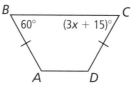

20.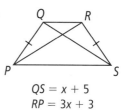

$QS = x + 5$
$RP = 3x + 3$

Algebra Find the lengths of the segments with variable expressions.

21.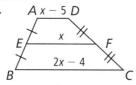

22.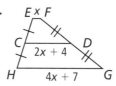

23.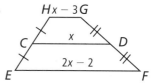

Algebra Find the value(s) of the variable(s) in each kite.

24.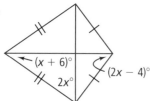

25.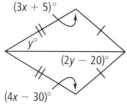

26.

STEM **Bridge Design** The beams of the bridge at the right form quadrilateral *ABCD*. △*AED* ≅ △*CDE* ≅ △*BEC* and $m\angle DCB = 120$.

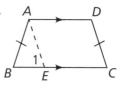

27. Classify the quadrilateral. Explain your reasoning.

28. Find the measures of the other interior angles of the quadrilateral.

Ⓖ Reasoning Can two angles of a kite be as follows? Explain.

29. opposite and acute

30. consecutive and obtuse

31. opposite and supplementary

32. consecutive and supplementary

33. opposite and complementary

34. consecutive and complementary

Ⓖ 35. Developing Proof The plan suggests a proof of Theorem 56. Write a proof that follows the plan.

Given: Isosceles trapezoid *ABCD* with $\overline{AB} \cong \overline{DC}$

Prove: $\angle B \cong \angle C$ and $\angle BAD \cong \angle D$

Plan: Begin by drawing $\overline{AE} \parallel \overline{DC}$ to form parallelogram *AECD* so that $\overline{AE} \cong \overline{DC} \cong \overline{AB}$. $\angle B \cong \angle C$ because $\angle B \cong \angle 1$ and $\angle 1 \cong \angle C$. Also, $\angle BAD \cong \angle D$ because they are supplements of the congruent angles, $\angle B$ and $\angle C$.

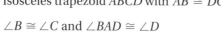

Proof 36. Prove the converse of Theorem 56: If a trapezoid has a pair of congruent base angles, then the trapezoid is isosceles.

Name each type of special quadrilateral that can meet the given condition. Make sketches to support your answers.

37. exactly one pair of congruent sides

38. two pairs of parallel sides

39. four right angles

40. adjacent sides that are congruent

41. perpendicular diagonals

42. congruent diagonals

Proof 43. Prove Theorem 57.
    Given: Isosceles trapezoid $ABCD$ with $\overline{AB} \cong \overline{DC}$
    Prove: $\overline{AC} \cong \overline{DB}$

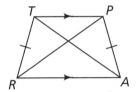

Proof 44. Prove the converse of Theorem 57: If the diagonals of a trapezoid are congruent, then the trapezoid is isosceles.

Proof 45. Given: Isosceles trapezoid $TRAP$ with $\overline{TR} \cong \overline{PA}$
    Prove: $\angle RTA \cong \angle APR$

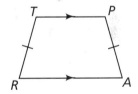

Proof 46. Prove that the angles formed by the noncongruent sides of a kite are congruent. (*Hint:* Draw a diagonal of the kite.)

Determine whether each statement is *true* or *false*. Justify your response.

47. All squares are rectangles.

48. A trapezoid is a parallelogram.

49. A rhombus can be a kite.

50. Some parallelograms are squares.

51. Every quadrilateral is a parallelogram.

52. All rhombuses are squares.

Ⓒ Challenge

Proof 53. Given: Isosceles trapezoid $TRAP$ with $\overline{TR} \cong \overline{PA}$; $\overline{BI}$ is the perpendicular bisector of $\overline{RA}$, intersecting $\overline{RA}$ at B and $\overline{TP}$ at I.

    Prove: $\overline{BI}$ is the perpendicular bisector of $\overline{TP}$.

For a trapezoid, consider the segment joining the midpoints of the two given segments. How are its length and the lengths of the two parallel sides of the trapezoid related? Justify your answer.

54. the two nonparallel sides

55. the diagonals

56. $\overleftrightarrow{BN}$ is the perpendicular bisector of $\overline{AC}$ at N. Describe the set of points, D, for which $ABCD$ is a kite.

14-7 Applying Coordinate Geometry

G.CO.11 Prove theorems about parallelograms. Theorems include: opposite sides are congruent . . . Also G.CO.10

Objective To name coordinates of special figures by using their properties

Solve It! Write your solution to the Solve It in the space below.

In the Solve It, you found coordinates of a point and named it using numbers for the *x*- and *y*-coordinates. In this lesson, you will learn to use variables for the coordinates.

Essential Understanding You can use variables to name the coordinates of a figure. This allows you to show that relationships are true for a general case.

In Chapter 13, you learned about the segment joining the midpoints of two sides of a triangle. Here are three possible ways to place a triangle and its midsegment.

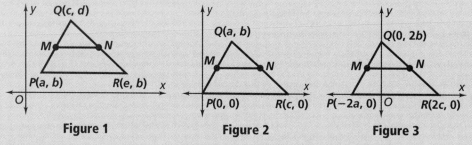

Figure 1 does not use the axes, so it requires more variables. Figures 2 and 3 have good placement. In Figure 2, the midpoint coordinates are $M\left(\frac{a}{2}, \frac{b}{2}\right)$ and $N\left(\frac{a+c}{2}, \frac{b}{2}\right)$. In Figure 3, the coordinates are $M(-a, b)$ and $N(c, b)$. You can see that Figure 3 is the easiest to work with.

To summarize, to place a figure in the coordinate plane, it is usually helpful to place at least one side on an axis or to center the figure at the origin. For the coordinates, try to anticipate what you will need to do in the problem. Then multiply the coordinates by the appropriate number to make your work easier.

Problem 1   Naming Coordinates

Got It?   What are the coordinates of the vertices of each figure?

a. *RECT* is a rectangle with height *a* and length 2*b*. The *y*-axis bisects $\overline{EC}$ and $\overline{RT}$.

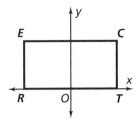

b. *KITE* is a kite where $IE = 2a$, $KO = b$, and $OT = c$. The *x*-axis bisects $\overline{IE}$.

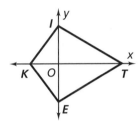

Practice Algebra   What are the coordinates of the vertices of each figure?

1. parallelogram where *S* is *a* units from the origin and *Z* is *b* units from the origin

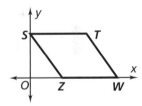

2. isosceles trapezoid with base centered at the origin, with base 2*a* and $OR = c$

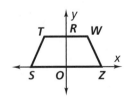

Got It? **a. Reasoning** In Problem 2, explain why the *x*-coordinate of *B* is the sum of 2*a* and 2*b*.

b. The diagram below shows a trapezoid with the base centered at the origin. Is the trapezoid isosceles? Explain.

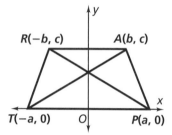

Plan

Which formula should you use to show that the trapezoid is isosceles?

Practice **3.** The diagram at the right shows a parallelogram. Without using the Distance Formula, determine whether the parallelogram is a rhombus. How do you know?

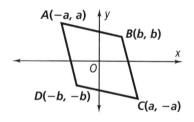

You can use coordinate geometry and algebra to prove theorems in geometry. This kind of proof is called a **coordinate proof.** Sometimes it is easier to show that a theorem is true by using a coordinate proof rather than a standard deductive proof. It is useful to write a plan for a coordinate proof. Problem 3 shows you how.

Problem 3 **Planning a Coordinate Proof**

Got It? Plan a coordinate proof of the Triangle Midsegment Theorem (Theorem 24).

Think

What conditions must be proved for the Triangle Midsegment Theorem?

Ⓐ Practice 4. Plan a coordinate proof to show that the midpoints of the sides of an isosceles trapezoid form a rhombus.

    a. Name the coordinates of isosceles trapezoid *TRAP* at the right, with bottom base length 4*a*, top base length 4*b*, and *EG* = 2*c*. The *y*-axis bisects the bases.

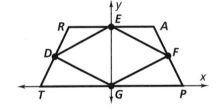

    b. Write the *Given* and *Prove* statements.

c. How will you find the coordinates of the midpoints of each side?

d. How will you determine whether *DEFG* is a rhombus?

Lesson Check

Do you know HOW?

Use the diagram at the right.

5. In ▱*KLMO*, *OM* = 2*a*. What are the coordinates of *K* and *M*?

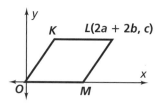

6. What are the slopes of the diagonals of *KLMO*?

7. What are the coordinates of the point of intersection of $\overline{KM}$ and $\overline{OL}$?

Do you UNDERSTAND?

8. Reasoning How do variable coordinates generalize figures in the coordinate plane?

9. Reasoning A vertex of a quadrilateral has coordinates (a, b). The x-coordinates of the other three vertices are a or $-a$, and the y-coordinates are b or $-b$. What kind of quadrilateral is the figure?

© **10. Error Analysis** A classmate says the endpoints of the midsegment of the trapezoid in Problem 3 are $\left(\frac{b}{2}, \frac{c}{2}\right)$ and $\left(\frac{d+a}{2}, \frac{c}{2}\right)$. What is your classmate's error? Explain.

More Practice and Problem-Solving Exercises

Ⓑ Apply

© **11. Open-Ended** Place a general quadrilateral in the coordinate plane.

© **12. Reasoning** A rectangle *LMNP* is centered at the origin with $M(r, -s)$. What are the coordinates of *P*?

Give the coordinates for point *P* without using any new variables.

13. isosceles trapezoid

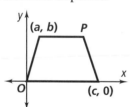

14. trapezoid with a right ∠

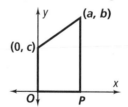

15. kite

© **16. a.** Draw a square whose diagonals of length 2*b* lie on the *x*- and *y*-axes.
  b. Give the coordinates of the vertices of the square.
  c. Compute the length of a side of the square.
  d. Find the slopes of two adjacent sides of the square.
  e. Writing Do the slopes show that the sides are perpendicular? Explain.

17. Make two drawings of an isosceles triangle with base length 2*b* and height 2*c*.
  a. In one drawing, place the base on the *x*-axis with a vertex at the origin.
  b. In the second, place the base on the *x*-axis with its midpoint at the origin.
  c. Find the lengths of the legs of the triangle as placed in part (a).
  d. Find the lengths of the legs of the triangle as placed in part (b).
  e. How do the results of parts (c) and (d) compare?

18. W and Z are the midpoints of $\overline{OR}$ and $\overline{ST}$, respectively. In parts (a)–(c), find the coordinates of W and Z.

a.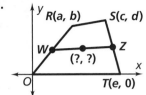

b.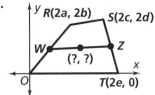

c.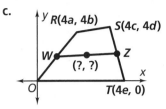

d. You are to plan a coordinate proof involving the midpoint of $\overline{WZ}$. Which of the figures (a)–(c) would you prefer to use? Explain.

Plan the coordinate proof of each statement.

19. Think About a Plan The opposite sides of a parallelogram are congruent (Theorem 40).
  - How will you place the parallelogram in a coordinate plane?
  - What formulas will you need to use?

20. The diagonals of a rectangle bisect each other.

21. The consecutive sides of a square are perpendicular.

Classify each quadrilateral as precisely as possible.

22. $A(b, 2c)$, $B(4b, 3c)$, $C(5b, c)$, $D(2b, 0)$

23. $E(a, b)$, $F(2a, 2b)$, $G(3a, b)$, $H(2a, -b)$

24. $O(0, 0)$, $P(t, 2s)$, $Q(3t, 2s)$, $R(4t, 0)$

25. $O(0, 0)$, $L(-e, f)$, $M(f - e, f + e)$, $N(f, e)$

26. What property of a rhombus makes it convenient to place its diagonals on the x- and y-axes?

STEM 27. Marine Archaeology Marine archaeologists sometimes use a coordinate system on the ocean floor. They record the coordinates of points where artifacts are found. Assume that each diver searches a square area and can go no farther than b units from the starting point. Draw a model for the region one diver can search. Assign coordinates to the vertices without using any new variables.

Challenge

Here are coordinates for eight points in the coordinate plane ($q > p > 0$). $A(0, 0)$, $B(p, 0)$, $C(q, 0)$, $D(p + q, 0)$, $E(0, q)$, $F(p, q)$, $G(q, q)$, $H(p + q, q)$. Which four points, if any, are the vertices for each type of figure?

28. parallelogram **29.** rhombus **30.** rectangle

31. square **32.** trapezoid **33.** isosceles trapezoid

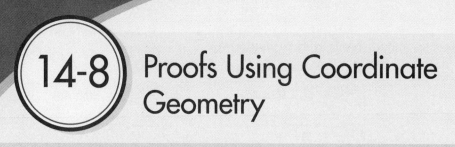

14-8 Proofs Using Coordinate Geometry

G.CO.11 Prove theorems about parallelograms . . . Also **G.CO.10**

Objective To prove theorems using figures in the coordinate plane

Solve It! Write your solution to the Solve It in the space below.

In the Solve It, the coordinates of the points include variables. In this lesson, you will use coordinates with variables to write coordinate proofs.

Essential Understanding You can prove geometric relationships using variable coordinates for figures in the coordinate plane.

Problem 1 Writing a Coordinate Proof

Got It? **Reasoning** Refer to the proof in Problem 1. What is the advantage of using coordinates $O(0, 0)$, $E(0, 2b)$, and $F(2a, 0)$ rather than $O(0, 0)$, $E(0, b)$, and $F(a, 0)$?

Think
What is the advantage of placing the legs of the right triangle on the axes?

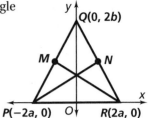

A Practice **Developing Proof** Complete the following coordinate proof.

1. The medians drawn to the congruent sides of an isosceles triangle are congruent.

   Given: $\triangle PQR$ with $\overline{PQ} \cong \overline{RQ}$, M is the midpoint of $\overline{PQ}$, N is the midpoint of $\overline{RQ}$

   Prove: $\overline{PN} \cong \overline{RM}$

   a. What are the coordinates of M and N?

   b. What are PN and RM?

   c. Explain why $\overline{PN} \cong \overline{RM}$.

In the previous lesson, you wrote a plan for the proof of the Trapezoid Midsegment Theorem. Now you will write the full coordinate proof.

 **Problem 2** Writing a Coordinate Proof

Got It? Write a coordinate proof of the Triangle Midsegment Theorem (Theorem 24).

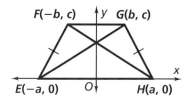

Think

How will you place the triangle in the coordinate plane and assign coordinates?

(A) Practice **Developing Proof** Complete the following coordinate proof.

2. The diagonals of an isosceles trapezoid are congruent.

Given: Trapezoid $EFGH$ with $\overline{EF} \cong \overline{GH}$

Prove: $\overline{EG} \cong \overline{FH}$

a. Find EG.

b. Find FH.

c. Explain why $\overline{EG} \cong \overline{FH}$.

Lesson Check

Do you know HOW?

3. Use coordinate geometry to prove that the diagonals of a rectangle are congruent.

    a. Place rectangle *PQRS* in the coordinate plane with *P* at (0, 0).

    b. What are the coordinates of *Q, R,* and *S*?

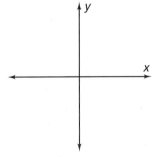

    c. Write the *Given* and *Prove* statements.

    d. Write a coordinate proof.

Do you UNDERSTAND?

  4. Reasoning Describe a good strategy for placing the vertices of a rhombus for a coordinate proof.

5. Error Analysis Your classmate places a trapezoid on the coordinate plane. What is the error?

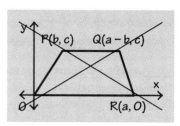

More Practice and Problem-Solving Exercises

Ⓑ Apply

Tell whether you can reach each type of conclusion below using coordinate methods. Give a reason for each answer.

6. $\overline{AB} \cong \overline{CD}$

7. $\overline{AB} \parallel \overline{CD}$

8. $\overline{AB} \perp \overline{CD}$

9. $\overline{AB}$ bisects $\overline{CD}$.

10. $\overline{AB}$ bisects $\angle CAD$.

11. $\angle A \cong \angle B$

12. $\angle A$ is a right angle.

13. $AB + BC = AC$

14. $\triangle ABC$ is isosceles.

15. Quadrilateral $ABCD$ is a rhombus.

16. $\overline{AB}$ and $\overline{CD}$ bisect each other.

17. $\angle A$ is the supplement of $\angle B$.

18. $\overline{AB}$, $\overline{CD}$, and $\overline{EF}$ are concurrent.

Proof **19. Flag Design** The flag design at the right is made by connecting the midpoints of the sides of a rectangle. Use coordinate geometry to prove that the quadrilateral formed is a rhombus.

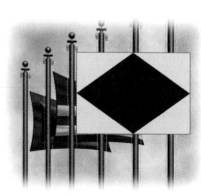

Ⓖ **20. Open-Ended** Give an example of a statement that you think is easier to prove with a coordinate geometry proof than with a proof method that does not require coordinate geometry. Explain your choice.

Use coordinate geometry to prove each statement.

Ⓖ **21. Think About a Plan** If a parallelogram is a rhombus, its diagonals are perpendicular (Theorem 50).
  • How will you place the rhombus in a coordinate plane?
  • What formulas will you need to use?

22. The altitude to the base of an isosceles triangle bisects the base.

23. If the midpoints of a trapezoid are joined to form a quadrilateral, then the quadrilateral is a parallelogram.

24. One diagonal of a kite divides the kite into two congruent triangles.

Proof 25. You learned in Theorem 31 that the centroid of a triangle is two thirds the distance from each vertex to the midpoint of the opposite side. Complete the steps to prove this theorem.

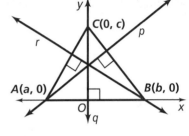

a. Find the coordinates of points L, M, and N, the midpoints of the sides of $\triangle ABC$.

b. Find equations of $\overleftrightarrow{AM}$, $\overleftrightarrow{BN}$, and $\overleftrightarrow{CL}$.

c. Find the coordinates of point P, the intersection of $\overleftrightarrow{AM}$ and $\overleftrightarrow{BN}$.

d. Show that point P is on $\overleftrightarrow{CL}$.

e. Use the Distance Formula to show that point P is two thirds the distance from each vertex to the midpoint of the opposite side.

Proof 26. Complete the steps to prove Theorem 32. You are given $\triangle ABC$ with altitudes p, q, and r. Show that p, q, and r intersect at a point (called the orthocenter of the triangle).

a. The slope of $\overline{BC}$ is $\frac{c}{-b}$. What is the slope of line p?

b. Show that the equation of line p is $y = \frac{b}{c}(x - a)$.

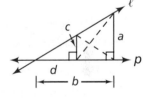

c. What is the equation of line q?

d. Show that lines p and q intersect at $\left(0, \frac{-ab}{c}\right)$.

e. The slope of $\overline{AC}$ is $\frac{c}{-a}$. What is the slope of line r?

f. Show that the equation of line r is $y = \frac{a}{c}(x - b)$.

g. Show that lines r and q intersect at $\left(0, \frac{-ab}{c}\right)$.

h. What are the coordinates of the orthocenter of $\triangle ABC$?

Ⓒ Challenge

27. **Multiple Representations** Use the diagram at the right.

a. Explain using area why $\frac{1}{2}ad = \frac{1}{2}bc$ and therefore $ad = bc$.

b. Find two ratios for the slope of ℓ. Use these two ratios to show that $ad = bc$.

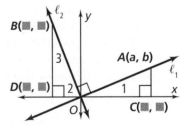

Proof 28. Prove: If two lines are perpendicular, the product of their slopes is -1.

a. Two nonvertical lines, ℓ_1 and ℓ_2, intersect as shown at the right. Find the coordinates of C.

b. Choose coordinates for D and B. (*Hint:* Find the relationship between $\angle 1$, $\angle 2$, and $\angle 3$. Then use congruent triangles.)

c. Complete the proof that the product of slopes is -1.

14-1 The Polygon Angle-Sum Theorems

Quick Review

The sum of the measures of the interior angles of an n-gon is $(n-2)180$. The measure of one interior angle of a regular n-gon is $\frac{(n-2)180}{n}$. The sum of the measures of the exterior angles of a polygon, one at each vertex, is 360.

Example

Find the measure of an interior angle of a regular 20-gon.

$$\text{Measure} = \frac{(n-2)180}{n} \qquad \text{Corollary to the Polygon Angle-Sum Theorem}$$

$$= \frac{(20-2)180}{20} \qquad \text{Substitute.}$$

$$= \frac{18 \cdot 180}{20} \qquad \text{Simplify.}$$

$$= 162$$

The measure of an interior angle is 162.

Exercises

Find the measure of an interior angle and an exterior angle of each regular polygon.

1. hexagon

2. 16-gon

3. pentagon

4. What is the sum of the exterior angles for each polygon in Exercises 1–3?

Find the measure of the missing angle.

5.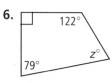

6.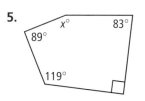

14-2 Properties of Parallelograms

Quick Review

Opposite sides and **opposite angles** of a **parallelogram** are congruent. **Consecutive angles** in a parallelogram are supplementary. The diagonals of a parallelogram bisect each other. If three (or more) parallel lines cut off congruent segments on one transversal, then they cut off congruent segments on every transversal.

Example

Find the measures of the numbered angles in the parallelogram.

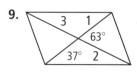

Since consecutive angles are supplementary, $m\angle 1 = 180 - 56$, or 124. Since opposite angles are congruent, $m\angle 2 = 56$ and $m\angle 3 = 124$.

Exercises

Find the measures of the numbered angles for each parallelogram.

7.

8.

9.

10.

Find the values of x and y in $\square ABCD$.

11. $AB = 2y$, $BC = y + 3$, $CD = 5x - 1$, $DA = 2x + 4$

12. $AB = 2y + 1$, $BC = y + 1$, $CD = 7x - 3$, $DA = 3x$

14-3 Proving That a Quadrilateral Is a Parallelogram

Quick Review

A quadrilateral is a parallelogram if any one of the following is true.

- Both pairs of opposite sides are parallel.
- Both pairs of opposite sides are congruent.
- Consecutive angles are supplementary.
- Both pairs of opposite angles are congruent.
- The diagonals bisect each other.
- One pair of opposite sides is both congruent and parallel.

Example

Must the quadrilateral be a parallelogram?

Yes, both pairs of opposite angles are congruent.

Exercises

Determine whether the quadrilateral must be a parallelogram.

13.

14.

Algebra Find the values of the variables for which *ABCD* must be a parallelogram.

15.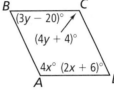

16.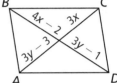

14-4 Properties of Rhombuses, Rectangles, and Squares

Quick Review

A **rhombus** is a parallelogram with four congruent sides.

A **rectangle** is a parallelogram with four right angles.

A **square** is a parallelogram with four congruent sides and four right angles.

The diagonals of a rhombus are perpendicular. Each diagonal bisects a pair of opposite angles.

The diagonals of a rectangle are congruent.

Example

What are the measures of the numbered angles in the rhombus?

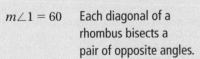

$m\angle 1 = 60$ Each diagonal of a rhombus bisects a pair of opposite angles.

$m\angle 2 = 90$ The diagonals of a rhombus are $\perp$.

$60 + m\angle 2 + m\angle 3 = 180$ Triangle Angle-Sum Thm.

$60 + 90 + m\angle 3 = 180$ Substitute.

$m\angle 3 = 30$ Simplify.

Exercises

Find the measures of the numbered angles in each special parallelogram.

17.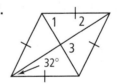

18.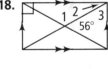

Determine whether each statement is *always*, *sometimes*, or *never* true.

19. A rhombus is a square.

20. A square is a rectangle.

21. A rhombus is a rectangle.

22. The diagonals of a parallelogram are perpendicular.

23. The diagonals of a parallelogram are congruent.

24. Opposite angles of a parallelogram are congruent.

14-5 Conditions for Rhombuses, Rectangles, and Squares

Quick Review

If one diagonal of a parallelogram bisects two angles of the parallelogram, then the parallelogram is a rhombus. If the diagonals of a parallelogram are perpendicular, then the parallelogram is a rhombus. If the diagonals of a parallelogram are congruent, then the parallelogram is a rectangle.

Example

Can you conclude that the parallelogram is a rhombus, rectangle, or square? Explain.

Yes, the diagonals are perpendicular, so the parallelogram is a rhombus.

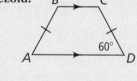

Exercises

Can you conclude that the parallelogram is a rhombus, rectangle, or square? Explain.

25.   26.

For what value of x is the figure the given parallelogram? Justify your answer.

27. Rhombus
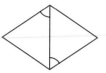
$(5x - 30)°$ $(3x + 6)°$

28. Rectangle
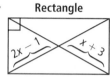
$2x - 1$ $x + 3$

14-6 Trapezoids and Kites

Quick Review

The parallel sides of a **trapezoid** are its **bases** and the nonparallel sides are its **legs**. Two angles that share a base of a trapezoid are **base angles** of the trapezoid. The **midsegment of a trapezoid** joins the midpoints of its legs.

The base angles of an isosceles trapezoid are congruent.

The diagonals of an isosceles trapezoid are congruent.

The diagonals of a kite are perpendicular.

Example

ABCD is an isosceles trapezoid. What is $m\angle C$?

Since $\overline{BC} \parallel \overline{AD}$, $\angle C$ and $\angle D$ are same-side interior angles.

$m\angle C + m\angle D = 180$ Same-side interior angles are supplementary.

$m\angle C + 60 = 180$ Substitute.

$m\angle C = 120$ Subtract 60 from each side.

Exercises

Find the measures of the numbered angles in each isosceles trapezoid.

29. 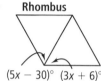 30.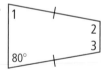

Find the measures of the numbered angles in each kite.

31. 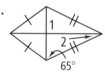 32.

33. **Algebra** A trapezoid has base lengths of $(6x - 1)$ units and 3 units. Its midsegment has a length of $(5x - 3)$ units. What is the value of x?

14-7 and 14-8
Applying Coordinate Geometry and Proofs Using Coordinate Geometry

Quick Review

When placing a figure in the coordinate plane, it is usually helpful to place at least one side on an axis. Use variables when naming the coordinates of a figure in order to show that relationships are true for a general case.

Example

Rectangle *PQRS* has length *a* and width 4*b*. The *x*-axis bisects $\overline{PS}$ and $\overline{QR}$. What are the coordinates of the vertices?

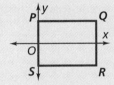

Since the width of *PQRS* is 4*b* and the *x*-axis bisects $\overline{PS}$ and $\overline{QR}$, all the vertices are 2*b* units from the *x*-axis. $\overline{PS}$ is on the *y*-axis, so $P = (0, 2b)$ and $S = (0, -2b)$. The length of *PQRS* is *a*, so $Q = (a, 2b)$ and $R = (a, -2b)$.

Exercises

34. In rhombus *FLPS*, the axes form the diagonals. If $SL = 2a$ and $FP = 4b$, what are the coordinates of the vertices?

35. The figure at the right is a parallelogram. Give the coordinates of point *P* without using any new variables.

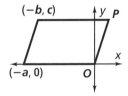

36. Use coordinate geometry to prove that the quadrilateral formed by connecting the midpoints of a kite is a rectangle.

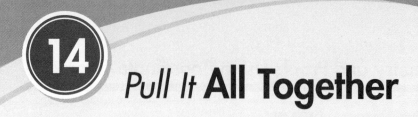

14 *Pull It* **All Together**

Building a Kite

Charles is building a paper kite. He needs another dowel to make the vertical support for the frame. He gives his friend Amy the measurements below but neglects to include the length of the support.

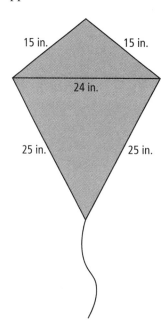

15 in.   15 in.

24 in.

25 in.   25 in.

Task Description

Find the length of the vertical support for this kite and the area of the paper used to make the kite.

- What is true about the diagonals of a kite? How can you use this information to find the length of the vertical support?

- How can you find the kite's area by decomposing the kite into smaller figures?

Postulates and Theorems

Postulates

Postulate 1
Through any two points there is exactly one line.

Postulate 2
If two distinct lines intersect, then they intersect in exactly one point.

Postulate 3
If two distinct planes intersect, then they intersect in exactly one line.

Postulate 4
Through any three noncollinear points there is exactly on plane.

Postulate 5
Ruler Postulate
Every point on a line can be paired with a real number. This makes a one-to-one correspondence between the points on the line and the real numbers.

Postulate 6
Segment Addition Postulate
If three points A, B, and C are collinear and B is between A and C, then $AB + BC = AC$.

Postulate 7
Protractor Postulate
Consider $\overrightarrow{OB}$ and a point A on one side of $\overrightarrow{OB}$. Every ray of the form $\overrightarrow{OA}$ can be paired one to one with a real number from 0 to 180.

Postulate 8
Angle Addition Postulate
If point B is in the interior of $\angle AOC$, then $m\angle AOB + m\angle BOC = m\angle AOC$.

Postulate 9
Linear Pair Postulate
If two angles form a linear pair, then they are supplementary.

Postulate 10
Area Addition Postulate
The area of a region is the sum of the area of its nonoverlapping parts.

Postulate 11
Same-Side Interior Angles Postulate
If a transversal intersects two parallel lines, then same-side interior angles are supplementary.

Postulate 12
Parallel Postulate
Through a point not on a line, there is one and only one line parallel to the given line.

Postulate 13
Perpendicular Postulate
Through a point not on a line, there is one and only one line perpendicular to the given line.

Postulate 14
Side-Side-Side (SSS) Postulate
If three sides of one triangle are congruent to the three sides of another triangle, then the two triangles are congruent.

Postulate 15
Side-Angle-Side (SAS) Postulate
If two sides and the included angle of one triangle are congruent to two sides and the included angle of another triangle, then the two triangles are congruent.

Postulate 16
Angle-Side-Angle (ASA) Postulate
If two angles and the included side of one triangle are congruent to two angles and the included side of another triangle, then the two triangles are congruent.

Theorems

Theorem 1
Vertical Angles Theorem
Vertical angles are congruent.

Theorem 2
Congruent Supplements Theorem
If two angles are supplements of the same angle (or of two congruent angles), then the two angles are congruent.

Theorem 3
Congruent Complements Theorem
If two angles are complements of the same angle (or of two congruent angles), then the two angles are congruent.

Theorem 4
All right angles are congruent.

Theorem 5
If two angles are congruent and supplementary, then each is a right angle.

Theorem 6
Alternate Interior Angles Theorem
If a transversal intersects two parallel lines, the alternate interior angles are congruent.

Theorem 7
Corresponding Angles Theorem
If a transversal intersects two parallel lines, then corresponding angles are congruent.

Theorem 8
Alternate Exterior Angles Theorem
If a transversal intersects two parallel lines, then alternate exterior angles are congruent.

Theorem 9
Converse of the Corresponding Angles Theorem
If two lines and a transversal form corresponding angles that are congruent, then the two lines are parallel.

Theorem 10
Converse of the Alternate Interior Angles Theorem
If two lines and a transversal form alternate interior angles that are congruent, then the two lines are parallel.

Theorem 11
Converse of the Same-Side Interior Angles Postulate
If two lines and a transversal form same-side interior angles that are congruent, then the two lines are parallel.

Theorem 12
Converse of the Alternate Exterior Angles Theorem
If two lines and a transversal form alternate exterior angles that are congruent, then the two lines are parallel.

Theorem 13
If two lines are parallel to the same line, then they are parallel to each other.

Theorem 14
In a plane, if two lines are perpendicular to the same line, then they are parallel to each other.

Theorem 15
Perpendicular Transversal Theorem
In a plane, if a line is perpendicular to one of two parallel lines, then it is perpendicular to the other.

Theorem 16
Triangle Angle-Sum Theorem
The sum of the measures of the angles of a triangle is 180.

Theorem 17
Triangle Exterior Angle Theorem
The measure of each exterior angle of a triangle equals the sum of the measure of its two remote interior angles.

Corollary
The measure of an exterior angle of a triangle is greater than the measure of each of its remote interior angles.

Theorem 18
Third Angles Theorem
If two angles of one triangle are congruent to two angles of another triangle, than the third angles are congruent.

Theorem 19
Angle-Angle-Side (AAS) Theorem
If two angles and a nonincluded side of one triangle are congruent to two angles and a nonincluded side of another triangle, then the two triangles are congruent.

Theorem 20
Isosceles Triangle Theorem
If two sides of a triangle are congruent, then the angles opposite those sides are congruent.

Corollary
If a triangle is equilateral, then the triangle is equiangular.

Theorem 21
Converse of the Isosceles Triangle Theorem
If two angles of a triangle are congruent, then the sides opposite the angles are congruent.

Corollary
If a triangle is equiangular, then it is equilateral.

Theorem 22
If a line bisects the vertex angle of an isosceles triangle, then the line is also the perpendicular bisector of the base.

Theorem 23
Hypotenuse-Leg (HL) Theorem
If the hypotenuse and a leg of one right triangle are congruent to the hypotenuse and a leg of another right triangle, then the triangles are congruent.

Theorem 24
Triangle Midsegment Theorem
If a line segment joins the midpoints of two sides of a triangle, then the segment is parallel to the third side and is half as long.

Theorem 25
Perpendicular Bisector Theorem
If a point is on the perpendicular bisector of a line segment, then it is equidistant from the endpoints of the segment.

Theorem 26
Converse of the Perpendicular Bisector Theorem
If a point is equidistant from the endpoints of a line segment, then it is on the perpendicular bisector of the segment.

Theorem 27
Angle Bisector Theorem
If a point is on the bisector of an angle, then the point is equidistant from the sides of the angle.

Theorem 28
Converse of the Angle Bisector Theorem
If a point in the interior of an angle is equidistant from the sides of the angle, then the point is on the angle bisector

Theorem 29
Concurrency of Perpendicular Bisectors Theorem
The perpendicular bisectors of the sides of a triangle are concurrent at a point equidistant from the vertices.

Theorem 30
Concurrency of Angle Bisectors Theorem
The bisectors of the angles of a triangle are concurrent at a point equidistant from the sides of the triangle.

Theorem 31
Concurrency of Medians Theorem
The medians of a triangle are concurrent at a point that is two-thirds the distance from each vertex to the midpoint of the opposite side.

Theorem 32
Concurrency of Altitudes Theorem
The lines that contain the altitudes of a triangle are concurrent.

Theorem 33
If two sides of a triangle are not congruent, then the larger angle lies opposite the longer side.

Theorem 34
If two angles of a triangle are not congruent, then the longer side lies opposite the larger angle.

Theorem 35
Triangle Inequality Theorem
The sum of the lengths of any two sides of a triangle is greater than the length of the third side.

Theorem 36
The Hinge Theorem (SAS Inequality Theorem)
If two sides of one triangle are congruent to two sides of another triangle and the included angles are not congruent, then the longer third side is opposite the larger included angle.

Theorem 37
Converse of the Hinge Theorem (SSS Inequality)
If two sides of one triangle are congruent to two sides of another triangle and the third sides are not congruent, then the larger included angle is opposite the longer third side.

Theorem 38
Polygon Angle-Sum Theorem
The sum of the measures of the angles of an n-gon is $(n - 2)180$.

> **Corollary**
> The measure of each angle of a regular n-gon is $\frac{(n - 2)180}{n}$.

Theorem 39
The sum of the measures of the exterior angles of a polygon, one at each vertex, is 360.

Theorem 40
If a quadrilateral is a parallelogram, then its opposite sides are congruent.

Theorem 41
If a quadrilateral is a parallelogram, then its consecutive angles are supplementary.

Theorem 42
If a quadrilateral is a parallelogram, then its opposite angles are congruent.

Theorem 43
If a quadrilateral is a parallelogram, then its diagonals bisect each other.

Theorem 44
If three (or more) parallel lines cut off congruent segments on one transversal, then they cut off congruent segments on every transversal.

Theorem 45
If both pairs of opposite sides of a quadrilateral are congruent, then the quadrilateral is a parallelogram.

Theorem 46
If an angle of a quadrilateral is supplementary to both of its consecutive angles, then the quadrilateral is a parallelogram.

Theorem 47
If both pairs of opposite angles of a quadrilateral are congruent, then the quadrilateral is a parallelogram.

Theorem 48
If the diagonals of a quadrilateral bisect each other, then the quadrilateral is a parallelogram.

Theorem 49
If one pair of opposite sides of a quadrilateral is both congruent and parallel, then the quadrilateral is a parallelogram.

Theorem 50
If a parallelogram is a rhombus, then its diagonals are perpendicular.

Theorem 51
If a parallelogram is a rhombus, then each diagonal bisects a pair of opposite angles.

Theorem 52
If a parallelogram is a rectangle, then its diagonals are congruent.

Theorem 53
If the diagonals of a parallelogram are perpendicular, then the parallelogram is a rhombus.

Theorem 54
If one diagonal of a parallelogram bisects a pair of opposite angles, then the parallelogram is a rhombus.

Theorem 55
If the diagonals of a parallelogram are congruent, then the parallelogram is a rectangle.

Theorem 56
If a quadrilateral is an isosceles trapezoid, then each pair of base angles is congruent.

Theorem 57
If a quadrilateral is an isosceles trapezoid, then its diagonals are congruent.

Theorem 58
Trapezoid Midsegment Theorem
If a quadrilateral is a trapezoid, then

  (1) the midsegment is parallel to the bases, and

  (2) the length of the midsegment is half the sum of the lengths of the bases.

Theorem 59
If a quadrilateral is a kite, then its diagonals are perpendicular.

Visual Glossary

English

Absolute value function (p. 219) A function with a V-shaped graph that opens up or down. The parent function for the family of absolute value functions is $y = |x|$.

Example

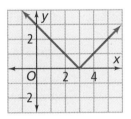

Accuracy (p. 49) Accuracy is the degree of how close a measurement is to the true value of the measurement.

Acute Angle (p. 460) An acute angle is an angle whose measure is between 0 and 90.

Example

$17°$

Adjacent angles (p. 466) Adjacent angles are two coplanar angles that have a common side and a common vertex but no common interior points.

Example

$\angle 1$ and $\angle 2$ are adjacent.

$\angle 3$ and $\angle 4$ are *not* adjacent.

Alternate interior (exterior) angles (p. 655)
Alternate interior (exterior) angles are nonadjacent interior (exterior) angles that lie on opposite sides of the transversal.

Example

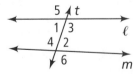

$\angle 1$ and $\angle 2$ are alternate interior angles, as are $\angle 3$ and $\angle 4$. $\angle 5$ and $\angle 6$ are alternate exterior angles.

Spanish

Función de valor absoluto (p. 219) Función cuya gráfica forma una V que se abre hacia arriba o hacia abajo. La función madre de la familia de funciones de valor absoluto es $y = |x|$.

Exactitud (p. 49) La exactitud es el grado de lo cerca que una medición está del valor verdadero de la cantidad que se mide.

Ángulo agudo (p. 460) Un ángulo agudo es un ángulo que mide entre 0 y 90 grados.

Ángulos adyacentes (p. 466) Los ángulos adyacentes son dos ángulos coplanarios que tienen un lado común y el mismo vértice, pero no tienen puntos interiores comunes.

Ángulos alternos internos (externos) (p. 655) Los ángulos alternos internos (externos) son ángulos internos (externos) no adyacentes situados en lados opuestos de la transversal.

English

Spanish

Altitude (p. 559)   *See* **parallelogram; trapezoid.**

Altura (p. 559)   *Ver* **parallelogram; trapezoid.**

Altitude of a triangle (p. 813)   An altitude of a triangle is the perpendicular segment from a vertex to the line containing the side opposite that vertex.

Altura de un triángulo (p. 813)   Una altura de un triángulo es el segmento perpendicular que va desde un vértice hasta la recta que contiene el lado opuesto a ese vértice.

Example

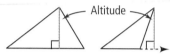

Angle (p. 458)   An angle is formed by two rays with the same endpoint. The rays are the *sides* of the angle and the common endpoint is the *vertex* of the angle.

Ángulo (p. 458)   Un ángulo está formado por dos semirrectas que convergen en un mismo extremo. Las semirrectas son los *lados* del ángulo y los extremos en común son el *vértice*.

Example

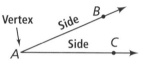

This angle could be named $\angle A$, $\angle BAC$, or $\angle CAB$.

Angle bisector (p. 471)   An angle bisector is a ray that divides an angle into two congruent angles.

Bisectriz de un ángulo (p. 471)   La bisectriz de un ángulo es una semirrecta que divide al ángulo en dos ángulos congruentes.

Example

$\overrightarrow{LN}$ bisects $\angle KLM$.

$\angle KLN \cong \angle NLM$.

Angle of rotation (p. 515)   *See* **rotation.**

Ángulo de rotación (p. 515)   *Ver* **rotation.**

Area (p. 545)   The area of a plane figure is the number of square units enclosed by the figure.

Área (p. 545)   El área de una figura plana es la cantidad de unidades cuadradas que contiene la figura.

Example The area of the rectangle is 12 square units, or 12 units^2.

Arithmetic sequence (p. 148)   A number sequence formed by adding a fixed number to each previous term to find the next term. The fixed number is called the common difference.

Progresión aritmética (p. 148)   En una progresión aritmética la diferencia entre términos consecutivos es un número constante. El número constante se llama la diferencia común.

Example   4, 7, 10, 13, … is an arithmetic sequence.

English

Auxiliary line (p. 687) An auxiliary line is a line that is added to a diagram to help explain relationships in proofs.

Example

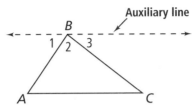

Auxiliary line

Average rate of change (p. 303) The average rate of change of a function over the interval $a \le x \le b$ is equal to $\frac{f(b) - f(a)}{b - a}$.

Example The average rate of change of the function $f(x) = x^2 - 2x + 2$ over the interval $1 \le x \le 4$ is $\frac{f(4) - f(1)}{4 - 1} = \frac{9}{3} = 3$

Axiom (p. 444) *See* **postulate.**

B

Base(s) *See* **isosceles triangle; parallelogram; trapezoid; triangle.**

Base angles *See* **trapezoid; isosceles triangle.**

Biconditional (p. 614) A biconditional statement is the combination of a conditional statement and its converse. A biconditional contains the words "if and only if."

Example This biconditional statement is true: Two angles are congruent *if and only if* they have the same measure.

Box-and-whisker plot (p. 394) A graph that summarizes data along a number line. The left whisker extends from the minimum to the first quartile. The box extends from the first quartile to the third quartile and has a vertical line through the median. The right whisker extends from the third quartile to the maximum.

Example

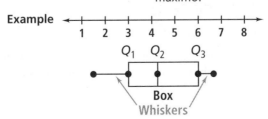

Spanish

Línea auxiliar (p. 687) Una línea auxiliar es aquella que se le agrega a un diagrama para explicar la relación entre pruebas.

Tasa media de cambio (p. 303) La tasa media de cambio de una función sobre el intervalo $a \le x \le b$ es igual a $\frac{f(b) - f(a)}{b - a}$.

Axioma (p. 444) *Ver* **postulate.**

Base(s) *Ver* **isosceles triangle; parallelogram; trapezoid; triangle.**

Ángulos de base *Ver* **trapezoid; isosceles triangle.**

Bicondicional (p. 614) Un enunciado bicondicional es la combinación de un enunciado condicional y su recíproco. El enunciado bicondicional incluye las palabras "si y solo si".

Gráfica de cajas (p. 394) Gráfica que resume los datos a lo largo de una recta numérica. El brazo izquierdo se extiende desde el valor mínimo del primer cuartil. La caja se extiende desde el primer cuartil hasta el tercer cuartil y tiene una línea vertical que atraviesa la mediana. El brazo derecho se extiende desde el tercer cuartil hasta el valor máximo.

Causation (p. 405) When a change in one quantity causes a change in a second quantity. A correlation between quantities does not always imply causation.

Causalidad (p. 405) Cuando un cambio en una cantidad causa un cambio en una segunda cantidad. Una correlación entre las cantidades no implica siempre la causalidad.

Center (p. 515) *See* **rotation.**

Centro (p. 515) *Ver* **rotation.**

Centroid of a triangle (p. 811) The centroid of a triangle is the point of concurrency of the medians of the triangle.

Centroide de un triángulo (p. 811) El centroide de un triángulo es el punto de intersección de sus medianas.

Example *P* is the centroid of △*ABC*.

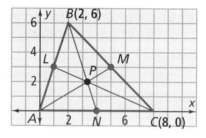

Circle (p. 460) A circle is the set of all points in a plane that are given distance, the *radius*, from a given point, the *center*.

Círculo (p. 460) Un círculo es el conjunto de todos los puntos de un plano situados a una distancia dada, el *radio*, de un punto dado, el *centro*.

Circumcenter of a triangle (p. 803) The circumcenter of a triangle is the point of concurrency of the perpendicular bisectors of the sides of the triangle.

Circuncentro de un triángulo (p. 803) El circuncentro de un triángulo es el punto de intersección de las bisectrices perpendiculares de los lados del triángulo.

Example

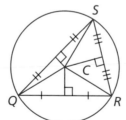

$QC = SC = RC$

C is the circumcenter.

Circumscribed about (p. 803) A circle is circumscribed about a polygon if the vertices of the polygon are on the circle. A polygon is circumscribed about a circle if all the sides of the polygon are tangent to the circle.

Circunscritoa (p. 803) Un círculo está circunscrito a un polígono si los vértices del polígono están en el círculo. Un polígono está circunscrito a un círculo si todos los lados del polígono son tangentes al círculo.

Example

⊙*G* is circumscribed about *ABCD*.

△*XYZ* is circumscribed about ⊙*P*.

English

Coefficient (p. 6) The numerical factor when a term has a variable.

Example In the expression $2x + 3y + 16$, 2 and 3 are coefficients.

Collinear points (p. 442) Collinear points lie on the same line.

Example

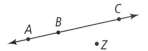

Points A, B, and C are collinear, but points A, B, and Z are noncollinear.

Common difference (p. 148) The difference between consecutive terms of an arithmetic sequence.

Example The common difference is 3 in the arithmetic sequence 4, 7, 10, 13, …

Compass (p. 591) A compass is a geometric tool used to draw circles and parts of circles, called arcs.

Complementary angles (p. 467) Two angles are complementary angles if the sum of their measures is 90.

Example

$\angle HKI$ and $\angle IKJ$ are complementary angles, as are $\angle HKI$ and $\angle EFG$.

Composition of transformations (p. 500) A composition of two transformations is a transformation in which a second transformation is performed on the image of a first transformation.

Example

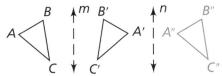

If you reflect $\triangle ABC$ across line m to get $\triangle A'B'C'$ and then reflect $\triangle A'B'C'$ across line n to get $\triangle A''B''C''$, you perform a composition of transformations.

Spanish

Coeficiente (p. 6) Factor numérico de un término que contiene una variable.

Puntos colineales (p. 442) Los puntos colineales son los que están sobre la misma recta.

Diferencia común (p. 148) La diferencia común es la diferencia entre los términos consecutivos de una progresión aritmética.

Compás (p. 591) El compás es un instrumento usado para dibujar círculos y partes de círculos, llamados arcos.

Ángulos complementarios (p. 467) Dos ángulos son complementarios si la suma de sus medidas es igual a 90 grados.

Composición de transformaciones (p. 500) Una composición de dos transformaciones es una transformación en la cual una segunda transformación se realiza a partir de la imagen de la primera.

Compound inequality (p. 70) Two inequalities that are joined by *and* or *or*.

Desigualdade compuesta (p. 70) Dos desigualdades que están enlazadas por medio de una *y* o una *o*.

Example $5 < x$ and $x < 10$
$14 < x$ or $x \le -3$

Compound interest (p. 311) Interest paid on both the principal and the interest that has already been paid.

Interés compuesto (p. 311) Interés calculado tanto sobre el capital como sobre los intereses ya pagados.

Example For an initial deposit of $1000 at a 6% interest rate with interest compounded quarterly, the function $y = 1000\left(\frac{0.06}{4}\right)^x$ gives the account balance y after x years.

Conclusion (p. 607) The conclusion is the part of an *if-then* statement (conditional) that follows *then*.

Conclusión (p. 607) La conclusión es lo que sigue a la palabra entonces en un enunciado (condicional), si ..., entonces. ...

Example In the statement, 'If it rains, then I will go outside,' the conclusion is 'I will go outside.'

Concurrent lines (p. 803) Concurrent lines are three or more lines that meet in one point. The point at which they meet is the *point of concurrency.*

Rectas concurrentes (p. 803) Las rectas concurrentes son tres o más rectas que se unen en un punto. El punto en que se unen es el *punto de concurrencia.*

Example

Point E is the point of concurrency of the bisectors of the angles of $\triangle ABC$. The bisectors are concurrent.

Conditional (p. 607) A conditional is an *if-then* statement.

Condicional (p. 607) Un enunciado condicional es del tipo *si ..., entonces.* ...

Example *If* you act politely, *then* you will earn respect.

Conditional relative frequency (p. 418) Conditional relative frequency is the quotient of a joint frequency in a two-way frequency table and the marginal frequency of the row or column in which the joint frequency appears.

Frecuencia relativa condicionada (p. 418) Frecuencia relativa condicionada es el cociente de una frecuencia conjunta en una tabla de frecuencias de doble entrada y la frecuencia marginal de la fila o columna en la que la frecuencia conjunta aparece.

Example

	Male	Female	Totals
Juniors	3	4	7
Seniors	3	2	5
Totals	6	6	12

The conditional relative frequency that a student is female given that she is a senior is $\frac{2}{5}$.

Congruence transformation (p. 774) *See* isometry.

Transformación de congruencia (p. 774) *Ver* isometry.

Congruent angles (p. 461) Congruent angles are angles that have the same measure.

Ángulos congruentes (p. 461) Los ángulos congruentes son ángulos que tienen la misma medida.

Example

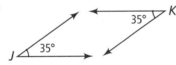

$m\angle J = m\angle K$, so $\angle J \cong \angle K$.

Congruent polygons (p. 709) Congruent polygons are polygons that have corresponding sides congruent and corresponding angles congruent.

Polígonos congruentes (p. 709) Los polígonos congruentes son polígonos cuyos lados correspondientes son congruentes y cuyos ángulos correspondientes son congruentes.

Example

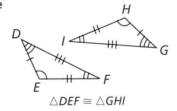

$\triangle DEF \cong \triangle GHI$

Congruent segments (p. 453) Congruent segments are segments that have the same length.

Segmentos congruentes (p. 453) Los segmentos congruentes son segmentos que tienen la misma longitud.

Example

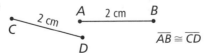

$\overline{AB} \cong \overline{CD}$

Visual **Glossary**

Conjecture (p. 600)   A conjecture is a conclusion reached by using inductive reasoning.

Conjecture (p. 600)   A conjecture is a conclusion reached by using inductive reasoning.

Example   As you walk down the street, you see many people holding unopened umbrellas. You make the conjecture that the forecast must call for rain.

Consecutive angles (p. 859)   Consecutive angles of a polygon share a common side.

Ángulos consecutivos (p. 859)   Los ángulos consecutivos de un polígono tienen un lado común.

Example

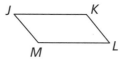

In $\square JKLM$, $\angle J$ and $\angle M$ are consecutive angles, as are $\angle J$ and $\angle K$. $\angle J$ and $\angle L$ are *not* consecutive.

Consistent system (p. 233)   A system of equations that has at least one solution is consistent.

Sistema consistente (p. 233)   Un sistema de ecuaciones que tiene por lo menos una solución es consistente.

Example

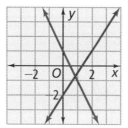

Constant (p. 6)   A term that has no variable factor.

Constante (p. 6)   Término que tiene un valor fijo.

Example   In the expression $4x + 13y + 17$, 17 is a constant term.

Constant of variation for direct variation (p. 176)   The nonzero constant k in the function $y = kx$.

Constante de variación en variaciones directas (p. 176)   La constante k cuyo valor no es cero en la función $y = kx$.

Example   For the direct variation $y = 24x$, 24 is the constant of variation.

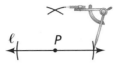
Construction (p. 591)   A construction is a geometric figure made with only a straightedge and compass.

Construcción (p. 591)   Una construcción es una figura geométrica trazada solamente con una regla sin graduación y un compás.

Example

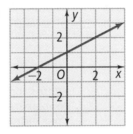

ℓ P

The diagram shows the construction (in progress) of a line perpendicular to a line ℓ through a point P on ℓ.

Continuous graph (p. 119)   A graph that is unbroken.

Gráfica continua (p. 119)   Una gráfica continua es una gráfica ininterrumpida.

Example

Contrapositive (p. 610)   The contrapositive of the conditional "if p, then q" is the conditional "if not q, then not p." A conditional and its contrapositive always have the same truth value.

Contrapositivo (p. 610)   El contrapositivo del condicional "si p, entonces q" es el condicional "si no q, entonces no p". Un condicional y su contrapositivo siempre tienen el mismo valor verdadero.

Example   **Conditional:** If a figure is a triangle, then it is a polygon.
Contrapositive: If a figure is not a polygon, then it is not a triangle.

Converse (p. 610)   The statement obtained by reversing the hypothesis and conclusion of a conditional.

Expresión recíproca (p. 610)   Enunciado que se obtiene al intercambiar la hipótesis y la conclusión de una situación condicional.

Example   The converse of "If I was born in Houston, then I am a Texan" would be "If I am a Texan, then I am born in Houston."

Conversion factor (p. 38)   A ratio of two equivalent measures in different units.

Factor de conversión (p. 38)   Razón de dos medidas equivalentes en unidades diferentes.

Example   The ratio $\frac{1 \text{ ft}}{12 \text{ in.}}$ is a conversion factor.

English

Spanish

Coordinate(s) of a point (p. 451)   The coordinate of a point is its distance and direction from the origin of a number line. The coordinates of a point on a coordinate plane are in the form (*x*, *y*), where *x* is the *x*-coordinate and *y* is the *y*-coordinate.

Coordenada(s) de un punto (p. 451)   La coordenada de un punto es su distancia y dirección desde el origen en una recta numérica. Las coordenadas de un punto en un plano de coordenadas se expresan como (*x*, *y*), donde *x* es la coordenada *x*, e *y* es la coordenada *y*.

Examples

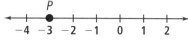

The coordinate of *P* is −3.

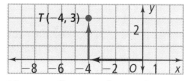

The coordinates of *T* are (−4, 3).

Coordinate proof (p. 907)   *See* **proof.**

Prueba de coordenadas (p. 907)   *Ver* **proof.**

Coplanar points (p. 442)   Coplanar points are points that lie in the same plane.

Puntos coplanarios (p. 442)   Los puntos conplanarios son los puntos que éstan localizados en el mismo plano.

Correlation coefficient (p. 404)   A number from −1 to 1 that tells you how closely the equation of the line of best fit models the data.

Coeficiente de correlación (p. 404)   Número de 1 a 1 que indica con cuánta exactitud la línea de mejor encaje representa los datos.

Example

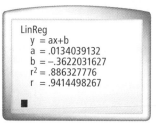

The correlation coefficient is approximately 0.94.

Corresponding angles (p. 655)   Corresponding angles lie on the same side of the transversal *t* and in corresponding positions relative to ℓ and *m*.

Ángulos correspondientes (p. 655)   Los ángulos correspondientes están en el mismo lado de la transversal *t* y en las correspondientes posiciones relativas a ℓ y *m*.

Example

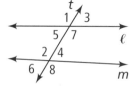

∠1 and ∠2 are corresponding angles, as are ∠3 and ∠4, ∠5 and ∠6, and ∠7 and ∠8.

Counterexample (p. 602) An example showing that a statement is false.

Contraejemplo (p. 602) Ejemplo que demuestra que un enunciado es falso.

Example **Statement:** All apples are red.
Counterexample: A Granny Smith Apple is green.

Cross products (of a proportion) (p. 53) In a proportion $\frac{a}{b} = \frac{c}{d}$, the products ad and bc. These products are equal.

Productos cruzados (de una proporción) (p. 53) En una proporción $\frac{a}{b} = \frac{c}{d}$, los productos ad y bc. Estos productos son iguales.

Example The cross products for $\frac{3}{4} = \frac{6}{8}$ are $3 \cdot 8$ and $4 \cdot 6$.

Cube root function (p. 356) A function containing a cube root with the independent variable in the radicand.

Función de la raíz cúbica (p. 356) Una función que contiene una raíz cúbica con la variable independiente en el radicando.

Cumulative frequency table (p. 375) A table that shows the number of data values that lie in or below the given intervals.

Tabla de frecuencia cumulativa (p. 375) Tabla que muestra el número de valores de datos que están dentro o por debajo de los intervalos dados.

Example

Interval	Frequency	Cumulative Frequency
0–9	5	5
10–19	8	13
20–29	4	17

D

Decay factor (p. 312) 1 minus the percent rate of change, expressed as a decimal, for an exponential decay situation.

Factor de decremento (p. 312) 1 menos la tasa porcentual de cambio, expresada como decimal, en una situación de reducción exponencial.

Example The decay factor of the function $y = 5(0.3)^x$ is 0.3.

Deductive reasoning (p. 622) Deductive reasoning is a process of reasoning logically from given facts to a conclusion.

Razonamiento deductivo (p. 622) El razonamiento deductivo es un proceso de razonamiento lógico que parte de hechos dados hasta llegar a una conclusión.

Example Based on the fact that the sum of any two even numbers is even, you can deduce that the product of any whole number and any even number is even.

Dependent system (p. 233)   A system of equations that does not have a unique solution.

Sistema dependiente (p. 233)   Sistema de ecuaciones que no tiene una solución única.

Example   The system $\begin{cases} y = 2x + 3 \\ -4x + 2y = 6 \end{cases}$ represents two equations for the same line, so it has many solutions. It is a dependent system.

Dependent variable (p. 103)   A variable that provides the output values of a function.

Variable dependiente (p. 103)   Variable de la que dependen los valores de salida de una función.

Example   In the equation $y = 3x$, y is the dependent variable.

Direct variation (p. 176)   A linear function defined by an equation of the form $y = kx$, where $k \neq 0$.

Variación directa (p. 176)   Una función lineal definida por una ecuación de la forma $y\, kx$, donde $k \neq 0$, representa una variación directa.

Example $y = 18x$ is a direct variation.

Discrete graph (p. 119)   A graph composed of isolated points.

Gráfica discreta (p. 119)   Una gráfica discreta es compuesta de puntos aislados.

Example

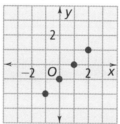

Distance between two points on a line (p. 451)   The distance between two points on a line is the absolute value of the difference of the coordinates of the points.

Distancia entre dos puntos de una linea (p. 451)   Ladistancia entre dos puntos de una lfnea es el valor absoluto de la diferencia de las coordenadas de los puntos.

Example

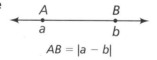

$AB = |a - b|$

Distance from a point to a line (p. 798)   The distance from a point to a line is the length of the perpendicular segment from the point to the line.

Distancia desde un punto hasta una recta (p. 798)   La distancia desde un punto hasta una recta es la longitud del segmento perpendicular que va desde el punto hasta la recta.

Example

The distance from point P to a line ℓ is PT.

English

Spanish

Distributive Property (p. 3) For every real number a, b, and c:

$a(b + c) = ab + ac$

$(b + c)a = ba + ca$

$a(b - c) = ab - ac$

$(b - c)a = ba - ca$

Propiedad Distributiva (p. 3) Para cada número real a, b y c:

$a(b + c) = ab + ac$

$(b + c)a = ba + ca$

$a(b - c) = ab - ac$

$(b - c)a = ba - ca$

Examples $3(19 + 4) = 3(19) + 3(4)$

$(19 + 4)3 = 19(3) + 4(3)$

$7(11 - 2) = 7(11) - 7(2)$

$(11 - 2)7 = 11(7) - 2(7)$

Domain (of a relation or function) (p. 135) The possible values for the input of a relation or function.

Dominio (de una relación o función) (p. 135) Posibles valores de entrada de una relación o función.

Example In the function $f(x) = x + 22$, the domain is all real numbers.

Elimination method (p. 247) A method for solving a system of linear equations. You add or subtract the equations to eliminate a variable.

Eliminación (p. 247) Método para resolver un sistema de ecuaciones lineales. Se suman o se restan las ecuaciones para eliminar una variable.

Example $3x + y = 19$

$\underline{2x - y = 1}$ Add the equations to get $x = 4$.

$5x + 0 = 20$ Substitute 4 for x in

$2(4) - y = 1 \rightarrow$ the second equation.

$8 - y = 1$

$y = 7 \rightarrow$ Solve for y.

Equiangular triangle or polygon (p. 852) An equiangular triangle (polygon) is a triangle (polygon) whose angles are all congruent.

Triángulo o polígono equiángulo (p. 852) Un triángulo (polígono) equiángulo es un triángulo (polígono) cuyos ángulos son todos congruentes.

Example

Each angle of the pentagon is a 108° angle.

Equilateral triangle or polygon (p. 852) An equilateral triangle (polygon) is a triangle (polygon) whose sides are all congruent.

Triángulo o polígono equilátero (p. 852) Un triángulo (polígono) equilátero es un triángulo (polígono) cuyos lados son todos congruentes.

Example

Each side of the quadrilateral is 1.2 cm long.

Equivalent statements (p. 610)   Equivalent statements are statements with the same truth value.

Enunciados equivalentes (p. 610)   Los enunciados equivalentes son enunciados con el mismo valor verdadero.

Example   The following statements are equivalent: If a figure is a square, then it is a rectangle. If a figure is not a rectangle, then it is not a square.

Even function (p. 144)   A function f is an even function if and only if $f(-x) = f(x)$ for all values of x in its domain.

Función par (p. 144)   Una función f es una función par si y solo si $f(-x) = f(x)$ para todos los valores de x en su dominio.

Example $f(x) = x^2 + |x|$ is an even function because
$f(-x) = (-x)^2 + |-x| = x^2 + |x| = f(x)$

Explicit formula (p. 150)   An explicit formula expresses the nth term of a sequence in terms of n.

Fórmula explícita (p. 150)   Una fórmula explícita expresa el n-ésimo término de una progresión en función de n.

Example   Let $a_n = 2n + 5$ for positive integers n. If $n = 7$, then
$a_7 = 2(7) + 5 = 19$.

Exponential decay (p. 312)   A situation modeled with a function of the form $y = ab^x$, where $a > 0$ and $0 < b < 1$.

Decremento exponencial (p. 312)   Para $a > 0$ y $0 < b < 1$, la función $y = ab^x$ representa el decremento exponencial.

Example $y = 5(0.1)^x$

Exponential function (p. 291)   A function that repeatedly multiplies an initial amount by the same positive number. You can model all exponential functions using $y = ab^x$, where a is a nonzero constant, $b > 0$, and $b \neq 1$.

Función exponencial (p. 291)   Función que multiplica repetidas veces una cantidad inicial por el mismo número positivo. Todas las funciones exponenciales se pueden representar mediante $y = ab^x$, donde a es una constante con valor distinto de cero, $b > 0$ y $b \neq 1$.

Example

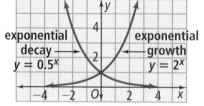

Exponential growth (p. 309)   A situation modeled with a function of the form $y = ab^x$, where $a > 0$ and $b > 1$.

Incremento exponencial (p. 309)   Para $a > 0$ y $b > 1$, la función $y = ab^x$ representa el incremento exponencial.

Example $y = 100(2)^x$

Exterior angle of a polygon (p. 689)   An exterior angle of a polygon is an angle formed by a side and an extension of an adjacent side.

Ángulo exterior de un polígono (p. 689)   El ángulo exterior de un polígono es un ángulo formado por un lado y una extensión de un lado adyacente.

Example

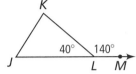

∠KLM is an exterior angle of △JKL.

Extrapolation (p. 401)   The process of predicting a value outside the range of known values.

Extrapolación (p. 401)   Proceso que se usa para predecir un valor por fuera del ámbito de los valores dados.

F

Flow proof (p. 672)   *See* **proof.**

Prueba de flujo (p. 672)   *Ver* **proof.**

Formula (p. 31)   An equation that states a relationship among quantities.

Fórmula (p. 31)   Ecuación que establece una relación entre cantidades.

Example   The formula for the volume V of a cylinder is $V = \pi r^2 h$, where r is the radius of the cylinder and h is its height.

Frequency (p. 371)   The number of data items in an interval.

Frecuencia (p. 371)   Número de datos de un intervalo.

Frequency table (p. 371)   A table that groups a set of data values into intervals and shows the frequency for each interval.

Tabla de frecuencias (p. 371)   Tabla que agrupa un conjunto de datos en intervalos y muestra la frecuencia de cada intervalo.

Example

Interval	Frequency
0–9	5
10–19	8
20–29	4

Function (p. 105)   A relation that assigns exactly one value in the range to each value of the domain.

Función (p. 105)   La relación que asigna exactamente un valor del rango a cada valor del dominio.

Example   Earned income is a function of the number of hours worked. If you earn \$4.50/h, then your income is expressed by the function $f(h) = 4.5h$.

Visual **Glossary**

Function notation (p. 137) To write a rule in function notation, you use the symbol $f(x)$ in place of y.

Notación de una función (p. 137) Para expresar una regla en notación de función se usa el símbolo $f(x)$ en lugar de y.

Example $f(x) = 3x - 8$ is in function notation.

G

Geometric sequence (p. 329) A number sequence formed by multiplying a term in a sequence by a fixed number to find the next term.

Progresión geométrica (p. 329) Tipo de sucesión numérica formada al multiplicar un término de la secuencia por un número constante, para hallar el siguiente término.

Example $9, 3, 1, \frac{1}{3}, \ldots$ is an example of a geometric sequence.

Glide reflection (p. 536) A glide reflection is the composition of a translation followed by a reflection across a line parallel to the direction of translation.

Reflexión deslizada (p. 536) Una reflexión por deslizamiento es la composición de una traslación seguida por una reflexión a través de una línea paralela a la dirección de traslación.

Example

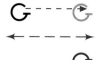

The blue G in the diagram is a glide reflection image of the black G.

Growth factor (p. 309) 1 plus the percent rate of change for an exponential growth situation.

Factor incremental (p. 309) 1 más la tasa porcentual de cambio en una situación de incremento exponencial.

Example The growth factor of $y = 7(1.3)^x$ is 1.3.

H

Height *See* **parallelogram; trapezoid; triangle.**

Altura *Ver* **parallelogram; trapezoid.**

Histogram (p. 372) A special type of bar graph that can display data from a frequency table. Each bar represents an interval. The height of each bar shows the frequency of the interval it represents.

Histograma (p. 372) Tipo de gráfica de barras que muestra los datos de una tabla de frecuencia. Cada barra representa un intervalo. La altura de cada barra muestra la frecuencia del intervalo al que representa.

Example

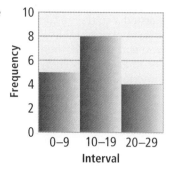

Visual Glossary

English

Hypotenuse (p. 753)   *See* **right triangle.**

Hypothesis (p. 607)   In an *if-then* statement (conditional), the hypothesis is the part that follows *if.*

Example   In the conditional "If an animal has four legs, then it is a horse," the hypothesis is "an animal has four legs."

I

Image (p. 495)   *See* **transformation.**

Identity (p. 24)   An equation that is true for every value.

Example $5 - 14x = 5\left(1 - \frac{14}{5}x\right)$ is an identity because it is true for any value of x.

Incenter of a triangle (p. 806)   The incenter of a triangle is the point of concurrency of the angle bisectors of the triangle.

Example

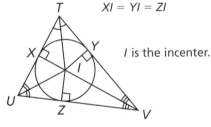

$XI = YI = ZI$

I is the incenter.

Inconsistent system (p. 233)   A system of equations that has no solution.

Example $\begin{cases} y = 2x + 3 \\ -2x + y = 1 \end{cases}$
is a system of parallel lines, so it has no solution. It is an inconsistent system.

Independent system (p. 233)   A system of linear equations that has a unique solution.

Example $\begin{cases} x + 2y = -7 \\ 2x - 3y = 0 \end{cases}$
has the unique solution $(-3, -2)$. It is an independent system.

Spanish

Hipotenusa (p. 753)   *Ver* **right triangle.**

Hipótesis (p. 607)   En un enunciado *si . . . entonces . . .* (condicional), la hipótesis es la parte del enunciado que sigue el *si.*

Imagen (p. 495)   *Ver* **transformation.**

Identidad (p. 24)   Una ecuación que es verdadera para todos los valores.

Incentro de un triángulo (p. 806)   El incentro de un triángulo es el punto donde concurren las tres bisectrices de los ángulos del triángulo.

Sistema incompatible (p. 233)   Un sistema incompatible es un sistema de ecuaciones para el cual no hay solución.

Sistema independiente (p. 233)   Un sistema de ecuaciones lineales que tenga una sola solución es un sistema independiente.

Independent variable (p. 103)   A variable that provides the input values of a function.

Variable independiente (p. 103)   Variable de la que dependen los valores de entrada de una función.

Example   In the equation $y = 3x$, x is the independent variable.

Indirect proof (p. 820)   *See* **indirect reasoning; proof.**

Prueba indirecta (p. 820)   *Ver* **indirect reasoning; proof.**

Indirect reasoning (p. 820)   Indirect reasoning is a type of reasoning in which all possiblities are considered and then all but one are proved false. The remaining possibility must be true.

Razonamiento indirecto (p. 820)   Razonamiento indirecto es un tipo de razonamiento en el que se consideran todas las posibilidades y se prueba que todas son falsas, a excepción de una. La posibilidad restante debe ser verdadera.

Example   Eduardo spent more than $60 on two books at a store. Prove that at least one book costs more than $30. **Proof:** Suppose neither costs more than $30. Then he spent no more than $60 at the store. Since this contradicts the given information, at least one book costs more than $30.

Inductive reasoning (p. 599)   Inductive reasoning is a type of reasoning that reaches conclusions based on a pattern of specific examples or past events.

Razonamiento inductivo (p. 599)   El razonamiento inductivo es un tipo de razonamiento en el cual se llega a conclusiones con base en un patrón de ejemplos específicos o sucesos pasados.

Example   You see four people walk into a building. Each person emerges with a small bag containing food. You use inductive reasoning to conclude that this building contains a restaurant.

Input (p. 103)   A value of the independent variable.

Entrada (p. 103)   Valor de una variable independiente.

Example   The input is any value of x you substitute into a function.

Inscribed in (p. 806)   A circle is inscribed in a polygon if the sides of the polygon are tangent to the circle. A polygon is inscribed in a circle if the vertices of the polygon are on the circle.

Inscrito en (p. 806)   Un círculo está inscrito en un polígono si los lados del polígono son tangentes al círculo. Un polígono está inscrito en un círculo si los vértices del polígono están en el círculo.

Example

$\odot T$ is inscribed in $\triangle XYZ$.

$ABCD$ is inscribed in $\odot J$.

English

Interpolation (p. 401)   The process of estimating a value between two known quantities.

Interquartile range (p. 392)   The interquartile range of a set of data is the difference between the third and first quartiles.

Example   The first and third quartiles of the data set 2, 3, 4, 5, 5, 6, 7, and 7 are 3.5 and 6.5. The interquartile range is $6.5 - 3.5 = 3$.

Intersection (p. 444)   The intersection of two or more geometric figures is the set of points the figures have in common.

Example

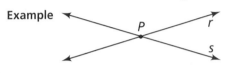

The intersection of lines r and s is point P.

Interval notation (p. 74)   A notation for describing an interval on a number line. The interval's endpoint(s) are given, and a parenthesis or bracket is used to indicate whether each endpoint is included in the interval.

Example   For $-2 \leq x < 8$, the interval notation is $[-2, 8)$.

Inverse (p. 610)   The inverse of the conditional "if p, then q" is the conditional "if not p, then not q."

Example   **Conditional:** If a figure is a square, then it is a parallelogram.
Inverse: If a figure is not a square, then it is not a parallelogram.

Isometric drawing (p. 433)   An isometric drawing shows a corner view of a three-dimensional figure. It is usually drawn on isometric dot paper. An isometric drawing allows you to see the top, front, and side of an object in the same drawing.

Example

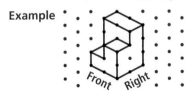

Spanish

Interpolación (p. 401)   Proceso que se usa para estimar el valor entre dos cantidades dadas.

Intervalo intercuartil (p. 392)   El rango intercuartil de un conjunto de datos es la diferencia entre el tercero y el primer cuartiles.

Intersección (p. 444)   La intersección de dos o más figuras geométricas es el conjunto de puntos que las figuras tienen en común.

Notación de intervalo (p. 74)   Notación que describe un intervalo en una recta numérica. Los extremos del intervalo se incluyen y se usa un paréntesis o corchete para indicar si cada extremo está incluido en el intervalo.

Inverso (p. 610)   El inverso del condicional "si p, entonces q" es el condicional "si no p, entonces no q".

Dibujo isométrico (p. 433)   Un dibujo isométrico muestra la perspectiva de una esquina de una figura tridimensional. Generalmente se dibuja en papel punteado isométrico. Un dibujo isométrico permite ver la cima, el frente, y el lado de un objeto en el mismo dibujo.

English

Spanish

Isometry (p. 532)   An isometry, also known as a *congruence transformation*, is a transformation in which an original figure and its image are congruent.

Isometría (p. 532)   Una isometría, conocida también como una *transformación de congruencia*, es una transformación en donde una figura original y su imagen son congruentes.

Example   The four isometries are reflections, rotations, translations, and glide reflections.

Isosceles trapezoid (p. 483, 894)   An isosceles trapezoid is a trapezoid whose nonparallel sides are congruent.

Trapecio isósceles (p. 483, 894)   Un trapecio isósceles es un trapecio cuyos lados opuestos no paralelos son congruentes.

Example

Isosceles triangle (p. 744)   An isosceles triangle is a triangle that has at least two congruent sides. If there are two congruent sides, they are called *legs*. The *vertex angle* is between them. The third side is called the *base* and the other two angles are called *base angles*.

Triángulo isosceles (p. 744)   Un triángulo isosceles es un triángulo que tiene por lo menos dos lados congruentes. Si tiene dos lodos congruentes, éstos se llaman *catetos*. Entre ellos se encuentra el *ángulo del vértice*. El tercer lado se llama *base* y los otros dos ángulos se llaman *ángulos de base*.

Example

Vertex angle
Leg   Leg
Base angle   Base angle
Base

J

Joint frequency (p. 414)   A joint frequency is an entry in the body of a two-way frequency table.

Frecuencia conjunta (p. 414)   Una frecuencia conjunta es una entrada en el cuerpo de una tabla de frecuencias de doble entrada.

Example

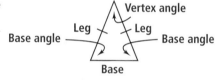

	Male	Female	Totals
Juniors	3	4	7
Seniors	3	2	5
Totals	6	6	12

3 and 4 in the first row, and 3 and 2 in the second row are joint frequencies.

Joint relative frequency (p. 416)   A joint relative frequency is a joint frequency in a two-way frequency table divided by the grand total of the entries in the table. It is also an entry in the body of a two-way relative frequency table.

Frecuencia relativa conjunta (p. 416)   Una frecuencia relativa conjunta es una frecuencia conjunta en una tabla de frecuencias de doble entrada dividido por el total de las entradas de la tabla. Es también una entrada en el cuerpo de una tabla de frecuencias relativas de doble entrada.

Kite (p. 483)   A kite is a quadrilateral with two pairs of consecutive sides congruent and no opposite sides congruent.

Cometa (p. 483)   Una cometa es un cuadrilatero con dos pares de lados congruentes consecutivos y sin laods opuestos congruentes.

Example

 L

Leg   *See* **isosceles triangle; right triangle; trapezoid**.

Cateto   *Ver* **isosceles triangle; right triangle; trapezoid**.

Like terms (p. 7)   Terms with exactly the same variable factors in a variable expression.

Radicales semejantes (p. 7)   Expresiones radicales con los mismos radicandos.

Example $3\sqrt{7}$ and $25\sqrt{7}$ are like radicals.

Line (pp. 441)   In Euclidean geometry, a line is undefined. You can think of a line as a straight path that extends in two opposite directions without end and has no thickness. A line contains infinitely many points. In spherical geometry, you can think of a line as a great circle of a sphere.

Recta (pp. 441)   En la geometría euclidiana, una recta es indefinida. Se puede pensar en una recta como un camino derecho que se extiende en direcciones opuestas sin fin ni grosor. Una recta tiene un número infinito de puntos. En la geometría esférica, se puede pensar en una recta como un gran círculo de una esfera.

Example

Line of best fit (p. 404)   The most accurate trend line on a scatter plot showing the relationship between two sets of data.

Recta de mayor aproximación (p. 404)   La línea de tendencia en un diagrama de puntos que más se acerca a los puntos que representan la relación entre dos conjuntos de datos.

Example

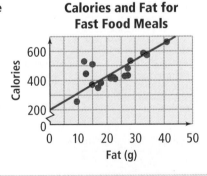

Calories and Fat for Fast Food Meals

Line of reflection (p. 508)   *See* **reflection**.

Eje de reflexión (p. 508)   *Ver* **reflection**.

Line of symmetry (p. 523)   *See* **reflectional symmetry**.

Eje de simetría (p. 523)   *Ver* **reflectional symmetry**.

English

Spanish

Line plot (p. 382)   A line plot is a graph that shows the shape of a data set by stacking X's above each data value on a number line.

Diagrama de puntos (p. 382)   Un diagrama de puntos es una gráfica que muestra la forma de un conjunto de datos agrupando X sobre cada valor de una recta numérica.

Example

Company A

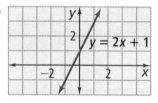

**Monthly Earnings
(thousands of dollars)**

Line symmetry (p. 523)   *See* **reflectional symmetry.**

Simetría axial (p. 523)   *Ver* **reflectional symmetry.**

Linear equation (p. 186)   An equation whose graph forms a straight line.

Ecuación lineal (p. 186)   Ecuación cuya gráfica es una línea recta.

Example

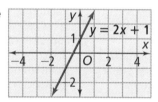

Linear function (p. 105)   A function whose graph is a line is a linear function. You can represent a linear function with a linear equation.

Función lineal (p. 105)   Una función cuya gráfica es una recta es una función lineal. La función lineal se representa con una ecuación lineal.

Example

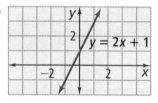

Linear inequality (p. 263)   An inequality in two variables whose graph is a region of the coordinate plane that is bounded by a line. Each point in the region is a solution of the inequality.

Desigualdad lineal (p. 263)   Una desigualdad lineal es una desigualdad de dos variables cuya gráfica es una región del plano de coordenadas delimitado por una recta. Cada punto de la región es una solución de la desigualdad.

Example

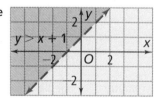

English   Spanish

Linear pair (p. 469) A linear pair is a pair of adjacent angles whose noncommon sides are opposite rays.

Par lineal (p. 469) Un par lineal es un par de ángulos adjuntos cuyos lados no comunes son semirrectas opuestas.

Example

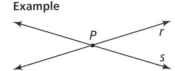

The intersection of lines *r* and *s* is point *P*.

Linear parent function (p. 186) The simplest form of a linear function.

Función lineal elemental (p. 186) La forma más simple de una función lineal.

Example $y = x$

Literal equation (p. 29) An equation involving two or more variables.

Ecuación literal (p. 29) Ecuación que incluye dos o más variables.

Example $4x + 2y = 18$ is a literal equation.

M

Marginal frequency (p. 414) A marginal frequency is an entry in the Total row or Total column of a two-way frequency table.

Frecuencia marginal (p. 414) Una frecuencia marginal es una entrada en la fila Total o columna Total de una tabla de frecuencias de doble entrada.

Example

	Male	Female	Totals
Juniors	3	4	7
Seniors	3	2	5
Totals	6	6	12

6 and 6 in the Total row and 7 and 5 in the Total column are marginal frequencies.

Marginal relative frequency (p. 416) A marginal relative frequency is a marginal frequency in a two-way frequency table divided by the grand total for the table.

Frecuencia relativa marginal (p. 416) Una frecuencia relativa marginal es una frecuencia marginal en una tabla de frecuencias de doble entrada dividido por el total de la tabla.

Mean (p. 379) To find the mean of a set of data values, find the sum of the data values and divide the sum by the number of data values. The mean is $\dfrac{\text{sum of the data values}}{\text{total number of data values}}$.

Media (p. 379) Para hallar la media de un conjunto de datos, halla la suma de los valores de los datos y divide la suma por el total del valor de los datos. La media es $\dfrac{\text{la suma de los datos}}{\text{el número total de valores de datos}}$.

Example In the data set 12, 11, 12, 10, 13, 12, and 7, the mean is $\dfrac{12 + 11 + 12 + 10 + 13 + 12 + 7}{7} = 11$.

Mean absolute deviation (MAD) (p. 388)
Mean absolute deviation is a measure of the spread of a data set. For data values $x_1, x_2, \ldots x_n$, the mean absolute deviation is given by $\frac{|x_1 - \bar{x}| + |x_2 - \bar{x}| + \ldots + |x_n - \bar{x}|}{n}$, where $\bar{x}$ is the mean of the data set.

Desviación absoluta media (p. 388) Desviación absoluta media es una medida de la dispersión de un conjunto de datos. Para los datos $x_1, x_2, \ldots, x_n$, la desviación absoluta media es igual a $\frac{|x_1 - \bar{x}| + |x_2 - \bar{x}| + \ldots + |x_n - \bar{x}|}{n}$, donde $\bar{x}$ es la media del conjunto de datos.

Measure of an angle (p. 460) Consider $\overrightarrow{OD}$ and a point C on one side of $\overrightarrow{OD}$. Every ray of the form $\overrightarrow{OC}$ can be paired one to one with a real number from 0 to 180. The measure of $\angle COD$ is the absolute value of the difference of the real numbers paired with $\overrightarrow{OC}$ and $\overrightarrow{OD}$.

Medida de un ángulo (p. 460) Toma en cuenta $\overrightarrow{OD}$ y un punto C a un lado de $\overrightarrow{OD}$. Cada semirrecta de la forma $\overrightarrow{OC}$ puede ser emparejada exactamente con un número real de 0 a 180. La medida de $\angle COD$ es el valor absoluto de la diferencia de los números reales emparejados con $\overrightarrow{OC}$ y $\overrightarrow{OD}$.

Example

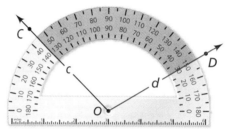

$m\angle COD = 105$

Measure of central tendency (p. 379) Mean, median, and mode. They are used to organize and summarize a set of data.

Medida de tendencia central (p. 379) La media, la mediana y la moda. Se usan para organizar y resumir un conjunto de datos.

Example For examples, see *mean*, *median*, and *mode*.

Measure of dispersion (p. 382) A measure that describes how dispersed, or spread out, the values in a data set are. Range is a measure of dispersion.

Medida de dispersión (p. 382) Medida que describe cómo se dispersan, o esparecen, los valores de un conjunto de datos. La amplitud es una medida de dispersión.

Example For an example, see *range*.

Median (p. 379) The middle value in an ordered set of numbers.

Mediana (p. 379) El valor del medio en un conjunto ordenado de números.

Example In the data set 7, 10, 11, 12, 12, 12, and 13, the median is 12.

Median of a triangle (p. 811) A median of a triangle is a segment that has as its endpoints a vertex of the triangle and the midpoint of the opposite side.

Mediana de un triángulo (p. 811) Una mediana de un triángulo es un segmento que tiene en sus extremos el vértice del triángulo y el punto medio del lado opuesto.

Example

Median

English

Spanish

Midsegment of a trapezoid (p. 896)   The midsegment of a trapezoid is the segment that joins the midpoints of the nonparallel opposite sides of a trapezoid.

Segmento medio de un triángulo (p. 896)   Un segmento medio de un triángulo es un segmento que une los puntos medios de dos lados del triángulo.

Example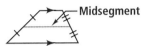

Midpoint of a segment (p. 454)   A midpoint of a segment is the point that divides the segment into two congruent segments.

Punto medio de un segmento (p. 454)   El punto medio de un segmento es el punto que divide el segmento en dos segmentos congruentes.

Example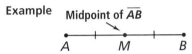

Midsegment of a triangle (p. 787)   A midsegment of a triangle is a segment that joins the midpoints of two sides of the triangle.

Segmento medio de un triángulo (p. 787)   Un segmento medio de un triángulo es un segmento que une los puntos medios de dos lados del triángulo.

Example

Mode (p. 379)   The mode is the most frequently occurring value (or values) in a set of data. A data set may have no mode, one mode, or more than one mode.

Moda (p. 379)   La moda es el valor o valores que ocurren con mayor frequencia en un conjunto de datos. El conjunto de datos puede no tener moda, o tener una o más modas.

Example   In the data set 7, 7, 9, 10, 11, and 13, the mode is 7.

N

Negation (p. 610)   The negation of a statement has the opposite meaning of the original statement.

Negación (p. 610)   La negación de un enunciado tiene el sentido opuesto del enunciado original.

Example   The angle is obtuse.
Negation: The angle is not obtuse.

Negative correlation (p. 399)   The relationship between two sets of data, in which one set of data decreases as the other set of data increases.

Correlación negativa (p. 399)   Relación entre dos conjuntos de datos en la que uno de los conjuntos disminuye a medida que el otro aumenta.

Example

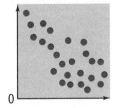

Net (p. 431)   A net is a two-dimensional pattern that you can fold to form a three-dimensional figure.

Plantilla (p. 431)   Una plantilla es una figura bidimensional que se puede doblar para formar una figura tridimensional.

Example

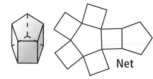

Net

The net shown can be folded into a prism with pentagonal bases.

No correlation (p. 399)   There does not appear to be a relationship between two sets of data.

Sin correlación (p. 399)   No hay relación entre dos conjuntos de datos.

Example

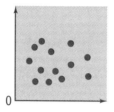

Nonlinear function (p. 110)   A function whose graph is not a line or part of a line.

Función no lineal (p. 110)   Función cuya gráfica no es una línea o parte de una línea.

Example

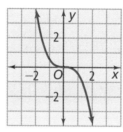

Obtuse angle (p. 460)   An obtuse angle is an angle whose measure is between 90 and 180.

Ángulo obtuso (p. 460)   Un ángulo obtuso es un ángulo que mide entre 90 y 180 grados.

Example   147°

Odd function (p. 144)   A function f is an odd function if and only if $f(-x) = -f(x)$ for all values of x in its domain.

Función impar (p. 144)   Una función f es una función impar si y solo si $f(-x) = -f(x)$ para todos los valores de x en su dominio.

Example   The function $f(x) = x^3 + 2x$ is odd because $f(-x) = (-x)^3 + 2(-x) = -x^3 - 2x = -f(x)$

English

Opposite angles (p. 858) Opposite angles of a quadrilateral are two angles that do not share a side.

Example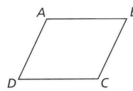

∠A and ∠C are opposite angles, as are ∠B and ∠D.

Opposite rays (p. 443) Opposite rays are collinear rays with the same endpoint. They form a line.

Example

$\overrightarrow{UT}$ and $\overrightarrow{UN}$ are opposite rays.

Opposite reciprocals (p. 214) A number of the form $-\frac{b}{a}$, where $\frac{a}{b}$ is a nonzero rational number. The product of a number and its opposite reciprocal is -1.

Example $\frac{2}{5}$ and $-\frac{5}{2}$ are opposite reciprocals because $\left(\frac{2}{5}\right)\left(-\frac{5}{2}\right) = -1$.

Opposite sides (p. 858) Opposite sides of a quadrilateral are two sides that do not share a vertex.

Example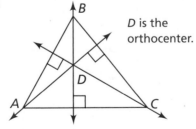

$\overline{PQ}$ and $\overline{SR}$ are opposite sides, as are $\overline{PS}$ and $\overline{QR}$.

Orthocenter of a triangle (p. 814) The orthocenter of a triangle is the point of concurrency of the lines containing the altitudes of the triangle.

Example

D is the orthocenter.

Spanish

Ángulos opuestos (p. 858) Los ángulos opuestos de un cuadrilátero son dos ángulos que no comparten lados.

Semirrectas opuestas (p. 443) Las semirrectas opuestos son semirrectas colineales con el mismo extremo. Forman una recta.

Recíproco inverso (p. 214) Número en la forma $-\frac{b}{a}$, donde $\frac{a}{b}$ es un número racional diferente de cero. El producto de un número y su recíproco inverso es -1.

Lados opuestos (p. 858) Los lados opuestos de un cuadrilátero son dos lados que no tienen un vértice en común.

Ortocentro de un triángulo (p. 814) El ortocentro de un triángulo es el punto donde se intersecan las alturas de un triángulo.

Orthographic drawing (p. 435)   An orthographic drawing is the top view, front view, and right-side view of a three-dimensional figure.

Dibujo ortográfico (p. 435)   Un dibujo ortográfico es la vista desde arriba, la vista de frente y la vista del lado derecho de una figura tridimensional.

Example The diagram shows an isometric drawing (upper right) and the three views that make up an orthographic drawing.

Top

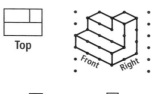

Front   Right

Front

Right

Outlier (p. 379)   An outlier is a data value that is much higher or lower than the other data values in the set.

Valor extremo (p. 379)   Un valor extremo es el valor de un dato que es mucho más alto o mucho más bajo que los otros valores del conjunto de datos.

Example For the set of values 2, 5, 3, 7, 12, the data value 12 is an outlier.

Output (p. 103)   A value of the dependent variable.

Salida (p. 103)   Valor de una variable dependiente.

Example The output of the function $f(x) = x^2$ when $x = 3$ is 9.

P

Paragraph proof (p. 639)   *See* **proof.**

Prueba de párrafo (p. 639)   *Ver* **proof.**

Example The output of the function $f(x) = x^2$ when $x = 3$ is 9.

Parallel lines (p. 212, 653)   Two lines are parallel if they lie in the same plane and do not intersect. The symbol ∥ means "is parallel to".

Paralle lines (p. 212, 653)   Dos rectas son paralelas si están en el mismo plano y no se cortan. El símbolo ∥ significa "es paralelo a".

Example $\ell \parallel m$

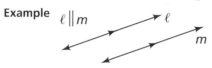

The red symbols indicate parallel lines.

English

Spanish

Parallelogram (p. 483, 858) A parallelogram is a quadrilateral with two pairs of parallel sides. You can choose any side to be the *base*. An *altitude* is any segment perpendicular to the line containing the base drawn from the side opposite the base. The *height* is the length of an altitude.

Paralelogramo (p. 483, 858) Un paralelogramo es un cuadrilátero con dos pares de lados paralelos. Se puede escoger cualquier lado como la *base*. Una *altura* es un segmento perpendicular a la recta que contiene la base, trazada desde el lado opuesto a la base. La *altura*, por extensión, es la longitud de una altura.

Example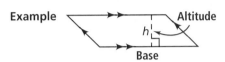

Parallel planes (p. 653) Parallel planes are planes that do not intersect.

Planos paralelos (p. 653) Planos paralelos son planos que no se cortan.

Example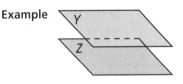

Planes *Y* and *Z* are parallel.

Parent function (p. 186) A family of functions is a group of functions with common characteristics. A parent function is the simplest function with these characteristics.

Función elemental (p. 186) Una familia de funciones es un grupo de funciones con características en común. La función elemental es la función más simple que reúne esas características.

Example $y = x$ is the parent function for the family of linear equations of the form $y = mx + b$.

Percentile (p. 395) A value that separates a data set into 100 equal parts.

Percentil (p. 395) Valor que separa el conjunto de datos en 100 partes iguales.

Percentile rank (p. 395) The percentage of data values that are less than or equal to a given value.

Rango percentil (p. 395) Porcentaje de valores de datos que es menos o igual a un valor dado.

Perimeter of a polygon (p. 545) The perimeter of a polygon is the sum of the lengths of its sides.

Perímetro de un polígono (p. 545) El perímetro de un polígono es la suma de las longitudes de sus lados

Example

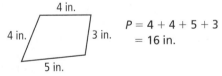

$P = 4 + 4 + 5 + 3$
$= 16 \text{ in.}$

Perpendicular bisector (p. 593) The perpendicular bisector of a segment is a line, segment, or ray that is perpendicular to the segment at its midpoint.

Mediatriz (p. 593) La mediatriz de un segmento es una recta, segmento o semirrecta que es perpendicular al segmento en su punto medio.

Example

$\overleftrightarrow{YZ}$ is the perpendicular bisector of $\overline{AB}$. It is perpendicular to $\overline{AB}$ and intersects $\overline{AB}$ at midpoint *M*.

English

Perpendicular lines (pp. 213, 593) Perpendicular lines are lines that intersect and form right angles. The symbol ⊥ means "is perpendicular to". Two lines are perpendicular if the product of their slopes is −1.

Example

Piecewise function (p. 357) A piecewise function has different rules for different parts of its domain.

Plane (p. 441) In Euclidean geometry, a plane is undefined. You can think of a plane as a flat surface that extends without end and has no thickness. A plane contains infinitely many lines.

Example

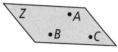

Plane *ABC* or plane *Z*

Point (p. 441) In Euclidean geometry, a point is undefined. You can think of a point as a location. A point has no size

Example • *P*

Point of concurrency (p. 803) *See* **concurrent lines.**

Point-slope form (p. 195) A linear equation of a nonvertical line written as $y - y_1 = m(x - x_1)$. The line passes through the point (x_1, y_1) with slope m.

Example An equation with a slope of $-\frac{1}{2}$ passing through $(2, -1)$ would be written $y + 1 = -\frac{1}{2}(x - 2)$ in point-slope form.

Point symmetry (p. 523) Point symmetry is the type of symmetry for which there is a rotation of 180° that maps a figure onto itself.

Polygon (p. 483) A polygon is a closed plane figure formed by three or more segments. Each segment intersects exactly two other segments, but only at their endpoints, and no two segments with a common endpoint are collinear. The *vertices* of the polygon are the endpoints of the sides. A *diagonal* is a segment that connects two non-consecutive vertices.

Spanish

Rectas Perpendiculars (pp. 213, 593) Las rectas perpendiculars son recta sue se cortan y frman angulos rectos. El símbolo ⊥ significa "es perpendicular a". Dos rectas son perpendiculares si el producto de sus pendientes es −1.

Función de fragmentos (p. 357) Una función de fragmentos tiene reglas diferentes para diferentes partes de su dominio.

Plano (p. 441) En la geometría euclidiana, un plano es indefinido. Se puede pensar en un plano como una superficie plana sin fin, ni grosor. Un plano tiene un número infinito de rectas.

Punto (p. 441) En la geometría euclidiana, un punto es indefinido. Puedes imaginarte a un punto como un lugar. Un punto no tiene dimensión.

Punto de concurrencia (p. 803) *Ver* **concurrent lines.**

Forma punto-pendiente (p. 195) La ecuación lineal de una recta no vertical que pasa por el punto (x_1, y_1) con pendiente m está dada por $y - y_1 = m(x - x_1)$.

Simetría central (p. 523) La simetría central es un tipo de simetría en la que una figura se ha rotado 180° sobre sí misma.

Polígono (p. 483) Un polígono es una figura plana compuesta or tres o más semgentos. Cada segmento intersecta los otros dos segments exactamente, pero únicamente en sus puntos extremos y ningúno de los segmentos extremos comunes son colineales. Los *vértices* del polígono son los extremos de los lados. Una *diagonal* es un segmento que conecta dos vértices no consecutivos.

Example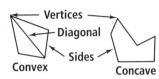

Vertices

Diagonal

Sides

Convex   Concave

Positive correlation (p. 399) The relationship between two sets of data in which both sets of data increase together.

Correlación positiva (p. 399) La relación entre dos conjuntos de datos en la que ambos conjuntos incrementan a la vez.

Example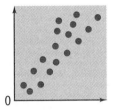

0

Postulate (p. 444) A postulate, or *axiom*, is an accepted statement of fact.

Postulado (p. 444) Un postulado, o *axioma*, es un enunciado que se acepta como un hecho.

Example Through any two points there is exactly one line.

Preimage (p. 495) *See* **transformation.**

Preimagen (p. 495) *Ver* **transformation.**

Proof (pp. 632, 639, 672, 907) A proof is a convincing argument that uses deductive reasoning. A proof can be written in many forms. In a two-column proof, the statements and reasons are aligned in columns. In a paragraph proof, the statements and reasons are connected in sentences. In a flow proof, arrows show the logical connections between the statements. In a coordinate proof, a figure is drawn on a coordinate plane and the formulas for slope, midpoint, and distance are used to prove properties of the figure. An indirect proof involves the use of indirect reasoning.

Prueba (pp. 632, 639, 672, 907) Una prueba es un argumento convincente en el cual se usa el razonamiento deductivo. Una prueba se puede escribir de varias maneras. En una *prueba de dos columnas*, los enunciados y las razones se alinean en columnas. En una *prueba de párrafo*, los enunciados y razones están unidos en oraciones. En una *prueba de flujo*, hay flechas que indican las conexiones lógicas entre enunciados. En una *prueba de coordenadas*, se dibuja una figura en un plano de coordenadas y se usan las fórmulas de la pendiente, punto medio y distancia para probar las propiedades de la figura. Una *prueba indirecta* incluye el uso de razonamiento indirecto.

Example E

F G

Given: $\triangle EFG$, with right angle $\angle F$
Prove: $\angle E$ and $\angle G$ are complementary.

Paragraph Proof: Because $\angle F$ is a right angle, $m\angle F = 90$. By the Triangle Angle-Sum Theorem, $m\angle E + m\angle F + m\angle G = 180$. By substitution, $m\angle E + 90 + m\angle G = 180$. Subtracting 90 from each side yields $m\angle E + m\angle G = 90$. $\angle E$ and $\angle G$ are complementary by definition.

Proportion (p. 52)   An equation that states that two ratios are equal.

Example $\frac{7.5}{9} = \frac{5}{6}$

Proporción (p. 52)   Es una ecuación que establece que dos razones son iguales.

Q

Quadrilateral (p. 483)   A quadrilateral is a polygon with four sides.

Example

Cuadrilátero (p. 483)   Un cuadrilátero es un polígono de cuatro lados.

Quartile (p. 392)   A quartile is a value that separates a finite data set into four equal parts. The second quartile (Q_2) is the median of the data set. The first and third quartiles (Q_1 and Q_3) are the medians of the lower half and upper half of the data, respectively.

Example   For the data set 2, 3, 4, 5, 5, 6, 7, 7, the first quartile is 3.5, the second quartile (or median) is 5, and the third quartile is 6.5.

Cuartil (p. 392)   Un cuartil es el valor que separa un conjunto de datos finitos en cuatro partes iguales. El segundo cuartil (Q_2) es la mediana del conjunto de datos. El primer cuartil y el tercer cuartil (Q_1 y Q_3) son medianas de la mitad inferior y de la mitad superior de los datos, respectivamente.

R

Radical expression (p. 344)   Expression that contains a radical.

Example $\sqrt{3}$, $\sqrt{5x}$ and $\sqrt{x - 10}$ are examples of radical expressions.

Expresión radical (p. 344)   Expresiones que contienen radicales.

Range (of a relation or function) (p. 135)   The possible values of the output, or dependent variable, of a relation or function.

Example   In the function $y = |x|$, the range is the set of all nonnegative numbers.

Rango (de una relación o función) (p. 135)   El conjunto de todos los valores posibles de la salida, o variable dependiente, de una relación o función.

Range of a set of data (p. 382)   The difference between the greatest and the least data values for a set of data.

Example   For the set 2, 5, 8, 12, the range is $12 - 2 = 10$.

Rango de un conjunto de datos (p. 382)   Diferencia entre el valor mayor y el menor en un conjunto de datos.

Rate (p. 37)   A ratio of a to b where a and b represent quantities measured in different units.

Example   Traveling 125 miles in 2 hours results in the rate $\frac{125 \text{ miles}}{2 \text{ hours}}$ or 62.5 mi/h.

Tasa (p. 37)   La relación que existe entre a y b cuando a y b son cantidades medidas con distintas unidades.

English

Spanish

Rate of change (p. 167)   The relationship between two quantities that are changing. The rate of change is also called slope.

rate of change = $\dfrac{\text{change in the dependent variable}}{\text{change in the independent variable}}$

Example   Video rental for 1 day is $1.99.
Video rental for 2 days is $2.99.

$$\text{rate of change} = \frac{2.99 - 1.99}{2 - 1}$$
$$= \frac{1.00}{1}$$
$$= 1$$

Tasa de cambio (p. 167)   La relación entre dos cantidades que cambian. La tasa de cambio se llama también pendiente.

tasa de cambio = $\dfrac{\text{cambio en la variable dependiente}}{\text{cambio en la variable independiente}}$

Ratio (p. 37)   A ratio is the comparison of two quantities by division.

Example $\frac{5}{7}$ and 7 : 3 are ratios.

Razón (p. 37)   Una razón es la comparación de dos cantidades por medio de una división.

Rationalize the denominator (p. 349)   To rationalize the denominator of an expression, rewrite it so there are no radicals in any denominator and no denominators in any radical.

Example $\dfrac{2}{\sqrt{5}} = \dfrac{2}{\sqrt{5}} \cdot \dfrac{\sqrt{5}}{\sqrt{5}} = \dfrac{2\sqrt{5}}{\sqrt{25}} = \dfrac{2\sqrt{5}}{5}$

Racionalizar el denominador (p. 349)   Para racionalizar el denominador de una expresión, ésta se escribe de modo que no haya radicales en ningún denominador y no haya denominadores en ningún radical.

Ray (p. 443)   A ray is the part of a line that consists of one *endpoint* and all the points of the line on one side of the endpoint.

Example

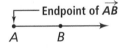

Semirrecta (p. 443)   Una semirrecta es la parte de una recta que tiene un *extremo* de donde parten todos los puntos de la recta.

Rectangle (p. 483)   A rectangle is a parallelogram with four right angles.

Example

Rectangle (p. 483)   Un rectángulo es un paralelogramo con cuatro ángulos rectos.

Recursive formula (p. 149)   A recursive formula defines the terms in a sequence by relating each term to the ones before it.

Example   Let $a_n = 2.5a_{n-1} + 3a_{n-2}$. If $a_5 = 3$ and $a_4 = 7.5$, then
$a_6 = 2.5(3) + 3(7.5) = 30$.

Fórmula recursiva (p. 149)   Una fórmula recursiva define los términos de una secuencia al relacionar cada término con los términos que lo anteceden.

English

Spanish

Reflection (p. 508) A reflection (*flip*) across line *r*, called the *line of reflection*, is a transformation such that if a point *A* is on line *r*, then the image of *A* is itself, and if a point *B* is not on line *r*, then its image *B′* is the point such that *r* is the perpendicular bisector of $\overline{BB'}$.

Reflexión (p. 508) Una reflexión (*inversión*) a través de una línea *r*, llamada el *eje de reflexión*, es una transformación en la que si un punto *A* es parte de la línea *r*, la imagen de *A* es sí misma, y si un punto *B* no está en la línea *r*, su imagen *B′* es el punto en el cual la línea *r* es la bisectriz perpendicular de $\overline{BB'}$.

Example

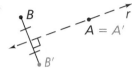

Reflectional symmetry (p. 523) Reflectional symmetry, or *line symmetry*, is the type of symmetry for which there is a reflection that maps a figure onto itself. The reflection line is the *line of symmetry*. The line of symmetry divides a figure with reflectional symmetry into two congruent halves.

Simetría reflexiva (p. 523) Simetría reflexiva, o *simetría lineal*, es el tipo de simetría donde hay una reflexión que ubica una figura en sí misma. El eje de reflexión es el *eje de simetría*. El eje de simetría divide una figura con simetría reflexiva en dos mitades congruentes.

Example

A reflection across the given line maps the figure onto itself.

Regular polygon (pp. 484, 852) A regular polygon is a polygon that is both equilateral and equiangular. Its *center* is the point that is equidistant from its vertices.

Polígono regular (pp. 484, 852) Un polígono regular es un polígono que es equilateral y equiangular. Su *centro* es el punto equidistante de sus vértices.

Example

ABCDEF is a regular hexagon. Point *X* is its center.

Relation (p. 135) Any set of ordered pairs.

Relación (p. 135) Cualquier conjunto de pares ordenados.

Example {(0, 0), (2, 3), (2, −7)} is a relation.

Relative frequency (p. 416) The ratio of the number of times an event occurs to the total number of events in the sample space.

Freuencia relativa (p. 416) La razón del número de veces que ocurre un evento número de eventos en el espacio muestral.

Example

Archery Results				
Scoring Region	Yellow	Red	Blue	Black	White
Arrow Strikes	52	25	10	8	5

$$\text{Relative frequency of spinning 1} = \frac{\text{frequency of spinning 1}}{\text{total frequencies}}$$
$$= \frac{29}{100}$$

English

Spanish

Remote interior angles (p. 689)   Remote interior angles are the two nonadjacent interior angles corresponding to each exterior angle of a triangle.

Ángulos interiores remotos (p. 689)   Los ángulos interiores remotos son los dos ángulos interiores no adyacentes que corresponden a cada ángulo exterior de un triángulo.

Residual (p. 411)   The difference between the *y*-value of a data point and the corresponding *y*-value of a model for the data set.

Residuo (p. 411)   La diferencia entre el valor de *y* de un punto y el valor de *y* correspondiente a ese punto en el modelo del conjunto de datos.

Rhombus (p. 483)   A rhombus is a parallelogram with four congruent sides.

Rombo (p. 483)   Un rombo es un paralelogramo de cuatro lados congruentes.

Example

Right angle (p. 460)   A right angle is an angle whose measure is 90.

Ángulo recto (p. 460)   Un ángulo recto es un ángulo que mide 90.

Example 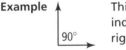 This symbol indicates a right angle.

Rigid motion (p. 495)   A transformation in the plane that preserves distance and angle measure.

Movimiento rígido (p. 495)   Una transformación en el piano que no cambia la distancia ni la medida del ángulo.

Example Translations, reflections, and rotations are rigid motions.

Rotation (p. 515)   A rotation *(turn)* of *x°* about a point *R*, called the *center of rotation*, is a transformation such that for any point *V*, its image is the point *V′*, where $RV = RV′$ and $m\angle VRV′ = x$. The image of *R* is itself. The positive number of degrees *x* that a figure rotates is the *angle of rotation*.

Rotación (p. 515)   Una rotación *(giro)* de *x°* sobre un punto *R*, llamado el *centro de rotación*, es una transformación en la que para cualquier punto *V*, su imagen es el punto *V′*, donde $RV = RV′$ y $m\angle VRV′ = x$. La imagen de *R* es sí misma. El número positivo de grados *x* que una figura rota es el *ángulo de rotación*.

Example

Rotational symmetry (p. 523)   Rotational symmetry is the type of symmetry for which there is a rotation of 180° or less that maps a figure onto itself.

Simetría rotacional (p. 523)   La simetría rotacional es un tipo de simetría en la que una rotación de 180° o menos vuelve a trazar una figura sobre sí misma.

Example   The figure has 120° rotational symmetry.

English

S

Same-side interior angles (p. 655)   Same-side interior angles lie on the same side of the transversal t and between ℓ and m.

Example

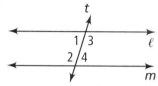

$\angle 1$ and $\angle 2$ are same-side interior angles, as are $\angle 3$ and $\angle 4$.

Scatter plot (p. 399)   A graph that relates two different sets of data by displaying them as ordered pairs.

Example

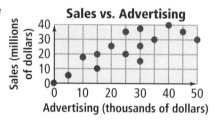

The scatter plot displays the amount spent on advertising (in thousands of dollars) versus product sales (in millions of dollars).

Segment (p. 443)   A segment is the part of a line that consists of two points, called *endpoints*, and all points between them.

Example   Endpoints of $\overline{DE}$

Segment bisector (p. 454)   A segment bisector is a line, segment, ray, or plane that intersects a segment at its midpoint.

Example

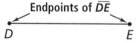 ℓ bisects $\overline{KJ}$.

Sequence (p. 146)   An ordered list of numbers that often forms a pattern.

Example -4, 5, 14, 23 is a sequence.

Side   *See* angle.

Spanish

Ángulos internos del mismo lado (p. 655)   Los ángulos internos del mismo lado están situados en el mismo lado de la transversal t y dentro de ℓ y m.

Diagrama de puntos (p. 399)   Grafica que muestra la relacion entre dos conjuntos. Los datos de ambos conjuntos se presentan como pares ordenados.

Segmento (p. 443)   Un segmento es la parte de una recta que tiene dos puntos, llamados *extremos*, entre los cuales están todos los puntos de esa recta.

Bisectriz de un segmento (p. 454)   La bisectriz de un segmento es una recta, segmento, semirrecta o plano que corta un segmento en su punto medio.

Progresion (p. 146)   Lista ordenada de numeros que muchas veces forma un patron.

Lado   *Ver* angle.

Visual **Glossary**

English

Spanish

Skew lines (p. 653) Skew lines are lines that do not lie in the same plane.

Rectas cruzadas (p. 653) Las rectas cruzadas son rectas que no están en el mismo plano.

Example

$\overleftrightarrow{AB}$ and $\overleftrightarrow{EF}$ are skew.

Slope (p. 168) The ratio of the vertical change to the horizontal change.

$$\text{slope} = \frac{\text{vertical change}}{\text{horizontal change}} = \frac{y_2 - y_1}{x_2 - x_1}, \text{ where } x_2 - x_1 \neq 0$$

Pendiente (p. 168) La razón del cambio vertical al cambio horizontal. pendiente cambio vertical cambio horizontal. $\text{pendiente} = \frac{\text{cambio vertical}}{\text{cambio horizontal}} = \frac{y_2 - y_1}{x_2 - x_1}$, donde $x_2 - x_1 \neq 0$

Example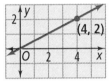

The slope of the line above is $\frac{2}{4} = \frac{1}{2}$.

Slope-intercept form (p. 186) The slope-intercept form of a linear equation is $y = mx + b$, *where m is the slope of the line and b is the y-intercept.*

Forma pendiente-intercepto (p. 186) La forma pendiente-intercepto es la ecuación lineal $y = mx + b$, en la que m es la pendiente de la recta y b es el punto de intersección de esa recta con el eje y.

Example $y = 8x - 2$

Solution of a system of linear equations (p. 231) Any ordered pair in a system that makes all the equations of that system true.

Solución de un sistema de ecuaciones lineales (p. 231) Todo par ordenado de un sistema que hace verdaderas todas las ecuaciones de ese sistema.

Example (2, 1) is a solution of the system
$$y = 2x - 3$$
$$y = x - 1$$
because the ordered pair makes both equations true.

Solution of a system of linear inequalities (p. 271) Any ordered pair that makes all of the inequalities in the system true.

Solución de un sistema de desigualdades lineales (p. 271) Todo par ordenado que hace verdaderas todas las desigualdades del sistema.

Example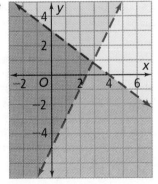

The dark shaded area shows the solution of the system $y > 2x - 5$
$$3x + 4y < 12.$$

English

Spanish

Solution of an inequality (two variables) (p. 263) Any ordered pair that makes the inequality true.

Solución de una desigualdad (dos variables) (p. 263) Cualquier par ordenado que haga verdadera la desigualdad.

Example Each ordered pair in the shaded area and on the solid red line is a solution of $3x - 5y \leq 10$.

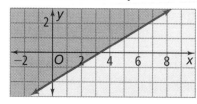

Space (p. 443) Space is the set of all points.

Espacio (p. 443) El espacio es el conjunto de todos los puntos.

Square (p. 483) A square is a parallelogram with four congruent sides and four right angles.

Cuadrado (p. 483) Un cuadrado es un paralelogramo con cuatro lados congruentes y cuatro ángulos rectos.

Example

Square root function (p. 354) A function that contains the independent variable in the radicand.

Función de raíz cuadrada (p. 354) Una función que contiene la variable independiente en el radicando.

Example $y = \sqrt{2x}$ is a square root function.

Standard deviation (p. 390) A measure of how data varies, or deviates, from the mean.

Desviación típica (p. 390) Medida de cómo los datos varían, o se desvían, de la media.

Example Use the following formula to find the standard deviation.

$$\sigma = \sqrt{\frac{\Sigma(x - \bar{x})^2}{n}}$$

Standard form of a linear equation (p. 203) The standard form of a linear equation is $Ax + By = C$, where A, B, and C are real numbers and A and B are not both zero.

Forma normal de una ecuación lineal (p. 203) La forma normal de una ecuación lineal es $Ax\ By\ C$, donde A, B y C son números reales, y donde A y B no son iguales a cero.

Example $6x - y = 12$

Step function (p. 358) A step function pairs every number in an interval with a single value. The graph of a step function can look like the steps of a staircase.

Función escalón (p. 358) Una función escalón empareja cada número de un intervalo con un solo valor. La gráfica de una función escalón se puede parecer a los peldaños de una escalera.

Straight angle (p. 460) A straight angle is an angle whose measure is 180.

Ángulo llano (p. 460) Un ángulo llano es un ángulo que mide 180.

Example

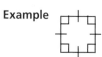

$m\angle AOB = 180$

English

Straightedge (p. 591)   A straightedge is a ruler with no markings on it.

Substitution method (p. 240)   A method of solving a system of equations by replacing one variable with an equivalent expression containing the other variable.

Example   If $y = 2x + 5$ and $x + 3y = 7$, then
$x + 3(2x + 5) = 7$.

Supplementary angles (p. 467)   Two angles are supplementary if the sum of their measures is 180.

Example

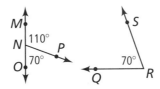

$\angle MNP$ and $\angle ONP$ are supplementary, as are $\angle MNP$ and $\angle QRS$.

Symmetry (p. 523)   A figure has symmetry if there is an isometry that maps the figure onto itself. *See also* **point symmetry; reflectional symmetry; rotational symmetry.**

Example

A regular pentagon has reflectional symmetry and 72° rotational symmetry.

System of linear equations (p. 231)   Two or more linear equations using the same variables.

Example $y = 5x + 7$
$y = \frac{1}{2}x - 3$

System of linear inequalities (p. 271)   Two or more linear inequalities using the same variables.

Example $y \leq x + 11$
$y < 5x$

Spanish

Regla sin graduación (p. 591)   Una regla sin graduación no tiene marcas.

Método de sustitución (p. 240)   Método para resolver un sistema de ecuaciones en el que se reemplaza una variable por una expresión equivalente que contenga la otra variable.

Ángulos suplementarios (p. 467)   Dos ángulos son suplementarios cuando sus medidas suman 180.

Simetría (p. 523)   Una figura tiene simetría si hay una isometría que traza la figura sobre sí misma. *Ver también* **point symmetry; reflectional symmetry; rotational symmetry.**

Sistema de ecuaciones lineales (p. 231)   Dos o más ecuaciones lineales que usen las mismas variables.

Sistema de desigualdades lineales (p. 271)   Dos o más desigualdades lineales que usen las mismas variables.

English

T

Spanish

Term (p. 6) A number, variable, or the product or quotient of a number and one or more variables.

Término (p. 6) Un número, una variable o el producto o cociente de un número y una o más variables.

Example The expression $5x + \frac{y}{2} - 8$ has three terms: $5x$, $\frac{y}{2}$, and -8.

Term of a sequence (p. 146) A term of a sequence is any number in a sequence.

Término de una progresión (p. 146) Un término de una secuencia es cualquier número de una secuencia.

Example -4 is the first term of the sequence $-4, 5, 14, 23$.

Theorem (p. 636) A theorem is a conjecture that is proven.

Teorema (p. 636) Un teorema es una conjetura que se demuestra.

Example The theorem "Vertical angles are congruent" can be proven by using postulates, definitions, properties, and previously stated theorems.

Transformation (p. 495) A transformation is a change in the position, size, or shape of a geometric figure. The given figure is called the *preimage* and the resulting figure is called the *image*. A transformation *maps* a figure onto its image. *Prime notation* is sometimes used to identify image points. In the diagram, X' (read "X prime") is the image of X.

Transformación (p. 495) Una transformación es un cambio en la posición, tamaño o forma de una figura. La figura dada se llama la preimagen y la figura resultante se llama la *imagen*. Una transformación *traza* la figura sobre su propia imagen. La *notación prima* a veces se utilize para identificar los puntos de la imagen. En el diagrama de la derecha, X' (leído X prima) es la imagen de X.

Example

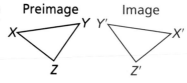

Preimage   Image

$$\triangle XYZ \rightarrow \triangle X'Y'Z'$$

Translation of a graph (p. 219) A translation (*slide*) is a transformation that moves points the same distance and in the same direction.

Traslación (p. 219) Una traslación (*desplazamiento*) es una transformación en la que se mueven puntos la misma distancia en la misma dirección.

Example

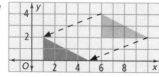

The blue triangle is the image of the red triangle under the translation $(-5, -2)$.

Translation (p. 498)   A translation is a transformation that moves points the same distance and in the same direction.

Traslación (p. 498)   Una traslación es una transformación en la que se mueven puntos la misma distancia en la misma dirección.

Example

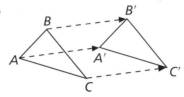

Transversal (p. 655)   A transversal is a line that intersects two or more lines at distinct points.

Transversal (p. 655)   Una transversal es una línea que interseca dos o más líneas en puntos precisos.

Example

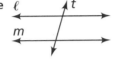

t is a transversal of *ℓ* and *m*.

Trapezoid (pp. 483, 894)   A trapezoid is a quadrilateral with exactly one pair of parallel sides, the *bases*. The nonparallel sides are called the *legs* of the trapezoid. Each pair of angles adjacent to a base are *base angles* of the trapezoid. An *altitude* of a trapezoid is a perpendicular segment from one base to the line containing the other base. Its length is called the *height* of the trapezoid.

Trapecio (pp. 483, 894)   Un trapecio es un cuadrilátero con exactamente un par de lados paralelos, l, as *bases*. Los lados no paralelos se llaman los *catetos* del trapecio. Cada par de ángulos adyacentes a la base son los *ángulos de base* del trapecio. Una *altura* del trapecio es un segmento perpendicular que va de una base a la recta que contiene la otra base. Su longitud se llama, por extensión, la *altura* del trapecio.

Example

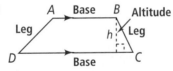

In trapezoid *ABCD*, ∠*ADC* and ∠*BCD* are one pair of base angles, and ∠*DAB* and ∠*ABC* are the other.

Trend line (p. 401)   A line on a scatter plot drawn near the points. It shows a correlation.

Línea de tendencia (p. 401)   Línea de un diagrama de puntos que se traza cerca de los puntos para mostrar una correlación.

Example

Positive   Negative

English

Truth value (p. 609) The truth value of a statement is "true" or "false" according to whether the statement is true or false, respectively.

Two-way frequency table (p. 414) A table that displays frequencies in two different categories.

Example

	Male	Female	Totals
Juniors	3	4	7
Seniors	3	2	5
Totals	6	6	12

Two-way relative frequency table (p. 416) A two-way relative frequency table shows joint relative frequencies and marginal relative frequencies for two categories of data.

U

Unit analysis (p. 39) Including units for each quantity in a calculation to determine the unit of the answer.

Example To change 10 ft to yards, multiply by the conversion factor $\frac{1\text{ yd}}{3\text{ ft}}$.

$$10\text{ ft}\left(\frac{1\text{ yd}}{3\text{ ft}}\right) = 3\tfrac{1}{3}\text{ yd}$$

Unit rate (p. 37) A rate with a denominator of 1.

Example The unit rate for 120 miles driven in 2 hours is 60 mi/h.

V

Vertex *See* **angle.** The plural form of *vertex* is *vertices.*

Vertex angle (p. 744) *See* **isosceles triangle.**

Vertical angles (p. 466) Vertical angles are two angles whose sides form two pairs of opposite rays.

Example

Spanish

Valor verdadero (p. 609) El valor verdadero de un enunciado es "verdadero" o "falso" según el enunciado sea *verdadero* o falso, respectivamente.

Table de frecuencias de doble entrada (p. 414) Una tabla de frecuencies que contiene dos categorias de datos.

Tabla de frecuencias relativas de doble entrada (p. 416) Una tabla de frecuencias relativas de doble entrada muestra las frecuencias relativas conjuntas y las frecuencias relativas marginales para dos categorías de datos.

Análisis de unidades (p. 39) Incluir unidades para cada cantidad de un cálculo como ayuda para determinar la unidad que se debe usar para la respuesta.

Razón en unidades (p. 37) Razón cuyo denominador es 1.

Vértice *Ver* **angle.**

Ángulo del vértice (p. 744) *Ver* **isosceles triangle.**

Ángulos opuestos por el vértice (p. 466) Dos ángulos son ángulos opuestos por el vértice si sus lados son semirrectas opuestas.

∠1 and ∠2 are vertical angles, as are ∠3 and ∠4.

Visual Glossary

English

Spanish

Vertical line test (p. 136) The vertical-line test is a method used to determine if a relation is a function or not. If a vertical line passes through a graph more than once, the graph is not the graph of a function.

Prueba de la recta vertical (p. 136) La prueba de recta vertical es un método que se usa para determinar si una relación es una función o no. Si una recta vertical pasa por el medio de una gráfica más de una vez, la gráfica no es una gráfica de una función.

Example

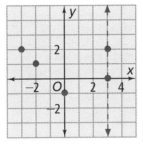

A line would pass through (3, 0) and (3, 2), so the relation is not a function.

X

x-intercept (p. 203) The x-coordinate of a point where a graph crosses the x-axis.

Intercepto en x (p. 203) Coordenada x por donde la gráfica cruza el eje de las x.

Example The x-intercept of $3x + 4y = 12$ is 4.

Y

y-intercept (p. 186) The y-coordinate of a point where a graph crosses the y-axis.

Intercepto en y (p. 186) Coordenada y por donde la gráfica cruza el eje de las y.

Example The y-intercept of $y = 5x + 2$ is 2.

Index

Index

Index

Index

Acknowledgments

Staff Credits

The people who made up the High School Mathematics team—representing composition services, core design digital and multimedia production services, digital product development, editorial, editorial services, manufacturing, marketing, and production management—are listed below.

Patty Fagan, Suzanne Finn, Matt Frueh, Cynthia Harvey, Linda Johnson, Roshni Kutty, Cheryl Mahan, Eve Melnechuk, Cynthia Metallides, Hope Morley, Michael Oster, Wynnette Outland, Brian Reardon, Matthew Rogers, Ann-Marie Sheehan, Kristen Siefers, Richard Sullivan, Susan Tauer, Mark Tricca, Oscar Vera, Paula Vergith

Additional Credits: Emily Bosak, Olivia Gerde, Alyse McGuire, Stephanie Mosely

Illustration

Jeff Grunewald: 101, 102, 134, 584, 613, 627, 643, 857, 872, 916; **Christopher Wilson:** 377; **Stephen Durke:** 439, 440, 450, 451, 464, 457, 479, 500, 556, 563, 674, 684, 690, 711, 720, 734, 741, 751, 768, 794, 797, 801, 805, 806, 810, 826, 835, 837, 839, 844; **Phil Guzy:** 525.

Technical Illustration

Aptara, Inc.; Datagrafix, Inc.; GGS Book Services

Photography

Every effort has been made to secure permission and provide appropriate credit for photographic material. The publisher deeply regrets any omission and pledges to correct errors called to its attention in subsequent editions.

Unless otherwise acknowledged, all photographs are the property of Pearson Education, Inc.

35, Reuters/Corbis; **158,** John Glover/Alamy Images; **158,** Bob Gibbons/Alamy Images; **352,** Laurie Neish/iStockphoto; **446,** Kelly Redinger/Alamy Images; **465,** Stuart Melvin/Alamy Images; **474,** Richard Menga/Fundamental Photographs; **514,** North Wind Picture Archives/Alamy Images; **522,** Alan Copson/City Pictures/Alamy Images; **620,** Material courtesy of Bill Vicars and Lifeprint; **643,** Jenny Thompson/Fotolia; **657,** Kevin Fleming/Corbis; **669,** photo courtesy of Frank Adelstein, Ithaca, NY; **677,** Robert Llewellyn/Corbis; **690,** Peter Cade/Iconica/Getty Images; **738,** Viktor Kitaykin/iStockphoto; **748,** John Wells/Photo Researchers, Inc; **759,** Image Source Black/Jupiter Images; **779 l,** M.C. Escher's "Symmetry E56" © 2009 The M.C. Escher Company-Holland. All rights reserved. www.mcescher.com; **779 r,** M.C. Escher's "Symmetry E18" © 2009 The M.C. Escher Company-Holland. All rights reserved. www.mcescher.com; **793,** Joseph Sohm/Visions of America, LLC/Alamy Images; **853 l,** Laurie Strachan/Alamy Images; **853 r,** BestShot/iStockphoto; **866,** Esa Hiltula/Alamy Images; **878 t,** Claro Cortes IV/Reuters/Landov LLC; **878 b,** Michael Jenner/Alamy Images; **892,** Rodney Raschke/Active Photo Service; **902,** Colin Underhill/Alamy Images.